HEROES & RASCALS

OF OLD OREGON

OFFBEAT OREGON HISTORY VOL. I

HEROES & RASCALS
OF OLD OREGON

OFFBEAT OREGON HISTORY VOL. I

By FINN J.D. JOHN

Copyright ©2019 by Finn J.D. John

All rights reserved. However, please note that most stories in this book are edited, revised, and augmented versions of stories that initially ran in the Offbeat Oregon History syndicated newspaper column under a Creative Commons Attribution-Share Alike license. Those earlier versions are still covered under the license, and can be easily found with a Google search.

For information about permission to reproduce selections from this book, write to Ouragan House Publishers, Post Office Box 77, Corvallis, OR 97339, or e-mail permissions@ouragan-house.com.

Softcover Edition: ISBN 978-1-63591-102-2

Other edition ISBNs:
Hardcover Multimedia Edition: 978-1-63591-101-5
E-book: 978-1-63591-104-6
Audiobook, retail: 978-1-63591-105-3
Audiobook, library edition: 978-1-63591-106-0
Interactive PDF: 978-1-63591-108-4

Dust jacket:

Dust jacket design by Fiona Mac Daibheid.

Ouragan House Publishers
An imprint of
Pulp-Lit Productions
Corvallis, Oregon

http://ouragan-house.com
http://pulp-lit.com

This softcover edition comes bundled with the e-book version*.

HERE'S HOW TO ACCESS IT:

EPUB or Interactive PDF:
Download the E-book in EPUB or Interactive PDF form at http://ouragan-house.com/102.

*Everyone who buys this multimedia bundle edition receives a lifetime non-alienable license to all the e-book editions, with the exception of the copy Amazon provides through the Kindle Matchbook program. **This includes people who buy it secondhand**, and it does not expire if you sell this copy to someone else: you keep your license, and the buyer receives a fresh one of his/her own.

TABLE OF CONTENTS:

Foreword xiii
Prologue xxv

Part I: Heroes 1
   Marie Aioe Dorion, Woodswoman 3
      #Oregon's Revenant   *#Astorian Party*
   Joel Munson, Lifeboat Rescuer 15
      #Lighthouse   *#Shipwrecks*
   Cheng, Smuggler 19
      #Chinese Mail Service   *#Gold Rush*
   Ing Hay, Healer 23
      #China Doctor of John Day *#Kam Wah Chung*
   "One-Eyed Charley" Parkhurst, Stagecoach Driver 29
      #Gold Rush   *#Disguise*
   Mary G. Leonard, Attorney at Law 35
      #First Woman Lawyer   *#Madness and Murder*
   Uriah B. Scott, Riverboat Captain 49
      #Riverboat Fire   *#Columbia River*
   Chee Gong, Chinese Tong Member 55
      #Tong Wars   *#Sacrificial Lamb*
   Lucinda Schroder, Homesteader 59
      #1894 Silver Lake Fire   *#Died rescuing people*

Charles T. "Buck" Bailey, Tugboat Captain 63
    #SS Washington   *#Columbia River Bar*

Fern Hobbs, Attorney and Law Enforcer 69
    #Governor Oswald West   *#Copperfield*

Harry Lane, United States Senator 77
    #First World War   *#Voted No*

Capt. Robert Pamphlet & al., Rumrunners 81
    #Canadian Rumrunner   *#Rescuer*

Thomas McAdams, U.S. Coast Guard Lifesaver 89
    #US Coast Guard   *#Motor Lifeboat*

Gordon Huggins & al., U.S. Coast Guard Lifesavers 95
    #Columbia River Bar   *#Motor Lifeboat Triumph*

Jim Wright, Engineer and Aviator 105
    #Howard Hughes' Plane   *#Cottage Grove*

Part II: Mavericks 119

"Uncle Joab" Powell, Frontier Circuit Preacher 121
    #Oregon Legislature   *#"Father, Forgive Them . . ."*

Lemuel Wells & al., Frontier Circuit Preachers 131
    #Bathtub Down Staircase   *#Father Wilbur*

Capt. Richard Hillyer, Oyster Pirate 143
    #Yaquina Bay   *#Siletz Indians*

"Colonel" T. Edgenton Hogg, Railroad Builder 149
    #Yaquina Bay   *#Alcatraz Prison*

George Wetherby & al., Real Estate Developers 159
    #Multnomah Falls   *#Logging Plans*

Lafayette "Lafe" Pence, Real Estate Developer 165
    #Guild's Lake   *#Water Rights*

Joe Knowles, Wilderness-Survival Guru 171
    #Bear Grylls of 1910s   *#Newspaper War*
Gilbert E. Gable, Promoter, "Governor" of Jefferson 181
    #Port Orford   *#Dinosaur Bone Hunter*
Art Lacey, B-17 Smuggler 191
    #Bomber Gas Station   *#Lacey Lady*

Part III: Rascals 197

Pvt. James W. Smith, Civil War soldier 199
    #Olney's Forty Thieves   *#Last Living Veteran*
Capt. James "Jemmy" Jones, D.I.Y. Naval Architect 203
    #Invented Steam Schooner   *#Stole His Own Boat*
William Johnson, Pioneer Moonshiner 209
    #Prohibition   *#Portland's First Business*
Edouard Chambreau, Gambler and Saloonkeeper 215
    #Blackleg Gambler   *#Temperance Crusades*
James Lappeus, Gambler, Saloonkeeper, Police Chief 225
    #Crooked Gambler   *#Saloonkeeper*
Walter Moffett, Saloonkeeper 231
    #Temperance Crusades   *#Sea-Captain*
Hank Vaughan, Gunfighter and Rustler 251
    #Gunfighter   *#Saloon Hell-Raiser*
Charles "Black Bart" Bolton, Stagecoach Robber 263
    #Gentleman Bandit   *#Highway Robber-Poet*
Donald McKay & al., Patent-Medicine Showmen 269
    #Ka-Ton-Ka   *#Warm Springs Indians*
Jefferson "Soapy" Smith, Swindler and Racketeer 281
    #Soap swindle   *#Klondike Gold Rush*

Maud Myrtle Johnson, Actress and Scammer 287
  #Insurance Fraud   *#Fake Injuries*
Edward F. Lee, Patent-Medicine Swindler 293
  #Fake Viagara   *#Mail Fraud*
Jonathan Bourne Jr., Political Boss 297
  #Votes For Sale   *#Initiative And Petition*
John M. Hipple (a.k.a. John H. Mitchell), U.S. Senator . . . 303
  #Fugitive from Justice *#Embezzler*
Sylvester Pennoyer, Governor of Oregon 311
  #"MYOB, Mr. President" *#Two Thanksgivings*
Joseph "Bunco" Kelley, Shanghaier and Entrepreneur 319
  #Opium smuggling *#Portland Waterfront*
F. Wallace White, Mining-Stock Swindler 329
  #Mail Fraud   *#Bourne*
Ellis Hughes, Meteorite Pirate 335
  #Willamette Meteorite *#Tomonowos*
Frank "Three Minute" Wagner & al., Prison Escapees . . . 339
  #Safecrackers   *#Shawshank Redemption*
Harry Virtue, Swindler and Quack Doctor 343
  #Fake Dr. Barber *#Gardiner-Reedsport*
George L. Baker, Vaudeville Impresario and Mayor 349
  #Posed with KKK *#Baker Stock Theatre*
Paul Remaley & al., Bootleggers and Jailbreakers 359
  #Whale Cove   *#Jailbreak*
Robert G. "Oregon Wildcat" Duncan, Radio Host 369
  #Sentenced for Swearing *#First Shock-Jock*
Jim Elkins & al., Racketeers [51] 35
  #Stole Pinball Machines *#Lost To Teamsters*
Allen Midgette, Andy Warhol Impersonator 379
  #Allen Midgette   *#Fake Andy Warhol*

FOREWORD:

The book you are holding in your hands is the fruit of a decision I made exactly 10 years ago (almost to the day), while strolling along the Old 804 Trail in Yachats, Oregon.

With your indulgence, I intend to share that "origin story" here in the foreword to the first volume in what I anticipate will be an eight-book series — collecting the stories that have filled the weekly Offbeat Oregon History newspaper column for the past decade in one updated, binge-friendly package.

The beauty of a foreword, as a place in which to indulge in this sort of thing, is that it is easily skipped over; so, if you find yourself glazing over as my voice drones on and on talking about myself, simply skip to the end and start right in on the first of the actual Oregon history stories. You see, I like to think I'm pretty good at picking out interesting stories to write about, and I hope once you've read on a bit, you'll agree. But you know, we all tend to find ourselves to be the most fascinating of topics; so, my radar is a little off when the target of my storytelling is Yours Truly. I can personally guarantee that the stories in this book will not be boring. I can make no such representation as regards the foreword.

But — being serious now — I strongly believe this information has to be here. Because today more than ever, any piece of information you take into your mind and make a part of your life has to have some sort of pedigree: you must know the source of the information before you can know if you trust it. I'm old enough (and maybe you are too) to remember a time when having a realistic-looking photocopy of a newspaper clipping was virtual proof that a story was truth. It's not like that any more, as you undoubtedly know well.

The summer of 2008 — as I write this, exactly 10 years ago — was when I first developed the idea for what would become Offbeat Oregon History.

I had been working in newspapers for years — except for a couple brief interludes during which I'd tried to become first a banker and then a magazine publisher, I'd been a newspaper guy since 1989 when I joined the staff of a student-run periodical at the University of Oregon. And over the years the business had been pretty good to me ... until there had come a time when it was not. My boss had been fired and replaced with a fellow who, though affable and professional, seemed not to fully trust me. It seemed clear that I would need to move on soon, and so I had applied for and been accepted into graduate school at the University of Oregon.

And so here it was, the summer of 2008, and I would be starting classes in a couple months.

I was excited to go. And yet I was a little apprehensive about leaving behind the business in which I had for so long toiled. This mood hung over me as I drove out to the beach with my wife and our then-8-year-old son for a weekend at Yachats, staying in one of our favorite haunts there — a hotel called The Overleaf.

The Overleaf stands right on a low bluff overlooking the sea, and there is a walking path behind it running from the beach, half a mile to the north, all the way back south to Yachats. I learned that this walking path was an old wagon road — County Road 804, a.k.a. the 804 Trail.

The next morning, while the rest of the family was still sleeping, I slipped out of the room for a walk along the sea. I stopped in the lobby of the Overleaf for a cup of coffee, and on the counter I found a stack of pamphlets produced by the hotel, which told the story of the 804 Trail.

I read it by the early morning light as I started my walk. Here, as briefly as I can make it, is what I learned from my reading:

In the days of the pioneers along the Oregon Coast, the residents of

The Overleaf Lodge in Yachats, as seen from the 804 Trail along the sea in 2018. (Image: offbeatoregon.com)

what's now Yachats got their supplies from Waldport, seven miles to the north. But there were no roads, and the geography of the Oregon Coast made it very difficult to build them; so they traveled back and forth on the beach.

The beach ran unimpeded from Waldport most of the way down to Yachats. But when it got almost there, it was replaced with a jagged line of rocky outcroppings jutting right out into the sea.

Fortunately, behind those rocks was a lovely flat shelf of land, and across that land there was already a footpath that paralleled the sea — the Native Americans of the area, faced with the same transportation challenges as the newcomers, had already solved the problem.

So the settlers simply widened the trail to make it a wagon road, and that road became County Road 804. It was in regular use until 1916, when an inland road was built (which would become part of Highway 101 later).

After that, the cars and trucks and wagons stopped using Road 804. But local residents continued to use it as a walking path, and for access to the sea. Anyone was, of course, welcome to bring a vehicle onto it at any time; but there wasn't really any need to.

So matters stood for 50 years. But then, in 1977, the Oregon Parks Department asked the county to officially vacate part of the road so that it could begin construction of Smelt Sands State Park — which they couldn't do while it was part of a county road.

The county didn't move fast enough for the Parks Department, so it

The 804 Road as it appeared in 1892. There is a shell midden in the foreground, and Horizon Hill is in the background. (Image: Lincoln County Historical Society)

took the extraordinarily heavy-handed step of asking the state attorney general to declare the road vacated, on the basis of there not having been any vehicular traffic on it for 50 years. The A-G obliged, and suddenly not just the Smelt Sands right-of-way, but all of the 804 Road was gone.

In blissful and happy ignorance of the damage they'd just inflicted on Yachats, the parks department got busy building Smelt Sands State Park. And, of course, several of the residents with property fronting on the 804 road got busy building fences across it.

This kicked off a ten-year-long legal civil war in Yachats, pitting neighbor against neighbor. Those favoring the trail argued that a public easement existed independent of the now-vacated road, essentially through squatters' rights, since it had been in continuous use for 60 years. What they hoped would be overlooked was the fact that the reason that use had gone unchallenged was that no one would ever challenge users of a county road the way they would squatters on private land.

804 Road opponents argued that it was now unencumbered private property, and vacating the road having extinguished the public's right to use it, they were within their rights to decide if they'd allow access or not; and, furthermore, they argued that letting anybody cross their property would invite trouble and vandalism unless it were policed, which there were no plans to do. What they hoped would be overlooked was the fact that as far

as anyone knew, no one had ever before tried to vacate a right-of-way for a road that was in active use.

Of course, the whole thing ended up in court. The result was, eventually, a victory for the public-access side of the argument; the property owners appealed the ruling to the state Supreme Court, which upheld it in 1985.

Finally, in 1990, after all the surveying and platting and planning was finished, the 804 Trail was handed off to the Oregon State Parks Department — and for the first time in 13 long years, residents of Yachats could walk the 804 trail unchallenged.

A half-dozen or so years later, after the wounds and scars of battle had healed a bit, the department negotiated to acquire an oceanfront right-of-way south of Smelt Sands, to extend the 804 trail all the way to the Yachats River. This trail had to be partly routed on roads, but they're nice quiet roads, and the overall experience isn't much diminished.

And so matters stood in the summer of 2008, when I stood on what I'd thought was a cute little walking path and learned the rest of its centuries-long story. Needless to say, when I lifted my eyes back up from the pamphlet and looked again at the modest walking path before me, I saw it in an entirely new light.

This history-catalyzed transformation got me to thinking. How many other interesting little story-nuggets about my home state were out there, relatively unknown, waiting for *someone* to pick them up and tell them?

I could be that someone. In fact, this idea was quite providentially

The 804 Trail as it appears today. (Image: offbeatoregon.com)

presenting itself to me at the exact time when I was actively looking for something like it in my life.

I had been working for 20 years as a writer of nonfiction. Now I was about to level up — joining a grad-school program in which I'd be doing nothing but telling nonfiction stories in longer and more complicated formats. This was exciting, but also a little daunting. Most nonfiction requires reporting skills, and I never have been a particularly talented reporter. I always made up for my lack of aptitude in that area with above-average writing and storytelling skills and by forcing myself way beyond my comfort zone; but I always knew reporting wasn't a job in which I could really excel. How could I make a practice for myself of nonfiction storytelling, working around such a critical weak spot?

It seemed to me that if I wanted to be a writer/storyteller not dependent on those shoe-leather reporting skills, I should develop an area of expertise, a channel into which to focus my creative energies — a channel that could be mine to take with me wherever I went. A channel that would, if I worked it long enough, make me a legitimate, recognized expert on something.

So on that early morning, strolling along the 804 Trail, I was already thinking about how I might solve this dilemma. And that pamphlet, with the story of the 804 Road, sparked an idea with which I was, by the end of the weekend, pretty much fully on fire.

As I strolled along beside the sea, the unseasonably big breakers crashing on the rocks a few dozen feet from me, I thought about it. I had the local roots. I was born in Oregon — not that where one is born makes any difference at all, as opposed to where one grew up or lived for years; I have no patience at all for that elitist "you're not really an Oregonian unless" crap one sometimes hears from bitter locals. But roots are roots; and my parents represent perfectly the two major influences of the Oregon of 50 years ago. My dad, who retired in the late 1980s after a 30-year run teaching painting and drawing at Clackamas Community College in "The O.C." (an ironic local reference to Oregon City with a snarky nod to Orange County, California) is about a third-generation Webfoot, and Grandpa used to work in the logging camps like Stewart Holbrook. My mom came out here in '66 or so from Illinois, where Other Grandpa was a vice president at Kimberly-Clark Paper, to teach English and writing at Mt. Angel College. I'd grown up in the woods outside the timber town of Molalla, surrounded by Blitz-drinking loggers, pot-smoking Back-to-the-Land hippies, rodeo cowboys and retired Vaudeville players hiding from the world. Then we'd moved to Southeast Portland and I'd soaked up some other cultures: quirky mayors, working-class urban folks, fresh young proto-hipsters, preppies in loafers and sock ties. Then I'd moved to Springfield in the fall of '86 for a

The 804 Trail to the south, as seen from the Overleaf, looking toward The Adobe Resort. (Image: offbeatoregon.com)

five-year on-again-off-again run at the University of Oregon.

I'd worked in sawmills and I'd worked in newsrooms. I'd even helped build the Alsea Bay Bridge — a significant percentage of the rebar in that bridge went through the powder-coating machine which I was paid $4 an hour to operate back in 1988 after I dropped out of college to join the U.S. Coast Guard. (It didn't work out; the Coast Guard kicked me out on a medical discharge after learning that I had a bum shoulder. That ended my dream of becoming a surfboat rescuer like Tom McAdams in Newport, but it more or less forced me to go back to college, so it's all good.)

Into this, throw my parents — academics both, and my dad a producing artist working mostly in oil paints — and I felt I had a pretty good basis for developing a real and fundamentally legitimate expertise in the story of my home state.

As I thought through the plan that was coalescing with uncanny swiftness in my mind, I remembered all the weird and quirky stories I had heard about Oregon: the exploding whale of Florence in 1970, the edgy and brazen Pixieland amusement park, the daredevil canoeist who paddled over South Falls in Silver Falls State Park. I knew there were more. I would dig them up and turn them into 350-word newspaper columns for the *Gazette-Times*. This would provide a thin trickle of income to help replace my salary — which would of course be going away when I went back to school, replaced with a wafer-thin stipend for my graduate teaching fellowship there.

And that is how Offbeat Oregon History got its very first start: as a weekly column in the Sunday edition of the Corvallis *Gazette-Times* called "Historic Oregon." It kicked off on Oct. 19, 2008, with a column headlined "Exploding whale? It's a true Oregon tale." (As of the time of this writing, you can still find it with a Google search for "Finn John Gazette-Times Exploding Whale.")

I'm still somewhat partial to that first column, although in general, the earliest columns were not very good. I found, in a bookstore, a copy of *A Roadside Guide to Oregon History* by Bill Gulick, and mined it ruthlessly for stories. The M.O. was usually to find an interesting story in Bill's book, and then do some exploratory research at the college library and on the Internet. If it turned out to be meaty enough to make a column from, I'd go for it.

Time went by. I joined my cohort at the university, threw myself into classes. But by the end of fall term, I was realizing something: I didn't want to be a part-time freelance columnist for the *Gazette-Times*. I wanted to make something that could be my own, to build a body of work that I could point to with pride and say, "I did that." This could only happen if I created something of my own ... a storytelling franchise.

So in December of 2008, roughly five months after that summer stroll by the sea on which I hatched the whole scheme, I took it (please pardon the cliché) to the next level. I went through the Oregon Newspaper Publishers Association Web site and from it developed a list of e-mail contacts for all the small community newspapers of the state. Then I reached out to them in a giant e-mail. Having been an editor at such a newspaper, I knew that occasionally small publications have a news hole that they need to fill. Sometimes it's a last-minute ad cancelation, sometimes it's a freelance writer flaking out; but whatever might be the cause, they end up, at the last minute, having to bodge together a house ad that says "Subscribe today" or something like that, just to fill the space. I thought, I can supply them with good-quality local-enough copy that can be kept on the back burner for just such emergencies. I also committed to finding and including at least one piece of art with each column.

What I basically was doing was launching a first-run syndication service.

My new syndicated column started in January 2009 with a short piece about the time Andy Warhol booked a speaking tour in Oregon and sent a friend in a white wig to impersonate him. (You'll find an updated version of this story in this book.)

At first I had just three newspapers regularly running the column, all in Lane County: The *McKenzie River Reflections*, the *Creswell Chronicle*, and the newspaper in Junction City, the *Tri-County Tribune*.

My initial plan was to charge a small fee for the column. But after a couple months I realized that this just made using the column require annoying coordination with the accounting department, which would surely reduce its use; and moreover, it made me feel obligated to it. I felt the subtle shift in my attitude, from that of a hobbyist expressing his creativity to that of a holder of a part-time job, and I didn't like it. I quickly made the column free of charge, in the process removing any obligation on my part to continue it if ever I were to decide it wasn't fun any more. That, of course, hasn't ever happened.

Well, by about halfway through 2009, I was progressing pretty well. Another half dozen newspapers had sampled my column and some of them were also running it regularly now: the papers in Myrtle Creek, Sutherlin and Redmond were regulars, and McMinnville and Astoria occasionally ran columns as well. Having Astoria on the list was an accident, and it hurt my adoption on the North Coast among the smaller papers that I'd intended the column for; seeing their regional daily on the distro list, they stayed away for fear that they'd end up running something that the overlapping daily was also using. Still, though, it was getting pretty good traction.

I have vacation memories of waking up early and "banging out copy" on my laptop in strange hotel lobbies. Once we took a weekend and went stormwatching in Lincoln City, and I found a book about Timberline Lodge in the lobby. I wrote my next week's column on the spot, while sipping coffee and waiting for my family to wake up. And then there was the hotel we stayed at while on a road trip to Louisiana. I'd planned ahead so I could have all the materials I'd need for it.

Week in, week out — since January of 2009 — I have not missed a single column.

At the same time I launched the new column, I built a Web page for it. It was awful. I hadn't used HTML since 1996, so of course I created a 1996-style page for it. Then I tried using something called Adobe GoLive, the results of which were even worse. But over time, I slowly started getting the hang of it — bought a copy of Dreamweaver, created something that was more or less good enough, and built from there. I'm still no Web designer, but I hand-code my CSS now and take a certain measure of pride in the leanness of my HTML code.

At the same time, I launched a Facebook page for the column. I was very new to Facebook myself; I'd created a MySpace page a few months before Rupert Murdoch bought and ruined it, but never got into it. However, every other graduate student was on Facebook, so to participate in their network I almost had to join them. Offbeat Oregon's presence on Facebook was pretty desultory at first. But by mid-2009 it was a regular part of my routine.

Also around mid-2009, the Gazette-Times quit running my Historic Oregon column. It was almost a relief; I could go from writing two a week to writing one, and it would be all mine.

Years went by. Columns rolled out. I was getting better. By mid-2010 I was looking back on my earliest efforts with actual chagrin. I guess this is how it works, right? You start on a new thing, you don't really know what you're doing but you do your research and you watch what the best people are doing and you give it your best shot. They say you have to "fake it till you make it," and I guess this is what they mean; but I wasn't faking it. I just wasn't as good as I could get yet.

I graduated from my program in June 2010 with a Master of Science degree in Journalism-Literary Nonfiction. My final project was a book proposal and first chapter covering the story of ex-Oregonian Herbert Hoover, who basically saved the nation of Belgium from starving to death during the First World War. This was a story I learned about while doing research for my column.

From then until now, basically I was all about two things: Growing my base of expertise in old funky Oregon stuff, and expanding the Offbeat Oregon History franchise. The most important breakthrough happened in late 2011, about a year after I'd joined the staff at Oregon State University's New Media Communications department. When I did that, I discovered to my chagrin that the only New Media thing I had any practical knowledge of was the Website I had wobblingly launched for my column. Other than that, I was pretty much Old Media all the way. I realized I needed to start expanding the franchise.

That is how I ended up launching a daily podcast, in late 2011.

I started out calling it "Offbeat Oregon du Jour." It only took about three episodes before I realized how incurably stupid that sounded. Not that it was out of place in the early podcasts, though. I mean to say, those early efforts were truly awful. I recorded them sitting in a blue leather recliner speaking into my Motorola Droid X cell phone. No earphones, no monitor, just a voice-memo-recording app running on a $20 phone. The sound was thin and boxy, my delivery was dorky and amateurish, and every time I moved the chair squeaked.

But for some reason I didn't give up on it. Instead I doubled down. I bought some new equipment. I asked advice from the sound guy at our department. I bought audio software. A colleague gave me a couple old dynamic microphones; one was broken, the other worked great. Within a single year, I was sounding, actually, pretty good.

Then, in 2012, something interesting happened. I found a book titled *Hidden History of Civil War Oregon*, by Randol B. Fletcher of Albany.

Thinking Randy was a neighbor, I dropped him a note, and learned he was familiar with my column and podcast, and had recommended me to the acquisitions editor at The History Press as a potential author.

That led to my first book: *Wicked Portland: The Wild and Lusty Underworld of a Frontier Seaport Town.*

Once that book was published, I began thinking of the possibility of narrating it as an audiobook. That was late in 2013, and by January 2014 it was ready. It didn't sell very well, but it opened the ways for me to develop a repertoire of audio production married to my other rising hobby — vintage pre-war pulp fiction — and the result was the founding, in 2014, of Pulp-Lit Productions. That, of course, is another story; but, you've surely noticed that the publishing imprint of this book, Ouragan House Publishers, is an imprint of Pulp-Lit.

When I first started off on this journey, I expected it would be a bit like *Star Trek:* A five-year mission. I fully expected to run out of interesting stories by then, if not before. The idea that there could be 150 or 200 weird, funny, tragic, ironic, and/or outrageous anecdotes from the history of such a young state — well, I thought it likely that I would run out of material long before I ran out of the inclination to continue.

That was 525 columns ago (at the time of this writing). There is still no end in sight.

Since at least 2014, I've been contemplating publishing a collection of the columns in book form. Once or twice I even went so far as to plan out what the table of contents might look like. I found, though, that as the list of columns grew longer, the project of categorizing and picking through them became more and more daunting.

Finally, in the summer of 2018, I blocked off some serious time to make the plans. The result of this — or, rather, the first of probably nine or 10 results of it — is the book you are listening to or reading right now.

So, there you have it: A little about me, a lot about the Offbeat Oregon History newspaper column, and, like a cherry on top of a delicious strawberry sundae, a bit of info about where this whole project is going. It's time now to turn to the first of our tales of Heroes and Rascals of Old Oregon.

Enjoy! And, thank you.

— Finn J.D. John

June 10, 2018
Corvallis, Oregon

PROLOGUE:

This volume is the first in a set of eight, possibly nine, which will be published under the Ouragan House imprint over the next several years.

Vol. 1: Heroes and Rascals of Old Oregon
Vol. 2: Love, Sex, and Murder in Old Oregon
Vol. 3: Bad Ideas and Horrible People in Old Oregon
Vol. 4: Larger-than-Life Characters of Old Oregon
Vol. 5: World Records and Famous People in Old Oregon
Vol. 6: Mysteries and Disasters of Old Oregon
Vol. 7: Plane Crashes and Shipwrecks in Old Oregon
Vol. 8: An Old Oregon Miscellany (may run to two volumes)

The eighth volume will consist mostly of stories that I have not yet written, but will be "banging out" for the next few years of weekly Offbeat Oregon History columns.

In this volume, you will find two broad categories of characters showcased: Heroes and Rascals.

Heroes, as I'm defining them, are people who sacrificed their own safety and in many cases their lives to try to help others.

It's an interesting thing about heroism: it always involves some sort of sacrifice. Heroes often don't survive. Of our 15 (plus the Coast Guardsmen involved in the Triumph incident, several of whom didn't survive) at least five sacrificed their lives. Theirs are probably the most compelling stories in the collection.

The word "Rascal" has a lot of conflicting connotations. It can refer to a terrible man like John M. Hipple, who served in the U.S. Senate under the alias "John H. Mitchell," which he adopted for criminal reasons after abandoning his wife and children, stealing several thousand dollars from his employer, and running away to the other side of the country with his mistress; or it can refer to a "lovable rogue," like Maud Johnson, "Queen of the Fakers," who bilked the railroads out of thousands of dollars by faking injuries on passenger trains.

The common element is a sort of brazenness, a charisma that our character trades on, a twinkle in the eye that takes the sting out of whatever shady thing he or she has done. Rascals are fun to read about. They aren't usually much fun to deal with in real life, of course; but most of them are hard to hate in spite of having done more than enough to deserve to be.

Some of the characters we're discussing here aren't exactly rascals; but they behave in such colorful and rascally ways that we have to include them in the category. Milwaukie businessman Art Lacey, with his adventures in buying and bringing home a war surplus B-17 bomber despite the best efforts of City Hall to stop him, is a perfect example of what I mean here. He was not a rascal; but he was most certainly a maverick, and so I have designated him here.

In this volume, we've got 32 tales of rascals and mavericks — so the bulk of this book is taken up with their stories.

The stories have been arranged chronologically, from oldest to newest; so we'll start out talking about a Hero who was a teenager when Lewis and Clark set out for the West Coast, and finish up talking about another Hero who died crashing his airplane in 2003.

Along the way, we'll meet some real memorable characters: an 1840s bootlegger who was the first resident and businessman of Portland; a lighthouse keeper who dedicated his life to getting a rescue service started; a ship captain who stole his own ship back from the U.S. Marshal Service after it was seized; a bootlegger who risked prison to save seven sailors' lives; a 1910s patent-medicine swindler peddling fake erectile-dysfunction remedies; an innocent Chinese man who stopped a brewing gang war by allowing himself to be hanged as a murderer; an early DJ who broadcasted with the microphone in one hand and a six-shooter in the other; and lots more.

Let's get started!

PART I:

HEROES.

MARIE AIOE DORION:

WOODSWOMAN.

The history of Oregon sometimes resembles an old manuscript from which every other page has been ripped out. Throughout the 1800s and much of the 1900s, most people only deemed stories worth preserving if they featured people who were wealthy, male, and of northern-European extraction — or unusually interesting to people who were.

But there are one or two individuals who have overcome this handicap through sheer colorfulness or competence.

One of these was Marie Aioe Dorion, the Ioway woman who accompanied the Astorian Party on its ill-starred overland journey from St. Louis to Astoria in 1810.

In a January 2016 article in the Portland Oregonian newspaper, writer Joseph Rose compared Marie Dorion to Hugh Glass, the character played by Leonardo DiCaprio in the 2016 movie *The Revenant*. The comparison is spot-on. If anything, Glass's story isn't extreme enough to measure up.

The records of Marie's birth and early years are scant and untrustworthy. We know she was born in roughly 1790, give or take a year or two. Some sources say she was *metis*, being the daughter of an Ioway mother and a

French-Canadian father; other sources say she was full-blooded Ioway. Even her maiden Ioway name isn't known for sure; some sources say it's "Wihmunkewakan," a Lakota word for "Holy Rainbow," but in a note on Marie's Wikipedia page the modern Ioway tribe argues that this is an error in the historical record resulting from someone getting Marie mixed up with her husband's first wife.

In 1806 she was married to a French-Canadian translator named Pierre Dorion. (Until her third husband, all Marie's marriages were under Ioway Nation law, so historians well into the twentieth century have refused to recognize them, calling her a "common-law wife." This, of course, is inaccurate.)

Pierre seems to have been a real rough-and-ready hard-drinking saloon-brawling tough guy. Whether he brought any of that home or not isn't known (except for one anecdote — more on that soon); but the couple seemed happy enough, and by 1810 they had two children, both boys: Paul, age 1; and Baptiste, age 4.

That's when the heroic part of Marie's story started: the year when the Astorian party was preparing to journey to the West Coast.

The Astorian party was a project of wealthy investor John Jacob Astor. His plan was to equip an expedition to follow in the footsteps of the Lewis and Clark expedition, establish a trading post at the mouth of the Columbia River, and use it to leverage a great worldwide trading empire. And he was in a hurry to do this, because certain British rivals were making similar plans up in Canada.

To establish his outpost, Astor equipped a sailing ship, the *Tonquin*, and sent it "around the horn" to Astoria to set things up. Meanwhile, he also outfitted a large overland expedition which would blaze a trail that others could follow, to establish trading posts along the way as part of his planned worldwide network.

It was this overland expedition that Marie Dorion was dragooned into. And that happened in an unusual way:

Marie's husband, Pierre, was approached by the leader of the overland expedition, a man named Wilson Price Hunt. Hunt offered Pierre a good salary and a $200 cash bonus to sign on as the Astorian party's translator and accompany it on its journey.

This might have represented a problem, because Pierre was already making plans to accompany another trading expedition under the direction of New Orleans native Manuel Lisa. But Pierre didn't see it that way. He saw it as a golden opportunity to rake in a quick $200 from this Eastern sucker and disappear in the night with Lisa's expedition, doubling his money.

An engraving from an 1838 edition of Edmund Fanning's book, Voyages to the South Seas, Indian and Pacific Oceans, China Sea, North-West Coast, *purports to show the attack on the* Tonquin *in a bay on Vancouver Island. (Image: W.H. Vermilye)*

Home he went to tell his wife, Marie, all about it, and to have her get the two boys ready for a surreptitious nighttime departure preparatory to meeting up with Lisa's expedition. And, of course, Pierre being Pierre, he stopped at a watering hole along the way to celebrate his scheme, and by the time he made it home, the $200 had been somewhat depleted and his mood had been correspondingly elevated.

But upon arrival, he found a buzz-harshing welcome from his wife. Marie was dead set against his scheme. Absolutely not, she told him; we will do nothing of the sort. If Pierre had engaged the family's word of honor to work for the Astorians, she told him, they would follow through on it. Stealing $200 and sneaking off into the woods with it was not an option.

Pierre, emboldened perhaps by the liquor, reacted poorly to this unexpected resistance, and apparently decided that the best way to make his point would be to rough her up a bit. Accordingly, he hit her — whether it was a punch or a slap is not clear. Whatever it was, Marie responded to it by picking up a club and laying her husband out cold.

While he was unconscious, Marie gathered all her necessaries, collected the two boys, seized for safekeeping the remainder of the $200, and slipped out the door.

When Pierre woke up, in a cold and empty house, he found his options considerably reduced. So, presumably with some reluctance, he presented himself as agreed a few days later, ready to embark on the Astorian expedition.

During this time Marie had been hiding out in the nearby woodlands with the two boys. When she saw that Pierre was going to honor his obligations, she strolled out of the woods and resumed her place at his side as if nothing had happened.

One thing, though, would never be the same. As historian Bill Gulick puts it in his book *A Roadside History of Oregon*, "There is no record that Pierre Dorion ever attempted to beat his wife again."

There is, by the way, another version of this story. In it, Pierre, when he gets home with the remainder of the $200, finds that Marie does not want to join the expedition, so he beats her to punish her for her reluctance. She then walks out on him, taking the boys with her. In this story, she is gone for two days, after which she returns chastened and ready to obey him. Now, this version may be accurate; but given what we know of Marie's temperament and character, it seems most likely that it's just a cover story that Pierre told to explain her extended absence without any humiliating loss of *machismo*.

But Marie may have had good reason not to want to go on this journey. Living in St. Louis as the Native American wife of a French-Canadian interpreter, she almost certainly moved in the same circles as the Shoshone wife of another French-Canadian interpreter living in St. Louis at the time — none other than Sacagawea, who had just returned from the Lewis and Clark expedition. And Sacagawea may have known — surely must have known — about a thing Meriwether Lewis did on the journey back, a deed that was like a modern echo of Odysseus' taunting of the blinded cyclops in *The Odyssey* — and that had not-entirely-dissimilar results.

While the Lewis and Clark party had been traveling through the lands of the Blackfeet tribe in northern Montana, a group of young Blackfeet had slipped up and tried to steal a horse and some rifles. They were spotted, and combat was engaged, and one Blackfeet man was stabbed and another shot and gravely wounded.

The brazenness of the incident put Lewis into a paroxysm of how-dare-they wrathfulness. So he hung a Jefferson Peace Medal around the corpse's neck, so that when it was found, the Blackfeet would know who had killed him.

This was a terrible idea — for practical as well as moral reasons. Theft, by the moral code of the Blackfeet, was more or less a lark. The tribe viewed its members' attempt to steal horses and guns from another group the way modern Americans would view a pack of local high-school kids climbing the town water tower in the night to paint it John Deere green.

But the moral code of the Blackfeet treated killing much more seriously. They were a warlike tribe. Blood was answered with blood. And the extra little touch of decorating the corpse with a medal made them furious.

A crew of expert boatmen tackles "La Riviere Enragee" — the Snake River in Hells Canyon — in May of 1973. You can imagine how dugout canoes would fare tackling rapids like these. (Image: Boyd Norton, US National Archives)

Since that time, the Blackfeet had been sworn enemies of the European-Americans from down the river. That meant the turf was well and thoroughly burned, and the Astor party would not be able to follow in the footsteps of the Lewis and Clark expedition. They would have to find another way.

Hunt, the expedition's leader, did not know this yet. But he would soon find out. And if Marie knew about it, possibly from talking to Sacagawea, she certainly would have had good reason not to want to go.

And as if that weren't enough, Marie was also four months pregnant.

Nonetheless, when the time came, she and the two boys were there with Pierre, ready to do their part.

Astor's plan was for the overland party to take about half a year blazing a suitable trail from St. Louis to the Pacific Ocean, noting good sites for trading posts along the way, which subsequent parties would later establish and operate. The trail would terminate at the mouth of the Columbia River where Lewis and Clark had camped.

Meanwhile, as the trailblazers were beating their way through the bushes, the crew of the sailing ship, *Tonquin*, would be on its way to Astoria via Tierra del Fuego — "around the horn" — a three-to-six-month journey given favorable winds. So, by the time the trailblazers arrived on the scene in late fall or early winter, the base in Astoria would be already established, ready to welcome the trail-weary travelers. They would settle in for a restful if soggy winter, and the following spring they would set about establishing overseas trading routes across the Pacific to the Far East, and get busy making enormous profits selling New World beaver and otter furs worldwide.

It was a neat scheme ... on paper.

Things went somewhat badly amiss, though, with both the land and the sea parties.

The sea party arrived on schedule in the 94-foot, 290-ton *Tonquin*, but in a state of near-mutiny; Jonathan Thorn, the captain of the ship, was a Navy officer on leave, and expected passengers and crew alike to behave like sailors on a Navy ship. Some of these passengers were investors in Astor's company, and considered themselves Thorn's bosses.

After dropping the Astorians off to build their trading post, Thorn sailed north, making for the Russian colony of New Arkangel (today's Sitka) to trade for supplies. He stopped on the way on Vancouver Island, where in trade negotiations he humiliated a First Nations chief — actually had him pitched overboard in a misguided attempt to teach him some humility. The natives, in retaliation, snuck aboard the Tonquin and attacked, killing most of the crew; one of the survivors blew up the powder magazine, killing himself and dozens of the boarding natives and sinking the Tonquin in the bay; and just like that, Fort Astoria was completely on its own.

Still, for the surviving members of the sea party, it could have been worse. They were at their destination, there was a sufficiency of food, and the natives, while not super-friendly, were at least not out for scalps.

The same would not be true for Marie Dorion and the overland party.

The overland party left the outskirts of St. Louis in the spring of 1811. There were a total of 60 of them, including the Dorian family — 61 if one counted the bun in Marie's oven.

Because Astor's Great Lakes fur empire was largely handled by French-Canadian voyageurs, this new expedition was staffed with quite a few of them. And for the first half of the journey, their watercraft skills stood the party in excellent stead. They made fine time working their way up the Missouri, until it was time to strike out overland to avoid the enraged Blackfeet. And even then, on horseback, they did as well as anyone might.

But then came a time when the party arrived on the banks of a broad and beautiful river, a river flowing northwest ... toward their destination. Correctly they divined that this was a tributary to the mighty Columbia. The voyageurs in the party became very excited.

There was some debate. Some members of the party who were not voyageurs felt that the overland journey, while not as easy and pleasant, was more of a bird in the hand — while who knew where this river might lead? For all they knew it could pour into a colossal sinkhole and run underground for hundreds of miles.

The argument was becoming heated, so party leader Hunt (who seems to have been reluctant to exercise actual leadership) tried to settle it by putting it to a vote. He needn't have bothered; there were far more voyageurs than anyone else in the party. Surely no one was surprised when the result was an overwhelming mandate to take to the water — and, just like that, the expedition was doomed.

As a side note, it is ironic that the overseas expedition failed because Captain Thorn was *too* decisive, while the overland expedition failed because Hunt was not decisive enough.

Back to our story:

The party camped there by the river for a few days while the voyageurs felled cottonwood trees and shaped them into canoes. Then, leaving their horses in the care of some nearby Native Americans, they took to the water.

They should have asked the locals first. Or, perhaps they did; but the voyageurs, born to the open water, the speeding canoe, and the flashing paddle, had high confidence in their ability to handle any kind of river. Even if the Native Americans had warned them about what was in store, they likely would have assumed they could handle it.

Well, for the first several days the party made thrilling progress: 60 miles one day, 40 miles the next (some rapids had to be portaged around), 50 on the third ... but the river was getting rougher and rougher.

By the time the river revealed its true colors, they were in what we know today as Hells Canyon, hundreds of miles downstream from where they had left the horses, and they had given the river a new name: *La Rivière Enragée* — Mad River. Today we know it as the Snake. It was not navigable. Not even for voyageurs.

The party split into two groups before striking out cross-country, hoping thereby to be better able to feed themselves as late autumn ripened into early winter. Even so, all of them soon were on the brink of starvation. They depended greatly on the Shoshone tribes in the area, but the high plateau terrain there is not fruitful, and the population was scant and had little to share. Nonetheless, share they did; all the members of the party would have died of starvation and exposure if not for Shoshone charity.

Throughout this time, Marie Dorion was preternaturally stoic, never complaining, always keeping up, while becoming more and more visibly pregnant. Finally, she went into labor; Hunt and the party forged ahead, leaving her and Pierre and the two boys behind somewhere near the location

The monument in honor of Marie Dorion placed at her gravesite in 2014 by the Champoeg chapter of the Daughters of the American Revolution. (Image: Andrew Parodi)

of present-day North Powder. A day or two later they rejoined the party, and Marie had her new baby in her arms.

The baby died eight days later. It seems likely that there simply wasn't sufficient nourishment for Marie to nurse him.

Finally, on Jan. 7, the reluctant Shoshone guides whom Hunt had bribed and shamed into helping them brought the first group into the Grand Ronde Valley, the little banana-belt pocket of lush grasslands and plentiful game tucked into the otherwise inhospitable Blue Mountains of Eastern Oregon — around what's now La Grande.

There they stayed for a week or two with charitable Native Americans, gorging on deer and elk meat and starchy roots, as the other members of the overland party straggled in.

Then they set out for the short journey to the banks of the Columbia, down which they would find their destination.

It was January 18, 1812, when the traders at Fort Astoria looked up and saw two canoes coming down the river toward them. The overland party had made it at last — or, rather, most of them had; of the original complement of 60 (61 if one includes Marie's baby), just 45 survived.

And a case could be made — based on circumstantial evidence, but lots of it — that that number would have been much smaller had Marie and her two boys not been with the party. The decision to abandon the horses and follow an unknown river should have been a fatal one. The main reason it was not was the charity of Shoshone and other Native American tribes. Would those tribes have been as responsive, as willing to share their own limited resources, without the faces of the children and Marie among the group of bedraggled, dirty, scraggly-bearded, scary men? Or would they have left them all alone to starve?

As for Marie, she may have thought her troubles were over when her husband and the boys arrived at the fort. She may also have thought that nothing could ever induce her to go back into that barren Snake River wilderness that had slain her baby and come so close to taking the rest of her family as well. But if she did think that, she was wrong.

In July of 1813 — literally the very next year — Marie and her husband, Pierre, were packing their two children up for another journey into the wilderness that had nearly killed them. This time, the plan was to set up a string of trading posts and start collecting beaver pelts to be turned into fetching headgear for well-dressed European gentlemen.

The beaver trappers and traders spent the summer and early fall getting trading posts built and establishing relationships with Shoshone tribe members in the Snake River area. And when winter came along, this time Marie and her kids were ready for it. With Reed and several other traders and trappers, they holed up in the expedition's main outpost, well supplied with everything they'd need to get through a high-country winter.

But then came the evening of Jan. 10, when a friendly Shoshone tribe member came to warn Marie that the neighboring Bannock tribe was making trouble. These "bad Snakes," as some sources call them, had started burning the Pacific Fur Company's outposts and killing the traders and trappers. The Bannock war party had just laid one of the camps to waste, and was on its way to another … the one at which Pierre Dorion was stationed.

Marie, very alarmed, thanked and fed the visitor, sent him on his way home, and packed her stuff. She and the two boys were going to go out into the snow, racing with the marauding Bannocks to get to Pierre in time to warn him.

She was three days getting there, trudging through knee-deep snow and leading her horse with the two boys sitting on it. And she got there just a few hours too late.

Trapper Gilles LeClerc met her as she approached the outpost, staggering in the snow, weak from loss of blood. He was the only survivor. Everyone else had been murdered.

Marie was now a widow.

There was nothing to do now but turn around and follow the trail Marie had broken through the snow, back to the main outpost. Luckily, the marauders hadn't quite managed to catch all the horses, and Marie was able to capture two of them; so all four of them were able to ride on the journey back.

Two days later, LeClerc succumbed to his injuries. Marie and the boys pressed on.

But at the post, they found not the welcoming fires and nourishing food they'd expected, but charred and blackened walls and mutilated bodies. The main trading post had been wiped out and burned down. Marie and the boys were now the only survivors of the beaver-trapping party, and they were on their own, a good 200 miles away from the nearest source of help, in the dead of a mountain winter.

Marie set out immediately, going northwest, making for the Columbia River area where she knew the Native Americans to be friendly.

They struggled through the snowdrifts to the Snake River, swam it (presumably 3-year-old Paul and 6-year-old Baptiste rode across the river on the horses, but Marie probably had to swim). They forged on through what's now eastern Oregon. But then, as they reached the Blue Mountains, one of the horses collapsed, unable to continue.

Marie decided it was time to stop. She built a rude but cozy shelter and installed her family in it. She built a fire to warm the boys, then slaughtered the horses and started smoking the meat.

The three of them lived in that tiny shelter in the snowy mountains, surrounded by drifts and battered by blizzards, for 53 days. They lived primarily on smoked horsemeat, of course, augmented by a few frozen berries, the inner bark of trees, and small rodents that Marie caught in snares made from horsehair.

An early spring thaw hit their camp in March, just as their horsemeat supply was almost exhausted. Marie packed up the children and the remaining horsemeat and the three of them left their little shelter.

But two days after that, a blizzard struck. Trying to forge on, Marie became snow-blind, and was forced to stop, rig up another shelter (cruder this time, because of course she was snow-blind while building it) and convalesce for three days.

Finally, the food exhausted, she ventured out with the boys for a final desperate push. And, fifteen days after they left their little shelter, they reached the plains. There, Marie saw campfire smoke.

Unsure if it was friend or foe, she cached the boys behind a rock and approached the village. By the time she reached it, her strength was gone and she was literally on her hands and knees.

Luck was with her. It was a friendly tribe of Walla Wallas.

Marie lived in the Oregon Territory for the rest of her life. In the late 1810s she married a fur trapper named Louis Venier, and the two of them had a daughter together, named Marguerite; but Louis was killed by Shoshone Indians in 1821, leaving Marie once again a widow.

Her third and final marriage was in Walla Walla to a French-Canadian interpreter named Jean-Baptiste Toupin, with whom she had two more children: François and Marianne.

In 1841 the family moved to a farm near the Willamette Valley community of St. Louis, where Marie settled into a quiet life, devoted to her family and the local Catholic church. When she died in 1850, she received the high honor of burial inside the walls of the church. She was only about 60 years old when she died, but the official church records listed her age at death as 100 years. This surely was an understandable error ... she had lived a full enough life to cover an entire century, and then some.

Perhaps because she lacks a charismatic name like "Sacagawea," Marie Dorion is not much talked about today, and has never appeared on U.S. currency or anything like that. But her feat of surviving over the winter in some of the most hostile wilderness in the continent with two small boys in tow made her famous in her day.

Sources and works cited:
- "*Four Arrows Draft Historical-Genealogical Report on Pierre Dorion,*" an article by Rarihokwats of Ontario, Canada, published Oct. 2, 2002, on the Historical Marker Database at hmdb.org;
- *Roadside History of Oregon*, a book by Bill Gulick, published in 1991 by Mountain Press of Missoula, MT;
- *Astoria: John Jacob Astor and Thomas Jefferson's Lost Pacific Empire*, a book by Peter Stark, published in 2014 by Ecco Press of New York;
- "*Marie Dorion and the Astoria Expedition,*" an article by Wayne Jewett published in the October 2000 issue of *Wild West* magazine.

CAPT. JOEL MUNSON:

LIFEBOAT RESCUER.

It was the Ides of March, in 1865. Captain I. Lewis, commander of the 300-ton barque *Industry*, was staring at the mouth of the Columbia River.

He'd been staring east at that river for two straight weeks, as the *Industry* tacked back and forth in the safe, deep waters beyond the notorious Columbia River bar, known (for good reason) as a graveyard of ships. Lewis was waiting for the bar pilots to send a boat with a pilot over to guide the big windjammer safely into the river.

But no pilot had come, and now the Industry's supplies of food and water were exhausted. Lewis couldn't wait any longer.

He gave the order to fall off the wind and sail into the bar.

At the top of the Cape Disappointment Lighthouse, on the Washington side of the river, the lighthouse keeper, Joel Munson, must have watched this with mounting anxiety. Captain Lewis was taking a huge risk, and no one knew that better than Munson. His duties at the lighthouse went beyond tending the light; it also regularly fell to him to retrieve and arrange for burial of the corpses of unlucky mariners that all too frequently washed up on the beach nearby. The prevailing winds on the Oregon coast come out of the southwest during shipwreck season, so when a ship foundered on the bar, the wreckage — human and otherwise — tended to be blown his way.

Sailing ships were especially vulnerable on the bar. There were unpredictable wind shadows, and many a ship would sail on in only to be suddenly becalmed at the worst possible moment.

And that's exactly what happened to the *Industry* an hour or so later. And although the wind picked back up, the current had shifted her position, and on the next attempt to tack, the Industry struck a sandbar, which tore off her rudder.

Now truly helpless, the *Industry* wallowed in the trough of the sea on the bar as the waves got bigger — probably as a result of the tide starting to go out. A lifeboat was launched and promptly capsized. The ship drifted further onto the sandbar and stuck there, pinned to the seafloor in ten or twelve feet of water as walls of what sailors call "green water" took turns slamming down on it. The survivors on the ship climbed into the rigging to escape from the pounding breakers, which soon had the decks cleared of everything, including even the cabins.

They waited

Cape Disappointment Lighthouse as viewed from the north. (Image: David Keyzer)

there all day and all night.

Finally, the next day, the seas were calm enough for the survivors to build rafts from the wreckage and float to shore. One raft made it; the other did not. Seven men lived; 17 died.

By the time the last mariner had drowned, it had been a good 48 hours since the Industry's rudder was stripped off. Munson, who had been unable to do anything but watch helplessly, now had something he could do: Go to the beach and look for corpses.

A portrait of Capt. Joel Munson. This photograph was made in his later years, probably when he was operating a steamer, circa 1880. (Image: Joseph Gaston)

But when he got to the beach, Munson found something else: A battered lifeboat — either the one that had capsized after launch, or one stripped off the Industry by a "comber" during the shipwreck.

Munson decided he'd take that lifeboat and use it to actually do something about the situation that he found so intolerable.

Munson was a gifted fiddle player — his nickname was "Fiddler Smith." He decided to use that talent, along with his new lifeboat, to get a lifesaving station started at "Cape D." And the next time a ship went down, he'd just row right out there and start fishing people out of the drink.

He booked a series of fund-raising dances in Astoria, charging $2.50 a head — equal to about $40 today. The community turned out in force to support the cause. He also talked the U.S. Lighthouse Service into building a boathouse for the lifeboat he was restoring, and put out a call to the community for volunteers to help him man it when there was rescuing to be done.

By the following spring, Munson could say with absolute confidence that if the *Industry* wreck were repeated, every hand would be rescued.

But he didn't have to boast. In May of 1866, another barque, the *W.B. Scranton* — ironically owned and captained by the same fellow who had owned the *Industry*, Paul Corno — came to grief on the bar in a similar manner.

Munson and his volunteers were ready. Several hours later, the entire crew of 13 men was safely on shore.

A few years later, Munson and his team rowed out again to rescue 10 mariners off the rigging of the *Architect*, a barque that simply filled with water for unknown reasons and sank to the bottom with its masts sticking up above the waves.

By 1877, Munson was getting a bit too old for this sort of thing, so he handed it off to his volunteers, retired from the lighthouse service and moved to Astoria.

There he built a small steamer, the *Magnet*, and went into business operating it until 1881, when he was appointed as lightkeeper at Point Adams, on the Oregon side of the river. He did this until 1898, when bad health forced him to leave the post; he died a short time later.

As for the life station he founded, it was staffed by community volunteers until 1882, when the U.S. government made it an official operation and hired career surfmen. An additional station was later built at Point Adams. The U.S. Coast Guard runs both stations today, using their famous unsinkable 47-foot motor lifeboats to rescue mariners in astonishingly hostile seas.

Over the years, thousands of mariners have been saved from the lonely, watery death that came to those 17 sailors on the *Industry*, almost 150 years ago. And it all started when the Pacific Ocean took away their lifeboat and gave it to Joel Munson.

Nobody wants to drown at sea. Still, if one has to die that way anyway, there's something special and noble about that death being part of something that saves the lives of so many others.

Sources and works cited:
- *Oregon Shipwrecks*, a book by Don Marshall, published in 1984 by Binford & Mort of Portland;
- *The Centennial History of Oregon, 1811-1912*, a book by Joseph Gaston, published in 1912 by S.J. Clark of Chicago;
- "Joel Munson, rescuer," an article by Elinor DeWire published in the February 2009 issue of *Focal Point* magazine.

CHENG:

SMUGGLER.

Cheng was on his way to a southern-Oregon mining outpost one evening just before the Civil War, during the heyday of the California Gold Rush, when he saw the wagon. It was slumped down in the road, hunched over a broken axle. But it obviously had only recently been abandoned; its canvas cover was still in fine shape. It would make a good shelter for the night, he thought.

He pulled open the flap. A terrified scream rang out. Peering inside, Cheng saw a starving, frightened woman holding a tiny newborn baby.

She soon calmed down when she saw that her visitor was just a mild, unassuming Chinese man, dressed in rags. Cheng did not look the least bit dangerous. He didn't look like much of anything, really. That was the secret of his success. In fact, it was probably the reason he was still alive.

Cheng opened his bag and started pulling things out. Food, of course, was the first order of business. But Cheng also had a wide assortment of herbs and extracts used for traditional Chinese medicine, and he used them to brew up a strengthening decoction for the woman and her baby.

They would need their strength to get out of the predicament they were in. Their wagon axle had broken a week before, and the woman's husband had taken the horses and set out to find help. There had been no sign of him since. Why he had taken both horses, instead of just one, wasn't clear; perhaps he wanted to avoid drawing attention to the wagon with his little family inside.

In any case, they couldn't wait for him. So the next morning, Cheng guided her to the nearest town.

He stayed just long enough to make sure she was safe there — staying with the local stabler's family while waiting and hoping for her husband to be found.

Then Cheng disappeared into the night like a phantom. The last thing he wanted was attention of any kind, good or bad. If he stayed in town, he could count on both — gratitude for saving two lives mixed with suspicion that he'd had something to do with the husband's disappearance. It didn't matter. Any kind of publicity could be deadly for him.

Cheng was a courier for the frontier Chinese community. During the Gold Rush, as many as 20 percent of miners in southern Oregon and northern California were Chinese. They worked the rejected tailings of less patient miners, getting surprising amounts of gold out of them. They tried to be as inconspicuous as they could, and they lived in little segregated camps in the field, hoping a combination of invisibility and numbers would help protect them from drunks, bullies and robbers.

And they needed all the protection they could get. In frontier American society, the law offered them almost nothing. In theory it treated all alike, but in practice it covered Chinese immigrants only barely and offered them protection in only the most egregious cases. A murder here, a robbery there — few non-Chinese people cared, and that included sheriffs and judges. And it certainly included jury members.

So Chinese miners couldn't just pack up their gold dust and ride to Portland to buy things with it; they were too tempting a target. To get their gold out of the field, and buy things they needed or wanted — Chinese herbs, exotic dried seafoods and vegetables, opium — they turned to professionals like Cheng. Cheng was part of an elite group of what you might call blockade runners. In effect, he was a smuggler — just not an illegal one.

On a visit to a camp, Cheng would pick up the miners' gold and bring it to one of the major Chinatowns — San Francisco and Portland. There, the gold would be handled by trusted shopkeepers — divided out on different miners' accounts, sent home to family members in China, and used to pay for supplies. Cheng would then return with the supplies. It was on such a return trip that he came across the starving woman.

To safely deliver such valuable cargo took a special kind of skill.

The Chinese apothecary shop in the Kam Wah Chung Company building in John Day. Chinese herbal remedies and supplements were one of the most important things couriers like Mr. Cheng supplied to Chinese miners in the gold fields. (Image: Ian Poellet)

"He was very cautious," Cheng's descendant, Dave Cheng, told magazine writer Robert Joe Stout in an interview, "and never wore good clothing or let on in any way that he was carrying thousands of dollars concealed among his rags."

The younger Cheng, a San Francisco resident, told Stout his ancestor made a point of not paying cash for things on the way. He'd trade labor for what he needed, like a 1930s hobo — working as a deckhand to earn passage on a steamboat, or shoveling out someone's stables in exchange for permission to sleep in them for the night.

Cheng made his rounds out of either Portland or San Francisco; typically from San Francisco he'd journey to Eureka and Weatherville, then cross the border through Ashland to Jacksonville, Gold Hill, and Roseburg; then north to Portland and sometimes on northward to one or more of the Puget Sound towns.

Dave Cheng's memories of family stories are probably the best documentation we'll find of the exploits of his remarkable ancestor and his colleagues. The fires that broke out after the 1907 earthquake hit San Francisco's Chinatown especially hard, and most of their records are now lost.

We still don't have basic information about how many Chinese people there were on the West Coast.

But it's possible — almost certain, in fact — that many more deeds of heroism and compassion done by Chinese pioneers have been utterly lost to history.

As for the woman in the wagon, her fate has mostly been lost to history too. But through discreet inquiries Cheng was able to learn that her husband never reappeared; she finally gave up and moved with her baby back to Tennessee with her parents. But Cheng also learned that before she left, she rose to his defense against several of the townspeople, who refused to believe Cheng hadn't had something to do with her husband's disappearance.

He had been right to leave when he did.

Sources and works cited:
- *"The Chinese Mail Service,"* an article by Robert Joe Stout published in Little Known tales from Oregon History: A Collection of 28 Stories from Cascades East Magazine *(ed. Geoff Hill), published in 1988 by Sun Publishing of Bend;*
- *"Never Far from Home: Being Chinese in the California Gold rush," an article by Sylvia Sun Minnick published in* Riches for All: The California Gold Rush and the World *(ed. Kenneth Owens), published in 2002 by the University of Nebraska Press in Lincoln, Nebraska.*

ING HAY:

HEALER.

In the decade or two following the 1849 gold rush, a sort of "bracero" program got started in the western U.S. Chinese laborers — called "coolies" after the Chinese term *ku li*, meaning "muscle strength"— poured across the ocean to the land they called "Gold Mountain," eager to do the dirty, menial and degrading jobs that were left to be done when all the European-Americans were off digging for gold or staking homestead claims.

Most frontier Chinese people had great difficulty learning English and spoke a pidgin version that the European-American settlers found amusing, but not very useful as a basis for social connections. And, of course, most of their records were destroyed when San Francisco burned. So there's a lot we don't know about them.

What is known, of course, is that the Chinese in early Oregon were treated as second-class citizens — openly so. And when the need for cheap muscle began to fade with the completion of the transcontinental railroad lines, the U.S. government hastened to slam the door with the Chinese Exclusion Act, locking their second-class-citizen status in by statute.

The Kam Wah Chung Company building in John Day as it appears today. (Image: Finetooth)

But in John Day, there was one Chinese man whom the local residents would "posse up" to protect, if they had to. His name was Ing Hay — better known as Doc Hay — and he was a skilled Chinese physician.

Hay was born in 1862 in the impoverished and opium-ravaged Guangdong province in China. He came to the U.S. twenty years later, leaving a wife and daughter in the old country.

At first Hay did *ku li* work in the Walla Walla area, but later he moved to John Day, where he met a fellow traveler from the same part of China, a man named Lung On.

Lung On — known to his Western friends as Leon — was a highly unusual man, and by all accounts a true genius. He arrived in the U.S. in 1882, and by 1887 he'd mastered English with enough fluency to fit in in mainstream society — most Chinese people never moved past crude pidgin jargon. He soon was riding with cowboys, wearing a six-shooter and bending elbows and playing cards with buckaroos in saloons. He moved easily and fluently between the two worlds — the underground world of Chinese expats living apart from the "barbarians," and the mainstream English-speaking world of farmers and merchants and cowboys. And pretty much everybody loved him.

When the first automobiles arrived on the scene shortly after the turn of the century, Lung On became an enthusiastic early adopter, and with a partner opened a Pontiac dealership — the first auto dealership in Oregon east of the Cascades.

In Ing Hay, Lung On knew he'd found a man as extraordinary as himself. Hay was a trained and successful pulsologist — meaning he was trained in diagnosing medical issues by just feeling the pulse of the patient in different parts of the body. Today, this sounds like new-age hokum, and so perhaps it is; but it's part of a long tradition of medical practice in China, and even there very few people were able to practice it. Hay was clearly one of them, and it enabled him to perform a sort of parlor trick to demonstrate his competence:

Dr. Ing Hay as he appeared as a young man, probably around 1890 or so.. (Image: Oregon Historical Society)

"Former patients of Doc Hay state that he often told them what was wrong with them before they said anything to him," Jeffrey Barlow and Christine Richardson report in their book. "In fact, Hay delighted in surprising his patients with this diagnostic technique."

This gifted but reticent healer and this boisterous and friendly showman soon went into business together, forming a company and a friendship that would last for the rest of their lives: The Kam Wah Chung company — which translates into "Golden Flower of Prosperity."

Hay proved especially effective in dealing with what was known, in the day, as "blood poisoning" — septic infections.

And septic infections were a big deal. Back then, every time you cut your hand or even pricked it on the wrong piece of barbed-wire fence, you faced a real risk of death. If you were unlucky, your hand would swell up the size of a grapefruit, red streaks would appear on your skin moving toward your heart, and you'd die. Western medicine, at the time, was

The kitchen in the Kam Wah Chung Company building in John Day. (Image: Ian Poellet)

essentially powerless against this. And everybody in Eastern Oregon was constantly working around livestock and barbed wire. Blood poisoning was a leading cause of death in rural 1880s Oregon.

Doc Hay's blood-poisoning cure was an herbal decoction that he cooked up at the Kam Wah Chung building and sealed up in quart beer bottles. A patient would pour out a 12-ounce draft of the stuff, which of course tasted horrible; but after faithfully following the course Doc Hay prescribed, the patient would get better — every time.

Some of his other remedies were not quite so satisfactory; there are a few letters among his personal effects from patients reporting things like "I received your medicine a few days ago and took it according to directions, but it nearly killed me." But far more of Hay's patients got better than worse.

He also supplied female patients with abortifacients when asked to do so. This was, at the time, highly illegal.

It wasn't always smooth sailing for Hay in John Day. In the first few years of the twentieth century, there was a big scare in mainstream American society over what you might call Chinatown-slum-culture mythology — stories of opium dens that reached out to trap unwary young men, sinister Fu Man Chu types ensnaring young women into a life of "white slavery" to be peddled as prostitutes, vicious "tong wars," and a variety of other exaggerated stereotypes and outright fictions that chilled the blood of many an early-1900s parent. Dime-novel heroes like Old and Young King Brady in Secret Service had been playing on these fears and at the same time stoking them since the 1880s.

All of this led to a few rough encounters with some of the more credulous members of the community in the very early 1900s.

In 1906 a mob stormed Kam Wah Chang in the middle of the night, seized Lung On and two other Chinese men, and hauled them to the local jail, where they persuaded the authorities to lodge them for the night on charges of possession of opium (which had just been outlawed). A delegation of the insurgents demanded that the entire Chinese population leave town immediately. But, nothing came of this — presumably someone realized that if the Chinese community went, so did Ing Hay — and Lung On and the others each paid a $100 fine for opium possession and went home the next day.

Trouble also came from the medical establishment. Over the first few decades of the twentieth century, conventional doctors joined the fledgling American Medical Association in trying to have Hay prosecuted for practicing medicine without a license, as part of their campaign against patent-medicine swindles and itinerant quack doctors. This should have been an easy case; Ing Hay had no license or formal credentials of any kind. The problem was, no jury in Grant County would convict him. For them, his record was license enough.

Another interesting side note: Old-timers in John

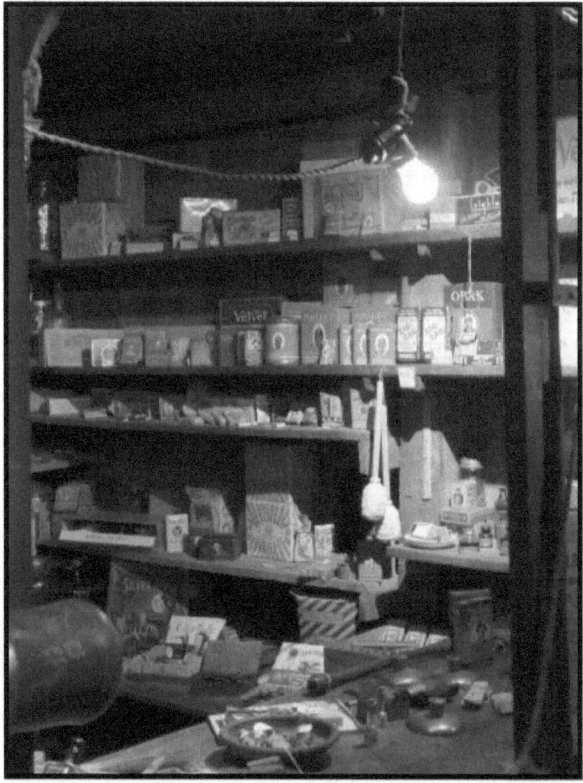

The tobacco counter at the Kam Wah Chung Company store, at the building in John Day. (Image: Ian Poellet)

Day told Barlow and Richardson that not a single one of Doc Hay's patients died during the terrible Spanish Flu epidemic that killed so many people around the world — about 3,500 of them in Oregon — in 1919. Not one.

Doc Hay and Lung On weren't perfect people, of course. As a young man, Lung On loved gambling of all types, from Fan Tan to Faro, but especially horse racing; he and Hay had some strident fights when he lost. And Doc Hay was an occasional opium smoker, right up until the drug was outlawed in 1905; in fact, the Kam Wah Chung building occasionally served as an opium den. Both men were big disappointments to their families back home in China, who wrote frequently begging them to come home — which they could not do, for fear of being prevented from returning — or at least send money, which they did only very sporadically.

The end came in 1940, when Lung On suddenly sickened and died, and nothing Doc Hay could do seemed to make a difference. Hay took this very hard, and very personally, as if he had failed his friend in his hour of greatest need.

Doc Hay continued practicing after that, but it wasn't the same, and he was plainly miserable without his lifelong friend. Toward the end, his eyesight started failing. By the time of his death, in 1952, at the age of 82, he was completely blind.

When Doc died, the Kam Wah Chung & Co. building was boarded up and deeded to the City of John Day. In 1967, the city belatedly realized it owned the place and had the boards removed. They found everything in place, like a time capsule. Under Doc Hay's bed was a box containing $23,000 in uncashed checks — checks from people who, he'd told a friend, needed the money more than he did.

They also found six cases of fine bourbon tucked away in the attic — Lung On's stash, no doubt.

Kam Wah Chung has since been turned into a museum, which is well worth visiting.

Sources and works cited:
- *"Kam Wah Chung," an episode of* Oregon Experience *produced by Beth Harrington and published by Oregon Public Broadcasting on May 14, 2009;*
- The China Doctor of John Day, *a book by Jeffrey Barlow and Christine Richardson, published in 1979 by Binford & Mort of Portland;*
- *"Oregon's China Doctor and his Assistant," an article by Daniel Lindley published in the February 2002 issue of* Wild West Magazine.

"ONE-EYED CHARLEY" PARKHURST:

STAGECOACH DRIVER.

In the frontier years before the arrival of railroads to the West Coast, the tough characters who drove the stagecoaches were among society's most admired citizens.

And among those stagecoach drivers there was one whose macho exploits had already passed into legend by the time he retired from the job: "One-Eyed Charley" Parkhurst.

Parkhurst was a natural with horses, able to get them to do nearly anything. His stagecoach driving was so precise that he was able to hit a silver half-dollar placed in the street as a target with both wheels on either side of his rig. (Remember, there was no steering wheel on a stagecoach; one could only "steer" it by controlling the horses.) With a whip, he could slice open an envelope from 15 feet away, or take a cigar out of a man's mouth without touching him.

He was pretty good with a pistol, too. A good driver had to be. Robbing stagecoaches was almost an industry back then, before more secure methods were developed for hauling large sums of money around, and oh yeah — large sums of money were constantly needing to be hauled around. Usually it was in the form of gold nuggets and dust being transported from the diggings to the branch mint in San Francisco; but sometimes it would be cash intended to cover payroll for railroad crews, logging operations, and other big undertakings.

To get it to its destination safely, the stagecoach would carry it in an "express box," a large locked wooden crate, into which would be loaded the gold, securities, and other valuable things.

The problem was, few things were easier for an enterprising desperado than to position himself on the uphill slope of a steep hill and step out in front of the stagecoach as it came, Winchester cocked and at ready, and order the driver to "throw down the box."

Few drivers ever objected. Perched up high on the bench, they made fabulous targets, and the robbers always had the drop on them. It's never smart to draw on a drawn gun. And so down would go the box, and the driver would be on his way; a glance behind would usually show the bandit chopping away at the express box with an ax.

The robbers avoided One-Eyed Charley's runs, though, because they knew he wouldn't play along. He'd proved it one day when, in response to the familiar old "Throw down the box," he "turned his wild mustangs and wicked revolver loose," according to a New York Times article, bringing the express box through unharmed. The bandit, a fellow known to history only by the nickname "Sugarfoot," staggered to a nearby cabin, where he told the whole story before dying from his wounds.

There were lots of other drivers who didn't risk their lives by shooting back, so after the Sugarfoot incident the bandits concentrated on them and left Charley alone.

And in general, alone is how Charley liked to be left.

"He was a man about 40 years old, rather short in stature, lame in one leg, and having but one eye," recalled Santa Cruz, California, resident Ed Martin in a newspaper article published about 50 years later. "Thus, you see, he had rather a peculiar appearance: the absence of any beard, save a very little on his upper lip, a falsetto voice, a face rather repulsive on first acquaintance, strikingly composed a make-up of such a character as to be remembered."

For the 15 years or so that he drove gold-country stagecoaches, Charley mostly worked California lines. But his duties frequently took him north into Oregon as well.

"Charley ... used the language of the 'knights of the whip,' swore at his horses as the occasion demanded, took his 'nip' at the stopping places, carried the United States Mail, conveyed messages from one settlement to another

An advertising flier for the Overland Mail Company, dating from around 1870 or so. (Image: Univ. of Central Missouri)

in his route, performed his duties faithfully, and was a general favorite on the road," Martin recalled.

But by the mid-1860s Charley, now well into his 50s, was feeling the effects of a long career of bouncing for days at a time on a hard wooden bench. Arthritis had developed and was making it hard to work. Plus, the railroads were being built, and replacing the stagecoach lines he'd helped establish; he could see the writing on that wall. It was time to quit, he decided.

So, "he started a half-way house, 'Refreshments for Man or Beast'; took care of the relay of stage horses; bought 25 acres of land on the Calabasas; and apparently settled down on his own ranch," Martin said. That was in around 1864.

Charley farmed the land for a decade and a half, getting by but certainly not getting rich. During the winter he augmented his income by working on lumberjack crews in the woods, where he was a tiger in spite of his age, commanding wages as high as anyone's.

But by the late 1870s, the end was near for the aging Charley. A cancerous tumor on his tongue had developed, probably in response to a lifetime of chewing tobacco; and his arthritis, now in all his limbs, kept him in constant pain. The formerly genial and popular old "whip" grew taciturn. Finally, in 1879, he died.

And then ...

"When the hands of the kind friends who had ministered to his dying wants came to lay out the dead body of the adventurous Argonaut, a discovery was made that was literally astounding," writes the reporter for the *California Call* newspaper, in the obituary article about Charley. "Charley Parkhurst was a woman, a perfectly formed, fully developed woman. ... The discoveries of the successful concealment for protracted periods of the female sex under the disguise of the masculine are not infrequent, but the case of Charley Parkhurst may fairly claim to rank as by all odds the most astonishing of all of them. That a young woman should assume man's attire and, friendless and alone, defy the dangers of the voyage of 1849, to the then-almost-mythical California — dangers over which hardy pioneers still grow boastful — has in it sufficient of the wonderful. That she should achieve distinction in an occupation above all professions calling for the best physical qualities of nerve, courage, coolness, and endurance — qualities arrogantly claimed as being almost exclusively masculine — and that she should add to them the almost romantic personal bravery that enables one to fight one's way through the ambush of an enemy, seems almost fabulous, and that for 30 years she should be in constant and intimate association with men and women, and that her true sex should never have been even suspected, and that she should finally go knowingly down to her death, without disclosing by word or deed who she was."

The article went on to add that Charley had registered to vote in 1867, just after the Civil War; so, she had probably been the first female West Coast resident to vote for a Presidential candidate. (The claim that she was the first American woman to vote is often made, but isn't true. In New Jersey in the late 1700s, only property owners were allowed to vote, and if a property owner happened to be a woman, she got to vote.)

"Charley," as it turned out, was short for "Charlotte," not "Charles": Charlotte Durkey (or Darkey) Parkhurst, born to Mary and Ebenezer Parkhurst in Sharon, Vermont. She was their third and last child; her mother either died giving birth to her or shortly thereafter, and her older brother, Charles, died a little later. Charlotte and her sister Maria were then placed up in an orphanage in Lebanon, New Hampshire. I haven't been able to learn what became of her father.

At the age of 12, Charlotte ran away from the orphanage, dressing as a boy to avoid detection and so that she could get a job in a nearby livery stable. Although she cannot have had many opportunities to work with horses in the orphanage, she found that she had a natural way with them — and her boss, Ebenezer Balch, noticed. Soon Balch asked her to drive a buggy;

and, when she easily did so, Balch moved her up to larger and larger rigs until she was driving a team of six.

By now Charlotte knew the score. As a little orphaned girl, with no family and no dowry, she had zero prospects in early-1800s society. But as a little orphaned boy, she could travel and work and make her way in the world.

So Charlotte Parkhurst disappeared into the mists of time, and a stocky, barrel-chested, piping-voiced lad named Charley took her place.

One-Eyed Charley's grave marker in the Watsonville (Calif.) pioneer cemetery. (Image: Wikicuda)

Charley spent the next 20 years or so working with horses on the East Coast. For a few years she was in Georgia with another driver, and there's some evidence that she tried to settle down and start a family at that time; some sources say physicians examining her after her death determined that she had given birth at some point (although frankly, given the state of the medical profession back then, there's ample reason to be skeptical about any 1879 doctor's claims about anything, medical or otherwise).

If she did start a family, though, it clearly ended in early tragedy, because she was back in New England in 1849 when news of the California Gold Rush broke. There, she met Jim Burch and Frank Stevens, and the three of them decided to go to California and get into the stagecoach business. And, in the words of an old cliché, The Rest is History.

The admiring tone of the *California Call* article wasn't universally adopted by the other newspapers covering the sudden posthumous revelation of Charley's womanhood. Other writers were more defensive. A wary, pugnacious article in the *Sacramento Record-Union* said the story was "seriously impeached" by the fact that the names of the attending physicians had not been included in the original report, but added (with an almost audible sneer) that there was "nothing intrinsically incredible in the story, for women have in many remarkable and well-authenticated cases played the part of men"; it finishes by opining that even if it was true, most likely Charley was a hermaphrodite — born with both male and female body parts, but really a man.

This response, while certainly ungallant, was kind of understandable. After all, what Charley had done was nothing less than to infiltrate the most macho, swaggeringly male-dominated profession of her day — and demonstrate that a woman could do it better.

Sources and Works Cited:
- Encyclopedia of Frontier Biography, *a book by Dan Thrapp, published in 1991 by the University of Nebraska Press of Lincoln, Nebraska;*
- "*Charley's Secret: A Stagecoach Driver's Sexual Identity Concealment,*" *an article by Shannon Moon Leonetti published in Vol. 32, issue 2, of* American History *magazine.*

MARY G. LEONARD:

ATTORNEY AT LAW.

Most Oregon professional women can point to a truly amazing pioneer who opened her profession up to women. Physicans (physiciennes?) can look to Bethenia Owens-Adair, who, despite her now-embarrassing enthusiasm for eugenics, was a giant in her field. Journalists (journalistes?) have Abigail Scott Duniway, about whom little more needs to be said.

But attorneys? Not so much — not, that is, if you believe the conventional wisdom on the subject. Oregon's first female attorney was a bit of an embarrassment ... or so they say.

The conventional wisdom on Oregon's first-ever "lady lawyer," handed down to us by people like early Oregon journalist Fred Lockley and pop historian Malcolm Clark, is that she was a grasping and crazy-eyed but somehow endearing borderline girl, grinding down all barriers through the sheer force of manic enthusiasm and pro-level nagging skills.

Oh, and she was a murderess, too, her biographers hint (or, in some cases, blithely assert) darkly. It seemed she'd gotten into the profession of law after acquiring her husband's large estate through the simple expedient of murdering him before their pending divorce could be finalized. Then, she moved to Portland and proceeded to make herself notorious — as a last-ditch defender for hookers, drunks, and brawlers in police court, as a hard-drinking and unladylike mascot at social gatherings of young male attorneys half her age, and — to top it all off — as an operator of boardinghouses marketed winkingly to working prostitutes.

Ah, stereotype. So comforting, so easy to laugh off. The truth of the Mary Leonard story will probably never be fully known, but it's a sure bet that it bears only a faint resemblance, at best, to the story Mary Leonard's contemporaries liked to tell about her.

It's not clear quite what it was about Mary Leonard's life that inspired all this tall-tale telling. But something certainly did. In *With Her Own Wings* (1948), Myrna Aldrich passes on one almost-entirely-untrue story:

> Mrs. Ledding, of Milwaukie, Oregon, who, as Florence Oleson, was admitted to the bar in 1897, relates this story as told to her by Captain Ives, master of the seagoing vessel "Tillie Starbuck," who knew Mary well:
>
> In the late Sixties, Mary, about 16 years of age, was shanghaied by a sea captain at a port in Italy. He brought this Italian girl to Portland, Oregon, where he held her in captivity. He treated her with extreme cruelty, and she grew to hate her abductor and threatened his life. One day he was found in his room, murdered, with the door locked on the inside. Mary was arrested and accused of his murder.
>
> Mary could not speak a word of English, but she had a keen mind. While in jail awaiting trial, she studied English and began reading law, presumably under the guidance of the attorney who had been appointed to defend her. Everyone knew how cruelly she had been treated, and public sympathy was in her favor. At the trial she was acquitted.
>
> Mary Leonard became a well-known character in Portland but she was never highly regarded, socially, because of her careless habits. . . .

Another thoroughly inaccurate story of Mary's life comes to us from the famous and popular *Oregon Journal* columnist Fred Lockley, writing three years after her death, who passes on as gospel fact a wildly augmented, almost-completely-untrue version of the story of the murder of her husband:

> "Something over 30 years ago Mary Leonard and her husband became mutually annoyed and Mary Leonard shot her husband. He fell and his wife thought she had killed him. After she had left the house her husband arose, dressed himself, and went to town. He was wounded, but not, as he supposed, seriously. He told, with considerable enjoyment, that his wife had shot him and that he had pretended to be dead to "fool the old lady and throw a scare into her." However, his wound bled internally and was more serious than he supposed, and he died from internal hemorrhage. Mary Leonard was tried for murder.

The case dragged its weary length and while she was in jail she studied law. She was finally cleared and decided to support herself by the practice of law...." (Jan. 31, 1915)

Not a single claim made in this story is true except for the phrases "The case dragged its weary length" and "she was finally cleared."

On some level this sort of storytelling excess is understandable. Mary's life was complicated and full of drama — on that, at least, everyone seems to agree — and she was a genuine character; by her personal style she had already done about half the work of turning herself into a Paul Bunyan-style tall-tale character. So it's not too surprising that lovers of a good juicy story would pick that up and run with it.

An old portrait of Mary Leonard, found in a family album in Switzerland in 1965, made in Portland in 1890 or 1891 when Mary was roughly 45 years old. (Photo: Oregon Historical Quarterly)

Plus, there are some yawning gaps in her early story. It's difficult to learn anything real about her early life. She was born in Alsace to Swiss parents: Johannes and Elizabeth Gysin. She was their second child, and because Johannes was a worker in a silk-weaving factory, money was tight; so Mary (or Marie, as she then called herself) emigrated to Portland when in her early 20s to work as a domestic. She was joined a few years later by her younger sister, Rosa, the grandmother of legendary Oregon State University atmospheric-science professor Fred Decker — from whom most of the actual trustworthy information about Mary's early life comes.

In 1875 Mary traveled up the river to The Dalles to meet, and subsequently marry, a prosperous ferryman, hotelier and restaurateur named Daniel G. Leonard. At the time, she was pushing 30 — an age at which Victorian-era women started worrying a great deal about spinsterhood. Leonard was roughly twice her age — again, this was not out of the ordinary by 1870s standards.

Their marriage lasted roughly two years before he sued her for divorce, claiming she was lazy and a spendthrift, and had started refusing him what he was pleased to refer to as his "marital rights." He claimed she had appropriated large sums of money and title deeds to property out of his safe. He also alleged that she had started sleeping regularly with a telegraph lineman who was staying in his hotel at the time.

She shot back that he had put her to work like a servant in the kitchen, worked her until her health broke and then refused to pay for necessary medical treatment, refused to give her money, and treated her with physical cruelty. She denied, of course, sleeping with the lineman.

While all this was being sorted out, the judge ruled that Daniel must pay separate maintenance, since they were living apart. This he refused to do, prompting her to fire off an angry letter to him in which she implied, essentially, that she would exact a terrible revenge if he did not obey the judge, and that he should, to use a modern turn of phrase, watch his back.

A few nights later, someone slipped into Daniel G. Leonard's house and plugged him in the head with a small-caliber pistol while he slept.

There was no actual evidence that Mary had done it. But everyone assumed she had. Daniel was apparently not a nice man, and the popular opinion on the subject was that he'd had it coming.

That popular opinion, though, was not shared by the mayor of The Dalles, N.H. Gates, who was Daniel's personal attorney. Gates joined forces with District Attorney L.B. Ison to get Mary charged with murder, and she was promptly tossed into the county jail to wait for trial.

And there she sat, for months, while Gates and Isom struggled to piece together a case against her.

It wasn't until five months into Mary's incarceration that the prosecution was able to get a grand-jury indictment against Mary and the lineman she'd allegedly slept with. She was charged with murder; he, with being an accessory. Mary's attorney, W. Lair Hill, successfully argued for separate trials, with Mary's coming first.

"The customs of the time were informal," writes Clark in a 1955 article in *Oregon Historical Quarterly*. "Occasionally, on a particularly fine day, she might be seen abroad on the streets of the town, taking the air on the arm of Sheriff Crossen."

This isn't quite accurate — had Mary been a man, she sure wouldn't have been allowed out. But much of the time she was the only woman in the joint, and the sheriff likely felt some chivalrous obligation to help ease her stay.

And by the time Mary's case came up, it had been eleven months — a long time for anyone, man or woman, to rot in jail waiting for trial.

She might have had to wait even longer, but in November, the delay came to the attention of Abigail Scott Duniway, the famous women's suffrage advocate and editor of the weekly *New Northwest* newspaper in Portland.

"This woman has been in jail since last February awaiting her trial on evidence purely circumstantial," Duniway wrote in an editorial, "for the murder of her husband, a monster whom for his treatment of women should have been slain by a woman, whether he was or not...."

When Mary's trial finally commenced, a possible reason for the delaying tactics became obvious: Duniway was right; there just wasn't much, if any, evidence. The closest thing the prosecution had to a smoking gun in the case, other than Mary's ambiguously worded angry letter, was, according to historian Clark, evidence that Mary "was somehow in the neighborhood when she ought to have been elsewhere."

The trial was not a long one: it lasted just three days. *The Dalles Inland Empire* newspaper called the evidence "flimsy and disjointed." So it must have been, for the jury of 12 men voted unanimously for full acquittal. Of course, it's entirely likely that they actually thought she was guilty, but voted to acquit because they felt Daniel Leonard had had it coming. So, maybe this was an early manifestation of "The Unwritten Law."

In any case, the acquittal didn't help Mary much. For Mary, the problem was that it wasn't so much an exoneration as a justification — not what you need if you want your neighbors to stop looking at you like you're Norman Bates. Daniel may have had it coming, but that didn't change the "fact" that she was a suspected murderess. No one could blame her for killing him, but no one could imagine what kind of a woman could actually pull that trigger.

Nor did it help that her defense attorney was widely reported to have conducted a "masterful" defense — the implication being that the verdict had more to do with his skills than her lack of provable guilt.

But more than anything, it was the timing of the crime that made it look bad for her. Had Daniel been murdered a few days *after* the divorce was final, she would have gotten nothing. But because he was murdered a few days *before* the ruling could be made, she was his sole heir — and he was a fairly well-off man.

Thus, in addition to means or opportunity, she had motive in spades, and that was good enough for the rumor mill. And in 1877, being known as an over-30 rumored-adulteress, murderess, almost-divorcee, and now jailbird — reputations didn't get much more ruined than that. Finding another husband was surely out of the question unless she went somewhere far, far away.

She may also have felt that her economic prospects in The Dalles weren't all that good — although most likely she could have continued to operate her almost-ex-husband's business, and most likely made a good living doing it. But apparently she had had about enough of Wasco County.

So instead, in 1878, she moved to Portland and went into business as the proprietress of a boardinghouse in the wild, seedy neighborhood known as the North End — the corner of town near the waterfront north of Stark Street, known as Old Town today.

In the 1880s the North End was the most dangerous part of town, home of Portland's skid road, peopled with sailors on shore leave, thieves and ruffians, laid-off loggers, temporarily-wealthy gold miners, and prostitutes of all kinds. It was to these folks that Mary now went into business renting out rooms.

And so, in 1878, at the age of 33 or so, Mary settled into her new role as a North End landlady. She apparently made her peace with singlehood; she never remarried, and if she carried on any sort of courtship or romance with anyone, she was most uncharacteristically discreet about it. Instead, five years after coming to Portland, she became a law student — first in Portland and then in Seattle, where she moved to study under renowned attorney J.C. Haines, leaving her boardinghouse behind for the time being.

Finally, in 1885, having passed the bar exam, Mary became the first woman ever licensed to practice law in Washington.

Then she turned back to her home state, applying to be licensed to practice there as well.

Judge Matthew Deady promptly ordered her admitted to practice in federal courts. (Historian Clark, indulging in pure speculation, claims — literally on the basis of there being no evidence — that he did this because she ground him down with a campaign of badgering and nagging: "In his diary, he noted simply, 'Friday (Mar. 27) ... Admitted Mary A. Leonard to the bar.' Judge Deady was no man of few words. There is resignation in the brevity of the entry."

Clark doesn't mention the possibility that the brevity of the entry may

This drawing from a 1888 edition of The West Shore, a literary magazine published in Portland, shows the neighborhood in which Mary Leonard ran her boardinghouse and later practiced law. This image is along Front Street facing south from Ankeny. One of Mary's several boardinghouses was located two blocks to the right along Ash, which is the intersection shown in this image, close to the present-day location of Dan and Louis's Oyster Bar. (Image: University of Oregon Libraries)

represent merely the fact that admitting Mary to practice in federal courts was no big deal. As Deady well knew, the United States Congress, six years before, had enacted an actual law requiring women to be admitted to the bar of the Supreme Court of the United States. By 1885 dozens, if not hundreds, of women had been admitted to federal bars in various states nationwide.

To get admission to practice at the state level, though, it was not to be so easy.

It had long been the state courts' practice to recognize the credentials of attorneys from other jurisdictions without requiring them to prove their merit and "good moral character." But now that Mary Leonard's application was before them, the state supreme court suddenly and conveniently decided to question whether that "exuberance of liberality" was appropriate, decided it was not, and denied it.

Mary responded by successfully lobbying in the state Legislature (a process historian Clark also manages to characterize, despite a lack of any actual evidence, as consisting primarily of her persistently and exasperatingly nagging the legislators) and getting a law passed that would require women to be admitted to the bar on the same basis as men. It passed overwhelmingly in both houses.

This drawing of what we know today as the Pioneer Courthouse in Portland appeared in 1888 in The West Shore *magazine. When this drawing was inked, Mary Leonard was a regular visitor to the courthouse. (Image: University of Oregon Libraries)*

The state Supreme Court responded to this development by hastily cooking up a brand-new one-year residency requirement and using that to deny Mary's application a second time.

This time, Mary argued her case in person before the court itself.

She started by pointing out that in the month since it had adopted the new rule, the court had made exceptions for 12 other (male) attorneys moving to the state.

"If in its discretion the court saw fit to treat these men with such consideration, then may I ask who is entitled to more consideration than I am?" she said. "Since I have been deprived of practicing my profession for the last twelve months, having made my arrangements and my calculations under the old rule, and knowing nothing else until a month ago, when the rules were published. I am now pleading to this court not to impose upon me a hardship which the court deems too hard for a strong, free and unfettered man to bear. I am not a free man, but since I belong to the protected sex, or oppressed sex, whichever you please ... I am asking for the pitiful privilege to be allowed to obtain a livelihood as best I can, which is a natural and God-given right and my right in law."

One of the things that historians have frequently said of Mary is that she was incompetent as an attorney. This was unquestionably true late in her career, when she was apparently suffering from some unknown and progressively worsening medical condition. And it was certainly true that she never was much of a detail person. But as this quote nicely shows, in the late 1880s she had some serious rhetorical skills, and she was hell on wheels in a closing argument.

Of course, the court admitted her. What choice did it have?

As a practicing attorney, Mary was not particularly successful, but she was most definitely noticeable. She did a vast amount of pro-bono work, especially early in her career before money became tight. She held an open office hour every Thursday, during which women who found themselves friendless and in legal trouble were invited to stop in for free legal advice. (Clark doesn't even mention this in his article on Mary.)

Her practice was mostly in the criminal courts, where she represented down-and-out prostitutes, gamblers, vagrants and laborers in trouble with the police. These clients had little or no money, but she was able to make ends meet by continuing to run her boardinghouse business and, at first, drawing on her inheritance. Her boardinghouse, by the way, had a bit of a reputation; many of her tenants were either working prostitutes, or prostitutes working to get out of the business (something that was notoriously difficult to do).

She was also famous for going out drinking with the young attorneys (the "knights of the green bag"), who seem to have regarded her as something of a mascot. She drank and caroused as wildly as any of them despite being in her late 40s — twice their age. But as far as I've been able to learn, there was no hint or rumor of anything sexual. There never was with Mary Leonard in Portland ... and as interested as everyone was in her eccentricities and scandals, that's saying something.

If Mary Leonard had been run over by a trolley at this point in her life — in the early to middle 1890s — she would have been remembered as a pioneering woman of considerable promise and talent cut tragically short in the prime of her career, and probably would have had a monument in her honor at Riverview Cemetery.

But as it turned out, fate had something considerably less glorious in store for her.

About 10 years after she was admitted to the bar, Mary's behavior started to change. She started feuding with people — neighbors, clients, the owner of the building in which her boardinghouse operated.

Other things were happening too. Mary's pleadings in court were getting increasingly erratic. She was getting arrested for things that ranged from stupid to bizarre — suborning perjury, embezzling $1.40 in witness fees from a client's mother, threatening bodily violence, menacing her landlord with a pistol. She started calling police to report that unseen enemies were conspiring against her. In 1909 a long-suffering policeman tried to get her judged insane and sent off to the asylum. (It didn't work.)

Her handwriting started to change. By the end of her career, it was completely different, and it wandered off the lines in strange and illegible ways.

Her famous oral arguments also started to lose their edge, fading into a chaotic style of wandering, garrulous griping. Her success rate in court dropped accordingly.

What was going on? Alcohol-induced dementia? Tertiary-stage syphilis? Early-onset Alzheimer's? It's just not possible to say, although I have my own theories — more on that in a bit.

Mary's law career ended just a few weeks before her death with complete humiliation in an attempt to claim title to some real estate in lieu of payment from a client who'd been judged insane.

By that time, Mary almost certainly should have been judged insane as well. Her habits and practices at the end of her career were totally different from those she'd shown at the beginning of it. And by the end, she'd apparently lost every friend she had.

The end came just days later, on Oct. 11, 1912, when Mary was admitted to Multnomah County Hospital. On her admission papers, the lines for the names of friends and family members are blank. Her coterie of young lawyers was gone; apparently they'd all stepped away from the awkward spectacle that she'd become. Her sister Rosa — Fred Decker's grandmother — still lived in town, but they never spoke and her children didn't even learn they had an aunt until decades after her death.

Two weeks later, she died in her hospital bed — alone, friendless, penniless. Cause of death was given in the newspapers at the time as nephritis (kidney failure); other sources say it was heart failure. Today, no one even knows where she's buried.

She was, however, commemorated with a small, inaccurate article buried deep in the Oct. 25, 1912, issue of the *Portland Journal*, headlined "Court House Misses 'Judge' Mary Leonard":

> *A near-sighted, bent little old woman with gray hair cut "Dutch," who affected rather manly dress, is missing about the courts and corridors of the county court house, for "Judge" Mary Leonard has passed to her last reward. Death occurred at the county hospital last night from nephritis. She was taken to the hospital by the visiting nurses Oct. 11, where she sank rapidly.*
>
> *Mrs. Leonard was a well known character at the court house, as she was a lawyer. Her knowledge of the law was gained years ago while she was in the county jail, held for*

shooting her husband, and she was later admitted to the bar. The charge of killing her husband was later dropped.

According to her statement she was 64 years of age and had been in Multnomah County for 35 years. At one time she was supposed to have had considerable property, but for years she lived in a dilapidated building on East Washington Street near Grand Avenue.

So that is the story of Mary Leonard, Oregon's first woman attorney. And at the time of her death, and for nearly a century afterward, smug journalists and pop-historians have had enormous fun with it, glibly portraying her as just another frontier Oregon character — an irresistible nagging machine that somehow got itself admitted to the bar, and thereupon spent a decade or two making all the poor, henpecked men around her miserable until she got her way.

But — what if they got it completely wrong? What if the woman they blithely pigeonholed as a garden-variety grasping nag was, in fact, a sort of Mother Teresa to the down-and-out prostitutes and working girls of Portland's notoriously seamy waterfront?

Looking over the historical record, it's at least a strong possibility. And it is that possibility that is the basis for Mary Leonard being included in the "heroes" category in this book.

The historical record of Mary's life is mostly extrapolation. We know a few facts, and the historian explains those facts by guessing at the reasons behind them. The most well known account, that of Malcolm Clark Jr., is full of that sort of thing.

As long as it's not labeled as proven fact, there's nothing wrong with extrapolation. The trouble is, these guesses about Mary come to us filtered through the eyes of 19th-century men (often newspaper reporters), and saturated with that odd (to us) mixture of dismissive condescension and self-interested gallantry with which those long-gone guys viewed women—especially "uppity" ones.

No great surprise: the resulting picture of Mary Leonard, passed down through the years to us, is of a stereotype-infused caricature, a ridiculous sort of extreme picture of a grasping, nagging, husbandless hag, bereft of brains but making up for it by trading on her protected status as a member of the "fairer sex" and getting her way by burying her opponents under mountains of impassioned but meaningless blather.

Well, today I'm going to do some extrapolation of my own. I'm proposing a theory of Mary's life. I can't prove any of it (or most of it, at any rate.) But I suspect it's at least closer to the truth than others have gotten.

Call it, if you will, the Mother Teresa theory:

In this, my historical theory, Mary may or may not have been her husband's murderer, but he did kill her: He infected her with syphilis, a case of which he had, in my theory, picked up earlier in his life; remember, he was pushing 60 when they were wed.

Mary is now forced to give up any plans she'd had for starting a family. Revulsion, anger and determination not to give birth to a syphilitic child cause her to cut her husband off from what he later referred to as his "marital rights," so he files for divorce and kicks her out of the house. And while that divorce is pending, someone — maybe it was even her! — slips into his house and shoots him in the head.

Now, charged with this crime, Mary is in the Wasco County Jail. She is, in a very real sense, ruined. She has twenty to forty years to live, and she knows it's quite likely she will die in a madhouse. She can never have a family; congenital syphilis is a horrible, disfiguring thing, and in the 1800s there's no cure. No future husband will want a syphilitic wife; romantically, she's done. She probably cries a lot.

She's in jail for a long time — roughly a year — while her case drags on. And during that time, she meets some other jailbird women, who blow through the joint on 30-day stretches or spend weekends there being held for trial. The stories they tell put hers to shame. She soon sees that, poorly as she's been treated, they're getting much worse, and they need a friend. She determines that, if she gets out of jail, she will be that friend.

Then she's declared innocent, handed her late husband's complete inheritance, and sent out into the community. She stays in The Dalles exactly zero days longer than she absolutely has to; that much we know. Conventional wisdom says that her reputation as a suspected murderess drove her out of town. But if that's the case, why would she not take her newly gotten money and go someplace where she was unknown, and could make a fresh start? Maybe open a store in a tiny town somewhere in Idaho or Nebraska, maybe meet a nice not-too-young widower and make a quiet, happy life there?

No. Instead of that, she moves to Portland — where, thanks to the excellent newspaper coverage of her murder trial, she is well known already — and plunges into the worst neighborhood in town and sets up a boardinghouse. A place for girls and women exactly like the ones she met in jail. As historian Clark rather boorishly puts it, a "*côte* for soiled doves."

Now, remember, this is a boardinghouse for the lowest-status people in the city. It's probably safe to assume that year after year, teenage girls are moving into her place, trying to work at the theater or factory, slipping into desperation, becoming prostitutes, getting raped and assaulted, turning to whisky and opium and fading away into oblivion and disappearing. Where do old prostitutes go, anyway? Had you asked Mary, it's a good bet she'd know. Because, I would argue, she'd made a deliberate decision to spend her life helping them.

She runs the boardinghouse for four years, and then she starts studying law. Now, why on Earth would she ever want to do that? To make money, perhaps? But at that time, there had never been a female attorney in the history of the state. There were a few of them around the country, but they weren't getting rich at it. And female lawyers were still illegal in most states, including Oregon; there was a strong possibility that she would never be admitted to the profession at all, and those years of study would be wasted. No, money couldn't be it.

Fame, then? Not likely. Mary'd had a bellyful of fame.

Clark suggests that maybe she thought she might need good legal advice again someday, and that it would be wise to grow her own, as it were. That theory works great ... as a punchline for a lame joke, that is. Two years of one's life is a crazy price to pay for free legal advice that one may never actually need.

The one explanation nobody's paid any attention to until just recently (a tip of the hat here to historian Kerry Abrams of Stanford) is Mary's own — delivered to Abigail Scott Duniway in an interview for an issue of *The New Northwest*:

"Many are the wrongs I have suffered in my time, and besides, so many inflicted upon others came under my observation that my heart went out to all womankind, and I resolved to do all I could to assist my sisters who were less fortunate," she told Duniway. "You just let me get a legal clutch on some of those who wrong and plunder members of my sex, and see if they long escape punishment."

This is the only explanation that makes any sense at all — essentially, that Mary got into law to help the helpless. A woman of independent means with a skeleton in her closet plunges into the worst neighborhood of Portland, starts taking in prostitutes and impoverished girls and women as boarders, decides she's going to learn to handle herself in a court of law, and then, upon admission, practices primarily in criminal courts representing those same impoverished women — you have to work very hard to make that pattern of facts add up to any other explanation.

Clark gives it a shot, implying dismissively that she practiced mostly in criminal court because she was too incompetent to do anything else. And we do know she wasn't a detail person. But it seems unlikely that an attorney with her known rhetorical skills — she did, after all, successfully argue for her own admission before both the state supreme court and the state legislature — would have had no more lucrative options available to her.

Later in her life, Mary seems to have declined slowly into madness. Her behavior got really erratic and more than a little unethical starting in the late 1890s. This can really only be explained as some sort of worsening medical condition. My theory, of course, was that it was the syphilis given her by her husband reaching the tertiary stage, the stage that sent Christopher Columbus over the edge of lunacy. Syphilis would explain why she never remarried or, so far as I've been able to learn, even indulged in any kind of romance after leaving The Dalles. It would also explain the ambiguity of her death — her crazy behavior in court followed two weeks later by checking into a hospital to begin a two-week terminal decline ending in what was probably multiple organ failure. This is right out of the playbook for death from syphilis.

In any case, her pitiful antics during these later years cast a big, ugly shadow on the legacy of what she had accomplished a few years before.

Mary is gone now, and remembered today — misremembered, that is — chiefly as a sort of adorably crazy old nag, to be smiled at indulgently and immediately dismissed, who just happened, through no fault or merit of her own, to have ended up as the first female attorney in the state of Oregon.

I can't represent my theory of Mary's story as truth; at best, as I said, it's informed guesswork. But I can guarantee this much: It's a lot closer to the truth than the conventional wisdom on her story.

Sources and Works Cited:
- *"The Lady and the Law,"* an article by Malcolm Clark Jr. published in the June 1955 issue of Oregon Historical Quarterly;
- *"Folk Hero, Hell Raiser, Mad Woman, Lady Lawyer,"* an article published by Kerry Abrams at womenslegalhistory.stanford.edu;
- *"Oregon's First Woman Lawyer,"* an article by Myrna Aldrich published in With Her Own Wings (ed. Helen Krebs), published in 1948 by Beattie & Co. of Portland;
- *"Discovered: A Photo and More Facts about Mary Leonard, Oregon's First Woman Lawyer,"* an article by Fred W. Decker published in the Summer 1977 issue of Oregon Historical Quarterly.

URIAH B. SCOTT:

RIVERBOAT CAPTAIN.

You might not think a fire on a riverboat would be that big a deal. After all, it's only a river, right?

But fire on a paddlewheel riverboat was a very serious matter. The stories of riverboats on American rivers are peppered with tales of fires, and nearly all of them come with a body count.

Oregon's most famous riverboat fire has a body count, too. It's 1.

But it would have been quite a bit higher had it not been for the quick thinking of its skipper.

Here's how it happened:

When launched in 1884, the sternwheeler *Telephone* was the fastest boat on the Columbia, and possibly the fastest in the country. With steam up, this rakish and palatial vessel could do considerably better than 20 miles per hour. Its owner, designer and skipper was the already-legendary Uriah B. Scott, the guy who brought true shallow-draft riverboats to the Willamette and later ate the lunch of Henry

Villard's would-be steamboat monopoly on the Portland-Astoria run with his other steamer, the *Fleetwood*.

The *Telephone* was even faster than the *Fleetwood*. And that speed would turn out to be vitally important on one particular voyage, on Nov. 20, 1887.

On that day, the *Telephone* was steaming toward Astoria as usual when Scott got a terse message over the speaking tube from the engine room.

"Engine room's afire," the engineer reported. "It's driving us away from the engines."

Scott now had a choice to make, and he had to make it in the next few seconds. He could muster the crew and try to put the fire out, or turn and make for shore at top speed.

If he tried to fight the fire, he could possibly save the *Telephone*, a very valuable piece of naval architecture indeed. And, of course, if all went well, he could then continue to Astoria and deliver his passengers as usual.

But to do this, and have any chance of success, he'd have to kill the engines so that the wind created by the speed of the *Telephone* wouldn't fan the flames. That meant that if firefighting efforts didn't go well, they'd be stuck in the middle of the widest part of the Columbia River while the boat burned to the waterline and sank. Yes, there would be lifeboats in the water, but people would die. They always did. Decks collapsed under them, they became overcome with smoke, they panicked and jumped overboard and drowned, or maybe they died of hypothermia in the chilly November river water. There were 140 of them; some of them would die.

And if the crew lost the fight with the fire, the end would come fast. Riverboats like the *Telephone* were made, of course, of wood. That wood was kept carefully dry, to prevent rot, and usually pickled in varnishes and flammable paints which, even after they dry out, help the wood catch and burn (and make the smoke deadlier).

Captain Scott was an old riverboat man. He knew what happens when one starts to burn.

He also knew what had happened to the *Eliza Battle* a couple dozen years before in Indiana. Efforts to fight that fire had failed, and by the time the skipper had realized he needed to make for shore, the rudder ropes had burned through and the boat could not be steered. Eighty people died on the *Eliza Battle*, and another 100 were badly hurt, while the boat blindly thrashed down the river, aflame from stem to stern, like a great fiery ghost ship.

If Scott opted to fight the fire, he might save the ship — or he might end up presiding over another *Eliza Battle* scenario and, if he survived, be

This photo from the early 1880s shows the Telephone as it looked before the fire. (Photo: Superior Publishing)

forever haunted by the sense of having staked his passengers' lives on a foolish, losing gamble to save his ship.

The alternative was to make for shore with all possible speed. But this would involve sacrificing any possibility of saving the boat. The wind created by the *Telephone*'s speed would fan the flames to an inferno, and by the time the boat hit the beach, there would be nothing to do but watch her burn.

Then, too, it was not clear that the *Telephone* could make it to shore in time. The *Telephone* could hardly have picked a worse place to catch fire. It was most of the way to Astoria when this happened, and the river was almost five miles wide. Scott had a good two miles of open water to cross, and he had to do it before the fire spread enough to start killing people. Could he make it? Maybe not.

The sternwheeler Telephone under way in San Francisco Bay, long after the vessel caught fire on the Columbia; the entire superstructure shown in this photo was built after the fire. The once-proud riverboat ended up in San Francisco Bay as a railway ferry for a time before being scrapped in 1918. (Photo: Superior Publishing)

Stay and try to save the boat, or run for shore and try to save the passengers? This doesn't seem to have been a hard decision for Captain Scott. He didn't even hesitate. "Put her full speed ahead!" he barked back into the speaking tube, and put the helm hard a-port.

The *Telephone* heeled over hard as the paddlewheel's thrashing intensified, and Scott strained to hold the rudder over. Around the slim vessel came, until its nose was pointing straight at the state of Oregon. The engine-room "black crew," having opened up the steam as wide as it would go, hustled through the smoke and fire to the top deck, where the passengers were already clustered around at the least fiery end of the boat —the one closest to shore.

From the pilothouse, Scott could look ahead at the patch of deck farthest from the flames, at the very bow of the boat, where the wind was sweeping the flames back and away. Soon everything behind and around his pilothouse was on fire. The rudder ropes had probably gone by now. In moments, the boat would be fully engulfed, and anyone still on deck at that time would start dying.

But he could see his gamble in making full speed for shore was going to pay off. The *Telephone* was going to make it in time.

Nobody was checking, of course, but it's a safe bet that the *Telephone* was moving faster than it ever had before (or would again). In a few moments it would be connecting with the riverbank at 20-plus. The passengers packed into the bow braced for impact as best they could.

Then the *Telephone* fetched up on the Oregon side of the river traveling at maximum speed.

Luckily, there was a gentle mud flat there, and it buffered the impact. Still the *Telephone* dealt the state of Oregon a mighty blow, and passengers went flying to the rapidly-heating-up foredeck. There probably were some injuries; the record doesn't say.

Whatever those injuries might have been, they weren't enough to keep a single passenger on that by-now-dangerously-hot deck once the boat hit the shore. Over the gunwales they went, splashing into the water and mud and clambering up on shore to watch the *Telephone* burn.

After watching the last of the passengers disembark, Scott turned to leave, but found to his consternation that the fire was surrounding the pilothouse and had burned away the steps. So he opened the pilothouse window and bailed out. Most sources say he executed a swan dive, but this seems unlikely given that the *Telephone* was stuck in mud. More likely, it was something on the order of a cannonball.

The *Telephone* burned to the waterline as the passengers watched and firefighters from Astoria did what they could. When all was done, they found one single body in the wreckage — that of an unfortunate fellow who had just picked a really bad time to get drunk, and had either passed out or been too befuddled to find his way upstairs.

Everyone else made it.

The *Telephone* was rebuilt, and continued to work the Astoria run for many years after that. It enjoyed a reputation for blinding speed right up until it was scrapped, in 1918. Still, after the rebuild the *Telephone* was never quite as fast as it had been before.

Luckily, it never had to be.

Sources and Works Cited:
- *Lewis & Dryden's Marine History of the Pacific Northwest, a book by E.W. Wright, published in 1895 by Lewis & Dryden of Portland;*
- *Pacific Steamboats, a book by Gordon Newell, published in 1958 by Superior Publishing of Seattle;*
- *Oregon Shipwrecks, a book by Don Marshall, published in 1984 by Binford & Mort of Portland.*

CHEE GONG:

CHINESE TONG MEMBER.

The late 1800s were a tough time to be Chinese in Oregon. Welcomed into the state as *ku li* workers in the railroad-building years when the demand for cheap muscle was limitless, they were, by the early 1880s, starting to face widespread resentment. The language barrier was high enough to make it very hard to assimilate. Towns and cities started passing "sundown laws" requiring Chinese residents to be off the streets at nightfall. The Chinese Exclusion Act was passed, and then renewed. And as if that weren't enough, in 1886, Sylvester Pennoyer successfully used anti-Chinese sentiment to win election as governor of Oregon.

By the mid-1880s the Chinese residents of Oregon all knew the justice system was virtually rigged against them. They could be robbed, beaten, or even murdered, without the perpetrators ever being held to account, if those perpetrators were European-Americans. They were, in other words, on their own.

So the frontier Chinese Oregonians did what any sensible group of people would do under the circumstances: They mobbed up.

That is, of course, oversimplifying things a bit. But the similarities between a Chinese tong and a Sicilian mafia family are notable.

The tongs, or "highbinder societies" as they were also called, were something like what you might get if the Crips merged with the International Order of Odd Fellows: a fraternal association based on family connections both natural and adoptive, with fierce loyalty and sometimes a disturbing willingness to spill blood.

And by 1886, that had happened often enough that the dime novels of the day were already entertaining their young readers with gripping stories of "tong wars" and "white slavery."

In Portland, though, one didn't have to be a regular Old King Brady reader to know something about "tong wars." Portland had started to develop into one of the most critical importation points for smuggled opium — before the early 1900s, the stuff was perfectly legal, but taxed at an extremely high rate. With such a lucrative source of income to contend for, the tongs of Stumptown were getting increasingly active, jockeying for a bigger slice of the action. And nearly 75 percent of Chinese residents belonged to one tong or another; so when fights broke out, they were hard to keep a lid on.

So that's what was going on in the Portland of late 1887, when a 20-year-old Chinese cook named Lee Yik got in a fight with his boss, the head cook at the Saddle Rock Restaurant in Portland, who was a member of a rival tong.

Yik promptly quit; but some time later, the head cook's cousin, Chee Gong, saw the Saddle Rock Restaurant's owner talking to Yik. Angrily, Chee Gong reported what he'd seen, and every member of his tong, including the head cook, quit the Saddle Rock in protest.

So the owner hired Lee Yik back, and Yik got to play Santa Claus to his brothers in the Luen Tu tong with the jobs of the rival tong members who'd quit.

But, of course, the other tong was hardly going to be willing to leave it at that. The ball was now in their court, and they intended to play it.

They made their play at Lee Toy's Chinese Vaudeville theater, on the corner of Second and Alder, on the evening of Nov. 6. Yik was watching the show, up close near the stage; and at one point five of the players on the stage simply leaped into the crowd and started beating him.

It's highly unlikely that the rival tong wanted to do more than just give Yik a beating — in public, at least. But someone — no one really knew who — got excited and pulled a knife. By the time order had been restored, Yik was mortally wounded, and the police had been summoned.

Lee Yik was able to identify two of his five assailants: Fong Long Dick, and Chee Gong. Police managed to come up with three more names, although it's still not clear that they got the right guys — Ching Ling, Yee

Long and Chee Son.

Of the suspects, police were only able to arrest three: Fong Long Dick, Chee Gong, and Ching Ling.

By that time, Yik had died of his wounds, so it was a murder case. The court promptly empaneled a jury — 12 men, not a single one of them Chinese — and got busy hustling up a trio of convictions.

After two days of desultory justice topped off with a 40-minute jury deliberation, they got two of those convictions; the third took an extra week. All three defendants were sentenced to hang.

This early pulp magazine cover shows the adventures of Old and Young King Brady, detectives, battling the members of a Chinese tong. (Image: Stanford University archives)

Their attorneys, of course, appealed, and at the last minute, 11 months later, the Oregon Supreme Court ruled that all three would have to be re-tried.

The second time around, Ching Ling was acquitted, and Fong Long Dick was sentenced to life in prison (but was pardoned out just nine days later).

Chee Gong was not so lucky.

But, looking over the records, luck doesn't seem to have had much to do with it. As historian Diane Goeres-Gardner points out, it's rather unusual for multiple witnesses to have stories that match up perfectly point by point ... almost as if they were working from the same script, furnished to them in advance.

And, in fact, after the inevitable conviction by a jury of 12 white

Portlanders of northern European ancestry, a number of Chinese residents prepared affidavits swearing that they had been forced to testify against Chee Gong — and given scripts to follow in doing so.

But by this time, the conviction was on the books, and Gong's only hope was that the governor would pardon him. The governor, at that time, was Sylvester Pennoyer ... who won the governorship in part by taking over an anti-Chinese protest and whipping it into a slogan-chanting, brick-throwing street riot. He certainly wasn't going to help any Chinese guy out.

And so, at 12:25 p.m. on Aug. 9, 1889, Chee Gong stood on the scaffold, prepared to take a rap that was pretty obviously pinned on him. Invited to speak, he told the crowd that although he was innocent, the member of his "family" — the tong — who had committed the crime had disappeared, and blood had to answer the blood. His blood had been selected for the sacrifice, and he accepted his fate.

Whether he committed the crime or not, by taking the rap as he did, Chee Gong probably ended the tit-for-tat exchange that could have escalated into an actual tong war.

Of course, that wasn't the end of highbinder-society violence in Portland. In late 1888, while all this was going on in Portland courts, members of the Hup Sing tong gunned down a member of the Hoo Leong tong on a sidewalk downtown; Hoo Leong members ran to avenge, and a riot broke out. A total of six people, including the assassinated Hoo Leong man, were killed.

All the violence was starting to cause serious public-relations problems. The leaders of the tongs knew well that if they kept too high a profile, bad things would happen. They knew they needed to keep a lid on things, to prevent other Portlanders from cracking down on them and interfering with their opium-smuggling and other quasi-legal operations. The Lee Yik incident had raised that profile, and something had to be done to lower it once again.

So Chee Gong was hanged, and his body goggled at and tittered over by street urchins as the hearse carried it to Lone Pine Cemetery for burial. Seid Back, the most prominent Chinese merchant at the time (who, by the way, would be a key player in the opium-smuggling scandal of 1893, in partnership with Oregon Republican Party chairman James Lotan), paid for his burial expenses.

Sources and Works Cited:
- *Necktie Parties: Legal Executions in Oregon 1851-1905*, a book by Diane Goeres-Gardner, published in 2005 by Caxton Publishers of Caldwell, Idaho;
- Portland *Morning Oregonian* archives, November 1887 and August 1889.

LUCINDA SCHRODER:

HOMESTEADER.

Being a real hero has a lot to do with luck — bad luck. After all, if everything is peaches and cream, a hero's services are not usually needed. It's only when something awful happens that ordinary people find themselves suddenly forced to make an extraordinary choice — to try to save themselves, or to try to save others.

Sometimes these heroes die and few others ever know what they really did.

And that's more or less what happened to the woman who was perhaps the most significant hero in the history of the community of Silver Lake.

Here's the story:

On Christmas Eve, 1894, nearly the entire population of Silver Lake and surrounding ranches was crammed into a 1,200-square-foot room above Chrisman Brothers Mercantile in Silver Lake. There were a total of 175 to 200 people in the hall.

The night was bitter cold — about 20 degrees below zero — but the room was warm, inviting, and festive. The "Christmas Tree Program" was being staged, starring the kids of the community and centering around a big Christmas tree piled with presents; the room was festooned with paper decorations and pine boughs.

The children of the community, some dressed in holiday costumes, were singing songs and performing little skits and plays, and the community choir was there to sing Christmas carols and other cheerful songs. Benches made of planks perched on chunks of wood had been set up so audience members could sit down and watch.

Around 8 p.m., just as the choir was winding down for the evening, one of the men in attendance — 18-year-old George Payne — got up to go outside and, finding his way blocked, hopped up on one of those benches to get around the crowd. As he made his way to the door, his head clipped one of the hanging Rochester kerosene lamps.

Coal oil sloshed out, covered the lamp, and dripped to the floor. The flame caught it. Fire surged to the ceiling.

The first of the evening's heroes now leaped into action. Francis Chrisman, the owner of the place, leaped up and grabbed the lamp — remember, it was essentially a fireball at the time — and, ignoring the burning oil blistering his hands and arms, started for the exit with it.

But there were many people in the hall, and some of them were trying to do something too. People batted at Chrisman's arms with coats trying to smother the flames, knocking the lamp from his hands — where, of course, its bowl broke, emptying the rest of its now-fiercely-burning oil onto the floor, and there was no stopping the fire after that. Worse, the fire was ignited close by the door, which Chrisman had almost made it to — so after a few minutes, the only exit from the room would be blocked by a wall of fire.

People started for the door, dodging around the spreading column of flames. It was the only exit, and it was at the end of a narrow corridor with a door that opened inward at the top of an outside staircase. As panic rose in the room above, people at one end of the hall started shoving, desperate to leave. The pressure threatened to force the door closed and pin people against it, like water fetching up against the check valve in a pump.

And that certainly would have happened were it not for the major hero of the evening, a pregnant woman named Lucinda Schroder. This intrepid woman, having escaped early, recognized the danger and forced her way up to the doorway, where she blocked the door open with her body, grabbing people as they came by and shoving them down the stairs toward the street.

At least 100 people escaped from the blaze through the front door. Given how the exit was set up, and the rising panic in the people still trapped inside, it's hard to imagine how more than a dozen or two of these lucky souls would have escaped without her help.

It's not clear how Schroder died. She may have been trampled to death. She may also have tried to go upstairs, into the burning building, thinking her husband was inside and hoping to help him get out — not realizing that he actually was working furiously and heroically at the other end of the building helping get people out the window. Although she certainly couldn't have made any headway against the crush of people trying to come down the stairs, she might have gotten far enough along for the door to close behind her and seal her doom. In any event, survivors in the street at one point looked up and saw the door closed and no sign of her.

Then the front stairs, heavy with people trying to help open the door of the burning building, collapsed. A little later, the porch roof that people had been climbing onto from the window collapsed. And after that, nobody got out of the building alive, except for one or two desperate souls who simply leaped out of the window into the darkness.

When the end came, the death toll was staggering in percentage terms. Out of a population in Silver Lake Valley of a little more than 200, 40 people were dead and another several dozen badly burned, injured in falls from the second floor, or both.

By this time, another hero of the moment was already in action. Local cowboy Ed O'Farrell, well before the fire had burned out, was on his horse and galloping through the snow and freezing weather toward Lakeview, 100 miles away, to get Dr. Bernard Daly to come and tend to the injured.

O'Farrell left well before midnight on Christmas eve and, after a 19-hour ride through snow that sometimes got quite deep, got to Lakeview at around 4 p.m. Christmas afternoon. One source reports that O'Farrell actually ruined the horse he was riding because he was pushing it so hard. This seems unlikely, though, since he stopped at livery stables in two towns on the way and would have been easily able to change horses there.

Daly dropped everything and was on his way within an hour, driving a buggy pulled by the best horses in town. They stopped for fresh teams at Paisley and Summer Lake — O'Farrell had made the arrangements on the way — so Daly and O'Farrell were able to get back to Silver Lake in just 13 hours, arriving at 6 a.m.

He was soon joined by Dr. W.M. Thompson, Silver Lake's town doctor, who had journeyed to Summer Lake; he returned as soon as he heard.

With Dr. Thompson's help, Daly was able to save the lives of all but three of the burn victims — who, added to the 40 who had already died in the fire, put the final death toll at 43. Dr. Daly's quick action and success won him statewide recognition and a medical journal published his account of how he treated the victims.

It was ten full years before the community of Silver Lake held another

Christmas celebration. Almost every family in the town and surrounding ranches had lost at least one member.

Four years later, a monument was installed in the town's cemetery, commemorating those who died in the fire. Lucinda Schroder's name is on it, along with that of her two-year-old son Eston, who disobediently followed his mother back into the building when she went to block the door open.

By the way, it was Central Oregon journalist Melany Tupper who unearthed the story of Schroder's heroism; without her work, the story might have quietly disappeared into the archives of various small-town newspapers.

But then, given the way true heroes so often feel about their actions, that might have suited Lucinda Schroder just fine.

Sources and Works Cited:
- High Desert Roses: Significant Stories from Central Oregon, *a book by Melany Tupper, published in 2013 by Central Oregon Books of Silver Lake;*
- The Oregon Desert, *a book by E.R. Jackman and Reub Long, published in 1964 by Caxton Press of Caldwell, Idaho;*
- Homesteading the High Desert, *a book by Barbara Allen, published in 1987 by the University of Utah Press of Salt Lake City.*

CHARLES T. "BUCK" BAILEY:

TUGBOAT CAPTAIN.

By the time Buck Bailey — or Captain Charles T. Bailey, as he was more formally known — of the tugboat *Tatoosh* arrived, the steam schooner *Washington* had been drifting helplessly toward Peacock Spit for 20 brutal, soggy, pounding, terrifying hours — and everyone but Bailey and his crew thought the 49 people on board were as good as dead.

The *Washington*'s troubles had started the day before, on the morning of Nov. 12, 1911. The weather had been heavy, but not heavy enough to prevent ships from crossing the bar. Loaded down with a heavy cargo of lumber both above decks and below, the little 539-ton freighter was beating her way out to sea into the teeth of the usual wintertime southwest wind when a big boarding sea tore loose the chains that dogged down the deck load on the port side. The lumber washed away into the sea, leaving the little ship with a badly unbalanced load that resulted in a terrifying list to starboard.

The crew rushed to cut loose the starboard deckload to even out the weight and put the ship back on an even keel — but as soon as the lumber on the starboard deck was gone, the ship's steam engine suddenly came to

The steam tugboat Tatoosh *under way, as seen from off the starboard beam, circa 1910. (Image: Univ. of Washington Libraries)*

a stop with a shriek of stressed metal. The deckload chains had fouled the drive screw, and probably torn off the rudder to boot — leaving the *Washington* dead in the water in the worst possible place. And to make matters worse, the wind had increased, becoming a serious gale.

The *Washington* drew 16 feet of water without her deckload on, and that's about how deep the water is on most of Peacock Spit — shallow enough to catch and break ships to pieces, but still plenty deep enough to drown their crews. It juts out miles into the open sea, and the water there hovers around 50 degrees — cold enough to incapacitate a swimmer in 15 to 20 minutes.

Captain George Winkel ordered the anchors dropped. They caught, and they held better than expected; the ship was still drifting, but very slowly. If help could only come, the 49 people on board — 25 passengers and 24 crew members — just might survive. If not — well, life vests or no life vests, they were all as good as dead. The lifeboats, of course, had been torn away by the pounding combers by this time.

On shore, old salts with binoculars and spyglasses were watching the ship being eaten time and again by walls of green water, and sadly shaking their heads. If there were any betting men among them, they weren't putting any money on a happy outcome.

HEROES.

On board the steam schooner, though, there wasn't time for thoughts of doom. The boiler fire had gone out, so the steam pumps were inoperative, and the water in the hull was rising with each wave that poured over the hull and into broken windows and hatches. Drenched and chilled, passengers and crew alike kept themselves warm by taking turns at the pumps, trying to keep the vessel afloat. They knew the more water was left in the bilges, the lower the ship would ride in the sea, and the more likely she would be to strike the seabed as the wind carried her over Peacock Spit.

One of the passengers, 69-year-old Mary Fullmer, rose to the occasion like a one-woman U.S.O., leading songs and cracking jokes to keep everyone's spirits up while they battled the rising waters and waited for the rescue they scarcely dared hope the next high tide would bring. All the while, the pounding waves continued breaking over the deck as the wind howled in the rigging, or what remained of it.

Finally, around noon the next morning, as the tide reached full flood, the exhausted passengers and crew looked out through the flying spray and saw, steaming cautiously toward them, the salvage tug *Tatoosh* — Buck Bailey's boat.

This map appeared in the Portland Morning Oregonian *on Nov. 14, 1911, showing the location where the* Washington *was when she was saved. (Image: Oregonian)*

Bailey's top priority, of course, was to get the passengers and crew off the stranded ship safely. And that would have been a tough enough task under the circumstances; the sandy bottom near Peacock Spit was constantly shifting, and at any moment Bailey and his crew might feel the dreaded thump of their own hull striking the bottom — the prelude to their own watery death, as well as that of the 49 exhausted souls aboard the *Washington* whose last hope for rescue they represented.

But after looking over the situation, Bailey decided he was not going to be satisfied with just rescuing the people. It looked to him like he could, at not much more risk and possibly considerably less, rescue the whole package — people, cargo, steamship and all. After all, the *Washington* wasn't aground … yet.

On the other hand, the more time he spent in the shoal waters near the *Washington*, the more likely the *Tatoosh* was to be stranded as well. Was it worth the added risk?

Captain Bailey decided it was. He brought his boat in within hailing distance of the *Washington* to see about getting the crew to take a towing hawser.

"As I approached the *Washington*, I could see 12 or 15 passengers huddled together on the after end with life preservers on," Bailey told author James Gibbs Jr., years later. "I asked the captain if he had any steam to use in heaving the hawser aboard. He told me no, that the fires were out. Then I called to the passengers huddled aft and asked them to go forward and help get the hawser aboard. They did so, all of them running over the debris like scared sheep."

As the old German proverb says, *Viele Haende machen leicht ein Ende* ("Many hands make light work"); and four dozen pairs of eager hands proved more than a match for the massive, waterlogged hemp towing hawser. It took only about 10 minutes to get it aboard the ship and fastened securely to the *Washington*. Then, Captain Bailey called for steam and pointed his powerful tugboat at the open sea. The water beneath its fantail roiled and frothed. The *Washington* gave a jerk; the crew members finished cutting the anchor chains; and slowly the *Washington* started to move.

"The passengers and crew acted like they were (crazy) when we got started — threw up their hands, gesticulated, and yelled at the tops of their voices," Bailey recounted. "I looked over to North Head, and at the lifesaving station, and there must have been a thousand people there watching the rescue."

The stricken steam schooner, when brought to the dock, was a shocking sight.

"The deck of the *Washington* is almost a complete wreck," the Oregonian's

The steam schooner Cosmopolis in the Hoquiam River sometime in the early 20th century. The Washington was a similar vessel in size and design. (Image: Univ. of Washington Libraries)

reporter recounted. "Her visible lumber cargo is a mass of broken kindling wood, part of the bridge and wheelhouse is washed ashore, every window and door on the ship was broken in, with water three and four inches deep covering the floors."

And yet the only casualty had been the ship's cat, which had been atop the deckload when it was washed into the sea.

Once back on shore, Captain Buck Bailey was the man of the hour. The story of the *Tatoosh*'s daring rescue was still being repeated over schooners of beer decades later — although Bailey would have probably been the first to point out that had the *Washington* not been carrying so many passengers, and had the passengers not behaved so coolly and competently under the stress of the moment (thanks, perhaps, to Mary Fullmer), the rescue would not have been possible.

When all was squared away, Bailey learned that the *Washington*'s owners had not been carrying insurance. That meant that, rather than filing a claim with a federally regulated third party of known financial reliability, the *Tatoosh*'s owners — Puget Sound Tow Boat Company — would have to present a bill to the actual owners of the *Washington*, hope they had the resources to pay it, and quite possibly sue to make them do so.

For his part, Bailey seemed almost to relish the thought of writing off his actions as a pro-bono voluntary service done to save lives regardless of profit. He wrote to the manager of the tugboat company that he didn't mind if he got not a cent for the job, but that he wanted his crew members to be rewarded for the great risk they'd taken at his command.

But as much attention as had been fixed on this case, the steam schooner's owners had little choice but to make whatever financial arrangements were necessary to pony up. And by the time they'd done so, Bailey and his crew had all been rewarded with lifesaving medals as well.

Sources and Works Cited:
- Pacific Graveyard, *a book by James Gibbs Jr., published in 1950 by Binford & Mort of Portland;*
- Portland Morning Oregonian *archives, November 1911, January 1912, April 1912, November 1912.*

FERN HOBBS:

ATTORNEY AND LAW ENFORCER.

All Oregonians owe former Gov. Oswald West a debt of gratitude for saving Oregon's beaches from being locked away in private ownership. He did that in 1913, by getting them declared state highways.

But the progressive "father-knows-best" impulses that inspired West to take that action didn't always lead in perfectly positive directions. In fact, when we're out looking to identify heroes and rascals in Oregon history, we'll find a little of both in Os West — although overall he was more hero than rascal, particularly early in his life.

But for West, the ends often did justify the means.

And that is how progressive hero Os West came to be the only governor in state history (so far as I have been able to learn) to actually issue a command to the Oregon National Guard to ignore a legally issued court order — in the spirit of Andrew "Now let him enforce it!" Jackson.

Oswald West isn't the real "hero" (or the "rascal") of this story. We'll meet her shortly; but first, we must get acquainted with the scene of her

Copperfield as seen from the Idaho side of the Snake River, across the footbridge. (Image: Baker County Library)

heroism: a town that legendary Oregon raconteur Stewart Holbrook once referred to as "the Gomorrah on the Snake (River)."

The town was called Copperfield.

Copperfield was first platted just after the turn of the twentieth century, on the banks of the Snake River a little more than 100 highway miles east of Baker City (if there had been highways back then). It was originally a small copper-mining town, or would have been if there had been enough copper nearby to bother about; but by 1907 or so, Copperfield was more or less a construction camp: a pair of very long tunnels were under construction nearby, one being built by the predecessor of the Idaho Power Company and the other by a local railroad.

The town quickly developed a reputation for lawlessness. At its peak, it boasted 11 saloons, 11 brothels, two hotels, three stores, and a four-cell jailhouse/drunk tank with a dance hall on the second floor. Holbrook writes that the employees of the power company and those of the railroad would sometimes indulge in gang-style bar fights with broken beer bottles and flying bricks; but even at his best Holbrook is more a storyteller than a historian, so we can't really take his word for this.

Then, starting early in 1910, the construction workers started leaving. The railroad tunnel was finished; the power plant soon was too. By late 1913 the town had dwindled from roughly 1,000 residents to just 100 or so. And this left the town's saloons and bordellos all gasping for business.

The majority of them quietly closed their doors, and their owners moved on to greener pastures. But the owners of the others — three saloons, and possibly a brothel or two as well — quickly realized that they could turn Copperfield's remoteness and bad reputation to their advantage, drawing visitors from nearby Baker City for a good time, the way Las Vegas does with Los Angeles. And this is where things started to go badly for them.

It turned out that, out of the 100-odd residents of the town, at least half did not approve of the saloon and bordello owners' new "sin tourism" business model.

Fern Hobbs as she appeared during the Copperfield affair. This may be a portrait made after her graduation from law school in 1913, as she appears to be wearing academic robes. (Image: Baker County Library)

Their complaints to Baker County Sheriff Ed Rand having gone unheeded, they sent a petition to Governor West with fifty signatures on it. They complained that the saloons were selling booze on Sundays and hosting illegal gambling. (They didn't mention the prostitution in the petition. Maybe it had gone away by then.)

West, a committed Prohibitionist who was at that very moment working to get booze outlawed in Oregon, was very sympathetic. He promptly issued an order to Sheriff Rand to take care of the problem immediately, and set a deadline date of Dec. 26.

Now, Rand, as an elected official, did not answer to the governor, so the order had no legal weight; but he tried to be diplomatic about it. What law should he invoke, he asked the governor? None of the residents were willing to be witnesses against the saloons in court, so he couldn't get a court order to close anyone. Without a court order, he couldn't legally close any business.

"That," writes historian Gary Diehlman dryly, "was not the answer that West wanted to hear."

So West announced his intention to send his secretary, Fern Hobbs, to take care of the matter for him.

Now, Fern Hobbs was 30 years old in 1913, but she looked about 22. She was a slender, petite woman, bespectacled, 5 feet 3 inches tall, with a classically beautiful, albeit still girlish, face. She would have looked rather like a cute young schoolteacher or librarian — if it weren't for those steady, steely eyes. The fact was, she was no ordinary secretary. As most historians have, over the years, neglected to mention, she was a licensed and practicing attorney (Willamette University, Class of '13).

And nobody had handed her any of that on a platter. She'd come to Portland in 1904 to work as a governess in a prosperous local banker's home; in her spare time, she'd studied stenography. Soon she was working as a stenographer in a title company; in her spare time, she studied law.

Now she was an attorney, one of just a handful of female lawyers in the state; and she was working as the governor's private secretary. And that's secretary, as in "Secretary of State," not secretary as in "typist in the secretarial pool." It was a job that had nearly always before been filled by a man.

She was also, incidentally, the highest-paid woman in public service in the United States.

Overall, Fern Hobbs, J.D., was the ultimate stealth package. When she stepped off the train car in Copperfield, the local businessmen had no idea what was about to hit them.

Governor West, of course, knew this well, and played it up at the press conference at which he announced the plan. He casually mentioned that Baker County Sheriff Ed Rand stood six and a half feet tall and weighed over 200 pounds, but still wasn't big enough to put the kibosh on the scofflaws of Copperfield.

"My secretary," he added, "Miss Hobbs, is five feet three and weighs 104 pounds."

In what must have been intended as an attempt to charm the "secretary," the locals had decorated the town with copious amounts of bunting and pink and blue ribbons, and a small welcoming committee of city councilmen stood by to greet her, each holding a bouquet of flowers, as she stepped onto the platform.

Their first nasty shock may have been the seven armed and grim-faced Oregon National Guard and Oregon State Police personnel who stepped off the train after her: five battle-hardened veterans of the Philippines insurrection, led by Lt. Col. B.K. Lawson and accompanied by Frank Snodgrass, captain of the Oregon State Penitentiary guards.

Hobbs declined the proffered bouquets, and, without any sign of either pleasure or discomfort, marched with her escort directly to the town's big dance hall.

Fern Hobbs, revisiting the site of Copperfield in 1959, poses for a photograph with a big Colt six-shooter tucked into her belt as writer Stewart Holbrook looks on. (Image: Baker County Library)

The details of what happened in the dance hall come to us from Stewart Holbrook, who was in later years a personal friend and next-door neighbor of Fern Hobbs and a close friend and admirer of Oswald West. Its general gist is reliable — but there are certain details that have the distinct air of having had no small measure of poetic license taken with them.

That said, here is what he says happened:

Almost the entire population of the town followed Hobbs in, and everyone arranged themselves in the hall to hear what she had to say as she stood on the stage and waited for everyone to settle down. Lt. Col. Lawson and two of the Guard soldiers stood at the back of the room, by the door.

"Miss Hobbs" came straight to the point. The governor of Oregon would be most appreciative, she said, if all three City Council members and the mayor would step down immediately; and she handed each City Council member a letter of resignation to sign. (Remember, these were elected officials, not gubernatorial appointees. Neither Hobbs nor West had any authority to demand the resignation of an elected official.)

They all, of course refused to step down.

The entire dance hall was silent for a moment. Then Hobbs opened her briefcase, extracted the proclamation of martial law from it, and called Lawson to the stage. When he reached it, she handed it to him, and he read it out loud. Then he declared the three council members and mayor under arrest.

"You will now disperse in an orderly manner," he boomed. "As you leave the room you will turn over your revolvers and other weapons to my men at the door."

This is one point at which Holbrook's account is probably exaggerated, for he reports that they collected more than 170 sidearms from residents as they left the room — a neat trick in a town with a population of 100 or so. Nonetheless, they did collect quite a few, presumably tagged and receipted so that the owners could reclaim their property later; and as the now-weaponless citizens filed into the street, they found that the other three Guardsmen and Snodgrass had been very busy while they'd been in the meeting. All the saloons and gambling establishments in the city now had their doors secured with chains and padlocks.

Lawson and his troops escorted Hobbs back to the depot in time to catch the 4 o'clock train to Baker City — where she checked into the Geiser Grand hotel and rebuffed all attempts to contact her.

Lawson and his troops then returned to Main Street and continued the process of confiscating all the liquor, weapons and gambling supplies in Copperfield.

Saloon owners Henry Stewart and William Wiegand (the town's mayor and one of its city councilors, respectively) promptly filed a suit to stop the confiscations. A circuit court judge filed an injunction to stop the process while its legality could be probed.

That's when Oswald West issued his infamous order to Lawson to ignore the court and carry on.

Lawson, worried about getting arrested by Sheriff Rand for contempt of court, requested and got reinforcements. They stayed in Copperfield, enforcing martial law and hauling off kegs and bottles and faro banks and roulette wheels and other miscellaneous Implements of Satan, for several weeks.

As you may have gathered, Stewart Holbrook strongly approved of all of this. So, in fact, did most of the news reporters in the western half of the state. But in Baker County, there was a distinct note of fear in the coverage of this unfolding affair. "MARTIAL LAW FOR BAKER NEXT," screamed a two-inch-tall headline on the front page of the Baker City *Morning Democrat* shortly after the raid.

"If the power and authority of our civil courts is to be thus treated," wrote the editor of the *Morning Democrat*, "then we certainly have a czar in the gubernatorial chair in Salem whose word and command is law, and we had just as well abolish our courts and turn over all affairs of state to the executive."

Meanwhile, having been told that Sheriff Rand was assembling a posse to enforce the court order, West tried to temporarily remove him from office. Nothing came of this, or of the rumored posse either. It seems rather unlikely such a posse was ever seriously considered. As Rand would have well known, the only way it could have enforced the order would have been to risk a firefight with more than a dozen of the best soldiers in the Oregon National Guard.

The whole affair finally made its way to court in Baker City, where the judge ruled that courts could not forbid a governor from declaring martial law, but that the saloon owners could file a civil lawsuit and collect damages afterward if a governor did so inappropriately. Whether they pursued this or not, I have been unable to learn.

The saloons never reopened; the very next year, in 1914, the voters of Oregon approved Prohibition, so there wouldn't have been much point. And the year after that, a fire of unknown origin swept through the business district, dealing the final *coup de grace* to the town of Copperfield. Today the old town site is a park operated by Idaho Power.

Sources and Works Cited:
- Wildmen, Wobblies and Whistle Punks, *a book by Stewart Holbrook, published in 1992 by Oregon State University Press of Corvallis;*
- "Copperfield," *an article by Gary Dielman published August 31, 2018, on* The Oregon Encyclopedia *at oregonencyclopedia.org;*
- "Copperfield Affair, 1913-1914," *an article by Gary Dielman published March 17, 2018, on* The Oregon Encyclopedia *at oregonencyclopedia.org;*
- Baker City Morning Democrat *archives, December 1913 and January 1914;*
- Albany Democrat *archives, January 1914.*

HARRY LANE:

U.S. SENATOR.

Many historians, when asked to cite the single biggest and most far-reaching government misstep in American history, will immediately start talking about the First World War.

By getting involved with that conflict — subtly at first, by lending money to the Allies, and later directly with American boots on French soil — we made it possible for one side to crush the other and impose its will, rather than simply fighting to an impasse and being forced to negotiate peace. The world is still trying to recover from the aftershocks of that — particularly in the Middle East.

Such historians and history buffs — and yes, I do count myself among them — smile a bit when the topic of Oregon Sen. Harry Lane comes up. Lane was one of a tiny handful of federal legislators who, for reasons of principle or partisanship, fought as hard as they could to prevent President Woodrow Wilson from taking the country into the fight.

It's a small smile, though. Because Lane paid a heavy price for it.

Dr. Harry Lane as he appeared at the age of about 60, when he was a U.S. Senator. (Image: Library of Congress)

Harry Lane was a well-known and respected Oregon politician, a medical doctor by profession, born in Corvallis, the grandson of the first territorial governor of Oregon — the somewhat notorious Joseph Lane. He'd been mayor of Portland just after the turn of the century, and had established a reputation as a man of principle — the worst enemy of the corrupt politicians, cops and shanghai artists that were virtually running the city when he arrived. Although he didn't leave much of a long-term impact on those forces of corruption, he was able to suppress them during his two terms of office — long enough to put on a spectacular show at the 1905 Lewis and Clark Centennial Exposition, at any rate — and today he's remembered as the father of the Rose Festival.

He also had a strong reputation as a supporter of women's suffrage and an advocate for more respectful treatment of the remaining Native American tribes in the state.

He was firmly opposed to any American involvement in the brewing conflict in Europe. And by early 1917, he was growing increasingly alarmed by Wilson's steps toward war.

Wilson had won re-election just a few months earlier in spite of his party's underdog status at the time, largely on the strength of the slogan, "He Kept Us Out of War." The war referred to was with Mexico — the revolution that made Pancho Villa famous was playing out very messily at the time, and there was a certain pressure for the U.S. to get involved — but, of course, war was war. Senator Lane, from deep inside the Capitol, would have been able to clearly see Wilson's growing enthusiasm for direct American intervention in the war in Europe. And the hypocrisy of running for re-election on a platform of implied commitment to peace while quietly gathering forces to take the nation to war (after the election was safely won, of course) was not lost on him.

So when, two months into his next term and after several months of steady war-drum beating, Wilson asked Congress to let him arm American merchant ships, Lane and a few other like-minded senators (most notably Robert LaFollette of Wisconsin) threatened to stop it with a filibuster. They told the White House they were willing to go along with the plan if one little change were made in it: They wanted those American ships to stop carrying munitions to sell to the Allies. And they wanted that written into the law: Arm the merchant ships, fine — but no more guns and bullets would cross the sea until after peace was achieved.

Well, of course, that was not at all what the White House had in mind. The word that came back surprised nobody: No deal.

So in early March, Lane and his colleagues filibustered — a good old-fashioned talking filibuster — and the bill died a-borning.

Wilson was furious. He lashed out at Lane and his colleagues personally, calling them a "little group of willful men, representing no opinion but their own" that had "rendered the great government of the United States helpless and contemptible."

Although he'd come to expect this sort of petulance from Wilson, Lane was shocked by the animosity this stand earned him from others, both in Washington, D.C., and back home in Oregon. Hate mail started pouring into his office. The Portland *Morning Oregonian* — a Republican organ at the time, and no friend to Democrat Lane under any circumstances — wrote an editorial that essentially apologized to the nation, on behalf of every Oregon voter, for having sent Lane to Washington. A recall movement was launched, and started growing.

A month later, Wilson got the pretext he needed to take the country to war when a bungling German diplomat named Zimmerman used British undersea cables to telegraph a proposal for an alliance against the U.S. to the Mexican government. The British, of course, promptly leaked it, and Wilson was soon before Congress asking for a declaration of war.

Lane was, by this time in his life, a very sick man. He had painful chronic kidney disease and advanced heart disease on top of it, and the stress of the hate-storm swirling around him following his filibuster had exacerbated his health problems. His physician urged him to stay home and rest in bed. But Lane was adamant. He would go to the Senate floor and he would vote against entering the war.

And so he did. In the Senate, there were just six "no" votes. His was one of them.

Seven weeks later, on his way home to Oregon, he suffered a paralytic stroke and died.

The *Oregon Journal*, upon his death, may have wanted to eulogize the intransigent pacifist — but a month and a half into hostilities, an increasingly pro-war public was in no mood for anything like that. So the paper contented itself with a short and poignant message:

"He paid for his choice with his life."

And perhaps he did. The stress of all the animosity his principled stand earned him weighed heavily on him, according to his friends' recollections. It may not have actually killed him … but most of them thought it did. It certainly didn't help.

Sometimes history's heroes are neither successful nor survivors. Sometimes they're the men and women who take up lost causes because their ethics leave them no choice. Like the ship captain who refuses to "fall into the lifeboat," they're forced to choose between a hopeless fight against a rising tide of evil, and becoming a part of that evil — and they make the hard choice instead of the easy one.

Such a man was Harry Lane. And Oregon should be very proud to claim him.

Sources and Works Cited:
- The Growth of a City, *a book by E. Kimbark MacColl, published in 1976 by Georgian Press of Portland;*
- To the Promised Land, *a book by Tom Marsh, published in 2012 by Oregon State University Press of Corvallis;*
- The Illusion of Victory, *a book by Thomas J. Fleming, published in 2003 by Basic Books of New York.*

CAPT. ROBERT PAMPHLET & AL.:

RUMRUNNERS.

Captain Robert Pamphlet and his crew were sailing south in a heavy sea en route to Mexico ... or, at any rate, they later claimed they were ... when they heard the distress calls. The 579-ton steam schooner Caoba, slugging it out with the gale off the mouth of the Columbia, had suffered a knockout blow: A wave had burst through and flooded the engine room, putting out the boiler fire. The ship was adrift, rolling in the trough of a very heavy sea, and filling with seawater. The crew had taken to the lifeboats.

Pamphlet was in perfect position to help. But there was just one problem: The hold of Pamphlet's 90-foot, 100-ton gasoline-powered schooner, the *Pescawah*, was crammed with Scotch whisky — a total of 12,876 bottles of it. And the date was Feb. 1, 1925 — Prohibition wouldn't end for another eight years.

Also, he wasn't really going to Mexico with it. Pamphlet and his crew were Canadian rumrunners. At the time, this was a going business, with big rewards and bigger risks.

Cargo ships like the *Pescawah* would leave British Columbia with a hold full of bonded liquor and head south, being careful to stay in the international waters twelve miles off the U.S. shore. When they reached the prearranged spot, they would offload their cargo and head back north again.

There were several ways the offloading was done, involving wildly diverging levels of risk to the ships and crew — both legal and physical risk. Sometimes small cargo ships like the *Pescawah* would sail south to one of the remote "doghole" ports of southern Oregon and northern California, anchor in some tiny coastal divot, unload the cases into waiting trucks, and race back west to the safety of the open sea — and then north to start the process all over again.

This, obviously, was the most dangerous method. Not only did the ship have to spend a lot of time in U.S. territorial waters, but the dogholes were notoriously difficult to navigate even in daytime. And if a ship did catch a reef and sink, its crew was stranded deep in hostile territory.

The other method, which was more common as the rumrunners got more into their groove, involved coordinating with locals to offload the cargo into small boats or launches which they'd rendezvous with in international waters. That way, if the cops showed up, they would be easier to dodge, and a small boat could get into all sorts of places a big ship could not.

The *Pescawah* and her crew were almost certainly working one of these supply lines. Specifically, they were most likely the supply ship for the regular Sauvie Island run.

The Sauvie Island rumrunning operation was one of the more frustrating violations of Prohibition for Oregon law enforcement. It was an ongoing operation in which millions of gallons of high-quality liquor were slipping up the Columbia River to supply the finer speakeasies of Portland and other large West Coast towns. It was a fabulously clever hustle, and police were nearly helpless to shut it down.

Here's how it worked: Canadian cargo ships, like the *Pescawah*, would come down and lurk off the mouth of the Columbia River — taking care to remain at least twelve miles offshore, in international waters. In the dead of night, a fleet of high-powered motor launches with heavily muffled engines would come out and rendezvous with the ships. The launches would be loaded with cases of liquor. Then they would, under cover of darkness, slip across the bar and race upriver to rendezvous points on Sauvie Island.

These launches were the cigarette boats of the day — faster than anything the Coast Guard could send after them. So the operation was highly successful, and also somewhat flagrant — characteristics not calculated to endear it to any law-enforcement bureaucrat's heart.

Most of the time, the cargo ships would carry destination paperwork to "prove" that their real destination was Mexico. But on this run, Pamphlet

HEROES.

The USS Algonquin under way off Unalaska, Alaska, on June 19, 1926. The Algonquin was the Coast Guard cutter that chased down and captured the Pescawah and her crew after they left international waters to rescue a lifeboat full of shipwrecked American sailors. (Image: US Coast Guard)

didn't have those papers to cover himself. If he got caught within U.S. territorial waters, without those papers, he could expect scant mercy.

So he was listening carefully to the radio to see if the crew of the *Caoba* was getting rescued — hoping he wouldn't have to get involved.

What he was hearing was at first reassuring. The tugboat *John Cudahy* had found and picked up a lifeboat with nine men in it. But Pamphlet knew a freighter the size of the *Caoba* would have more than nine men on her crew. There had to be another lifeboat out there.

Nobody else seemed to think so, though. Responding to the distress call, two other freighters came to the *Caoba*'s aid. One after the other, they tried diligently to get towing hawsers on the wallowing ship, ignoring the need to rescue its crew. Apparently by this time it had become obvious that because of the flotation of the lumber in its hold, the *Caoba* was not going to sink after all. Now, crewless and adrift, ship and cargo belonged to whoever could get a line on her, under the law of salvage rights. So first the *Forest King* and then the *Thomas P. Beal* came alongside and tried to take the stricken ship in tow. Then, having failed, they just went on their way.

From Pamphlet's wheelhouse, it sounded like the scramble for those salvage rights was at the top of everyone's list, and the sailors on the second lifeboat — somewhere out there being tossed around in a gale, if they hadn't already overturned and drowned — could just look out for themselves.

Pamphlet got out his map and plotted wind directions and currents. Based on where the *Caoba* was abandoned, as best he could know in those pre-GPS (and pre-Loran) days, he figured out the patch of ocean in which the boat was most likely to be found — close by the entrance to Willapa Bay, it looked like, on the southwest corner of Washington State.

Then he gave the order to fall off the wind and sail due east. Eyes wide open, the *Pescawah* plunged into the 12-mile danger zone.

After a search, the Canadians found the lifeboat right where Pamphlet had figured it would be, and rescued its occupants (sources differ on how many — seven or nine).

We can only imagine what it must have been like for the rescued crew members, who went from tossing around in an open boat, wet and cold and exhausted from trying desperately not to overturn and drown, to the warm dry cabin of a ship crammed to the hatches with bonded Scotch.

But there was no time for celebration; they were still at least ten miles inside the twelve-mile danger zone. Leaving the empty lifeboat tossing upon the waves, the *Pescawah* turned west and, under full canvas hauled close to the southwest wind and probably with the gas engine running wide open as well, started for the open sea as fast as she could go.

It wasn't fast enough. The 1,181-ton, 16-knot Coast Guard cutter *Algonquin*, which had also plotted the winds and currents to search for survivors, got to the scene a short time later and saw a sinister-looking black schooner, canvas virtually bursting as she raced westward ... and it was all over for the *Pescawah*.

Pamphlet, of course, told the *Algonquin*'s officers that he was taking the liquor to Mexico; but he didn't have the all-important paperwork to back that claim up, so he was promptly arrested, along with the other crew members.

Hoping it would help him legally, Pamphlet declined to sail into Astoria; so the *Algonquin* put a prize crew on board to sail the *Pescawah*, and back to Astoria the schooner went at the heels of the *Algonquin*.

When they arrived at Astoria, they were greeted by a cheering crowd, including the rest of the *Caoba's* crew. After all, it was only with a bit of luck that the *Pescawah* had found the tiny lifeboat bobbing in the sea; if Pamphlet and his men had stayed in safe waters, the Coast Guard cutter might not have spotted them in time, and half of them might very well be dead.

The popular show of support might have been gratifying, but it did not help the Canadians' cause. The cheering infuriated the district immigration officer, who responded by jailing the *Pescawah's* crew and throwing everything he had at the men — including a charge of entering port without inspection

This photograph from shortly after the ship was built shows the Caoba — *then named the* Coastal — *under way. When the Caoba came to grief, the low area amidships was piled high with a deck load of lumber and there were, fortunately, far fewer passengers on board. (Image: Superior Publishing)*

and failure to carry the proper entry visa. This charge, of course, wouldn't stick, because Pamphlet's men hadn't entered the port — the prize crew from the *Algonquin* had. But it proved the wisdom of Pamphlet's refusal to voluntarily sail his ship into port.

In response, calls for clemency came from all over the U.S. and Canada. The Canadians had put themselves in jeopardy to save these sailors after two freighters turned their backs on them in an unlovely scramble for booty; it didn't seem right to most folks that the only people on the water that day who did the right thing should pay for their heroism with prison sentences.

Furthermore, there was some reason to suspect the *Pescawah* had made it into international waters, and that the Coast Guard cutter had made the arrest outside its jurisdiction.

It wasn't enough. The American officials were bent on convicting them, and the Canadian government didn't want to escalate to an international incident over a crew of men that, despite all the extenuating circumstances, everyone really knew had been breaking the law.

So to prison they went — with no regrets.

"If I was off the coast with a cargo of liquor, and the whole Yankee fleet was in your waters, and I saw that I could save the life of one poor fisherman, I'd sail in and do it again," Pamphlet said. "That's the training of the sea, my boy."

As for the *Caoba* — the lumber schooner for whose crew members the *Pescawah*'s crew risked and gave all — all the salvage attempts failed. The strong southwest wind blew her up onto the coast of Washington, and she fetched up near Ocean Park. Today, you can still find the ship's rusty boiler if you know where along the shore to look for it.

Pamphlet died at age 59 in 1932, a few years after his release from prison; though a solid healthy specimen at the time of his capture, he caught tuberculosis in the hoosegow, and it killed him. He really had, it turned out, given his life to save those sailors.

Jack Benny and Rochester (Eddie Anderson) from the television version of The Jack Benny Show, look over Jack's 1908 Maxwell in this publicity photo from 1951. The Maxwell car engine which Victor Riley was using to power the Pescawah probably was out of a much newer model than this. Incidentally, on Jack Benny's radio show, the sounds of the old Maxwell were provided by Oregon animation legend Vance "Pinto" Colvig. (Image: CBS)

The *Pescawah* came to a bad end as well. After about a decade of weathering at a dock in Portland, she was sold to an Oregon City man named Victor Riley. Riley planned to use the *Pescawah* to sail to the Arctic and hunt whales — an activity that, in the mid-1930s, was not frowned upon as it is today.

Riley recruited a crew of college students to help him in this adventure. Finding the *Pescawah*'s sturdy 100-horsepower Union marine power plant to be non-operational (probably seized), he disconnected it and replaced it with a four-cylinder automobile engine scavenged from an old Maxwell. The Maxwell engine was stationed up on the ship's deck, driving the prop shaft with a long belt — a remarkably janky and unseaworthy DIY setup. But, then as now, a good rebuild job cost a lot more than a used auto engine lugged home from the local wrecking yard; and perhaps Riley couldn't afford to do the job right.

Maxwell made its last car in 1925, so the engine was at least eight years old and probably more like 10 or 12 when Riley & Co. pressed it into service, in late February 1933. The most common Maxwell engine in the late 1910s and early 1920s was a 3-liter, 25-horsepower flathead mill, made to push a 1,500-pound car around at speeds of 30 to 40 miles per hour. Most likely, the *Pescawah*'s new engine was one of these.

This junkyard engine was simply not up to the job of muscling 100 tons of 90-foot schooner around — even when it was running. Which, before too long, it was not. On the *Pescawah's* way across the bar, at the moment it was most needed, the old flivver motor quit and the storied old sailing ship was washed into the North Jetty. Captain Riley was killed in the crash, crushed against the rocks while trying to launch the lifeboat; the other crew members managed to swim to shore.

Sources and Works Cited:
- Oregon Shipwrecks, *a book by Don Marshall, published in 1984 by Binford & Mort of Portland;*
- *"Americana," an un-by-lined article published in the July 1932 issue of* The American Mercury.
- Capital Journal *archives, February 1933;*
- Eugene Register *archives, December 1927.*

THOMAS McADAMS:

U.S. COAST GUARD LIFESAVER

Legendary Coast Guard motor lifeboat operator Master Chief Thomas McAdams always knew the weather could have a big impact on his life.

What he wasn't expecting was for a fog bank to make the difference between getting reprimanded and possibly demoted, and being awarded the Coast Guard's top lifesaving medal.

But that's exactly what happened one June day in 1957, when McAdams and his crew saved four people from drowning in the surf near the mouth of Yaquina Bay.

McAdams is a legend in the Newport area, and probably the most famous Coast Guard enlisted man ever. He started his career as a raw Seaman Recruit in 1950, and by the time he retired with the rank of Master Chief Petty Officer in 1977 he'd participated in some 5,000 rescues and saved at least 100 people from drowning. He'd survived nine rolls — in which his motor lifeboat was fully capsized by the surf and he had to hold his breath and wait for it to roll back upright. After his retirement, he helped design the standard 47-foot Coast Guard motor lifeboat that's used in rescues today.

This photograph, taken from "Chicken Hill," shows through a gap in the trees the scene of Tom McAdams' dramatic 1957 rescue. The boats were just off the beach, about three-quarters of the way to the end of the jetty, roughly in the center of the frame. (Image: offbeatoregon.com)

Crew members who went out with him said you could always tell how much trouble you were going to be in by watching the big cigar he always kept burning in his mouth. If he took it out of his mouth, turned it around and put the lit end into his mouth, you knew you were about to get very wet. And if you ever saw him spit it out, you took a deep breath, braced for impact, and held on, because the boat was about to get rolled.

On this particular day, McAdams got a call from the Coast Guard's observation tower that there was a pleasure boat in trouble just off the north reef. Almost every boat the life station had just then was out helping or rescuing somebody, and the only boat available for McAdams to take out was the brand-new 52-foot motor lifeboat, the biggest boat in the station, the pride of the Coast Guard, the most expensive boat it had ever built.

This 52-footer was completely unlike the older wooden 52-footer stationed up at Point Adams on the Columbia River Bar, the *Triumph* — which sank on the bar four years later. This one had a steel hull and twin screws — and unlike the *Triumph*, it was made to roll.

McAdams and his crew climbed aboard this brand-new boat, got the twin screws turning, and roared off to the rescue.

The beach and jetty were full of onlookers all helping point the Coasties to the spot, and it was a good thing, too, because the fog was fairly thick and visibility was short.

When they got to the scene, McAdams knew the situation was serious.

"I could see the bottom of a 16- to 18-foot capsized boat and then I'd seen a couple of heads by it," McAdams said, according to a Coast Guard oral-history interview. "And I thought, 'Oh my God, they're in the inter-breakers. We've got to get them out. They'll never make it.'"

The problem was, they were in about 10 feet of water, with heavy swells, and the boat drew six feet.

Master Chief Tom McAdams stands near the steering station of a Coast Guard boat. (Photo: US Coast Guard)

There was a pretty good chance, even with McAdams at the helm, that the boat — the gorgeous, new, super-expensive 52-foot twin-screw rescue lifeboat, the pride and joy of the U.S. Coast Guard — would end up ignominiously stranded on the beach.

McAdams doesn't seem to have even considered that. Let four people drown to save a Coast Guard asset? Nope. Into the breakers he went, cigar firmly fixed in his teeth.

He kept the boat in the crest of a swell and got within six feet of the upside-down boat, then dropped into the trough and sure enough, the boat bounced hard on the sandy bottom.

"I could see four people in the water and there was a man holding his wife and his wife was not in very good shape," McAdams said. "Her head was kind of going down and he's yelling, 'Help!'"

McAdams left the helm, ran to the rail, leaped onto the upside-down hull of the capsized boat, and sprang off of it, diving out into the surf. He swam to the struggling couple and dragged them back through the sea to the lifelines of the rescue boat. The whole time, the boat was rolling heavily in the water, occasionally pushing the three of them under water.

"I yelled to the fellows on deck and they grabbed the woman and they pulled her on up," McAdams said. "Well, they got the woman up and I got up myself and I heard 'Help' off the bow. ..."

The 52-foot motor lifeboat Victory *passes the Cape Disappointment Lighthouse in February 2003. This is the boat Thomas McAdams used to rescue the four drowning boaters just off the beach at the mouth of Yaquina Bay in 1957, when it was virtually brand-new. (Photo: Kurt Fredrickson/US Coast Guard)*

It was the other two people, a man and a woman. Again the woman was almost done for, and the man was fading fast as well.

This time McAdams sent one of the other guys to get them — rescuing people was hard work, and he needed to catch his breath — and soon strong hands were pulling them aboard: first the woman, who wasn't breathing, and then, while a crew member resuscitated her, the man. Then McAdams and another crew member went and pulled the first man on board.

"Then I got him up on board and I said, 'Okay, we've got everybody,' and then I heard, 'Help!'" McAdams remembered. "Well, I said, 'Who else is yelling help?' Well, it was my seaman who I had sent overboard" — to rescue the second couple — "and he's so tired now and cold from being in the water that all he could do is barely hang on the lifelines."

Once the rescuer was safely rescued, McAdams sent everyone below decks except one crew member — a big, muscular Black seaman named Schmidt.

"I'm going to need you to help me get this boat off the beach," McAdams told Schmidt. The rescue boat was still bouncing on the sand with every passing wave.

McAdams now looked up for the first time and realized the fog had lifted. All around "Chicken Hill" — the park where the Yaquina Bay Lighthouse is — and on the bridge, people and cars were stopped and watching the rescue. They'd seen the whole thing: McAdams' dramatic leap to the upside-down hull and dive to pull the first couple to the boat; the second couple being pulled aboard, the woman being worked on to get her breathing again, their obvious success in saving her — everything.

Now they were going to watch McAdams and Schmidt either triumphantly get the boat out of the breakers and off the beach, or ignominiously wash ashore and have to trudge back to the boathouse in disgrace to get a salvage rig.

The two of them got busy.

Once McAdams got on the power, the screws dug a big hole in the sandy bottom, so there was plenty of water under the boat. He just couldn't get out of the hole. Finally he turned the boat around with the stern pointing out to sea — thinking, "If I can turn around and get my stern to the sea and get over that hump I built, I'll probably tear the steering out of the boat but I've got twin screws."

It worked — on both counts. The spinning screws pulled enough sand out of the way for the boat to get through, but enough sand was left to rip the rudder off the boat. McAdams brought the damaged vessel triumphantly back into port, steering it with the two throttles.

The local Coast Guard brass — the group commanding officers, in charge of the life stations — were furious.

"They were upset because I'd taken the most expensive lifeboat the Coast Guard had and beached it and could have lost the boat on the beach," McAdams said. "I said, "But we saved four lives, what are they worth?"

One of the Coast Guard's legendary 36-foot motor lifeboats is on display in front of Coast Guard headquarters in Newport. This was the type of rescue boat Tom McAdams usually used when he went out to save people.

Meanwhile, some of the people who'd been watching the show from the bridge and from Chicken Hill turned out to be VIPs. Telephone calls started pouring into the district admiral's office, including one from Governor Robert Holmes and another from the commander of the Oregon State Police. The local officers, fearing they'd get in trouble, hadn't told the district admiral's office any of the details, so the admiral didn't know what to say.

"The admiral's getting' all these calls. All he's got is this little message," McAdams told author Dennis Noble. "When the officers find out the admiral is asking about the rescue they say, 'Yes, we're goin' to hang those guys.'"

The admiral's office quickly set the local officers straight on that score. They had something else in mind: Two gold lifesaving medals, and two silver ones. McAdams and his crew were heroes.

But in 2005, when he talked to Noble, McAdams was still sounding a bit bemused by the role that fog bank played.

"If the fog hadn't lifted, I'd probably have been busted," he said.

Sources and Works Cited:
- Rescued by the U.S. Coast Guard, *a book by Dennis L. Noble, published in 2005 by the Naval Institute Press in Annapolis;*
- *"The Champion Lifesaver of the Pacific Coast," an article by Stephanie Young published July 25, 2012, in* Coast Guard Compass: The Official Blog of the U.S. Coast Guard.

GORDON HUGGINS & AL.:

U.S. COAST GUARD LIFESAVERS.

It was the worst disaster in the history of the U.S. Coast Guard in Oregon. Three rescue boats, including two of the legendary "unsinkable" motor lifeboats, went out to rescue someone — and none of them returned. Five "Coasties" died.

And yet it all started as a routine rescue, late in the afternoon on Jan. 12, 1961.

The call that started it off came in at a little after 4 p.m. to the Cape Disappointment Life Station, on the Washington side of the Columbia River entrance. Two Ilwaco men, brothers Bert and Stanley Bergmann, had lost the rudder on their crab-fishing boat, the 34-foot *Mermaid*, just when they needed it most — while crossing the bar on their way back in. They'd dropped anchor, but the current was dragging them slowly toward Peacock Spit anyway.

No problem. Conditions were pretty good for January on the bar: winds in the 35-knot neighborhood, the seas in the 10- to 12-foot range. There was a small-craft advisory in effect, but nothing that would stop anything

This steel-hulled, twin-screw 40-foot utility boat is of the same type as the one launched to rescue the Mermaid. These boats could do almost 25 knots in protected waters. (Photo: US Coast Guard)

the Coast Guard had, and the weather service was expecting to cancel the advisory around 5. Speed was critical, though. Once the Mermaid hit the outside line of breakers on Peacock Spit, it would be all over.

So the life station immediately sent two boats out to the rescue: a 40-foot utility boat, and one of the Coast Guard's legendary 36-foot motor lifeboats.

The fact that the 40-footer was sent testifies to the utter unexpectedness of the disaster that was about to unfold. The 40-footers were fast general-purpose boats built for protected waters, not for surf operations and bar rescues. But at this point, the weather was reasonable and the mission looked simple. They'd be back on shore with their grateful rescuees in a couple hours ... right?

Before continuing, I have to explain in more detail what it is that can make the Columbia River Bar so deadly. Essentially, it's three factors: shallow water, swift current and a steady, strong wind that nearly always blows toward the north side of the river. The shallowness means the big, deep waves that have pulsed all the way across the Pacific Ocean start to get compressed into just a few feet of water, just like they do in surf on the beach. When they do, the current coming out of the river sort of pushes their feet out from under them, creating a sort of a circular swirl with the top moving shoreward and the bottom moving seaward. The stronger the current, the more it pushes, and the bigger the waves grow as they come shoreward — because, essentially, more water is being pushed into the bottom of each wave.

On a clear day with a calm sea, this swirling motion isn't even noticeable in the middle of the channel, especially if the tide is slack or flooding and the river is at low summertime flow rates. But winter storms off the Columbia regularly generate hurricane-class wind speeds, and whip up waves to match. When the seas get big, and the river flow is high, and the tide is going out and taking with it all the tidewater for miles up the river, you get some incredible breakers on the bar, breaking all the way across the channel — up to 70 feet tall with a powerful undertow right in front of them. When a boat or small ship is tackling one of these waves, what can happen is the undertow can grab the boat by the taff rail and pull the stern into the face of the wave while the top of the wave pushes the boat over — what sailors call a "pitch-pole," or end-over-end flipping. The hydraulic pressure this puts on a boat or ship is unbelievable, especially if the water is shallow enough for one end of the vessel to dig into the sandy bottom as it goes over. Ships have been known to actually break in half.

As the waves come into the bar on a nice day, they form breakers in the shallows along each side of the channel. As the weather gets heavier, the breakers spread farther into the middle of the channel, so that less of the water in the bar is left unbroken. When the weather gets really nasty, the waves break all the way across the channel, and boats and ships alike have to heave to and wait for it to settle down again. Only the Coast Guard's motor lifeboats are truly seaworthy in those conditions, and they almost expect to get rolled once or twice.

Then there's the wind. It's almost always blowing out of the

Another view of the 36-foot motor lifeboat on display at the Newport Coast Guard station. This was the same type as the motor lifeboat that accompanied the 40-footer out to rescue the Mermaid.

An early version of the Coast Guard's legendary 36-foot motor lifeboats. The boat sent out to rescue the Mermaid was very similar, but lacked the small furled sail this one sports. (Photo: US Coast Guard)

south-southwest, usually blowing hard. That means if you are trying to cross the bar and lose your propulsion, you're headed for Peacock Spit.

Which is exactly what had happened, and was happening, to the Mermaid on that day.

The speedy 40-foot utility boat got across the bar and onto the scene first, and towed the *Mermaid* far enough offshore to be out of danger from the breakers. Then the rescuers and rescuees conferred. The tide had turned and was starting to rough up the bar. So there were two options, they figured: First, they could take the Bergmann brothers aboard the 40-footer, turn the *Mermaid* loose to drift ashore wherever it wanted, and bring everyone to the Columbia River Lightship, anchored several miles offshore. The other possibility was to tow the Mermaid to the lightship.

At this point, nobody knew how much trouble they were in. The seas were high, but not bad by bar standards. The Bergmann brothers naturally didn't want to lose their boat. So the decision was made, by default, to tow the boat to the lightship and moor it there until daylight and flood tide the next day.

And here we come to a crucial point in the story. Because somewhere up the anonymous chain of command at the U.S. Coast Guard, several years earlier, some nameless functionary had ordered that rescue vessels would no longer carry drogues.

A drogue is a special sea anchor designed to make a vessel track straight in the water and stay pointed upwind while under tow. Because the Mermaid had lost its rudder, a drogue was needed to make it tow straight behind the 40-footer rather than yawing out to one side and taking seas on its beam.

The Coasties tried trailing crab pots out behind the boat to increase its drag. This worked OK, but slowed the pace of the boats to the point of barely making headway. They would have been all night making their way to the lightship. They decided they needed more power. And weather conditions were, by this time, getting pretty bad.

So they called up the biggest, toughest rescue boat the Coast Guard had at its disposal in 1961: the 52-foot motor lifeboat *Triumph*, stationed on the Oregon side at Point Adams Lifestation.

The *Triumph*, with six Coast Guard surfmen aboard, chugged out into the towering seas to lend a hand and take over the tow. Of those six men, five would not come back.

Point Adams Life Station in Hammond as it appeared in the early 1970s, a decade or so after the Triumph was stationed there. (Image: U.S. Coast Guard)

When the call came in at the Point Adams Life Station for the *Triumph* to come out and lend a hand, engineman Gordon Huggins was about to go off shift. The seas were burly, but nothing too alarming … yet. It all sounded pretty routine.

Huggins was the new guy at the station, and he was eager to get some experience in the 52-footer. So he asked the engineman on duty, a veteran of many rescues, if he could take his place.

Huggins would have wanted to spend as much time with the Triumph as possible, because he didn't have any experience with this type of motor lifeboat. He couldn't have; the boat was almost unique. Only one other 52-footer like it was built — and there was a reason they didn't build more. In most circumstances, the wooden 52-footers were fantastic rescue boats. They certainly looked, felt and handled as if they could take on anything.

But astonishingly, the 52-footers were not self-righting. Flip one over, and it would stay over. And not only that, but there was no provision to prevent seawater from flooding the air intake for the boat's diesel engines if it did flip over, so even if you could get it back right-side-up, it was still done for.

Now, granted, the boat was extraordinarily stable. It would take tremendous force to roll it over, and it was large and powerful — able to rescue up to 160 people at a go. It certainly was useful on rescues. But it's hard to understand why the Coast Guard thought it would be OK to station a boat like this in the one spot on the North American continent where any motor lifeboat, of any size, can count on being rolled at least once.

Whatever the reasoning behind it, five Coasties were about to pay the tab for that decision.

Out to sea the *Triumph* chugged. The seas were much bigger now; the boat was clawing its way over (and through) the tops of 35-foot breakers as it made its way seaward.

Finally it reached the 40-foot utility boat, which had been dragging the *Mermaid* through the sea for two and a half hours. With the crab pots dragging behind the *Mermaid* to keep her tracking straight, the 40-footer didn't have the power to make much headway. The rescuers hoped the bigger 52-footer would.

By now the waves were breaking all the way across the bar.

The *Triumph* took over the tow, heading out to sea in the direction of the lightship, dragging the *Mermaid* slowly behind. The 40-footer, accompanied by the 36-foot motor lifeboat, started heading for shore.

At this point, the conditions on the bar had gotten bad enough that trying to cross the bar with the 40-footer was a very bad idea. But by this

HEROES.

The Coast Guard only built two 52-foot wooden motor lifeboats. One was the Triumph, which sank during the 1961 attempt to rescue the fishing vessel Mermaid. This photograph is of the other one, the Invincible. (Image: US Coast Guard)

time it was dark outside, and perhaps the boat's skipper wasn't aware of how bad it had gotten; or, maybe he thought he could stay between the waves and make it through.

As the two boats reached the line of breakers across the mouth of the river, visibility got bad enough that they lost sight of each other. The faster 40-footer was in front, the slower 36-footer behind, but it didn't much matter; you could only cross the bar as fast as the waves would let you.

As they got to the most dangerous point in the crossing, trio of giant swells came up behind the boats and broke over the bar. The first two were fearsome, but slipped beneath the boats before they broke. The third did not.

On the 40-footer, crew member Darrell Murray looked behind and saw a huge breaker bearing down on them from behind. Fifty years later, at the age of 76, looking back on an entire career of rescuing people on the Columbia River Bar, Murray still remembered this one particular wave as the biggest breaker he'd ever seen, in an interview with journalist Erika Weisensee.

It could have been worse. It could have broken over the transom of the 40-footer. But instead, it broke right behind — probably because the skipper got on the throttle trying to get out of the way. The boiling foam picked the stern of the boat up high into the air and it rocketed down the wave

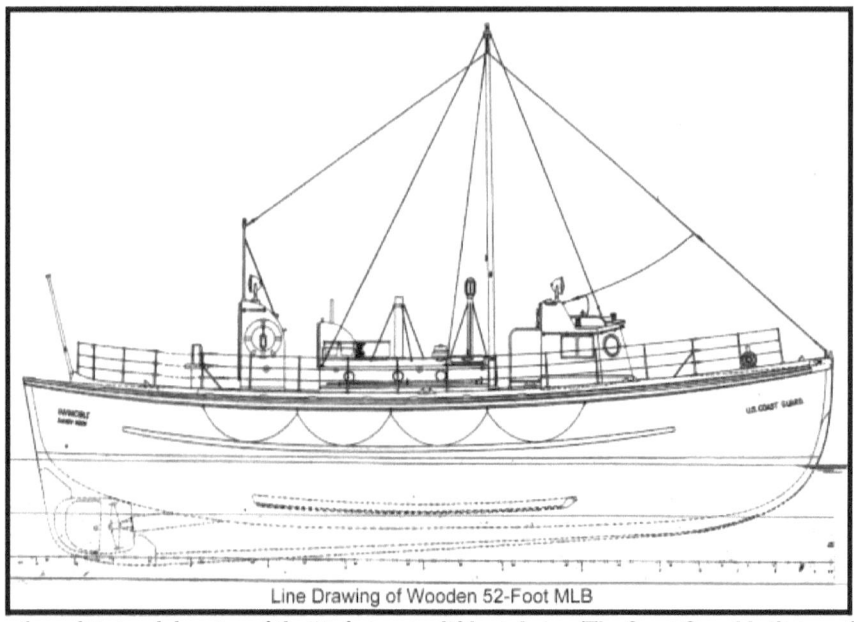

An architectural drawing of the 52-foot motor lifeboat design. The Coast Guard built two of these boats; one was the ill-fated Triumph. (Image: US Coast Guard)

face like a surfboard — and the bow lanced into the sea in front of it, catching the undertow — and the breaker pushed the stern up and over and down.

The three Coast Guardsmen managed to get out from under the upside-down boat and clung to it, waiting to be swept off by the next massive comber — waiting, essentially, for death.

Then the 36-footer came over a wave, slamming hard into the upside-down 40, and its crew members pulled all three of them to safety.

But by now the 36-footer was in trouble, too. Its aft compartment had sprung a leak in the collision with the 40-footer, and was now half full of water. Giving up on crossing the bar, the Coast Guardsmen turned around, leaving the 40 behind, and headed for the Columbia River Lightship as fast as they could go — which, as the aft compartment filled up more and more with water, was not very fast.

By the time they got there, the aft deck was fully awash. They moored there and clambered aboard the big lightship, grateful to be alive. The next morning, they found the motor lifeboat had completely sunk and disappeared — and there was no trace of the *Triumph* or the *Mermaid*.

The *Triumph* had been towing the *Mermaid* toward the lightship, crab pots and all, and the big motor lifeboat had enough power that the *Mermaid* was finally making headway. But, as it turned out, the *Triumph* had a little too much power — the towing hawser broke. The *Mermaid* was then carried by the relentless wind into the breakers on Peacock Spit — which by this time were enormous.

Well, no motor lifeboat crew was afraid to go into breakers; that's what motor lifeboats were made for, right?

Not this one.

Gordon Huggins, the engineman, had gone below decks to take care of a nosebleed when he felt the boat roll onto its side. He thought nothing of it — until the boat paused a moment and then finished the roll. Huggins stood there on the ceiling, now thoroughly alarmed. The engine conked out, of course, and a few minutes later the lights went out. He was left in the inky blackness, with water slowly leaking in through the companionway. He tried to open it, but it wouldn't budge: the pressure of the water held the hatches closed. He was trapped.

Several minutes later, miraculously, another wave hit the boat and rolled it back upright. Huggins tried the latch again and this time it opened for him.

He was alone on the deck of the Triumph. Everyone else was gone.

Huggins stayed with the boat as long as he could as the wind blew it closer to Peacock Spit. He knew he would inevitably end up in the 50-degree water, and that when he did, he'd have about 15 minutes before he'd go hypothermic and die. Every minute that the boat stayed upright, drifting closer to the shore, was another five minutes or so that he wouldn't be trying to swim through the freezing surf; so he rode it as long as he could.

Then another giant wave hit the Triumph and rolled it again, pitching Huggins into the sea. He floated in his life jacket, eyes on the breakers, curling up into a ball whenever one approached, getting colder and colder.

Then he felt the sandy bottom beneath him and staggered ashore on Peacock Spit. He was the only survivor of the Triumph's crew.

Two more 36-foot motor lifeboats from Point Adams came and tried to take the *Mermaid* and its crab pots in tow. Again, they made almost no progress. Finally a huge comber broke over the *Mermaid*, snapping the tow line and somersaulting the helpless fishing boat, breaking it into pieces. On board were the two brothers who owned the boat, and one member of the *Triumph's* crew whom they'd rescued after the boat rolled.

The Coast Guard searched all night for survivors, but found nothing and nobody. The total death toll was seven — five of the six *Triumph* crew members, plus the Bergmann brothers from the *Mermaid*.

Crew members of the Coast Guard motor lifeboat Triumph II lay a wreath on the sea in a 2008 memorial service commemorating the loss of the first Triumph's crew members 47 years earlier. (Photo: David Marin/U.S. Coast Guard)

There's a sort of odd afterword to this story. Remember the 36-foot motor lifeboat that sank after just barely getting the six Coast Guard guys to the lightship? According to an old motor-lifeboat Coastie named Thomas Dye, that wasn't the end of its story. According to Dye, the sunken boat actually washed ashore by the Nehalem River and was claimed by a local fisherman named Wes Shelton. Dye says he bought it in 1975 after recognizing it by its serial number as the lost motor lifeboat from the *Triumph* incident.

Dye said he sold the boat sometime in the early 2000s. When last he heard, Dye said the historic vessel was being used as a pleasure boat by a fellow in Garibaldi.

Sources and Works Cited:
- Rescued by the Coast Guard, *a book by Dennis Noble, published in 2005 by the Naval Institute Press of Annapolis;*
- *"Fiftieth Anniversary: One of the Coast Guard's Greatest Sea Tragedies," an article by Erika Weisensee published in the Jan. 10, 2011, issue of* Natural Resource Report;
- *Personal correspondence from Senior Chief Boatswain's Mate Thomas Dye, USCG.*

JIM WRIGHT:

ENGINEER AND AVIATOR.

I.

Jim Wright was just trying to make it home.

To get him there, he was depending on an airplane called a Hughes H-1, a sleek, streamlined machine that looked as if it belonged in an aviation museum. And, in fact, the only other one like it was in the Smithsonian, and hadn't flown since 1937.

That older plane had been built by Howard Hughes in 1934 to set a new world speed record. To no one's surprise, it did so the following year. Hughes then tucked it away in a dusty hangar, where it remained for the rest of his life.

The newer plane, the one Wright was flying now — well, he'd built that one himself, in 2002, faithfully following every detail of Hughes' original. And now, a little over a year later, it was a beautiful, clear day and he was soaring over the Rocky Mountains in it.

Wright was flying back home to Cottage Grove from the legendary annual air show at Oshkosh, Wis. There, as everywhere else he'd brought his airplane, it had been the toast of the event, a perfect replica of one of

Jim Wright flies a low pass over the airfield at what was then known as the Cottage Grove State Airport, in 2002. Since then, the airport has been renamed Jim Wright Field. (Image: Finn J.D. John)

the most important planes in history, with a one-digit serial number — 2. Airplane enthusiasts and history buffs alike had found the replica to be like a time machine. Everything on it, they'd noted, was either a custom-made replica or a lovingly restored original component from the early 1930s: The enormous round radial engine, the cockpit controls, even the twin-blade Hamilton Standard constant-speed propeller hub that was modified in exactly the same way Hughes' had been to complement the plane's 1,000-horsepower engine.

It was that insistence on authenticity that would, a little later that day, destroy Jim's priceless aircraft and make a widow of Betty, his wife.

II.

Now that I've given you an idea of where this story is going, I'm going to let down the Fourth Wall for a minute. Unlike most of the stories in this book, this one includes me personally. My role was far from central, but I *was* there; so, although having references to myself tucked into the narrative here and there feels a little weird for a history story, it also feels like the right thing to do for this one.

I first met Jim Wright in 2002, when he was putting the finishing touches on the H-1. At the time, I was the editor of his hometown newspaper, the weekly *Cottage Grove Sentinel*. A tiny town at the very southernmost tip of the Willamette Valley, with farmland to the north and timberlands to the south, east, and west, Cottage Grove has a correspondingly small newspaper. There were three of us in the newsroom — me, reporter Matthew Treder, and photographer Jared Paben. Technically it was Treder's story, but naturally we were all very interested — a major national sensation was brewing up right in our own little town.

And it was no exaggeration to call the H-1 that. It was an astonishing piece of industrial art, like a shining silver snub-nosed rocket made of polished aluminum with electric-blue wings and sitting on tall, spindly landing gear, the cockpit pushed way back toward the tail. Sitting there on the tarmac, with that massive, blunt engine thrust up into the air, it had an austere, uninviting, all-business look, like an unmanned missile with a propeller on the front. In the air, though, with the landing gear up and the fuselage level, it looked like a different airplane, in the spirit of the very finest industrial sculpture of the art-deco 1930s — sleek, streamlined, fabulous.

Yet it was not designed with looks in mind. The H-1's beauty was strictly incidental to its real purpose. The long, liquid lines in gleaming polished aluminum weren't there to be admired; they were there to slip the air past faster so that an extra two miles per hour could be squeezed from it. The cowl was round because that was the shape of the most powerful engine available at the time. The wing lines flowed out of the fuselage not for looks, but so that the wings could carry the structural load, saving a few dozen pounds. Just sitting there on the ground, pointing skyward at a 30-degree angle, it was an irrefutable demonstration that form and function live in the same place and may even be married to each other.

Wright himself was as quiet and unassuming as his airplane was striking and spectacular. A self-taught engineer who'd never bothered to go to college, Wright was mechanically a natural, having started out working on lawn-mowers at a very young age.

"He was a real smart, real affable guy," Treder remembered later. "Generous with his time." Treder, who interviewed Wright several times for stories, called the aviator a "natural-born storyteller."

Wright was half of the husband-and-wife team that started Wright Machine Tools in 1976. During the 25 years that followed, they built it into a lucrative business that still exists today, producing machines that sharpen and maintain industrial carbide saws, among other things. By the late 1990s it had become the kind of business that quietly overshadows the place in which it's located. It might have occupied an unassuming beige building on the outskirts of a tiny Willamette Valley timber town, but it was a multi-million-dollar enterprise.

Throughout the period of time that passed between the founding of the company and the building of the H-1, Wright himself didn't change much. Most of the time, his face wore one of two expressions: A huge, open grin or a focused look of intense concentration. Though he liked himself just fine and loved exotic toys, he showed no signs of the kind of egoism one expects from someone that successful. His office was modest, a bit cramped, dusty, stocked largely with cheap-but-serviceable furniture made of particle board covered with vinyl printed to look like oak. The computers there had originally been beige, but had turned yellow with age and exposure to sunshine. Wright's desk faced the wall, making his office look like a workstation, rather than a command center.

And through a window on that wall, Wright could look out at the airport and watch planes come and go. It was no coincidence that his business was located right next to the little community airport that today is named after him. Wright's father was an aviator, and passed the "bug" on to his boy; Wright bought his first plane, a Taylorcraft that at the time of his death he still owned, when he was just 21 years old.

As his business grew, Wright started acquiring more fast, exotic things: a rare Honda CBX six-cylinder motorcycle from the early 1980s, a red Corvette that he used for his regular driving, even a street-legal Formula race car that he drove around on special occasions — a gift from Betty, that last one.

On the airfield outside his shop was parked an early-1950s Beechcraft Bonanza, one of those V-tailed hot rods of the sky like the one Ritchie Valens and Buddy Holly crashed in. In his hangar he kept a Glassair III, a sleek kit-built plane that flew two and a half times faster than an entry-level Cessna.

But the Hughes racer: That was to be the highlight, the crown jewel in his hangar.

He'd dreamed of building the plane since 1978, when he'd read about it in a magazine article from the 1930s. And he'd been fascinated by the Hughes plane since he was young — its blinding speed, its secretive inventor who hurried to hide it from the world after breaking his second record with it in 1937, the persistent rumors — given extra weight by Hughes himself — that its design had been sold or leaked to Japan and had inspired the dreaded Type Zero fighter from World War II.

By the late 1990s, Wright's business was successful enough that he was able to pursue that dream.

III.

Howard Hughes is still best remembered today as a reclusive and aged billionaire with severe mental issues. Although that description hardly fit Jim Wright, the Cottage Grove entrepreneur shared several traits (positive ones) with the long-dead aviation pioneer. He had the same lean, lanky build, the same passion for things well-built and fast, and flying skills that — well, let's face facts, Hughes was one of the best flyers of all time. But Wright was no slouch either.

Wright also shared Hughes' ability to get the best out of the people who worked for him. This probably had something to do with Wright's attitude. It was quite a bit different from the "I'm better than you" hit one sometimes gets from CEOs. His attitude was more like, "I love people, including myself — and you too." You could see that attitude in his office layout, in his casual style of dress (he greatly favored long-sleeve plaid Western shirts and Panama hats) and in the morale of the people he led.

But the most important thing Wright shared with Hughes was ownership of a machine-and-tool company. That meant anything Wright needed, he could simply machine for himself — just as Hughes had done.

Now he focused all of these critical assets on replicating Hughes' airplane.

The original had been tucked away in an obscure hangar at Hughes Aircraft immediately after it broke its last record — the transcontinental record — in 1937; and it had been out of the public's sight until 1975, on the eve of Hughes' death, when it had been donated to the Smithsonian Institution.

Blueprints? Plans? All long gone. But Smithsonian officials Robert van der Linden and Bill Reese were willing to let Wright's team come to Washington, D.C., and examine the original to reverse-engineer a new set of plans. They were even allowed to disassemble parts of the plane to get better measurements — a huge demonstration of trust, as the H-1 is one of the Smithsonian's crown jewels.

"The director of the Smithsonian told me that if he could have one plane in the Smithsonian, it wouldn't be the Wright (Brothers) Flyer," Wright once told a reporter from the *Gillette* (Wyoming) *News-Record*. "It would be the Hughes Racer."

Wright assembled a team of experts to help build it. Two of his employees, Guy Ralstin and Dennis Parker, worked on computer-aided design drafting so that parts could be machined by digitally-controlled machining mills. He rounded out the team with experienced aircraft builders and flyers Mike Mann, Dave Payne and Al Sherman, and hired Ron Englund to direct the team.

For a few special tasks, experts had to be hired. A man from Arkansas with legendary skills as a panel-beater spent a full year using a ball-peen hammer to beat sheets of aluminum into the highly complicated shape required for the engine cowl. Another old-style craftsman from California carved part of the wooden tail section. A local craftsman, Steve Wolf from Creswell, spent 3,000 hours building just the wings.

For the propeller, Wright's team had some difficulty finding a unit that could handle the power of the H-1's engine. They started with the heaviest Hamilton Standard prop they could find, and it wasn't heavy enough. Eventually they found a vintage Hamilton Standard hub of the same type Hughes had used and fitted it with blades from an Italian military plane. Just like Hughes before them, they would have trouble with that propeller.

In addition to the subcontracted parts, the team poured 35,000 man-hours into the project — the equivalent of 17 years. Total cost? Just shy of $2 million — but, of course, if Wright hadn't owned a machine shop, it would have been much more than that.

IV.

By the spring of 2002, the plane was finally nearly ready, and Wright was starting to think about getting it into the air.

Finally, in mid-June, surrounded by a small group of admiring aviators and the entire newsroom staff of the *Cottage Grove Sentinel*, the plane was rolled out onto the airfield and, with that smoky belch characteristic of all radial engines, the monstrous power plant started up. Cottage Grove's airport echoed for the first time with the rough, belligerent roar of the Hughes H-1's massive engine.

It was the beginning of several months of continuous testing and development. Low-speed taxi testing, medium-speed taxi testing, brake checks .... Neighboring residents and businesses started getting used to the racket.

After the first medium-speed taxi run, reporter Treder found Wright looking distinctly rattled.

"The airplane is intimidating. It is incredibly powerful," he said. "I've never had my hand on the throttle of anything that had quite so much power. ... The Hughes feels scarily powerful. In your mind, you can visualize things going wrong."

Wright said he'd fed the engine a bunch of throttle to test the brakes, and the massive torque had tilted the whole plane, squashing down the landing-gear struts.

He turned to veteran test pilot and air racer Jimmy Leeward, of Leeward

The Hughes H-1 Racer replica, parked on the tarmac outside Jim Wright's hangar. To the left of the picture is Wright's street-legal Formula race car. (Image: Finn J.D. John)

Air Ranch in Florida, for some help handling his high-powered plane.* Leeward flew one of his P-51 Mustangs to Cottage Grove to help. Leeward used the Mustang to fly after Wright's plane and observe how it was flying, helping iron out minor issues in preparation for the H-1's first flight beyond Cottage Grove.

"Overall, there have been very minor problems, and those that have cropped up have been normal teeth-cutting items that happen to any newly constructed plane with only 15 hours of flight time," Leeward wrote in an update letter to *All Aviation Flightline Online*, an enthusiasts' website.

Leeward didn't mention what those issues were, but at the local paper, we did mention one of them — the tailwheel melted, causing a little repairable damage to the tail.

Another thing Leeward didn't mention was Wright's nagging worry that something bigger than a "minor problem" might be lurking. And indeed, though he kept his positive attitude up at all times, Wright had some reason to suspect there might be an actual, unknown problem with the plane. Hughes' life's biggest passion, in his younger days, was airplanes. He had built the fastest, best, most exciting airplane in the world. Why didn't he use it? Why did it end up tucked away in an obscure hangar at Hughes

---

* *Jimmy Leeward, by the way, was the pilot of the heavily modified P-51 named "Galloping Ghost," which on Sept. 16, 2011, crashed into the tarmac in front of a set of grandstands at the Reno Air Races, killing 11 people and injuring 69 others. It was the worst crash in Reno Air Races history.*

Aircraft and forgotten about? It made no sense. It was like Mario Andretti having Ferrari custom-build a one-of-a-kind supercar for him and then never driving it.

"There was always the nagging fear that the reason Howard flew (the H-1) only 42 hours was because there was some serious problem, which he never would have said anything about," Wright told *Air & Space Magazine*. "Was there a bear trap waiting for us?"

If that bear trap were to spring, Wright did not want the local newspaper to be there to witness it. Or anybody else, for that matter.

And that is surely why, a few days later, as I sat at the breakfast bar in my house nursing a cup of coffee early one morning and reading the *Eugene Register-Guard* (the regional daily paper that covered my town), I heard the distinctive sound of the plane flying over my house — sounding like a gang of Hells Angels doing subcontractor work for Santa Claus. Wright had left the airfield early that morning for the plane's maiden voyage, headed 70 miles north to Corvallis. No one had told us, so our photographer, Jared Paben, wasn't there.

Of course, reporter Treder hastened to get an after-the-fact article ready for the next week's paper. In it, Wright painted a glowing picture of the plane's handling on the flight: "What a hoot! It handles so good. It flies just incredible," he told Treder. "It was going 190 miles per hour at 30 percent power — you know it's just going to scoot!"

To scoot, that was, after the propeller problems were ironed out. Mindful of the publicity, Wright didn't tell Treder everything about the flight, but he did tell an *Air & Space Magazine* reporter about it later. It seemed Wright was getting that 30 percent power at 100 percent of the engine's allowable speed, because the prop wasn't taking big enough "bites" of air. As a result, the engine was running uncomfortably hot, and Wright at one point was looking for places to make an emergency landing. Luckily, the temperature stabilized, and he made it to Corvallis.

After the champagne celebration was over, Wright got back to work. To let the propeller function as it was supposed to with such a powerful engine, it needed bigger counterweights — one on each propeller blade. Without them, the centrifugal force of the propeller would make the blades take smaller bites of air.

Wright put bigger counterweights on the plane, which helped a lot.

HEROES.

The first propeller used on the H-1 was this heavy Hamilton Standard constant-speed prop, which now hangs on the wall of the Oregon Aviation Historical Society Museum in Cottage Grove. Behind it are pictures of Jim Wright with the plane, and an image of the H-1 shattering a speed record at the Reno Air Races. (Image: offbeatoregon.com)

v.

Jim and Betty Wright and their engineering team had a couple goals in mind. In 2002, they wanted to go to the Reno Air Races and break the world speed record. Not the "unlimited" one Hughes broke with the original H-1 70 years earlier — that one has been well out of reach for any gasoline-powered plane since about 1945 — but the record in the H-1's size class, which was 266 miles per hour, set in 1969.

Wright had already had his H-1 above 300 while testing it around Cottage Grove.

So when the time came, the development team saddled up and headed for Reno. Wright made his hometown newspaper — us — an offer: If a *Sentinel* staffer could get to Reno, he'd provide a hotel room.

This was a big deal. Booking a room in Reno during the weekend of the Air Races was almost impossible.

It took some fancy talking and some heavy-duty promising, but I secured permission from our publisher, Brad Chambers, to empty out the newsroom for the weekend. All three of us — reporter Treder, photographer Paben and I — bundled into a borrowed Volkswagen Euro-Van and launched ourselves on a road trip to Reno.

When we got there, we found the Wrights holding court. Or rather, court was holding them. They weren't trying to be the center of attention, but their airplane had the effect of emptying out all the other areas of the airshow. It was parked right next to a Bell P-63 Kingcobra, a rare and exotic mid-engined World War II fighter plane. The Bell got very little attention in the shadow of the H-1 — but its owner, delighted at the chance to look the historic replica over at close range, didn't seem to mind in the least.

At Reno, there's an air show on the ground — where visitors can look over historic and interesting planes and eat cotton candy — at the same time air races are going on above, with pilots roaring around pylons with wide-open throttles and jockeying for position in a quest for the checkered flag. Wright, of course, would never endanger his plane by racing it against other aircraft, so he stuck with the air show part of the program.

Treder, Paben and I watched the air races from the tarmac with him and the rest of the H-1 team. I was doing something else, not paying any attention to the planes buzzing overhead, when an electric current seemed to go through the crowd and I felt, rather than heard, a collective gasp.

I looked up. A tall plume of dust was rising from the desert floor on the opposite side of the airfield. I couldn't see it, but at the bottom of that plume was what was left of an airplane that had just broken apart in midair and hammered into the ground. There was no parachute. There were no survivors. It was a sobering reminder that this wasn't a stamp collecting convention — these people were here to do something that, sooner or later, would kill some of them.

We went back to the hotel after that, and had a couple drinks.

And very early the next morning — again, without telling us what he was up to — Wright took the plane out again, and shattered the record he'd come to break.

Disappointed but getting used to it by now, we hurried home and splashed the news all over the front page.

Wright's speed was 304 miles an hour. He said he could have gone faster, but the propeller still wasn't quite working right, and he could only get about 65 percent power to it. Maybe even bigger counterweights were needed.

VI.

I never saw Wright again after that day in Reno. Shortly afterward, I was transferred to the Corvallis *Gazette-Times*, and left Cottage Grove. But I followed Wright's exploits avidly in the *Sentinel*, where Treder had taken over as editor.

Wright, his first record broken, now had set his sights on the transcontinental record, the one Hughes had broken back in 1937 — a race against

HEROES.

A plastic model of the Hughes Racer, the plane of which Jim Wright's plane was an exact replica, hangs in the Oregon Aviation Historical Society museum. (Image: offbeatoregon.com)

the clock from one side of the North American continent to the other — which still seemed within striking distance of the H-1's capabilities.

But first, there was a summer full of appearances and airshows, starting with the Experimental Aviation Association show in Oshkosh, Wis., early in August 2003. This was the big one, and Jim wouldn't miss it for anything. So he fired up his plane and headed for Oshkosh.

The plane was, of course, the highlight of the show, as it had been everywhere. Pilots and spectators lined up to gawk at it. Jim grinned happily and proudly. It was the fulfilment of a dream.

On the way home from the show, Wright landed in Gillette, Wyo., where he and his plane "caused a mild sensation," according to the local paper.

But the paper reported that Wright said something ominous: He was having propeller trouble. Again.

"The air's thin enough here that the propeller gets stuck in low gear," he said. "I'm just trying to get home."

By this he meant that the counterweights, once again, wouldn't let his propeller take big enough bites of air. Things were fine when he took off from lower elevations, but high up in the Rocky Mountains, he was having trouble again.

Wright climbed up on a ladder and worked the propeller hub over, making sure it was well lubricated. No doubt he figured that, worst-case scenario, he'd have to limp home at 30 percent power again — no fun, but he'd done it before.

Then, his parachute on — he always said if there were ever trouble, he'd bail out — he strapped himself back into the airplane and took off.

An hour or so later, at Yellowstone National Park, a group of tourists was looking at geysers when they heard a very loud airplane engine start up with a sudden, shaggy roar. It sounded troubled and uneven and very, very close. Then, with a cough, it went silent again.

Looking up, they saw a silver airplane right above the treetops. It was headed right for them. Its wings were wobbling as if it were about to stall and crash.

What they didn't know was what would come out in the National Transportation Safety Board's analysis of the wreckage later on: The propeller had thrown off one of those two counterweights. As a result, one blade was taking tiny nibbles of air and the other was taking big bites. Running the engine with the propeller like that would shake an airplane so violently that it could actually break apart.

Apparently, when this had happened, Wright had cut the power and let his plane glide. It made a fabulous glider. But, of course, Wright needed to find a place to glide it to — or he'd have to bail out and let it crash. He was ready to do that — that's what the parachute was for.

But Wright's friends think he looked down and saw that geyser basin and thought, "I can land on that." So he stayed in the plane and lined it up for an emergency landing — gear up, so that it would bounce on the ground like a skipping stone rather than sticking in the field and tumbling end over end, and going just as slow as possible to reduce the impact damage.

Then, the theory goes, when he got close enough, he saw the tourists, at least 20 of them, standing right where he needed to land. If he put the plane down there, he'd mow them down like cornstalks in October.

He started the engine up again. The plane shook violently. Wright's crippled plane couldn't make enough power to save itself without shaking itself to pieces. He shut the plane off again.

He was flying as slow as the plane would go without stalling — standard procedure for an emergency landing. He was just a few hundred feet off the ground. Every time an airplane turns, it loses a little speed. If he tried to turn anyway, the plane would stall out and spin straight into those people. So, turning his plane away from the people to land it on another part of the geyser basin was not an option. He had just two choices: Save himself and

HEROES.

The sign posted at the entrance to the airport identifies it as Jim Wright Field — the name given it to honor Wright after his death. The building behind the sign is the Oregon Aviation Historical Society's museum. (Image: offbeatoregon.com)

his plane by covering it with their blood — or put it into a dive to gain enough speed to turn it away from them, knowing it would slice into the ground wing-first at 100 miles an hour if he did.

No one who knew Jim Wright would be surprised by the choice he made.

VII.

The news of Jim Wright's death hit Cottage Grove hard. Everyone in the community had heard him roaring overhead in that distinctive-sounding airplane. Hundreds of people drove to nearby Springfield for his memorial service, and the City Council immediately started the process of renaming the Cottage Grove State Airport. It's now known as Jim Wright Field.

Around the same time, a letter arrived to Wright's bereaved family. It was from the Chen family — Ning and Mei-Ling and their 12-year-old son Ian — who were among those tourists in the clearing. They described the scene in a letter forwarded to Wright's family by a Yellowstone Park ranger:

"The plane was heading directly towards my wife and several other people on the boardwalk," Ning Chen wrote. "The plane was about 500 feet away from her with a height of 300 to 400 feet. She and other people were directly under the flight path. The next thing I observed was that the plane all of a sudden veered to its right … after two or three more seconds, I saw a huge explosion from the creek next to the main road."

"The plane started to swerve away from the boardwalk, flipped perpendicular to the ground, and crashed into a small hill near the river, wing first," wrote young Ian. "Later my family figured that the pilot swerved away so he would not endanger the lives of the people on the ground, which also included my mom."

"I realize Mr. Wright really spared the lives of the people on the ground," wrote Mei-Ling Chen. "It must (have been) really hard for him to make that decision that final moment. I'm writing this letter to let you know (what) an honorable man he was. Our family is very grateful for his actions."

Sources and Works Cited:
- "*Silver Bullet,*" *an article by Preston Lerner published in the May 2003 issue of* Smithsonian Air & Space Magazine;
- "*NTSB Identification: DEN03FA138,*" *an accident report published in 2003, by the National Transportation Safety Board at ntsb.gov;*
- Cottage Grove Sentinel *archives, June through September 2002;*
- Gillette (Wyoming) News-Record *archives, August 2003;*
- *Personal correspondence: E-mail from Dennis Parker to Oregon Magazine, October 2002; personal recollections of Matthew Treder and Finn J.D. John.*

PART II:

MAVERICKS.

"UNCLE JOAB" POWELL:

FRONTIER CIRCUIT PREACHER.

About halfway between Crabtree and Lacomb, tucked into the side of a gentle hill, stands an old and somewhat austere-looking little white building known as Providence Pioneer Church.

The "pioneer" part of the name is somewhat superfluous. Just one look at it suffices to tell it's an old-style church of the kind built 150 years ago by people who'd come to Oregon in covered wagons. There is no stained glass, no icons or statuary — just four simple sash windows along each side, a steep roof, a simple belltower and steeple rising from the front. Simple, but welcoming, especially now that a covered port-cochere has been added to its front.

It's old, but it's not the original Providence Pioneer Church. That structure was built of logs back in 1854, and according to legendary Oregon pop historian Ralph Friedman, it "had an air of vigilant righteousness, as though erected by Jeremiah and maintained by avenging angels."

And, as Friedman goes on to note, that's not far from the actual truth.

There will surely never be a second Jeremiah. But the man who led the congregation of missionary Baptists who built Providence Church may have been the closest the world has come to producing one.

Joab Powell, better known as Uncle Joab, stood over six feet tall, with a great barrel chest enclosing a pair of lungs whose capacity was already legendary when he arrived in the state via covered wagon in 1852.

Uncle Joab is probably best known in Oregon today for a sequence of political "firsts," not all of which would have met with his approval. The main ones are these: He was the first chaplain in the state Legislature, in the year Oregon became a state; and, of course, he led the lawmakers in offering up the Legislature's first prayer.

But interesting as these little factoids may or may not be, they're far from the most interesting part of Uncle Joab's story.

Joab Powell was born in 1799 in the hills of Tennessee — Claiborne County, north of Knoxville, close to the Kentucky state line. His was a Quaker family, and he was brought up in the classic manner of the plain-dressing, plain-speaking Society of Friends, bitterly opposed on Biblical grounds to the institution of slavery, the consumption of alcohol, and the treatment of black people and Indians as something other than brothers and sisters under God.

These moral characteristics seem to have soaked deep into his bones, for when he left the Quakers and became a missionary Baptist, he brought them with him — except for the plain-speaking part, the 1600s-style use of "thee" and "thou," which in the mid-1800s was already starting to look a bit like an affectation.

In 1817, he married Anna Beeler; and the two of them got started building a family that would, by the time they were finished, number 14 members.

Anna was a critical and usually-forgotten part of the Uncle Joab story. For one thing, Joab Powell was illiterate: he had no formal schooling at all. But he had an uncanny ability to absorb and remember information. So Anna would read to the family from the Bible; he would absorb and memorize whole books of it; and, at Sunday services, out it would come — somewhat imperfect word-for-word, but spot-on in spirit and intent, and delivered with enthusiasm and fire.

Not surprisingly, he was promptly called into the ministry.

He had been preaching in Tennessee for six years when, in 1830, the family moved to Missouri — which was pretty much the frontier at that time — and took a 640-acre land claim, which he started in farming as a sort of side hustle. His real avocation in Missouri was, of course, as a circuit preacher, riding all over the frontier to hold services. Anna essentially financed this avocation by managing their farm with the help of their growing brood of children.

Twenty years passed. Then the Oregon Trail opened, and the Powells, living right there in Missouri, were perfectly positioned to join the throng. They promptly did so, crossing the plains in the approved Oregon Trail fashion and taking up a land claim at the forks of the Santiam River — where Anna set up her farming operation anew with the help of her now-mostly-grown children and, in several cases, their spouses.

Immediately upon arriving, Uncle Joab joined several other members of the party — missionary Baptists all, of course — to establish Providence Church. Then, onto his long-suffering horse he hopped, and set out into the wilderness to obey the Great Commission.

It took a stunningly short amount of time for Uncle Joab Powell to become the most famous preacher in the West. He had, as you will no doubt have gathered, that magical combination of ferocious passion and brotherly love that good Baptist preachers are known for — and he seemed to have more of both than anyone else alive. To that, add his prodigious lung capacity — it was said, only half in jest, that when he was preaching a sermon in Scio it could be heard in downtown Jefferson, ten miles away — and you can imagine what the Forces of Evil found themselves up against.

He would start off by singing a hymn — or, perhaps it would be more accurate to say, roaring one. His pitch, several sources say, was not as good as his memory; but he made up for any such deficiency with volume. Nor did he care: He was there to save souls, not to get Christina Aguilera to turn her chair around for him.

Next he would start into a sermon, and hold the congregation spellbound. His imperfectly remembered Bible verses would come out "translated" into frontier English — which the homesteaders always related to better than they would have the original King James text.

"When he went on a preaching trip he always took one of the brethren with him," recalled his granddaughter, Rachel Arminta Peterson, in a 1939 interview with a Works Progress Administration writer. "They went two by two just as the early disciples did at Jesus' command. In many of the places where they went there was no church building, so they preached in log cabins, in schoolhouses, in court-houses or out of doors under the trees. At

Lebanon he often held meetings in the old Santiam Academy building. ... His journeys took him south as far as California."

When Uncle Joab rode into a town, he typically would stay with a relative or friend, and then put the word out. He didn't follow a schedule; he just dropped in, preached a "sarvice," and moved on the next day to do it all again somewhere else.

"He always came unexpectedly; we never knew when he was coming," Peterson recalled. "He always spent the night with us and as soon as he came it was the business of us children to start out and notify all the neighbors that there would be preaching at Father's house that night. We children would run everywhere and by evening when the meeting began there would be a good housefull. That is the way he went all over the country."

On occasions when there wasn't a river nearby for purposes of baptism, tanks built of planks were sometimes knocked together and filled with water. Uncle Joab was a stickler for baptism, and at every service the opportunity to get "soaked and saved" had to be ready to hand.

Back at home in Linn County, Providence Church had swelled to more than 400 members — an enormous congregation for the population of Linn County at the time. And by 1859 — on the eve of Oregon's finally becoming a state — Uncle Joab was far and away the most famous clergyman in the territory.

So, naturally, when the first state Legislature convened and thoughts were turned to the need to start meetings off properly with bowed heads and folded hands, his was the first name to come to mind. An invitation was dispatched to him forthwith, offering a $30 fee for his services as the new state's first official man of God — the Chaplain of the Legislature. It was just as promptly accepted.

It became clear, though, immediately upon his arrival, that the Legislature had had no idea what sort of preacher they were hiring when they sent for him.

They would learn, the hard way, over the next few weeks.

Immediately upon Uncle Joab's arrival, it was obvious that he was not going to fit in. When he arrived, he was dressed in the same homemade clothes he always wore — simple working farm garments; he looked very out-of-place among the well-tailored lawmakers. Several sources claim he also smelled a bit farm-ish, as he had been shoveling manure when the summons came; but this is exactly the sort of detail that often gets added to stories like this by over-eager storytellers, so whether it's true or not isn't clear.

What's very clear, though, is that the Legislators were taken aback by Uncle Joab's frankness.

The tension started immediately, at the very first session of the very first Legislature. The meeting was called to order, and Uncle Joab took the floor to deliver the invocation. The Legislators folded their hands like good little churchboys. And then that famous voice boomed out over their bowed heads:

"FATHER, FORGIVE THEM," Uncle Joab roared, "FOR THEY KNOW NOT WHAT THEY DO."

An inset portrait of Uncle Joab Powell published in 1919 in John B. Horner's book, Oregon: Her History, Her Great Men, Her Literature. *(Image: Gazette-Times)*

As you are likely aware, this was the prayer Jesus offered up for the Roman soldiers who were about to crucify him, according to Luke 23:34. The implications of this — Uncle Joab praying *for* them rather than *with* them, analogizing them to ignorant pagans, and literally telling Almighty God that they didn't know what they were doing — cannot have failed to register with the Legislators. It's hard not to speculate, too, on the possibility that Uncle Joab was responding with subtle wit to some ill-concealed condescension on the part of the legislators, who certainly considered his social station to be far lower than their own and, having jumped to the conclusion that he was an idiot, may not have been at great pains to hide the fact.

I haven't been able to find a source that describes their reaction, but it must have been something to see.

Well — however insulting this inaugural prayer might have been, it was at least short. And if Uncle Joab's subsequent prayers had stayed that way, they might have found a way to live with him. But Uncle Joab's services were not ordinarily known for brevity, and it very soon became obvious that that first one had been something of an outlier in that respect.

Nor were Uncle Joab's sermons known for obsequiousness or deference to worldly power. Uncle Joab had not gotten to be the most popular pastor in the state by rendering unto Caesar the things that were God's. It was clear that in the course of his official duties he would be denouncing some sins and calling out some sinners ... present company most emphatically *not* excepted.

That made for some rather uncomfortable moments. Many of these frontier legislators were saloonkeepers and owners of stores that sold liquor. One or two were, or had been, professional gamblers. Other legislators were slavery-friendly or even slave "owners." And, of course, most of them patronized prostitutes, had mistresses, engaged in sharp dealing, or otherwise deviated discreetly from the straight and narrow. From Uncle Joab's perspective, they were a pack of preening sinners in fancy clothes, standing in grave need of some plain talk. And he was just the man to give it to them. The more uncomfortable they were

A granite monument that stands before Providence Pioneer Church commemorating "Uncle Joab" Powell and his fellow church founders. (Image: offbeatoregon.com)

when he did, the more he knew his tough-loving words of guidance and wisdom were hitting home.

Very soon, it was clear that inviting Uncle Joab to Salem had been a dreadful mistake, and the sooner he was sent off home the better. A group of legislators, seeking safety in numbers, formed a sort of ad-hoc committee to slip him the sad news.

Perhaps to their surprise, Uncle Joab was very professional about it. Absolutely no trouble at all, he told them. Just pay me my $30 and I'll be on my way.

(In point of fact, he was probably delighted. Although being the Legislature's first chaplain was a great prestige gig, by now Uncle Joab knew very well that he wouldn't be saving anyone's soul — Old Scratch had his hooks into these law-making rascals but good. He likely was very much looking forward to getting back on the circuit and putting up some more numbers for the Lord.)

Providence Pioneer Church, the church founded by "Uncle Joab" Powell, as it appeared in 1954. This church building was constructed some time after Powell's death; it dates from 1898. (Image: Ben Maxwell/ Salem Public Library)

But, say, um, about that $30. You see, it was like this: They didn't actually have the money. If Uncle Joab had been the Oregon Legislature's first chaplain, and supplied its first prayer, he had also been the occasion of a less auspicious Oregon "first": its first act of deficit spending.

Flummoxed, the committee reported back to the assembly. It was a dilemma. They could have passed a kitty and paid Uncle Joab off out of pocket, but nobody wanted to do that. Yet trying to put him off with an IOU would make them look and feel like a ridiculous lot of deadbeats.

Finally, Senator (and saloonkeeper) Victor Trevitt hatched an idea: They would solve this problem with yet another "first" (are you keeping track? That's four so far). They would hold the state's first political fundraising event — a "grand entertainment" starring Uncle Joab, with a modest admission fee charged at the gate. They estimated crowd size, and calculated a cover charge that would, they figured, add up to about $30.

Now, the rest of this story is rather heavily tinged with folklore. The bones of the tale are probably accurate; but, it has the distinct air of a story that's been augmented a little over the years of being passed around. So, keep that in mind as we continue.

Opening night came, and with it more evidence that Uncle Joab had been right — the Legislators knew not what they were doing. Specifically, they'd seriously underestimated Uncle Joab's fame. When word got around that the famous man of God would be preaching in Salem, the residential district of the town emptied itself out. On opening night, a very nervous group of legislators watched the venue fill to overflowing.

The financial problem was solved, several times over. But a new issue taxed them now: What if Uncle Joab bombed? They well remembered the ten-word opening prayer he'd boomed out on that first day, and fretted. What if he did that again? Insulted the audience and sat down? Would they riot? What would happen?

Senator Trevitt had another plan. He collected together all the small coins taken in at the gate, and distributed handfuls of them to a group of children. These he instructed to work their way to the front of the crowd and, if Uncle Joab showed any signs of winding down early, to shower him with money and shout, "Encore! Encore!"

Whether this worked, or whether Uncle Joab just delivered a great sermon as he always did, the show was a big hit. Uncle Joab went on home to his wife's farm, pockets nicely lined with his $30 plus all the "tips" showered on him by the urchins; and the Legislature got back to work, having chalked up yet another Oregon political "first" — the first act of Throwing Money at a Problem to Make It Go Away.

But they weren't done yet. The last and greatest Oregon political "first" to come from Uncle Joab's brief political career — number six — was the one the man himself would most disapprove of. You see, the gate receipts from Uncle Joab's "grand entertainment" were considerably over $30 — in fact, the total had come to roughly 10 times that much. And, being as loath as many of us are to follow the 10th Commandment too assiduously, the

Providence Pioneer Church as it appears today. It is now the home of Providence Vineyard Christian Fellowship. (Image: offbeatoregon.com)

Legislators had gone ahead and hung onto all of the surplus, paying Uncle Joab only the $30 they owed him. But now something had to be done with it, and it couldn't be seen to benefit any one legislator disproportionately.

So, taking one of the as-yet-unused committee rooms in the capitol building, they did a little remodeling project — stocking it with a fine assortment of wines and spirits as a sort of private lounge. It was Oregon's first Legislative den of iniquity — the sixth and final legislative "first" associated with the brief and colorful political career of Uncle Joab Powell.

Sources and Works Cited:
- *"WPA Interview: Peterson, Rachel Powell Arminta," a government document transcribed by Patricia Dunn in 2000 and published on the Linn County Genealogical Society Website;*
- *Joab Powell: Homespun Missionary, a book by Leona M. Nichols, published in 1935 by Metropolitan Press of Portland;*
- *Roadside History of Oregon, a book by Bill Gulick, published in 1991 by Mountain Press of Missoula;*
- *In Search of Western Oregon, a book by Ralph Friedman published in 1990 by Caxton Press.*

LEMUEL WELLS & AL.:

FRONTIER CIRCUIT PREACHERS.

In the early years of Oregon Country, back before it was a state — back even before Idaho and Washington were separate territories — newly arrived settlers found themselves completely on their own. There were some circumstances in which Native American tribes might help out, but most of the time, the early arrivals had to shift for themselves as best they might.

That meant, of course, that folks had to grind their own wheat, whipsaw their own lumber, and birth their own babies without any kind of professional assistance. For the most part, they made do pretty well.

But one category of professional was in particularly short supply, especially in the more rough-cut districts and mining camps of Eastern Oregon: Preachers.

Now, preachers might not seem, to a secular modern reader, to be nearly as important as, say, doctors, or even blacksmiths. But to those old-time pioneers, they very much were. Especially in the gold fields. There was a whole lot of sinning going on in those mining camps on Saturday nights. And yes, once in a while there was a funeral to be preached on a Sunday

The Rt. Rev. Lemuel Wells as he appeared in the early 1920s, from a photo published in Up to the Times Magazine in 1923. (Image courtesy Joe Drazan, Bygone Walla Walla)

morning as a result — but most Sundays there were just several dozen grimy miners with emptied purses and repentant headaches, trying to get close enough to the Almighty to sort of whisper an apology in His ear before taking up the pickaxe and pan for another week in the toils.

To help these poor souls get back into Heaven's good graces, a cadre of itinerant clergymen took up the task of ministering to their souls. Called "circuit riders," these preachers would travel from village to town to camp, making a regular circuit; upon arriving, they'd usually stay with a local family for the night, preach a rousing sermon the next day, perform any marriages and other ceremonies that might be required, and ride on for the next town.

Marriages, in particular, posed a problem in pioneer communities. Legally, the local Justice of the Peace could do the job; but the quality of that experience varied rather widely from place to place. One J.P., in the town of Murphy (in what's now Idaho), employed a ceremonial style with minimal input from the bride and groom, dispensing entirely with that whole "I do" rigmarole. "Take hold of hands," he'd instruct the happy couple. "What God and me put together nobody can put asunder. Now you buss (kiss) her. Now you're married!"

Like the crystal-clear frontier moonshine dispensed in the nearby saloon, this ceremony was a bit rough, but it got the job done. Well, most of the time it did. On at least one occasion, the Justice of the Peace accidentally grabbed the wrong dressed-up gent, and twelve seconds later — before anyone could interrupt him — he'd married the bride off to the best man.

But even at its best, this quasi-legal swearing-at lacked a certain dignity and solemnity which many affianced couples looked for in a wedding celebration. So they'd wait for a week or two, and present themselves ready for their nuptials when the circuit preacher arrived in town.

In their later years, most old frontier circuit riders looked back on their itinerant-preacher years through a nostalgic haze from a considerable distance — as most of us do when we get older. Days of mud and misery and discouragement went forgotten; days of joy and exhilaration and success were relived at every family gathering and church event (often growing noticeably more joyful and exhilarating and successful at each retelling).

These recollections are, of course, just as unreliable as any other kind of memoir. Although they hold themselves to a higher standard than most of us do, preachers are only human.

But their stories do make for very interesting reading.

Of course, the most common kind of story they tell is the inspirational kind, of the "Rogue River Jim swore he'd never come to Jesus, but after I pulled him out from under a landslide the Lord spoke to his heart and he got saved on the spot" sort. Such stories are all well and good if one is in the mood for them; but, and let's be honest here — they're far from the most entertaining.

Luckily, some of those old preachers kept a lively frontier sense of humor, and passed on a few less respectable yarns.

One particular circuit rider — Lemuel H. Wells, who would one day become Episcopal bishop of Spokane — seemed to have a particular knack for getting into strange situations (or maybe he just had a great talent for telling a good story, and perhaps a little human weakness when it came to strict adherence to the letter of the Ninth Commandment). In fairness, these episodes weren't always random misfortune. Some poor decision-making on his part occasionally played a role.

On one day, the Rev. Wells arrived in the town of Weston, near Pendleton; and he was invited to stay for the night at the home of a local Episcopalian family. When bedtime came along, he found the arrangements very crowded: two beds in a single room, with Mama and Papa in one and their three children in the other. Wells was to sleep on the bed with the children.

In the middle of the night, though, the four-year-old boy started having a nightmare, and with a shriek kicked out, catching poor Wells in the solar plexus. This happened two more times, and the last time, the exasperated and exhausted Wells secured a length of cord from his valise and set about

A LAST HOPE.

An illustration from an 1874 book about circuit riders showing a suspected horse thief, about to be lynched, being rescued by a circuit preacher. (Image: Schribner & Sons)

tying the lad's feet to the bedpost.

Now the boy really did start to scream, bringing his parents running. Upon arriving at his bedside, they found their son lashed to the bed and Wells guiltily fumbling at the knots.

We can only imagine how the subsequent conversation went. In fact, we have to, since Wells doesn't give the details; nor does he mention where he spent the rest of the night. But, "they never came to church again," he writes. "And I never received another invitation to their home."

The next time Wells came to Weston, he was on his own for a place to stay — word having apparently gotten around. So he bedded down for the night in a haystack, piled up against a fence to which he tied his horse.

The horse, who knew a good thing when he saw it, spent the evening taking bites of the hay and yanking them over the fence so that he could enjoy them at leisure. Sometime in the wee small hours, having developed a desire for a midnight snack, the horse stretched his neck over and got a big mouthful of hay — with Wells' trouser cuff in it. The horse gave a lusty yank, and the snoozing Wells came flying over the fence and down into a heap at his horse's feet.

Circuit riding was, obviously, a young person's game.

Quite possibly Wells' most picturesque misadventure — and, I'd argue, the one that it's hardest to believe consists purely of plain, unadorned Gospel truth — was one that he had in a small town in northern Idaho. In the hotel there, he requested a bath, and was told a tub would be ready for him in the morning at the head of the stairs. Upon coming out the next day, he found the tub — one of those giant galvanized-steel washbasins that one sometimes sees miner-'49er types taking baths in in old Western movies — half full of water. It was the dead of winter, and the foyer of the hotel was about 20 degrees; so, shivering in the chilly air, the Reverend leaped into the tub to get his morning ablutions over with as fast as possible, so that he might put clothes on and get warmed back up.

An illustration from an 1874 book about circuit riders shows a mining-camp preacher being accosted by two hostile miners demanding that he leave. (Image: Schribner & Sons)

He immediately made two unpleasant observations.

The first was that the water in the tub was just above freezing; he broke through a skim of ice on his way into it. It seemed the hotel owner had prepared the bath the night before, so as not to have to bother with it in the morning; so it had had all night to get very cold in the pre-dawn winter's chill of the unheated hotel lobby.

But the second discovery made Wells forget all about the coldness of the water. It seemed the tub leaked a little. It had been leaking out onto the floor throughout the night, forming a small puddle which had then frozen like black ice on a highway. When Wells had hopped into the icy water, the momentum of his leap had set the tub into motion on that sheet of ice. Majestically and inexorably it sailed straight toward the top of the staircase ....

And so the Reverend Lemuel H. Wells, shivering cold and stark naked and helpless in the hands of a cruel fate, rode a half-full washtub down the stairs of the hotel, tumbling with it to the bottom and ending up with the tub perched triumphantly atop his battered and shivering body in a great puddle of freezing water on the landing below.

This was, of course, hardly a silent procedure. The crashings and thumpings of the tub, and the terrified shrieks of its helpless passenger, roused every person in the building and probably several neighbors to boot. Luckily, Wells wasn't badly hurt. He was escorted back to his room as discreetly as was possible under the circumstances, where he tried to warm himself as best he could and get ready for a day's preaching of sermons to people who had, a few hours earlier, seen him naked under the most undignified of circumstances.

Just another day on the job, right?

When trying to minister to the spiritual needs of a crowd of hard-sinning miners and sailors, it was sometimes necessary to resort to unorthodox tactics — tactics not often seen among men of the cloth in more civilized times.

Or, at least, so Rev. Wells likely assured himself on the occasions when he found himself resorting to such tactics. As you will have gathered, Wells had a bit of the lovable rogue in him.

At one point in his career he found himself in Tacoma, up in Washington Territory, helping with the founding of Trinity Church. When it was built, the community wasn't quite as welcoming as had been hoped, and Wells found he was having difficulty filling the pews.

Not to worry: Wells had a plan. Under his direction, the ushers of Trinity arranged themselves in ambush at the front of the church on Sunday morning and waited for passers-by to walk along the street.

"They selected the most pleasing man in the congregation," Wells recalls in his memoir, "who would stand in front of the church and when anyone appeared in the street passing by, would step up to him and say, 'This is Trinity Church, I suppose you are looking for it,' and without waiting for a reply would take him by the arm, volubly telling him what a fine lot of men we had, and what a good fellow the clergyman was and what a fine preacher, until in spite of resistance he would firmly but gently push the would-be passer-by toward the church steps. The ushers would rush out to join the party, shake hands with the stranger — and help with the pushing. The protests of the victim would be drowned out by the cordiality of the ushers and before he knew it the poor man would be seated in the front pew.

"Strange to say, this method was rather liked by the victims," Wells adds, "and many an attendant and eventually a communicant was gained in this way."

Other itinerant men of the cloth found it convenient to cooperate with the proprietors of the more secular temples at which frontiersmen were wont to worship: saloons. Another future Episcopal bishop, Ethelbert Talbert, built a church in Murray, Idaho, right next door to the local saloon. Both buildings were quite flimsy and very close together, so the prospect loomed of noisy barroom activity disrupting services. Fortunately, the Rev. Talbert got along very well with the bar owner next door, and soon had worked out an arrangement: At the time for services, on Sunday morning, the saloonkeeper would close up shop for two hours. "That's all for now, gents," he'd holler. "Let's all step over and hear the Reverend talk!"

The cover picture from the Oct. 12, 1867, issue of Harper's Weekly, drawn by Alfred R. Waud, shows a Methodist circuit rider on the job. (Image: Library of Congress)

Out the door and around the corner would go the crowd of day-drinkers to sit down in the pews next door and soak up some religion, before returning to resume their matutinal bacchanals.

"Many of the fellows fresh from their drinks were hardly able to realize just where they were," Talbert later recalled.

On one particular occasion, Talbert selected a sermon on the parable of the Pharisee and the Publican — a gracious nod to his saloonkeeper friend next door.

"I proceeded to condemn the pride and self-complacency of the Pharisee, and, in correspondingly strong language, to praise the publican for his humility and self-abasement," Talbert said.

But it soon became clear that one of his audience members — one of the saloon patrons who'd come next door when the bar closed — was not

GOING TO CONFERENCE.

An illustration from "The Circuit Rider," an 1874 novel, showing a Methodist circuit preacher traveling. (Image: Schribner & Sons)

having any of that. As the sermon continued, he glared fiercely, then started muttering angrily to himself as his fellow congregants eyed him nervously. Finally he leaped to his feet, apparently able to endure no more.

"Tha'sh all wrong," he yelled resentfully, and would have gone on, but the other bar patrons — perhaps pleased to have an opportunity to leave the church without offending the keeper of the only saloon in town — leaped to their feet and hustled him, still incoherently protesting, out the door.

Back in the saloon, everything became clear. The disruptive day-drinker was a hard-core Democrat, and all the praise of the 'Publican Party without so much as a nod to the 'Emocrats had simply been more than he was willing to stand for.

Of course, it was all well and good for an Episcopal pastor to make friends with the saloonkeeper. For preachers of denominations with less worldly attitudes toward Demon Rum, that sort of thing would have been unthinkable.

Legendary Methodist circuit rider James H. Wilbur — better known as Father Wilbur — illustrated the tone of his denomination's attitude in the Umpqua gold fields in the 1850s, during the California gold rush. Wilbur was leading a team of Methodist ministers holding a week-long tent-revival event for nearby miners, and had attracted a considerable crowd. This crowd had, in turn, attracted the attention of a duo of itinerant liquor peddlers.

These two gentlemen had a wagon loaded with distilled spirits and a big tent they'd pitched beside it, forming a portable saloon; the wagon sides served as the bar. Like modern tailgaters partying in the parking lot at a Beavers game, they now came and set up this booze wagon as near to the revival tent as they dared, ready to slake the miners' always-prodigious thirst as they were coming and going from the revival.

You can imagine how this went over with the Methodists.

The men of the cloth tolerated the interlopers for several days, putting up with the nearby whoops and howls of drunken revelry during services in hopes that the booze-wagon soon would move on; but finally, several days into the revival, things came to a head.

The event that set it off was a gang of drunken miners, fresh from the grog-wagon, who decided to attend services. At the back of the congregation, they started laughing and disrupting the meeting. Finally Father Wilbur could take no more.

"Sing something," he muttered to the other preachers. "I'll be right back."

Slipping out the back of the tent, Wilbur made his stealthy way to the booze wagon. He caught its two proprietors alone — their customers having all apparently gone to the revival — and completely unawares.

Fired up with righteous wrath, the good pastor seized a bottle of whiskey and, using it as a club, set about getting the local earthworms drunk as skunks. Shards of glass flew; cheap whiskey and rum spattered everywhere. The two liquor peddlers, belatedly realizing they were under attack, leaped upon Wilbur; but Wilbur was a very large and powerful man, and more than a match for two half-drunk liquor peddlers even when he was not animated with a spirit of crusading fury. They didn't have a chance.

Wilbur didn't stop swinging until he saw that every bottle had been broken. Then, bleeding from several cuts inflicted by flying glass, he ordered the two liquor men to pack up and move on (which they meekly did, on the spot), and returned nonchalantly to his congregation — where, his face and shirt smeared with blood and his entire person doubtless reeking of cheap rotgut, he finished his sermon as if nothing had happened.

Let's finish out our overview of the adventures of frontier preachers with another story about Rev. Lemuel Wells. This one is from late in his career, after he had settled down in Tacoma, in the mid- to late-1880s.

On that day, Wells was approached by a deputation from the local Longshoremen's Union. The burly dockworkers had a sad story to tell, and a request for the Reverend's spiritual help. It seemed one of their members, while stumbling home following an epic spree, had fallen in the water and drowned. His body having been retrieved, the longshoremen now wanted Wells to give their poor deceased pal a decent Christian burial service.

Now, at this time, Tacoma was a booming new port city servicing a growing blue-water sailing fleet. Its fortune had been made in 1873 when it had become the terminus of the Great Northern Railroad, and in 1885 it had only been an incorporated city for about 10 years, during which time it had doubled in population about six times.

And although its waterfront sordidness was not yet in a class with Portland or Astoria, it was catching up fast. In his memoirs, Wells recounts an early-1880s incident that would have been worthy of Portland's legendary Joseph "Bunco" Kelley (whom we will be getting to know quite a bit more later in this book): It seems a boardinghouse operator named Brown stole a corpse from the local undertaker's parlor and, representing it as a drunk sailor sleeping soundly in the forecastle, cashed it in for a $10 "blood money" bonus from a ship captain.

Of course, that would never have happened in Portland or Astoria. In either of those towns, at that time, the "blood money" bonus demanded would have been at least four times that amount.

In any case, that was the scene in which the longshoremen in Wells' office earned their daily bread. Like most West Coast 1880s waterfront workers, they were hard-punching, hard-drinking, bluff and hearty men, as quick with a joke as they were with a fist. But they were also sentimental in ways that a modern reader might not expect. The untimely loss of their friend had hit them hard, and they wanted to do right by him — to say their goodbyes and send him off with what they considered to be proper respect.

Wells was, of course, happy to help. He followed the dockworkers back to a rough, cheap saloon in what today is Old Town Tacoma, where he found the drowned man laid out in a room upstairs.

"There was a staircase running down into the saloon from the room and a stream of longshoremen passing up and down," Wells writes in his memoirs. "The group around the body was weeping and saying, 'Poor Bill, he was a fine fellow, poor Bill; let's have a drink,' and down they would go into the saloon below. When they came up again they would be still more grief-stricken. Each visit to the bar would increase their tears and call out longer eulogies and greater professions of sorrow. I said to the president of the longshoreman's union, 'We'd better begin right away or these fellows will be too drunk to attend the funeral.'"

Accordingly, the president called for order; Wells led the mostly-sozzled mourners in a calming prayer; pallbearers were selected; and the drear burden was taken up. Down the stairs they solemnly went, through the saloon and out to the waiting hearse.

But when the pallbearers went to climb into the hack that had been brought to carry them to Trinity Church for the funeral, they found their seats had been hijacked by drunken longshoremen, who stubbornly refused to give them up.

Protracted negotiations ensued with the president of the union. These talks ended with the president agreeing to provide hacks for the members so that they would not have to walk.

That worked fine for getting this particular crew of squatters out of the pallbearers' seats. But by this time there were a lot of longshoremen on the scene, and even if the union president could have swung it financially, he couldn't have found and hired enough hacks for all of them to ride. Some of them were still going to have to walk.

So when the hired hacks started to appear, there followed a huge, drunken melee among aspirants to their seats.

"They all tried to get into the first one, and a free fight ensued, and when the cab was filled they dragged off the driver and two mounted the box and drove off," Wells recounts. "The crowd made a rush for the next vehicle and so on until they were all (filled)."

It was doubtless difficult to salvage some dignity for the solemn occasion after that display, but Wells did his best, and soon the funeral procession of hijacked cabs was on its ponderous way through the streets of Tacoma, surrounded by resentful, footsore longshoremen exchanging hostile glares with their comfortably seated comrades.

Upon arrival at the church, the pallbearers declined to leave their seats and take up their sorrowful burden to bring the body into the church. They knew the minute they did so, their envious comrades would pounce upon those coveted seats, and they'd have to walk the rest of the way.

So Wells and his undertakers, joined by the president of the union, lugged the body into the church with what slender ceremony they could muster, and Wells preached the funeral service to the rows of empty pews, while the members of the congregation eyed one another warily in the parking lot outside.

"On returning with the body to replace it in the hearse, we saw the men all grimly seated in the carriages waiting for us," Wells recalls. "When we arrived at the grave nobody would get out of the carriages, so the undertakers and I had to bury the deceased."

Once the graveside service was preached, and Wells and his helpers were throwing dirt onto the top of the coffin, the men in the hacks drove off, followed by the longshoremen on foot — leaving to Wells and his helpers the task of moving about five cubic yards of earth into the open grave and tamping it down as best they could.

This kept them busy for some time — probably half an hour or so. Afterward, they climbed aboard their hearse and started back toward the church.

But before they even got out of the cemetery, they saw something that has to have provoked a curse word or two from even a mild, kindhearted man of the cloth like Lemuel Wells:

"Just outside the cemetery gate there were a number of roadhouses, as they were called — disreputable places with bars for the sale of liquor," Wells writes. "When we reached the roadhouses, the carriages were all standing empty in front of them."

The fact that none of those grim riders clinging stubbornly to their seats in the hijacked cabs would bestir themselves to help bury their friend, even though the roadhouses were just a few hundred yards away from the cemetery gates, has to have rankled Wells. And although he claims no responsibility for what followed, it's hard not to wonder if he perhaps had a little something to do with it:

"Just then something startled one of the teams," he writes, somewhat coyly; "which ran away and ran into the next one and started that and so on down the line till they were all running at top speed; running into one another and wrecking and making sad havoc. The longshoremen's union had to pay several hundred dollars for the damage."

Wouldn't you just love to know exactly what that "something" was?

Sources and Works Cited:
- A Pioneer Missionary, *a book by Lemuel H. Wells, published in 1930 by Progressive Publishing of Seattle;*
- The Pioneer Campfire, *a book by G.W. Kennedy, published in 1913 by Marsh Printing of Portland;*
- *"Frontier Humor: Plain and Fancy," an article by Erik Bromberg published in the September 1960 issue of* Oregon Historical Quarterly.

CAPT. RICHARD HILLYER:

OYSTER PIRATE.

Like most tourist-friendly destinations on the Oregon Coast, the town of Newport is well stocked with kitschy pirate gear.
Unlike most other spots, though, Newport has a real history involving pirates — specifically, oyster pirates. Well, and the other kind too, but we'll get to that in the next chapter.

Now, in spite of their romantic name, oyster pirates really weren't pirates in the cutlass-and-pistol sense of the term. They were more like pirates in the rip-a-copy-of-a-Katy-Perry-album-and-share-it-with-all-your-friends sense. They were, in effect, poacher-thieves.

Oysters are unusual beasties in that although they do occur naturally, to be commercially viable they more or less have to be farmed. Doing this requires something like a public-private partnership. A legitimate oyster farmer gets the state's permission to control a piece of seafloor in a shallow bay or estuary, then inoculates it with tiny seed oysters. These then grow to a nice palatable size, at which point they are harvested and sold.

The trouble is, many members of the public object to the idea of a private operator asserting this level of control over public property. So some of them simply disregard it, telling themselves (and anyone else who will listen) that XYZ company has no right to tell anyone else they can't take fish in public waters ... and they become oyster pirates.

Most people who have heard of oyster piracy think of the stories of Jack London's youth, when he borrowed money to buy a small sloop and went into the "business" down in San Francisco Bay. (This was something of a different kind of "piracy," in that London and his friends were actually horning in on naturally occurring oyster beds, not farms.) Or they may think of the long and occasionally bloody struggles between oystermen and oyster pirates in Chesapeake Bay, on the East Coast, which were still straggling on as late as the 1950s.

But Newport's relationship with oyster piracy actually predates the city of Newport. It goes all the way back to the days of the Civil War, when Yaquina Bay was just starting to be noticed by European types — ship captains and traders whose rough, temporary settlement at the back of the bay was known as Oysterville.

And there was another important difference, too. These oysters weren't some big aquiculture company's private property. They belonged to a sovereign Indian tribe, by international treaty.

For the coastal Native American tribes, oysters had always been an important food. There were natural oyster beds generously distributed all over the bay, and the oysters that grew there seeded themselves and provided the Indians with all they could eat.

Unfortunately, though, two things became a problem after the European-Americans (or "Bostons" as the Indians called them in the Chinook jargon) started moving in. First, demand for oysters went from a few bushels a week to, essentially, infinity. The city of San Francisco, a few days' sailing journey away, would buy and devour every oyster it could get its hands on. So professional oystermen, with large sailing ships and industrial oyster-harvesting techniques, got very interested in the fishery.

The second problem — which, unfortunately, wouldn't become obvious until too late — was that those delicious, exotic West Coast oysters (the variety known as "Olympia" oysters) were very slow to reproduce and grow. This is why Yaquina Bay no longer has a commercial native oyster fishery today (although restoration efforts are beginning to bear fruit in other places, notably Netarts Bay).

By 1863, the Siletz Indian Reservation had been created, and included all of Yaquina Bay, oysters and all. So the Indians contracted with two commercial oystermen — captains Solomon Dodge of the sloop *Fanny* and

MAVERICKS.

James J. Winant of the schooner *Annie G. Doyle* — to exploit the resource for them.

Dodge and Winant had a great deal. They paid the tribes a total royalty of $1.15 per bushel of oysters, hauled the tasty shellfish to San Francisco, and sold them for $10 a bushel.

The problem was, they had unwanted company on the oyster beds back home in Yaquina Bay, in the form of Richard Hillyer.

Richard Hillyer, captain of the schooner *Cordelia Terry*, was Yaquina Bay's resident oyster pirate. Hillyer not only helped himself to the Indians' oysters, but did so with brazen hostility, asserting (according to Don Marshall in his book, *Oregon Shipwrecks*) the "free right of all citizens to take fish in American waters." He considered himself to owe the Indians nothing for the oysters, and he paid them nothing, and considered

No,— clothes alone won't make a gentleman, and probably it would be claiming too much to say that an oyster's wardrobe alone would be sufficient to make him welcome in discriminating homes. But

A promotional pamphlet for Pabco Oyster Pails, printed for the Paraffine Companies, Inc., sold by T. W. Jenkins & Co, wholesale grocers at Front & Pine Streets, Portland, OR, c.1917. The oyster drawn here is clearly an Olympia. (Image: Oregon Historical Society)

An engraving from Harper's Weekly magazine, March 1, 1884, showing oyster pirates at work on Chesapeake Bay in the dead of night. (Image: Library of Congress)

Dodge and Winant suckers for having agreed to do so.

After some fruitless attempts to talk things over with Hillyer, the Siletz Indian Agent, Ben Simpson, wrote to his supervisor asking for help enforcing the law. Soon a small company of U.S. Army soldiers was on its way over the Coast Range from a post on the Yamhill River.

The soldiers settled into an encampment near Oysterville, enjoyed a hearty dinner courtesy of the grateful Dodge and Winant, and retired for the night. And the next day they sallied forth to pay a courtesy call on the Dread Pirate Hillyer, aboard his schooner.

Hillyer received them with a smooth and unctuous welcome, and they dutifully presented their orders to him: an injunction to desist from further oyster piracy in Tribal waters on pain of arrest and prosecution. Hillyer cheerfully agreed to comply with everything, and the soldiers headed back to camp satisfied that they'd achieved their goal.

Then they found out that Hillyer had secretly arranged to dose their chow that night with enough laudanum to keep them all asleep until noon the next day. The plan was, while the soldiers snoozed and the other oystermen raged, he'd be frenetically loading his ship with oysters and standing out across the bar headed for San Francisco — and one last big payday.

The soldiers avoided the doped food, and bright and early the next morning, to Hillyer's surprise, they came to see him.

Hillyer, thinking on his feet, hastily tried to call the soldiers' bluff, loading his ship with oysters and essentially daring them to arrest him. When they borrowed a skiff and rowed out to do so, he hoisted a British flag — apparently in an attempt to bluff them into thinking arresting him would cause an international incident. They ignored this, boarded the ship and arrested him, then unloaded his ship and hauled him off to Corvallis.

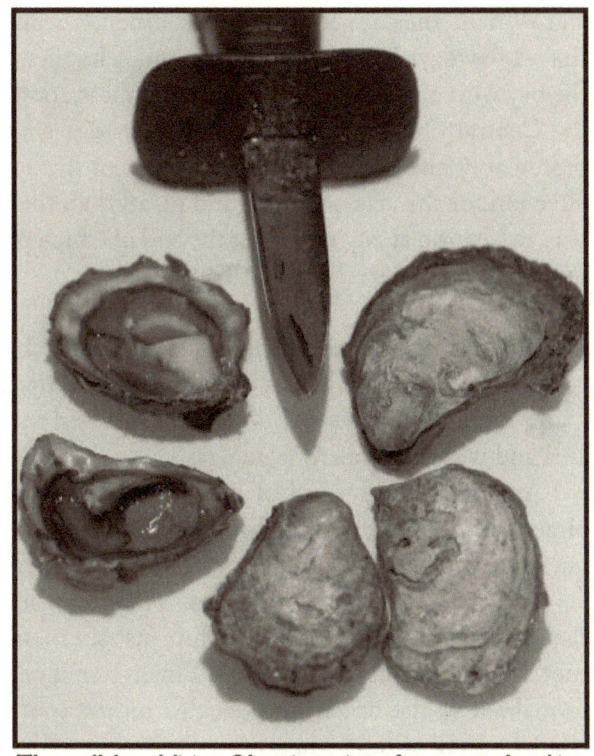

The small-but-delicious Olympia variety of oyster was the subject of Yaquina Bay oyster pirate Richard Hillyer's ardor. These oysters are still prized today, but are hard to come by, because they were harvested almost to extinction in the late 1800s; commercially grown oysters are usually of the large, fast-growing Pacific variety. (Image: Vancouver Island University)

Hillyer filed some lawsuits and criminal complaints, none of which really went anywhere, although he was soon released from prison. Meanwhile, he was officially banned from entering Yaquina Bay. Grudgingly, he returned to his ship and went off to try his luck in more northerly fisheries.

Hillyer's other oyster-thieving enterprises must not have worked out very well, though, because in September of 1864 he was back in Yaquina Bay with a crew of hard-fisted fighters, ready to take what was "rightfully" his by force. Simpson again summoned the Army — but their services turned out not to be necessary.

Historical records of this engagement are sparse; if someone left a full account of this final battle of the Yaquina Bay Oyster War, I have not been able to find it. But it seems, reading between the lines, that captains Dodge and Winant, the bay's legitimate oystermen, had anticipated something like this. A few days later, Winant sailed his schooner, the *Annie G. Doyle*, into the bay with a crew of the roughest, toughest, rootin'-tootin'est bar fighters the Central Oregon Coast had yet known. A short, sharp action ensued, presumably involving fisticuffs — pirates of the oyster beds having far less affection for the arts of cutlass and pistol than their colleagues of the high seas, in Oregon at any rate — at the end of which pirate captain Hillyer was in full retreat across the bar and out to sea.

Two weeks later, perhaps seeking a rematch, he was on his way into the bay when he ran onto the bar, and the *Cordelia Terry* broke up and sank beneath his feet. He survived the shipwreck, but left the area and was never heard from again.

And that was the end of the Yaquina Bay Oyster War, and of oyster piracy there — unless, of course, you include the U.S. government's subsequent theft of all of Yaquina Bay, oysters and all, from the Siletz Indians.

As a side note, Captain Winant's schooner, the *Annie E. Doyle*, suffered the same fate as Hillyer's pirate ship, just six months later — in the same spot. Meiert Wachsmuth, one of Winant's crew members, barely managed to make it to the beach, and decided on the spot to leave the sea for the relative safety of oyster harvesting in Yaquina Bay. His business grew and thrived, and eventually led to his son, Louis Wachsmuth, founding Dan and Louis' Oyster Bar in Portland.

Sources and Works Cited:
- Oregon Shipwrecks, *a book by Don Marshall, published in 1984 by Binford and Mort of Portland;*
- *"Oregon's Only Native Oyster, the Olympia, Makes a Comeback after Near Extinction," an article by Katy Muldoon published in the July 20, 2013, issue of the* Portland Oregonian.

"COLONEL" T. EDGENTON HOGG:

RAILROAD BUILDER, DEVELOPER.

Next time you're heading over Santiam Pass from the Willamette Valley, you might take a second to glance over at the side of the big potato-shaped promontory around which the highway bends as you pass Three Finger Jack.

If you do, you'll likely see something unexpected. Running along its side is an old railroad grade, painstakingly built up out of loose rock. And if you get out of your car and follow the track, you'll find it starts in the middle of nowhere west of the pass, crosses over the summit, and ends in the middle of nowhere on the east side.

The sawed-off mountaintop the railroad grade traverses as it does this is named after the man who built that track — a colorful and audacious character named "Colonel" Thomas Edgenton Hogg (pronounced "hoag").

Colonel Hogg was, at one time or another, a pirate, a shipping magnate, a jailbird lifer (in Alcatraz, no less) and a railroad baron. And he was, it seems, always a hustler.

It was as a railroad baron that he was best known in Oregon, during his time there. And although everyone knew he was a Confederate veteran, he was always a little reticent about going into the details.

There was a reason for that reticence.

Hogg's friend Wallis Nash, who spills a good bit of ink praising him in his book, *A Lawyer's Life on Two Continents*, writes that he held the rank of colonel in the Confederate forces, and describes him as "rather tall, lean, nervous, with curly brown hair, a full beard, good forehead, large pale-blue eyes, a repressed manner at first meeting."

Hogg told Nash that he had been a prisoner of war at Alcatraz during the war. After the war ended, he'd been transferred to San Quentin for another year or so. Finally released in 1866 after being granted amnesty, he'd returned to New Orleans, where he had been a fairly prosperous merchant back in 1861, to find that nothing remained of his property there. So he'd headed back to San Francisco again, seeking out his brother, a prosperous financier who had supported the North during the war.

Whatever might have passed between the brothers during the Civil War, now that it was over the two were reconciled, and Hogg, with his brother's backing, headed north in search of new opportunities. Upon arriving in Corvallis, Hogg quickly grasped the potential for a railroad link from Corvallis to Newport, and the tremendous possibilities that could be realized if that link kept on going over Santiam Pass to Boise ... and the rest, as historian Keith Clark puts it, is history.

A portrait of Colonel T. Edgenton Hogg as he appeared in 1862, when he was a confederate privateer. (Image: Oregon Historical Society)

MAVERICKS.

The 150-year-old rock cribbing on the side of Hogg Rock as it appeared around 2010, leading up to and over the pass and ending in the middle of nowhere. (Image: Curtis Irish)

All of this was true … it was just that it was, shall we say, somewhat incomplete.

The rumor mill wasn't nearly as reticent as Hogg was, of course, when it came to the spicy parts of his story. And Hogg's status as an ex-Rebel, plus the fact that his railroad enterprise put him at odds with some of the powerful Portland businessmen who were writing Oregon's official history, resulted in several of those rumors finding their way into the historical record — such as the one that claimed he and his crew had been captured while trying to raid opium ships. Had his plans been successful, he certainly would have had a go at any ship, whether it carried opium or not; but as it happened, he never had the chance.

Nevertheless, the real story is so much more bonkers than that, that one wonders why the rumor-passers even bothered with making things up.

Hogg's war story was unearthed somewhat painstakingly by historian Clark, a faculty member at Central Oregon College (now Central Oregon Community College) in the late 1970s and early 1980s. Clark, in his *Oregon Historical Quarterly* article, compares the whole thing to a rip-roaring B-movie Western, and he is not even slightly wrong about that.

T. Edgenton Hogg was from Baltimore originally, and was in his early 30s when the Civil War broke out. Shortly thereafter, he moved to New Orleans, where he went into business as a merchant.

But a couple years later, probably feeling the pinch of the Yankee blockade, Hogg left that business and embarked upon a brand-new career:

Piracy.

With five companions, he traveled to Matamoras, Mexico. Upon arrival, the six of them booked passage on a Yankee-registered schooner, the *Joseph P. Gerrity*. The schooner was bound for New York with a cargo of cotton.

Of course, Hogg's little band of maritime desperadoes had no intention of going to New York. Instead, on the second night out, the six of them armed themselves, commandeered the ship, marooned its crew on the coast of Yucutan, and sailed north to Belize. There, representing the ship as a Confederate blockade runner bringing a load of cotton in from Texas, Hogg sold the cargo and pocketed the receipts.

But the crew of the *Joseph P. Gerrity* had by this time found their way through the remote stretches of coastline where they'd been dumped, to an American embassy in Sisal. Word of the "conquest" of their ship reached the British colonial government in Belize while Hogg was still in port.

What Hogg and his pals had done had certainly been very irregular as naval operations go, but all was fair in love and war, right?

Well, not quite. Had Hogg not sold off the cargo, the British likely would have shrugged it off as simple military action, a *ruse de guerre*. But hijacking loads of cargo, selling it, and pocketing the proceeds is not much of a naval-warfare job. It's more of an opportunistic-highway-robber job. Also, Hogg was not yet an offical member of the Confederate military; he and his colleagues were totally freelancing. The British were very displeased to learn they'd bought stolen property, and immediately set out in hot pursuit, aiming to arrest Hogg for larceny.

Four of his companions were promptly arrested, but Hogg managed to skip town with one of his fellow pirates just a step or two ahead of the law, making for Colombia — then a brand-new country formed out of the ashes of the old Spanish viceroyalty of New Granada — which did not cooperate with extradition requests. And they made it, foiling their pursuers.

Now at loose ends again, Hogg sent a proposal to the Confederate consul in Havana, offering his services to do the same thing again, but playing for a legitimate war prize this time — to capture a modern Yankee steamer, outfit it as a commerce raider with guns and everything, put on an actual Navy uniform, and start attacking Yankee shipping in the Pacific. This time, of course, he would pass on any spoils of war to the proper authorities rather than pocketing them.

The proposal went up the chain of command all the way to the Confederate Secretary of the Navy, Stephen R. Mallory. Mallory responded by commissioning Hogg as an official Confederate officer and instructing

Santiam Pass as seen from Hoodoo. The potato-shaped promontory in the foreground is Hogg Rock; the highway traveling nearly all the way around it is U.S. Highway 20; and the peak in the background is Three Finger Jack. (Image: Shaun Che)

him to do exactly as he had suggested.

(As a side note, I haven't been able to learn whether "Colonel" was Hogg's official military rank, or a courtesy title he affected later, as many Southern men did after the Civil War. Although "Colonel" is not a naval rank, it's possible Hogg's service branch was the Confederate marine corps rather than its navy.)

Obtaining an official commission surely seemed like a smart move on Hogg's part. It would save him from being arrested and prosecuted as a pirate by the British, should he encounter them again. But it had the unanticipated effect of bringing the entire plot to the attention of an unknown highly placed Yankee spy, somewhere in Richmond.

As a result, when Hogg and six fellow Confederate Navy men booked their passage on the American steamer *San Salvador* in the territorial waters of neutral Colombia (the part we know today as Panama), the Yankees knew, in great detail, exactly who they were and what they were scheming to do.

Of course, Colombia being Colombia, they couldn't just haul off and collar them on the spot. A ruse would be necessary to bait the rebels out into international waters, where arresting them wouldn't create an international incident.

No problem. The plans were in place well before the rebels arrived; when they did, the Yankees were waiting for them.

Commander H.K. Davenport, skipper of the *USS Lancaster*, was put in charge of laying the trap. Leaving his warship to steam on ahead into international waters, Davenport and a small contingent of officers and men stealthily boarded the *San Salvador* just a few minutes before the ship was to cast off. So that they could do this undetected, the captain of the San Salvador, who had also been put wise to the plot, summoned all the passengers to his cabin to examine their tickets and brief them on the voyage; while they were doing this, the troopers from the *Lancaster* were discreetly ransacking the entire ship, hoovering up every scrap of paper they could find. (One of the pieces of paper they found was the letter from Secretary Mallory commissioning Hogg to do the job.) Presumably then they retreated to the cargo hold or some similar place out of view of the piratical Southerners.

Davenport then introduced himself to the pirates as an administrative officer from the ship's owners, on board making sure everything was all right and that the captain and crew were doing their jobs properly; and as the *San Salvador* slipped away from the dock, he mingled freely with the passengers, chatting them up and putting them at their ease.

All the while, the *San Salvador* was edging closer and closer to the boundary of Colombia's territorial waters.

Sometime that night, they caught up with the *Lancaster*, and all was in readiness for the springing of the trap. Davenport quietly gave the necessary orders and prepared to re-introduce himself to the *San Salvador's* passengers ... as the skipper of an American warship.

"At daylight the next morning," Davenport wrote, in his subsequent report on the operation, "being some 12 miles outside the territorial jurisdiction of New Granada, on the broad bosom of the Pacific Ocean, I ordered the ensign to be hoisted, assembled all the passengers, and then informed them that, in virtue of my commission, being now under the American flag, I desired the pleasure of the company of several of them on board my ship."

The would-be privateers were caught utterly flat-footed. They and their leader — T. Edgenton Hogg, Acting Master, Confederate States Navy — were out of action for the duration of the war.

Hogg and his fellow privateers were brought to San Francisco for trial, where a military tribunal sentenced them to hang as irregular combatants in violation of the rules of war — that is, essentially, as spies. But even in the face of death the famous Hogg charm must have been broadcasting at full strength, because Union General Irwin McDowell decided to commute their sentences — Hogg's to life on The Rock, and his accomplices to 10 years.

All of them were out and free just a few years later, of course, when they received amnesty at the end of the war. And Hogg, finding himself at loose ends in the most dynamic part of the country and with the backing of a wealthy brother, must have marveled at the change in his circumstances a few short years had brought.

Hogg spent the years after the war working with his brother out of San Francisco on various projects. One of these, in the early 1870s, brought him to the town of Corvallis.

There he found an interesting opportunity: The town was desperate for a way to connect with a deepwater seaport. Progress was passing Corvallis by as the Oregon and California Railroad chose to cut through Albany, on the other side of the river; the few remaining riverboats that chugged up the Willamette mostly didn't even bother to stop there on their way to Eugene City; and the only way to get products out to the world markets was to send them down the river to Portland and out to sea, which was very expensive.

So Hogg threw himself into raising the money to build a railroad line across the Coast Range, from Corvallis to Newport. He called it the Corvallis and Yaquina Bay Railroad.

This turned out to be a rather difficult proposition because of the geography of the Coast Range, which was very prone to landslides, especially after its vegetation has been disturbed. It took Hogg four years to finish the line. To finance it, he sold $25,000 bonds, and there was enough Gold Rush money still in Oregon to get the job done that way.

By the time the line was finished, Hogg had renamed it the Oregon Pacific Railroad — and he'd made some new plans for it. The thing was, at the time — roughly 1884 — travelers and freight coming to San Francisco from back east were having to come through Portland.

Hogg envisioned a transcontinental railroad line coming directly from Boise to Newport over Santiam Pass, which would shave 300 miles off the journey and, for goods and people going by sea, avoid the always-chancy Columbia River Bar. And the federal government was still offering huge grants of land to entrepreneurs willing to build railroads.

So Hogg went to the government and made a deal; the lands would become his as soon as he established service over the Santiam Pass.

Then Hogg started making the rounds of Eastern venture capitalists, deploying the legendary Hogg charm. He returned with big money behind him, ready to finish up the local railroad line.

But some of the business leaders in Portland had gotten wind of what Hogg had in mind. They now moved to block his next move, by buying up

The S.S. Yaquina City, T. Edgenton Hogg's steamer, stranded on the beach by the entrance to the bay after a rudder cable snapped at an inopportune time. (Image: Salem Public Library)

a big swath of land through which he would have to run his railroad to get to its planned terminus at Newport.

So instead Hogg terminated his railroad at the very back of the bay, named the resulting town Yaquina City, bought a big steamboat to connect with it there, and started providing passenger service to San Francisco. Then, with a steady stream of revenue coming in from that service, he turned to his next project: The transcontinental.

Crews got busy on the line, pushing it out as far as Idanha. Then, in 1887, disaster struck: Hogg's steamship, which connected with the rail line for passenger service to San Francisco, ran aground. While navigating the Yaquina Bay bar, the ship suffered a broken rudder cable, and drifted north and beached herself on the sand below Chicken Hill (where the Yaquina Bay Lighthouse is). The surf soon pounded her to pieces.

The loss was insured, but losing the cash flow of the successful passenger route was going to hurt.

In desperation, Hogg had his workers stop working on the rail line and sent them all up to the summit of the pass. There, they started work on a railroad line from nowhere to nowhere: A randomly selected spot on the west side, a randomly selected spot on the east side, and a mile or two of track crossing over the pass.

Then Hogg disassembled a passenger car and had a team of mules pack it up to the pass. There, it was reassembled and set on the rails.

The mules then pulled the car across the pass a couple times with workers on board, the workers having "paid" for tickets; and with that, Hogg was ready to report to the federal government that he had done it — established service over the pass.

The next step, he knew, was to receive those massive grants of land, sell them, and use them to finance the completion of the railroad.

This little swindle would probably have worked — actually, it did work, and provided Hogg with the income he would depend upon for his retirement. But it turned out not to matter. As the steamship Hogg had bought with the insurance money was being towed into the bay, a cable snapped (again) and the ship was washed onto the South Jetty. Again, it was a total loss.

Two snapped cables, two stranded ships, in two months ... what were the odds? Plenty of people thought this wasn't a coincidence. Suspicion naturally fell upon the Portland business crowd, since Hogg's plan would have meant a healthy slice of the Port of Portland's business would move to Newport; but, of course, nothing could be proved.

In any case, the second stranding dealt the *coup de grace* to Hogg's transcontinental aspirations. The construction was abandoned, and Hogg concentrated on keeping his existing rail service going.

Shortly thereafter, after failing to make the interest payments on his bonds, Hogg's railroad was forced into receivership. It filed bankruptcy in 1890 and was bought out by lumber magnate A.B. Hammond in 1894.

Sources and Works Cited:
- *"Colonel Hogg's Great Railroad to the Pacific,"* an article by Oregon Coast Aquarium Oceanscape Network, published in 2018 at oceanscape.aquarium.org;
- *"The Rise and Fall of Yaquina City,"* a research paper by Rich Sandler written for Geography 422 at Oregon State University, 2008;
- *"T. Edgenton Hogg — A Footnote,"* an article by Keith Clark published in the September 1983 issue of Oregon Historical Quarterly;
- A Lawyer's Life on Two Continents, *a book by Wallis Nash published in 1919 by Gorham Press;*
- *Personal correspondence with Marcola-area historian Curtis Irish.*

GEORGE WETHERBY & AL.:

REAL-ESTATE DEVELOPERS.

William C. Griswold surely thought he had a fortune in timber on his hands.

It was the late 1800s, and Griswold had homesteaded a heavily timbered 142-acre plot of land high on a bluff overlooking the Columbia river. And, even better, there was a large creek running through the property, for powering flumes to take the logs to the river below — where they could be easily and cheaply floated downstream for sale to one of the many sawmills there.

There was a problem, though. He quickly found out that the most powerful people in Portland were dead set against his plan, and were pulling every string they could reach to stop him.

The reason?

Scenic beauty.

No, really.

You see, the creek that ran through Griswold's property was the creek that runs over Multnomah Falls — at 620 feet, the tallest waterfall in Oregon, and already widely known as the "jewel of the Gorge."

A vintage 1950s postcard view of Multnomah Falls Lodge with the falls just behind. (Image: Postcard)

In Oregon at the turn of the twentieth century, scenic beauty was not usually a highly prized commodity. But Multnomah Falls was an exception. This was partly because of its unusual character; but the main reason was because it was making some very powerful people a whole lot of money.

As the city of Portland had grown larger and more squalid over the years, the residents there had started looking for nearby places to get away from it and get back to the natural scenic beauty that was so much a part of the attraction of the Pacific Northwest. One of their favorite Sunday afternoon pastimes was to board a steamboat or excursion train and travel east on the Columbia River Gorge, soaking up the scenery and maybe stopping for a picnic lunch or a short nature walk along the way. And the highlight of that short excursion was Multnomah Falls.

This had been going on since the late 1870s. By the early 1880s there was a steamboat dock in the river, and a stopping spot for outbound excursion trains. A well-developed trail led from those points up to the falls, crossing a rickety wooden bridge between the upper and lower falls along the way.

Would those upper-middle-class Portlanders don their Sunday best and board an excursion train for a trip to picnic in a stump-strewn field by an almost-empty streambed, noshing on their lunches to the rumbling sound of logs passing over their heads on leaky, rickety flumes?

The Oregon-Washington Railway and Navigation Company and the Union Pacific rather thought that they would not. And so these most powerful of Portland industrialists were dead set against Griswold's plan.

The fight dragged on. Finally, Griswold and his investors ran out of money and had to give up on the scheme. Griswold moved back east and gave the land to his daughter, Jennie Griswold, an artist from Washington, D.C. She, quite sensibly, gave up on the timber-harvest fantasy and started charging the visitors 10 cents each (a lot of money in those days) to visit and picnic there.

Then, in 1904, a Colorado mining lawyer named Lafayette "Lafe" Pence moved to Portland and, before anyone knew what he was up to, claimed the water rights to every creek in the hills around Portland — including, famously and very briefly, Bull Run, the city's water supply.

Multnomah Falls as it appeared a few years after the Simon Benson Bridge was constructed. (Image: Postcard)

Pence's plan, which we'll get into in more detail in the next chapter, was to use the water to wash and blast the northwest hills down to fill in Guild's Lake so that he could develop it as industrial land. This scheme ended in dismal failure just a few years later; but it gave Portland land developers a real education in water-rights law. It turned out you didn't have to own a piece of property to claim water rights on it, or even get permission from the person who did; you just had to file.

So, the very next year, a Portland developer named George Wetherby did just that: claimed the water rights in Griswold's land. Then, having thus gotten his foot in the door, he negotiated a lease from Griswold in early 1906. He claimed he was planning to install a water-powered sawmill at the foot of the waterfall.

It isn't clear just what Wetherby was trying to do here. Oregonian writer Joseph Rose takes his assertion at face value, calling him a "ruthless industrialist"; but this is hard to buy. Although most times of year Multnomah Creek provides enough water power for a modest sawmill, its location is extremely inconvenient for any timber not harvested directly up the hill from it. It is remotely possible that Wetherby planned to use the falls to generate electricity, which would then power a sawmill located several hundred yards away on the banks of the Columbia; but that seems a tremendous expense to undertake to do what a moderate-sized boiler and steam engine could easily and cheaply do, partly powered by the sawmill's own trimmings and waste; moreover, a steam engine could be made as large as necessary, whereas there was only so much power available from the creek. Indeed, with a few massive exceptions like the mills at Willamette Falls in Oregon City, water-powered mills were rare by this time.

Possibly this was the story Wetherby had to tell Griswold to get the lease approved — that with the sawmill in place it would finally be possible to harvest her father's timber. Possibly the sawmill was his cover story for having claimed the water rights (under the law, the proposed use had to be "beneficial").

It's also possible that he was trying to use the sawmill scheme as leverage to get the railroad to buy the place for an inflated price, to keep the tourist attraction intact. If that's the case, it didn't work out quite like he planned. Instead of buying him out, the railroad pulled some strings and the state Legislature promptly passed a law forbidding the diversion of Multnomah Creek for any reason. That was the end of the sawmill idea — and, most likely, Wetherby's water right as well, since he no longer had a "beneficial" use for it.

But Wetherby was still leasing the property in 1913, when the Columbia Gorge Highway was platted. At that time, with the encouragement and sponsorship of Simon Benson, the City of Portland opened negotiations to buy the property.

Wetherby, of course, promptly exercised his option to buy the place, anticipating marking it up sharply before selling it to the city for a tidy windfall profit. But this hope, too, was dashed, and by an unexpected person. It was Jennie Griswold, who, no doubt excited by all the interest and hoping to make a much larger profit than she could have made by delivering on her deal with Wetherby, refused to comply with the option agreement. A brief court battle ensued, which Wetherby lost. And just like that, he was out.

Jennie Griswold now claimed the place was worth $50,000. Benson thought $2,500 was more like it. And there things stood until suddenly someone figured out that the City of Portland could actually condemn the property under Eminent Domain, even though it wasn't in city limits.

With that threat in the air, Griswold settled for $5,250 and the city officially acquired the falls. (A persistent version of the story claims Benson bought it from Griswold and then donated it to the city, but he did not; he just acted as a broker in the deal.)

I haven't been able to learn what Wetherby's lease-option price was. It would be deliciously ironic if it were more than $5,250.

After that, Multnomah Falls as a public park was all but in the bag. The railroad donated the land at the foot of the falls, with the stipulation that a lodge be built there costing no less than $12,500. This was done (the enthusiastic city actually spent $40,000 on it). The wooden footbridge having long since decayed and fallen away, it was replaced with the bridge that's there now — one of the first continuous-pour bridges ever built, and named after Simon Benson. And in early 1915, inspired by a speech from legendary highway engineer Samuel Lancaster, the Progressive Business Men's Club of Portland took on as a fund-raising project the construction of what would become Larch Mountain Trail, the first 1.1 miles of which are the trail to the top of the falls.

The City of Portland owned the park until 1939, when it was transferred to the U.S. Forest Service (Benson Park was transferred to the state of Oregon). And so it has been ever since.

Sources and Works Cited:
- *"How Multnomah Falls was Saved from a Ruthless Industrialist,"* an article by Joseph Rose published in the Sept. 10, 2015, issue of The Portland Oregonian;
- *"Multnomah Falls Lodge and Footpath,"* a nomination for inclusion on the National Register of Historic Places submitted to the U.S. Department of the Interior in 1981.

LAFAYETTE "LAFE" PENCE:

REAL-ESTATE DEVELOPER.

In the story we just finished, the one about Multnomah Falls, I mentioned a sharp-eyed 61-year-old hustler named Lafayette "Lafe" Pence, who gave the city of Portland a real education in water-rights laws. This is the story of how he did that.

Lafe Pence stepped off a train in downtown Portland for the first time in 1904. He was there for a meeting of the National Mining Congress.

The conference he was attending has been long forgotten. But had the group chosen Seattle or Bakersfield to hold it, the very shape of the hills in Portland would be different today.

Pence had the kind of colorful Western background that you'd expect in a man who sets out to literally move mountains. He was born in Indiana just before the Civil War, and moved to Colorado to practice law when he was 24 years old. He became a specialist in mining law, and — likely representing the desires of his clients in the matter, as well as his own investments in silver mines — a strong advocate of the "Free Silver" movement.

For a while he looked like he'd have a political career, and he was elected to the U.S. House of Representatives in 1892 on the Populist Party ticket;

This old hand-tinted postcard image shows the full layout of the 1905 Lewis and Clark Centennial Exposition, with the steep adjacent mountains that inspired Lafe Pence's scheme. His plan was

but he lost his bid for re-election two years later, and not long afterward, Populist party membership and Free Silver sentiments became insurmountable barriers to political advancement. So he retired back to private practice and the management of his mines.

His 1904 visit to Portland found him at loose ends, ready for a new project. And in P-town, he found one — one that could really make him rich.

Portland, at the time, was in a frenzy of preparation for the 1905 Lewis and Clark Centennial Exposition. The whole thing was scheduled to be held in a sort of park-like patch of wetlands just north of the city on the west side of the river, called Guild's Lake ("Guild" was pronounced to rhyme with "Wild"). Mindful of the expense, the city had merely leased the land for a year, ignoring calls for the city to buy it and make it a permanent park.

One of the most persistent voices calling for Guild's Lake to be made a city park was Colonel L.L. Hawkins, chair of the Portland Parks Board. Hawkins, who lived just up the hill from Guild's Lake next to the newly formed Macleay Park (now part of Forest Park), even helped bring the Olmstead Brothers into town from New York to help the Parks Board make its case. Although the city had opted for the cheap lease, he still hoped the lake might eventually end up as parkland.

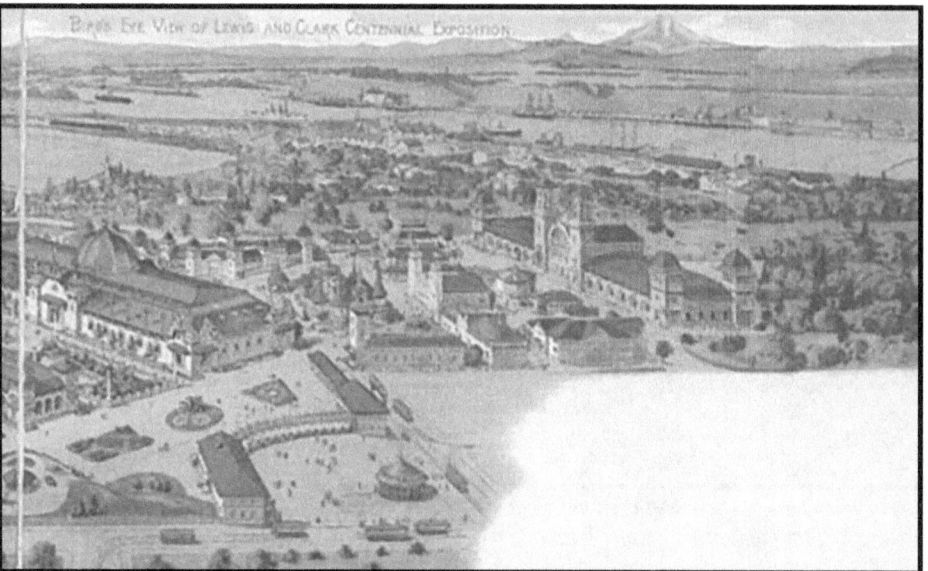
to wash those mountains down to fill the horseshoe-shaped lake that's visible in the foreground on the left-hand side. (Image: Postcard)

But the Expo grounds were right next to the busiest commercial part of the city, full of railroads and factories. Had it not been for the lake and surrounding marshy wetlands, it would have been not only in the path of progress, but on its very doorstep.

Well, Pence noticed a few very interesting things about Guild's Lake. First, it was not very deep; it was basically a low spot on an alluvial plain by the river. Secondly, it was surrounded by some remarkably extreme geography. The surrounding hills towered over it, steep and close at hand; yet they were made mostly of soil and clay, not rock.

The other thing he noticed was that despite Oregon's thriving hard-rock mining industry out east and down south, nobody in this, its biggest city, seemed to understand how water rights worked. Every river and stream in the city flowed free and unclaimed. The city hadn't even bothered to claim water rights on the Bull Run River, on which its domestic water supply depended.

To Pence, this all added up to a spectacular opportunity. The Exposition was about to catapult the town to nationwide prominence. To make the expo work, they would need water by the acre-foot, piped in from somewhere, to keep the lake deep enough to navigate on during the entire summer and to power the expo's many fountains and water features. He could acquire all the unclaimed water rights and use them to supply that demand, cementing connections with Portland's commerce-happy business elites; then, after the expo, with their support, he could put those massive water rights to work

Lafe Pence's land-moving operation as it appeared in spring of 1907. The long sinuous forms crisscrossing the landscape are water flumes. (Image: Portland Morning Oregonian)

sluicing down cubic acres of those nearby hills, filling the lake in so that the city's business district could expand.

With this plan in mind, Pence returned back east and got to work hustling the venture to investors. When he returned, later that year, he was ready for action.

The first thing Pence did was file water-rights claims on nearly every river, creek and spring in Multnomah County.

This came as rather a shock to most Portlanders, who hadn't realized that one could simply do that. They likely wouldn't have minded, but for one terrible public-relations blunder: Pence tried to claim water rights on Bull Run.

Pence backed off this claim when he realized how poorly it was playing with the public — which still remembered drinking from the Willamette and had a strong sense of ownership in the Bull Run water system. But the damage was done — and it was severe. Most of Portland now thought of him as a fresh-off-the-boat land shark who'd tried to use a legal technicality to snake the city's water supply out from under it and ransom it back.

But Pence's plans to be of service to the Expo were proceeding nicely. Using his water rights on Balch Creek and other water sources uphill from the grounds, he supplied all the water the fairgrounds could possibly need, and by the time the expo came to a triumphant conclusion late in 1905, he'd almost made up for the Bull Run blunder.

Then, at the head of his consortium of local and national investors, Pence bought the fairgrounds and started putting his plans into effect.

His crews got busy tearing down the fairgrounds structures and using the scavenged wood to create a massive system of flumes — fourteen miles of them — leading back up into the West Hills to the sources of water he controlled. With these, he fed a colossal high-pressure hose. He would use dynamite to loosen the soil, then wash it down into the lake in a muddy, swirling torrent. Blast, rinse, repeat. Day after day, all through the rainy season.

Naturally, this played poorly with the neighbors.

It played especially poorly with Colonel L.L. Hawkins — remember him?

Hawkins was already extremely displeased that his park dream had been definitively scotched by Pence's scheme, and the constant drumbeat of dynamite charges wasn't helping his mood.

Pence also had some trouble with the government. Denied permits for his system of flumes, he built them anyway, knowing if he missed the rainy

Aviation pioneer Thomas Scott Baldwin's airship returns from a trip over the Exposition grounds during the 1905 Lewis and Clark Centennial Exposition. The hillsides that Lafe Pence dreamed of moving into the lake are visible to the left. (Image: Library of Congress)

season, he'd be done for. This resulted in some hard feelings at City Hall. Luckily for Pence, Mayor Harry Lane overplayed his hand when he personally helped destroy a section of Pence's flume system that he mistakenly thought was inside Macleay Park; Pence graciously met him at the site with a team of surveyors who demonstrated that his flume was not encroaching, and the embarrassed Lane helped him fix it and removed further bureaucratic hurdles.

There was also a horrifying episode when a section of flume collapsed, precipitating several workmen to their deaths on the ground several dozen feet below.

Nonetheless, by the end of the rainy season (1906-1907), Pence was very bullish on the venture. His operation had all but removed a hill called Scotch Nubbin, and dumped over 200,000 cubic yards of dirt into the lake. At that rate, he expected to have the job fully finished well before the six years he'd promised his investors.

But it was not to be. In summer of 1907, a bank panic broke out, and the bank that was his primary backer closed its doors. Suddenly gasping for cash, Pence found himself unable to make payroll, and with the bankruptcy trustees trying to claw back the money the bank had previously advanced to him. Seeing the writing on the wall, Pence closed up shop and headed back east, where he finished out his life as a railroad lawyer.

As for the lake, when the property reverted to the sellers they sold it to a duo of Seattle hydraulic contractors, who finished part of the job and called it good. Then in the early 1920s, the Port of Portland filled in the rest of the lake when it dredged the river channel and used the lake as the repository for 20 million cubic yards of silt from the river bottom. Today, Guild's Lake is an industrial neighborhood, and Northwest Yeon Avenue (Highway 30) runs right through what used to be the middle of it.

Sources and Works Cited:
- *"The Reclamation of Lafe Pence," an article by Gabriel Liston accompanied by images of original art published on November 2014 at lastwater.net.*
- *"Lafayette Pence," an article by Kathy Tucker published March 17, 2018, on* The Oregon Encyclopedia *at oregonencyclopedia.org;*
- Portland Morning Oregonian *archives, March 1907.*

JOE KNOWLES:

WILDERNESS-SURVIVAL GURU.

On the morning of Tuesday, July 21, 1914, deep in the heart of the wilderness of the Siskiyous near the little hamlet of Holland, a naked man was soberly shaking the hand of an official-looking gentleman as several others looked on.

Then the naked man turned and padded away into the woods — barefoot.

Mr. Birthday Suit's name was Joe Knowles. He was, in essence, the Bear Grylls of the 1910s — an expert woodsman and wilderness-survivalist getting ready to demonstrate his skills for a nationwide audience. Like Bear Grylls, he was the real thing — but he'd been caught cutting some corners on his last show. This was the beginning of the demonstration that he hoped would prove once and for all that he could do it. At the same time, he hoped it would be an answer to a question that was much on Americans' minds back then, in the twilight years of the "long nineteenth century" — "Is civilization making us soft and degenerate?"

Joe hoped to prove that it was not, at least not yet; and that a healthy American man, equipped only with what the good Lord had given him, could

Joe Knowles as he appeared after emerging from the wilderness of northern Maine, wearing the skin of the bear he killed there. (Image: Small, Maynard & Co.)

step out into a howling wilderness and carve out of its natural bounty a comfortable life for himself.

"In attempting to live this life that no one else has attempted to live before in our age, my real purpose is to demonstrate the fact that the power of modern man has not deteriorated," Joe had explained, in an article published in the *Sunday Oregonian* (among other newspapers nationwide) a few days before. "To prove that the man of today, although handicapped by civilization, is the physical equal of his ancestors. I believe he has not lost that resourcefulness that in early days brought nature into subjection."

But Joe's other motivation for his Oregon demonstration was probably the real reason — and it wasn't one he alluded to in the newspapers. He very much wanted to redeem his reputation.

That reputation — for good and for ill — had been forged the previous year when he had plunged naked into the wilderness of northern Maine.

At the time, Joe was living in Boston. For years he'd been getting by as a wilderness guide, and he was augmenting his income by working part-time for the *Boston Post* as a commercial artist.

The plan for the "Nature Man" stunt was developed with a friend and co-worker at the *Post* named Michael McKeough. It was worked out in great detail, pitched and sold to the *Post*, and put into practice in the summer of 1913: Joe would plunge into the wildest wilderness, stark naked but for a loincloth, and prove that he could wrest a living from Nature's reluctant hands. Each week, Joe would drop off a stack of correspondence — drawings done on birchbark with a charred twig from his fire, and letters written the same way — in a designated location under a stump. McKeough, for whom the *Post* had rented a cabin

One of the charcoal-on-birchbark drawings Knowles left for the newspapers to publish. (Image: Small, Maynard & Co.)

near the stump to serve as a sort of "Joe Knowles bureau office" and who was enjoying a sort of paid working vacation in the woods, would retrieve the birchbarks, type them up, and convey them to the *Post*, which would then, of course, publish them.

The *Boston Post* was soon very glad it had said yes to McKeough and Knowles. Over the course of the stunt, circulation shot up by over 30,000 copies, and Joe's updates were the hottest thing on the AP wire. They were onto something really big; the whole thing was playing very well with the American public. The drama and romance of Joe's quest had captured the imagination of an America that still hadn't quite gotten used to not being a frontier country any more. Mountain men were already a distant memory, now remembered only on the labels of patent medicines and the pages of history books; cowboys were a dying breed; and Indians were a tiny and demoralized remnant of a once proud and powerful presence in

Another birchbark drawing, of a bobcat stalking deer by the lake. (Image: Small, Maynard & Co.)

The newspaper photo montage with which the Morning Oregonian told of Joe Knowles' departure into the wilderness of the Siskiyou Mountains, on July 24. (Image: Oregonian.)

the land. But now, here came Joe Knowles, the "American Adam," to prove that a naked American man could still take on a howling wilderness and thrive there, just as well as his ancestors could.

And there was another thing. The average American liked his/her modern comforts — streetcars, steam heat, indoor plumbing — but according to the then-recently-popularized theories of eugenics, the gene stock of a "race" of people was only kept strong through adversity and struggle. Would a soft modern life cause Americans to degenerate into soft, decadent people? Was it our destiny to slowly tranform into a bunch of immoral pleasure-seekers and drug addicts, as had happened (so the average American of the day thought) with China and Ottoman Turkey and various eastern European and Slavic cultures? (This sounds ridiculous to the modern ear; but in 1914 there were tenured Ivy League college professors teaching this theory as "science," and it was being actively used to decide on immigration policy at Ellis Island.)

Joe Knowles was there to prove that if degeneracy were indeed the destiny of "the race," it hadn't happened yet.

And when, two months later, a scruffy, thickly bearded Knowles emerged from the woods wearing sandals woven from tree bark, a bearskin taken from a bear that he had trapped in a pit and clubbed to death, and other garments made from the hide of a deer that he'd caught and killed with his bare hands, the whole country cheered and celebrated.

Well, not the whole country. The *Boston Post*'s rival newspaper, the *Boston American*, was extremely skeptical — and envious. It promptly published an article presenting a strong argument — backed by some circumstantial evidence — that Joe hadn't spent the entire two months in the wilderness. It pointed out that McKeough had had a very handy cabin, well stocked with Joe's favorite brand of beer; and it claimed that his animal skins had been tanned by a commercial process, and had bullet holes in them. He had, the *American* claimed, simply stayed in the cabin with McKeough for two months, working on his tan and growing his beard and sketching scenes he'd made up in his head.

This claim was shortly thereafter piled onto, with devastating effect, by McKeough. Joe's friendship with him did not survive the summer. The two men were bitter enemies almost immediately after Joe's return to civilization. This may have had something to do with the fact that almost immediately upon returning from the woods, Joe quit his job at the *Boston Post* and went to work for his erstwhile nemesis, the *Boston American* — and its owner, William Randolph Hearst.

It is very difficult to suss out the truth from the conflicting accounts of Joe's two-month wilderness sojourn. The bitter McKeough soon was claiming that Joe essentially moped around the cabin the entire time until the game wardens showed up (bears and deer were out of season, and he'd essentially confessed in the *Post* to poaching one of each, although McKeough claimed the deer had been roadkill). The picture he painted of his ex-friend was so unflattering and bitter, and claimed him to be so incompetent and thick-witted, that it's really not credible.

But neither is Joe's "official" account. Now as then, it seems very likely that Joe cheated, at least a little and probably a lot. If nothing else, the allegations that the animal skins were commercially tanned could be tested by taking them to a neutral third party (say, a chemistry professor at Cornell or Amherst) to examine them; the fact that this was not done, so far as I've been able to learn, is particularly damning.

There was, however, one other thing that even Joe Knowles had to admit. As a longtime trapper and wilderness guide in the north Maine woods, Joe knew the country "like an open book," as he put it. Even if he had played the whole thing straight, was it really a fair test for him to plunge into a woodland whose every plant and shrub he knew, the poisonous from the nutritious; and the habits of whose animals he was intimately familiar with?

Arguably, no.

But America wouldn't have to just wonder about this. Because now that Joe's experiment in the Maine woods was over, his new employer had a proposition for him. Hearst had, a few years earlier, founded and sponsored the American Boy Scouts as a paramilitary-and-woodcraft organization. He'd done this at roughly the same time that other community and business leaders had founded the Boy Scouts of America, and the two organizations were locked in a battle for the hearts and minds of American youth — a battle Hearst was losing thanks to one of his Boy Scouts, who'd murdered another Boy Scout with his Official Boy Scout Rifle at an official Boy Scout meeting a few years before. The incident inspired all the Scout groups to pivot away from the paramilitary stuff, and toward woodcraft and outdoor skills.

Hearst thought Joe Knowles would be a great "founding father" for his Scouting outfit. But until those rumors of cabin-lounging and beer-drinking were put to rest, he'd be more of a liability than an asset to the ABS. Joe Knowles was going to have to put those rumors to rest — not necessarily to prove he didn't cheat in the woods of Maine, but certainly to prove that he hadn't had to, and that his woodcraft was real and not just pub talk and yellow-newspaper puffery.

No problem — Hearst would redeem Joe by sponsoring a second experiment. Joe would plunge naked into a wilderness a continent away from his friends and their suspicious stocks of beer. There would be third-party observers in the form of well known university professors. Joe would prove his bona fides once and for all, and silence the critics.

Hearst's entire newspaper empire was at the ready. "WILD BEASTS ROAR INVITATION TO JOE KNOWLES," howled a banner headline in the *San Francisco Examiner*. Other newspapers — such as the *Portland Morning Oregonian* — carried the news on their front pages under more

The photo spread welcoming Joe Knowles back after his ordeal was considerably smaller — but, of course, it was now competing with news of the war. (Image: Oregonian.)

conventional headlines: "NATURE MAN STARTS TUESDAY," for instance.

So once more into the woods went Joe — and immediately made the single biggest mistake of his career as a public woodsman.

"Joe Knowles' first action in going to the woods is to pick up a sharp stone," explained Prof. T. T. Waterman of the University of California, one of the professors who was monitoring the experiment. "The second is to hack through the bark of a white cedar, pull loose a long strip of bark and extract the fiber. As he presses forward into the forests he twists this fiber into string as he walks. Before he has gone five miles he will have this fiber twisted into sandals."

The problem was, during this five-mile barefoot meander, Joe was apparently strolling through fields of small woody plants with glossy oak-shaped leaves clustered in groups of three. He didn't recognize them; why should he? Poison Oak doesn't grow in the north Maine woods.

Now, a really bad case of poison oak is bad enough. But when it's all over the feet, that's quite a bit worse. A miner who came across him halfway through his month told reporters he couldn't believe Joe hadn't contracted blood poisoning from it.

Joe had hoped to emerge from the woods on this attempt wearing another bearskin, or even — his fondest hope — leading a bear cub that he'd befriended. With his feet in the condition they were in, though, he quickly found himself subsisting on fish and huckleberries. These got the job done, but not much more than that.

Then, a little over a week into the ordeal, a second blow fell, and it would be this one that would essentially end Joe's bid for enduring national fame:

Half a world away, the particularly arrogant and thick-headed hereditary ruler of Germany sent his army over the border into Belgium on an ill-fated quest to take France by surprise. The First World War was under way.

With a story like that unfolding in real time, there was no room on the front pages of America's newspapers for the woodland adventures of some naked guy beating through the bushes of Southern Oregon.

The *Morning Oregonian* kept a steady flow of news coverage going, but it was no longer on the front page. And when the 30th day came along, and Joe had completed what he'd committed to, he abandoned his plan to extend his sojourn, and came in.

Other than the Portland and San Francisco papers, hardly anyone noticed. Herbert Hoover was making headlines rescuing stranded Americans in London; German troops were pouring through Belgium; there was a very real possibility that Paris would fall. Joe Knowles was just no longer news.

With Hearst's help, Knowles tried again in 1916, in the Adirondacks of upstate New York; this time, he served as a wilderness-survival trainer for two "Dawn Girls" who were going to plunge into the wilderness naked (under the supervision of a chaperone, of course); at the same time, several miles away, Knowles would be making a third demonstration of his own. But one of the Dawn Girls dropped the project before it even started, and the other lasted only a week or two before throwing in the towel — she couldn't stand the mosquitos. And when she quit, so did almost all of the media coverage.

For several years after this last stunt, Joe made regular personal appearances at talks and lectures as "The Famous Nature Man" at theaters and halls. But when Stewart Holbrook found him, a couple decades after his woodcraft demonstrations, he was living with his wife on the coast of Washington just north of Cape Disappointment, in a funny little cabin built with driftwood and bits of wrecked ships.

He hadn't lost his old streak of romanticism, either. "Mother Ocean

MAVERICKS.

Advance coverage of Joe Knowles' final 1916 wilderness plunge included this photo with Audreta Griswold and Emily Hammerstein (misidentified here as "Emily Hammus"), the two "Dawn Girls" who he was training. Griswold dropped out before the experiment was to begin; Hammerstein, complaining of mosquitos, quit a week or two later. (Image: Oregonian.)

supplies all my wants," he told *The New Yorker* writer Richard Boyer in 1938. "All I have to do is sit and wait, and she throws up what I need at my door. She gave me driftwood for my house. The other day she gave me a can of kerosene for light. She gives me clams and fish and crabs. The pancakes I had for breakfast this morning were made out of flour from a wrecked ship. And one time last summer Mother Ocean brought me in some of the finest etching paper I have ever used."

Since most of these things were coming to him courtesy of shipwrecks on the Columbia River Bar, which his cabin was just downwind from, one has to wonder if Mother Ocean ever brought him the bodies of drowned mariners as well. If so, he apparently didn't mention it to Boyer.

For things that Mother Ocean didn't supply, Knowles worked as a freelance commercial artist, specializing in wildlife and Western art, most often for magazines.

To the end of his days, he maintained that his demonstration of woodsmanship in Maine was the real thing. And he told Holbrook that he had just two regrets: First, that he didn't manage to befriend a bear cub; and second — that stupid war.

But although almost nobody remembers Joe Knowles today, he was probably the very first wilderness-survival showman. And as a form of spectator entertainment, the genre he pioneered has never been more popular than it is today. From Bear Grylls' various TV shows, to reality-show fare like *Survivor* and *Alone*, the wilderness-survival genre is alive and well. There's even one (*Naked and Afraid*, on Discovery) in which the "Dawn Girl" stunt is re-created — minus the chaperone, of course.

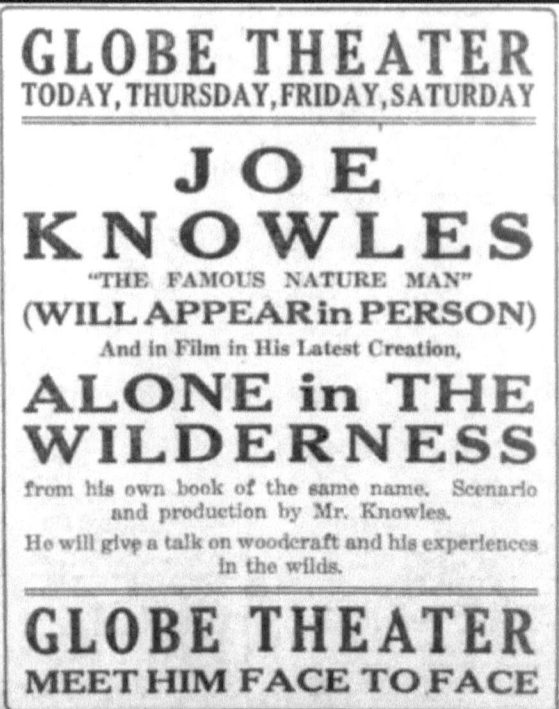

This advertisement, from the June 20, 1917, issue of the Oregonian, was for a wilderness-survival lecture to be given by Joe Knowles. This was a year after his last "naked in the wilderness" sojourn. (Image: Oregonian)

Sources and Works Cited:
- Wildmen, Wobblies and Whistle Punks, *a book by Stewart Holbrook, published in 1992 by Oregon State University Press;*
- Desperate Journeys, Abandoned Souls, *a book by Edward E. Leslie, published in 1998 by Houghton Mifflin;*
- Alone in the Wilderness, *a book by Joseph Knowles, published in 1913 by Small, Maynard & Co. of Boston;*
- "Where Are They Now? Nature Man," *an article by Richard Boyer published in the June 18, 1938, issue of* The New Yorker.
- Portland Morning Oregonian *archives: June—September 1914; July 1916; June 1917.*

GILBERT E. GABLE:

PROMOTER, "GOVERNOR" OF THE STATE OF JEFFERSON

I.

Most Oregonians know about the State of Jefferson — in general concept, at least: a small group of Southern Oregon people got together in 1941 to proclaim a new state, made up of southwest Oregon and northwest California, called Jefferson; just as they got started, the Japanese attacked Pearl Harbor; and the idea just never got off the ground.

All of which is true enough. But it barely touches the real story of Jefferson — and it's not even the most interesting part.

The fact is, the 1941 move for statehood was mostly a publicity stunt. It was crafted over drinks by two guys who seem right out of central casting for a Hollywood movie — a high-rolling, back-slapping business promoter and a hard-drinking, wildly imaginative newspaper man.

The newsman actually won a Pulitzer prize for his part in the affair. His name was Stanton Delaplane; he wrote for the *San Francisco Chronicle*.

The business promoter was a stocky, dynamic man named Gilbert E. Gable, onetime dinosaur egg hunter, movie maker, NBC radio-show star and (he claimed) honorary Navajo Indian chief. In 1941, he was mayor of the tiny Oregon town of Port Orford and, for a brief and shining moment, governor of the Great State of Jefferson.

Gilbert Gable at the mike.

Gilbert Elledy Gable was born in Pennsylvania in the late 1880s. Although he never went to college, he quickly found his way into public relations, and spent nine years as a publicity man for Theodore Vail's Bell Telephone Company. During this time, under Vail's direction, Bell transitioned from the most hated company in the nation to one of the most trusted, publicly committed to using its market dominance to bring telephone service to the remotest outposts of America. That story is more than we can get into here, but it's one of history's greatest public-relations triumphs. And Gable was a part of it — although I have been unable to learn how big a role he played.

An NBC promotional drawing of Gilbert Gable in 1931, for his radio show. (Image: Radio Digest Magazine)

The phone business must have been good to him, though, because after the war Gable became an explorer and amateur paleontologist — something it took money to do. He discovered a vast assortment of dinosaur tracks in Arizona, as well as a lost ancient Indian village, and claimed to have been made an honorary chief of the Navajo people — a claim he supported, when challenged on it, by displaying a certificate that he said was "written in human blood." He made a number of dinosaur-hunting expeditions to the Painted Desert area, until in 1929, the governor of Arizona ordered police to prevent "Dr. Gable" from removing any more fossils or artifacts.

He also made movies. In 1927, as vice-president of Bray Motion Pictures, he won publicity for the silent movie "Menace" by bringing a film crew down the wild Colorado River on a boat through the Grand Canyon, a feat that was breathlessly described in the papers as fraught with deadly peril.

By the early 1930s, Gable had gotten involved in the new world of radio broadcasting with an NBC show called "Highway of Adventure" (sometimes listed as "High Road to Adventure"), in which he recounted spine-tingling anecdotes — some of them no doubt true — from the previous dozen years of hunting for dinosaur eggs and exploring unknown landscapes. He also sought and won the hand of Miss Paulina Stearns, daughter of a wealthy Michigan timber family.

And then, in 1933, he went to Port Orford — probably to search for the legendary Port Orford Meteorite.

He didn't find the meteorite, of course — no one has; but he seems to have decided that the real treasure in Port Orford was the town itself.

"To the amazement of its 300 inhabitants, Gilbert Gable appeared at Port Orford, Ore., and formed six companies to promote it as the only natural deep-water harbor on the rugged coast between Puget Sound and the Golden Gate," reports TIME Magazine in its somewhat supercilious April 1938 article.

Gable hit Port Orford like a temperate-zone hurricane. He was convinced the nearby countryside was peppered with deposits of copper, gold and other resources, all covered over with billions of board-feet of old-growth timber.

The town of Port Orford as it appeared shortly before Gilbert E. Gable came to town. (Image: Port Orford Historical Photos archive, www.sixes.net/351)

The Port Orford harbor dock as it appeared in 1938. (Image: Port Orford Historical Photos archive, www.sixes.net/351)

The harbor, having no river bar to complicate navigation, was just one measly million-dollar jetty away from becoming the perfect port ... but, of course, it would also need a railroad line.

For a few years things went very well indeed. "Since 1935, Gilbert Gable has wrought such changes in Southwestern Oregon that the region has been called his 'empire,'" Time Magazine reported in its article about him.

But: "Last week, Emperor Gable was dethroned by the Interstate Commerce Commission," the article continued.

It was the railroad line that took Gable down — the railroad line, and the sea. Just three months after Gable (now mayor of Port Orford) dedicated the harbor in a splendid ceremony before dignitaries from all over the state, the massive new Trans-Pacific and Port Orford Dock and Terminal Line breakwater collapsed in a huge storm. A temporary pier was soon built, but it didn't afford the kind of protection the harbor would need, and Gable's backers weren't willing to invest in a railroad line to service a harbor that might not be capable of functioning as more than a temporary port of refuge.

In 1938, an ICC examiner quashed the whole plan, opining that Port Orford was never going to be an important center of commerce, and pulling Gable's "certificate of convenience and necessity" — and with that, his permit to build the railroad line.

Now Gable was caught in a catch-22. Without a railroad connection, his backers wouldn't help him finance the necessary repair and beefing-up of the harbor jetty. Without a beefed-up jetty protecting the harbor, the ICC wouldn't issue a permit to build a railroad.

An increasingly desperate Gable looked to the state for help in getting highways improved, so that the mining, logging and shipping companies that he'd founded could get their produce out to markets over land with heavy trucks.

But politicians in Salem could barely be bothered to even notice the tiny port city of under 1,000 residents that still cherished hopes of superseding Portland's harbor. Roadbuilding dollars remained in scarce supply.

By fall of 1941, Gable was watching his dream slip from his fingers for want of a transportation link. He started thinking about ways to bring pressure on the state to help him out. He started advocating for Curry County to split off from Oregon and become part of California — a suggestion that seems to have yielded amusement, alarm and ridicule in roughly equal measures from the governments of both states, but nothing more.

The suggestion did bring something else, though. It brought a visit from one of the West Coast's most enterprising and colorful newspapermen — Stanton Delaplane.

Gable and "Del" hit it off immediately. Soon, the two of them were cooped up together in a cozy office with a bottle of 150-proof rum as a hard winter rain pounded the roof ... hatching a breathtakingly audacious plan.

II.

The editorial writer for the Portland *Morning Oregonian* was trying to be sarcastically dismissive, but between the lines, a discriminating reader could pick up on signs of real concern.

"Curry (County) would of course immediately acquire the glorious climate of California and become a haven for retired Midwest farmers," he wrote. "Gold Beach would become a metropolis with offensive slums, and Latin quarters, and traffic problems and police scandals and what-not. ... The Curry County plan to become a county of California is so full of potential disaster that once again its people are beseeched to pause and consider."

The plan the paper was inveigling against was the idea Gable had floated a few days before — the idea Stanton Delaplane had found interesting enough to prompt a personal visit: Curry County would leave Oregon and join California — which, Gable hoped, would invest the road-building and harbor-development resources needed to unlock the mineral and timber resources with which the county was blessed.

Gable's hope had been to shame Salem into stepping up with those resources; he probably never entertained a California Anschluss as a serious possibility. And indeed, the main result in both Salem and Sacramento was little more than scornful laughter.

But the gambit also raised Gable's profile, and suddenly other nearby counties were interested in his plan.

A delegation from Josephine County (home of Grants Pass and the Oregon Caves) suggested joining Josephine and Curry counties in an entirely new state: "Cavemania." South of the California border, Del Norte County, home of Crescent City — another promising seaport that had been scorned by the powers that be — also wanted in.

But it was in Siskiyou County, and especially in Yreka, that that State of Jefferson movement started getting serious traction. Yreka was a town where resentment of Sacramento's neglect had simmered for decades. Now, with a skillful P.R. man like Gable to rally behind, the Yreka 20-30 Club took the State of Jefferson on as a project.

It wasn't called Jefferson yet, though. Some people had been calling it "Mittelwestcoastia," but that, of course, would never do. The Yreka Daily News, eager to help, announced a "name the state" contest, which yielded what historian Richard Reinhart called "a field of equally repulsive entries including Orofino, Bonanza, Del Curiskiou, Siscurdelmo, New West, New Hope and Discontent" — along with Jefferson. Jefferson, perhaps unsurprisingly, won.

Gilbert E. Gable in his office at the Trans-Pacific administration building in 1935. (Image: Port Orford Historical Photos archive, www.sixes.net/351)

Members of the Yreka 20-30 Club, sporting Western attire, staff the roadblock as "State of Jefferson Border Patrol" officers during the first Secession Thursday. This obviously-staged photograph shows a motorist accepting a copy of the "Proclamation of Independence" from one of the men. (Image: San Francisco Chronicle)

And Gable now found himself in the role of chief executive of the new proposed state — in effect, governor. As such, he started issuing executive orders in press releases to newspapers: Jefferson would be free of sales tax, income tax and liquor tax; labor strikes would be outlawed (no big surprise coming from the guy who owned almost all Curry County industry); and slot machines would be outlawed — not because they were immoral, but because they competed unfairly with local taverns' and saloons' "stud poker industry."

He was striking just exactly the right note of irreverent jocularity, iconoclastic thinking, and earnestness — the magic combination that conjures populist enthusiasm and renewed hope from a demoralized and underrepresented population.

The Oregonian gnashed its teeth in editorial fury, but Delaplane and his editors at the San Francisco Chronicle found the whole concept very droll. At first they expected his coverage to be fun and fluffy — "like an A.A. Milne report on political upheaval at Pooh Corner," as author Richard Reinhardt put it.

It was a little like that. But it was also, as Delaplane quickly learned, much more.

Delaplane discovered that, under the tutelage of the PR wizard Gable, things had already gotten very interesting.

PROCLAMATION OF INDEPENDENCE:

Following is the text of the "Proclamation of Independence" handed out by the "Jefferson Border Patrol" at roadblocks during Secession Thursdays:

> *You are now entering Jefferson, the 49th state in the Union.*
>
> *Jefferson is now in patriotic rebellion against the states of California and Oregon.*
>
> *This State has seceded from California and Oregon this Thursday, Nov. 27, 1941. Patriotic Jeffersonians intend to secede each Thursday until further notice.*
>
> *For the next hundred miles as you drive along Highway 99, you are traveling parallel to the greatest copper belt in the Far West, 75 miles west of here.*
>
> *The United States government needs this vital mineral. But gross neglect by California and Oregon deprives us of necessary roads to bring out the copper ore.*
>
> *If you don't believe this, drive down the Klamath River Highway and see for yourself. Take your chains, shovel and dynamite.*
>
> *Until California and Oregon build a road into the copper country, Jefferson, as a defense-minded State, will be forced to rebel each Thursday and act as a separate State.*
>
> *(Please carry this proclamation with you and pass them out on your way.)*
>
> —*State of Jefferson Citizens Committee*
> *Temporary State Capitol, Yreka*

After their late-night rum-fueled collaboration, things would get even more so.

The most visible and memorable part of the Jefferson gambit was the "State of Jefferson Border Patrol," organized by the Yreka 20-30 Club. Members of the patrol dressed up in Western outfits and strapped on target pistols for their "duties," of which the primary one was a series of public-relations events called "Secession Thursdays."

The first one of these was held on Nov. 27, and it was handled with remarkable preciseness and professionalism. The "border patrol" set up roadblocks to stop cars on the highways, next to barrels of burning kerosene. Drivers were given a few copies of a "Proclamation of Independence," urged to hand them out to all their friends, and sent on their way with a friendly Western-show smile. And, of course, a few carefully staged "car stops" involving fetching-looking female motorists and wholesomely-Western-looking "Border Patrol officers" were photographed for distribution to the national media.

"This state has seceded from California and Oregon this Thursday, November 27, 1941," the handbill reads. "Patriotic Jeffersonians intend to secede each Thursday until further notice."

Just as he and Gable had planned, Delaplane found himself the first national reporter on the scene of a story that was suddenly blowing up rather big. Newsreel companies were scrambling to get film crews out for the next Secession Thursday. The Yreka Daily News carried instructions for local residents on how to receive the national media — instructions that might as well have been penned by the great public-relations master Edward Bernays himself: "Please wear Western clothes if they are available," it read. "Two hundred people in Western costumes will be selected to march past the camera for close-ups."

Upon arrival, the film crews handled the crowd like extras at a movie shoot. "Get over there and be looking at the map," a man with a bullhorn yelled at them. "Don't be looking at the camera ... We have too many children. Can't we have a few more adults in here? ... Show a little enthusiasm! Wave your arms!"

The State of Jefferson had never seemed more like a real movement than it did at that moment, on the second Secession Thursday. But what the national media didn't realize was that it was already done. The movement's heart — the brilliant, colorful, and rascally character whose public-relations savvy had made everything possible — was gone.

It happened the day after reporter Delaplane left to go back to San Francisco with his story. Gilbert E. Gable had been up late the night before with Delaplane, comparing notes and talking about how the two of them were going to manage the public-relations bonanza that was bursting around their ears. Delaplane was going to win a Pulitzer; Gable was going to win approval for the railroad that was holding him back from becoming the wealthiest man on the West Coast; and the residents of Curry County were going to win statehood. The two of them talked, and drank, long into the night.

And the next day, unexpectedly, Gilbert Gable just dropped dead. The official cause of death was "acute indigestion," but that, of course, probably meant a heart attack.

Delaplane did win the Pulitzer Prize for his coverage of the secession movement. But the movement itself, without Gable, was lost. And when, just three days later, the Japanese attacked Pearl

HEROES *and* RASCALS *of* OLD OREGON.

Harbor, Jefferson's new duly elected governor (Judge John Childs of Crescent City) announced that Secession Thursdays — along with all other activities relating to the new state — would cease until further notice, as the U.S. now had bigger fish to fry.

Today, the State of Jefferson remains a fond memory for some; a fond hope for others; and for a few remaining die-hards, a serious goal. For most of us, though, it's a fascinating piece of the frontier history of Oregon and California, and an excellent excuse to visit the most gloriously untraveled part of the Oregon Coast.

Sources and Works Cited:
- The Elusive State of Jefferson, *a book by Peter Laufer, published in 2013 by Twodot Press;*
- *"Gable's Gold Coast," an un-by-lined article published in the April 4, 1938, issue of* TIME;
- *"Thrills," an article by Gilbert Gable published in the March 1931 issue of* Radio Digest;
- *"The Short, Happy History of the State of Jefferson," an article by Richard Reinhardt published in the May 1972 issue of* The American West.

ART LACEY:

B-17 BOMBER SMUGGLER.

Art Lacey was in serious trouble.

It was the summer of 1947, and he was about 50 feet above an Oklahoma airfield, at the controls of the biggest airplane he'd ever flown — a four-engined Boeing B-17G Flying Fortress, one of hundreds of the heavy bombers that the government was selling as surplus in the wake of the Second World War.

This one was his; he had just bought it for $13,000. But now the landing gear were stuck in the retracted position, and it looked like he was about to crash it.

This wouldn't have been such a big deal if it weren't for his "co-pilot." Art, not wanting to bother with getting someone to tag along with him, had brought a dressmaker's mannequin borrowed from a friend, dressed it in flight gear, and propped up in the seat, to fool the airfield manager into thinking there were two guys in the cockpit — like one of those modern "carpool lane cheaters" who are occasionally busted for driving in the carpool lane with an inflatable dummy in the passenger seat.

After crashing the plane and 'fessing up to this bit of deception, Art knew he would be in a less-than-optimal bargaining position vis-à-vis the defect in the plane he'd bought.

Still, that was all in the future. For now, the number-one goal was to not die in a giant fireball following a botched attempt at a gear-up landing. He lined the plane up as best he could with the runway and prepared to do his best.

Art's whole crazy scheme had its genesis when he first learned about the surplus B-17s. They were super-cheap, selling for not much above their scrap value, because there just weren't very many practical civilian uses for an obsolete heavy bomber. Art, already a successful Milwaukie businessman, had started stewing over how he might take advantage of the low prices on the big warbirds. The more he thought about it, the cooler he thought it would look to have one of them perched above the gas pumps at his gas station on McLoughlin Boulevard. The wings could serve as a roof over the pumps, and there would be room for a lot of them. And best of all, it wouldn't cost that much more than a stick-built structure of similar size.

According to Art's daughter, Punky Scott, in an interview with KATU-TV Channel 2 News, the scheme he developed remained just a scheme until someone put money on the line. At his birthday party, he shared his vision of a "Bomber Gas Station" with a friend, who laughingly told him he was dreaming. Art promptly put up a $5 bet, which was just as promptly accepted, and just like that the whole crazy dream was turned into a serious plan.

Art immediately turned to a friend who, Punky suggested, was well connected with the dark side of Portland business — untaxed liquor, gambling, pinball machines, that sort of thing. "Got any money on you?" he asked. "I need $15,000."

"And the guy had it on him," Punky said in her interview. "I don't know how that translates into today's money, but it's got to be a lot."

It is. $15,000 in 1947 is the equivalent of $160,000 today — a pretty impressive wad for "walking-around money."

Loaded down with this borrowed loot, Art made the journey to Oklahoma to buy his B-17. He had $13,000 for the plane and $2,000 for fuel and miscellaneous expenses on the way back.

Trouble started immediately upon arrival. After selling him the plane, the manager told him to bring his co-pilot the following day and he'd have the bird gassed up and ready. But Art hadn't realized he'd need a co-pilot, so he hadn't brought one.

The Bomber as it appeared just a few years after Art Lacey installed its signature airplane in 1947. (Image: Postcard)

He also hadn't given much thought to the fact that he'd never flown a four-engine bomber in his life. He was a skilled private pilot of single-engine planes, but this was a very different prospect.

Still, Art was determined to have his plane. So he returned the next day with the borrowed mannequin, strapped it into the copilot's seat, breezed into the manager's office to sign last-minute papers, and walked out ready to fly home.

Hoping to familiarize himself with the big aircraft a bit before he started flying it for real, he started out with a few passes, touch-and-gos, and gentle turns — literally holding the yoke in one hand and the flight manual in the other. And it was going pretty well, he thought.

But that's when he realized that the landing gear was stuck.

He flew the plane around for a while, trying to figure out how to get it unstuck. If his co-pilot hadn't been a dummy, he could have sent it down to try to pry something loose or bang on things; but that wasn't an option, and he certainly wasn't comfortable leaving the controls to try it himself. Finally he realized he'd just have to bring the plane in on its belly and hope for the best.

So down came Art Lacey in his new, doomed warbird, landing in a shower of sparks with a screech of tearing metal.

We can only imagine the relief that must have coursed through Art's veins and shimmered up and down his spine when he realized he was on the ground, no longer moving, and not on fire.

Although the cat was now out of the bag, the manager felt bad about the broken landing gear — and probably a little relieved, too, since his customer wasn't dead.

"He turned to his secretary and said, 'Have you written up the bill of sale yet on that B-17?'" Punky recounted. "And she said no, and he said, 'Worst case of wind damage I've ever seen.' And so he sold him a second B-17."

The second plane set Art back just $1,500 — a special deal the manager made him, knowing he'd spent all his money on the first one. But, of course, Art hadn't reduced the value of the bomber much by crashing it. $11,500 was probably roughly equal to the value of the scrap metal in the plane.

Of course, faking the copilot was no longer going to work, so Art called his wife long-distance and asked her to send two of his friends down in a car with a case of whiskey. The booze was to be used to bribe the local fire department to use their fire truck to pump the fuel out of the old B-17 and into the new one. It was a powerful enticement; Oklahoma was still a dry state at the time.

Everything worked as planned, although Art had to kite a check in Palm Springs to refuel the big plane; luckily, he made it home in time to cover his paper before it could bounce.

But when he arrived at PDX, Art found his troubles there had just begun. The city of Portland wouldn't issue permits to bring the plane from the airport. It was just too big, even after the wings were dismantled.

But Art was in so deep now, there was no turning back. He scheduled the move for the dark of night, well after the bars had all closed. He hired two teenagers with hot cars to accompany the motorcade, with instructions to floor it and race off recklessly into the night if the police should appear — the idea being to draw the cops away from the plane. The truck drivers were instructed that under no circumstances were they to stop before they arrived at the gas station, no matter who ordered them to. And he promised to pay any tickets anyone was written by any cop for his or her part in the move.

The move's only mishap was a drunk driver who, seeing an airplane bearing down on him, thought he'd accidentally driven out onto an airfield and panicked and skidded into the ditch.

And the next day, the morning sun dawned on a sight that must have stopped traffic: A genuine B-17 Flying Fortress bomber parked by McLoughlin Boulevard, right in the middle of town.

The Bomber as it appeared just a few years after Art Lacey installed its signature airplane in 1947. (Image: Postcard)

City Hall officials were, of course, furious. But after their initial attempts to punish Art resulted in some very unflattering newspaper coverage, they gave it up, fined him $10, declared victory and went home.

Art was able to pay half his fine with the $5 collected from his friend. He promptly had his airplane mounted above the gas pumps and renamed the place "The Bomber." And there it sat for the next 63 years, bringing in hundreds of thousands of curious gawkers and customers alike.

Over the years the Laceys added a restaurant and a small hotel. In the early 1990s they closed the gas pumps, and the big B-17 started to look increasingly forlorn up there, exposed to the weather and the occasional predations of vandals.

Then, in 1996, the family decided to do something about it — and the B-17 Alliance was born, dedicated to restoring the "Lacey Lady," as they've dubbed the bomber.

Currently (as of summer 2018) the bomber is in the B-17 Alliance Museum and Restoration, located at McNary Airfield in Salem (3278 25th St. S.E.). The museum is open Fridays through Sundays from 10 a.m. to 2 p.m. The multi-million-dollar restoration still has a ways to go before it's successfully completed, and the Alliance is working to raise the necessary funds to get it done; when it is, the Lacey Lady will be one of just seven B-17s remaining in flyable condition. Full details of their project are at www.b17alliance.com.

Sources and Works Cited:

- "The 'Lacey Lady' B-17 Bomber, a Milwaukie Landmark, Comes Down from its Perch," an article by Michael Bamesberger published in the Aug. 13, 2014, issue of the Portland Oregonian.
- "Lacey Lady's New Home," an article by Ellen Spitaleri published in the Nov. 10, 2014, issue of the Portland Tribune;
- "The Art Lacey Story," an article published by the B-17 Alliance Foundation at B17alliance.com.

PART III:

RASCALS.

PVT. JAMES W. SMITH:

CIVIL WAR SOLDIER.

If you had told James W. Smith of Lebanon that people would one day visit his grave to pay tribute to his service in the Union Army during the Civil War, he might have laughed.

He might also have run for the door ... you see, the unit of the Union Army in which Smith served had a bit of a reputation. During their three-month operating career, before the Army wised up and fired them all, Smith's unit — led by brothers Nathan and Orville Olney — became known among regular Army units as "Olney's Forty Thieves."

The story of the Forty Thieves company is an obscure one, and it hasn't been studied much; there isn't a whole lot of information about it out there. But what we do know is that it formed as a unit of 40 citizen-soldiers under the command of the Olney brothers late in the war, in July 1864. Its official name was "Olney's Detachment of the Oregon Cavalry," and it was tasked with patrolling and providing security for important parts of the Columbia River Gorge.

This it may have, in fact, done. But it's tempting to think the Olney

Detachment's real contribution to history was the invention (or at least, the refinement) of the art of security theater.

Today, of course, a modern form of security theater is performed daily in hundreds of airports across the country. A stranger in an official-looking hat pats you down for imaginary weapons, talks to you like a New Orleans cop interrogating a murder suspect, and confiscates your bottle of Efferdent tablets before letting you on the plane. The idea is to inconvenience you so much that you think the security guys are really on the ball, and quit worrying about the headline you read a few weeks earlier about a loaded .38 Special falling out of someone's luggage at LAX.

The Olney Brothers were early adopters of a different form of security theater, which they practiced up and down the Columbia River Gorge. They had it working so that not only did it provide a pantomime of security-related action on their part, it paid nice financial dividends as well. Here's how it worked:

At the time, Union Army soldiers enjoyed some of the finest clothing to be found on the frontier, including long, heavy blue wool coats that were much prized. The Olney boys developed a nice little scam in which the company would sell off its coats and other valuable Army stuff in one town, then go to another. There, they would claim to have just returned from action against Indians, in which all their supplies had been seized by the enemy. Then they would send word to the Army that they needed more.

They ran this scam this several times.

They also acquired a reputation for, as historian Randol B. Fletcher puts it, "fundraising" from the citizens they were supposed to be protecting. Surely we can't credit the Olney company with having invented the "protection racket," but it appears they weren't exactly strangers to the concept, either.

And this is probably why, in October 1864, at a time when the Union Army needed every man it could get hold of, it canned these 40 outright. Some of them may have found their way into other military units, but Olney's company as such ceased to exist eight months before the war itself did.

Now, let's skip ahead to September 1950. The commander of the Grand Army of the Republic, Theodore A. Penland of Portland, has just died. The state of Oregon grieves the loss of what it thinks is its last surviving veteran of the American Civil War.

Penland was the kind of veteran that makes a state proud. As a lad of 16, in Illinois, he desperately wanted to join the Army and fight, but he wasn't the kind of kid who can tell a lie and feel OK about it, so he was turned away twice when they asked him his age. Finally he actually wrote the number "18" on two pieces of paper and stuck one into each boot, so

The grave marker of James W. Smith, Oregon's last surviving Civil War veteran, as it appears today in Lebanon's IOOF cemetery. (Photo: Randol B. Fletcher)

that he could tell the recruiter that he was "over 18 now." And that did the trick.

After the war, Penland moved out West and joined the Grand Army of the Republic, the exclusive Civil War veterans' association. In the GAR, Penland distinguished himself as he'd never been able to in the actual Army. By the time he moved to Portland, in his 70s, he was already high in the organization's rankings, a sought-after public speaker and radio personality who loved to talk about his experiences in the war and the time he saw President Abraham Lincoln.

In 1949, at the very last annual GAR meeting, the surviving members of the GAR voted Penland Commander in Chief, a title he held until he died. So Theodore Penland of Portland was the last Commander in Chief of the Grand Army of the Republic.

When he died, the state of Oregon grieved, thinking it had lost its last Civil War veteran. But some time later, somehow it came to the state's attention that it had missed one.

That's right — Oregon's last surviving Civil War vet was not the heroically active and patriotic Penland, but — not to beat around the bush too much — one of Olney's Forty Thieves.

That would be James W. Smith.

After being booted out of the Army with his comrades/co-conspirators, Smith had settled in Lebanon and lived a quiet, law-abiding life. He never applied for a pension; he apparently never even contacted the GAR. Perhaps he was embarrassed by the wildness of his youth. Or perhaps he thought he might have warrants. Who knows?

Smith died at the age of 108, six months later than Penland. And it took a while for Oregon to figure out its mistake. But on June 23, 2010, the Sons of Union Veterans officially rectified it when they gathered around his modest grave in the Odd Fellows cemetery in Lebanon and, in a graveside service including a musket salute, affixed a brass plaque to the stone identifying him as Oregon's last Civil War vet.

It's hard not to notice what a great metaphor Smith was for his home state of Oregon — wild and more than a little notorious in its youth, grown mature and mellow with age, but still with that old rascally twinkle in its eye.

Sources and Works Cited:
- Hidden History of Civil War Oregon, *a book by Randol B. Fletcher, published in 2010 by The History Press;*
- Lebanon Express *archives, July 2010.*

CAPT. JAMES "JEMMY" JONES:

D.I.Y. NAVAL ARCHITECT.

There was no reason why the U.S. Marshal should spend the night on board the *Jenny Jones*, the cramped, smelly little freight schooner he was in charge of. After all, the ship was anchored in a semi-civilized town — Steilacoom, near Tacoma in the Washington territory — and there were several decent hotels there. The next day he'd have a few hours' cruise to Seattle, where the ship would be sold to pay the debts of its owner, Captain James "Jemmy" Jones.

(Got that? "Jenny Jones" was the ship; "Jemmy Jones" was its skipper. Confusing, yes? Jemmy named it after his wife, of course. But, back to our story:)

It seemed that the previous year, when his ship was aground on the deadly Columbia River bar, Captain Jones had thrown a bunch of freight overboard to lighten the ship and float it free of the sand. The freight's owners in Portland had been able to convince a judge that it was through Jones's recklessness in choosing to cross the bar without a pilot that this had to be done. This was probably a miscarriage of justice — the reason there was no pilot available was because conditions in the open sea beyond the

Unknown artist's rendering of Steilacoom's waterfront in 1858. Picture is from the collection of Mrs. Clyde V. Davidson, Steilacoom resident. The steamboat is the Enterprise, which traded between Olympia and Steilacoom. (Image: Tacoma Public Library)

bar were too dangerous to send one out. In any case, Jones had shown no sign of complying with the judge's order to pay up, and now the government had seized his ship.

It had been easy to seize, too. Jones had gotten himself into some trouble in Canada just before the marshal moved in. At that very moment, he was languishing in a jail cell up in the town of Victoria, far off to the north. By the time he made bail, his ship would be history and his debts would be paid — at least, that's what the marshal thought as he checked into his hotel room for the night.

What he didn't know was that Captain Jemmy Jones, one of the most colorful skippers in West Coast maritime history and one of the most resourceful as well, had escaped. With the help of some friends, he'd tarted himself up in a dress and bonnet, strutted unnoticed past the guards, and then actually paddled across the Strait of Juan de Fuca in a canoe — across 11 miles of open sea, in February! — to get back home to the U.S.

That's when he'd learned that his ship had been seized by the U.S. Marshal's office.

Time to give up? Not for Jemmy Jones. The intrepid (or maybe just plain crazy) captain had headed down to Olympia, found his repossessed ship — and, finding that the marshal was making a little extra money by selling tickets, booked passage on it as a passenger.

So, unbeknownst to the officer, Jemmy had been on board the whole time.

It's tempting to picture Jemmy that night, with a hat pulled low over his forehead to hide his face, furtively watching and smiling as the marshal stepped ashore and walked out of sight.

The marshal left the ship in the charge of his assistant. And when, early the next morning, the assistant went ashore to talk to his boss about something at the hotel, leaving the ship wholly unsupervised, Jemmy saw his chance. After getting reacquainted with the schooner's crew, the wily skipper got right to work implementing Phase 2 of one of his most audacious plans ever: The theft of his own ship, from right under the nose of the law.

Welshman James "Jemmy" Jones had come to the West Coast in 1849 for the California Gold Rush. He'd been lucky in the fields, and soon had a grubstake together big enough to outfit himself with a freight ship and go into business as a skipper.

As a sea-captain, Jemmy turned out to be a marvel — in a "19th-century Han Solo" kind of way. Historian James McCurdy calls him "a veritable stormy petrel, always in some trouble or another on the high seas." Five of his ships sank or broke up beneath his feet. His third shipwreck earned him a place in the geography books when he crashed his schooner into a small island right in the harbor at Victoria — the island that today is known as Jemmy Jones Island. The incident on the Columbia bar, had it gone the way such groundings usually did, would have been a shipwreck as well — and, given the survival rates for ships broken up on the bar, probably his last.

That incident on the bar may have been Jemmy's inspiration for the innovation that would put him in the history books as well as the geography ones. Crossing the bar in a sailing ship was, and still is, a very dangerous endeavor; the area is peppered with wind shadows in which a sailing ship can suddenly find itself drifting becalmed at the mercy of the currents, which run right across sandbars too shallow for a ship. Sidewheel steamers had a much easier time staying in the channel, but their big paddlewheels got in the way and made all but the simplest sailing moves impracticable. But a new kind of propulsion system had just recently been invented — the screw propeller — that solved that problem. So, why not put a steam engine in his sailing ship?

And so it was that, in 1864, the *Jenny Jones* became the first ship of the type that would become known as a "steam schooner," a trim wooden sailing schooner with a modest steam engine below decks. Jemmy had invented probably the most important type of ship in the history of the West Coast. You'll sometimes hear the invention of the steam schooner credited to a less disreputable innovator who did the same thing to a lumber schooner in San Francisco 15 years later, but that's simply incorrect. Jemmy did it first.

(Actually, Jemmy himself may not have been the first to do this. Historian Gene Barron, an expert on the West Coast steam schooner fleet, says there were a number of steam-powered fishing schooners in British Columbian waters around the same time. This could explain where Jemmy got the idea for his ship, but it also casts some doubt on the claim that Jemmy's was first. As with so many things from the 1860s, we'll probably never know.)

With his innovative new power setup, Jemmy started making profitable runs from Portland to Victoria late in 1864.

But apparently he wasn't making the money fast enough to pay his Portland creditors. They'd called upon the law to help them collect, and as a result, if Jemmy Jones wanted his schooner back, he was going to have to steal it.

In Steillacoom that day, Jemmy got busy doing exactly that.

Having a steam engine on board made Jones' escape that much easier. They must have been building steam already for the day's journey to Seattle — or perhaps the crew had been secretly getting ready all along. In any event, as soon as the long arm of the law headed off to breakfast, the *Jenny Jones* headed off to the open sea.

The reaction of the lawmen when they saw the empty slip where they'd left their 95-foot, several-hundred-ton charge is lost to history. Perhaps it's just as well.

Meanwhile, Jones and his crew were out at sea with very little fuel in the bunkers and not much food in the cupboards, and they were now wanted men in both the U.S. and Canada. Jones managed to get the ship to Port Ludlow, where they loaded a couple cords of firewood on board and cast off again quick. This load was enough to get the ship to Nanaimo, which Jemmy apparently hoped would be remote enough to not yet know him as an outlaw.

No such luck. Although they didn't try to arrest him at Nanaimo, neither would they sell him coal. So instead, he hired some Native Americans to help him load about 12 tons of coal dust from a nearby abandoned coal dump. Another stop in a third port brought a big load of cordwood to mix with the coal dust, and the Jenny Jones was ready for the open sea — and Mexico, the only country in North America that didn't have a warrant out for his arrest.

Along the way, the outlaw mariners encountered a waterlogged sloop, the *Deerfoot*, whose exhausted crew of three had been laboring mightily trying to keep her afloat and were steadily losing the battle. The crew begged to be taken off, and Jones was happy to oblige; they also took off the sloop's cargo of food provisions. With that, the crew of the little steam schooner had everything they needed for their journey.

Under sail and steam both, the Jenny Jones headed south, arriving in Mexico 25 days later. There, Jones started running freight again, but after some labor-related drama involving the rescued crew of the *Deerfoot*, in which someone stole the rudder off his ship, Jones gave it up in disgust, sold the *Jenny Jones* for the princely sum of $10,000 and headed for home.

When the ship Jemmy was on got to San Francisco, he stepped boldly and casually onto the shore, as if he had nothing to hide and nothing to worry about. The records are silent on this, but one imagines him as unworried, confident, a little cocky — like James Garner's character in "The Rockford Files."

Of course, he was arrested almost immediately when the authorities realized he was in town, and promptly hailed into court.

In court, Jemmy's defense was that he had not actually escaped from the marshal — rather, the marshal had abandoned his charge and he, finding it unattended there in the harbor, had simply recovered his property. The judge agreed, the case was dismissed, and Jones' creditors had to sue the marshal for their $4,600. (I haven't been able to learn if they got it or not.)

Jones was also arrested and tried on criminal charges in Steilacoom, but acquitted there as well.

The *Jenny Jones* disappeared into obscurity in Mexico. Perhaps she was simply too ahead of her time; another steam schooner would not be built until roughly 1880, at which time the type would revolutionize West Coast transportation.

As for Captain Jemmy, he moved back to British Columbia and, for years, skippered a small schooner — not a steamer this time — called *Industry*, aboard which he almost died in a fifth and final shipwreck in 1878.

He died a few years later, in his early 50s, after having become mentally unhinged. It must be said that in Jemmy's day, most often when men in late middle age went crazy and died, syphilis was the cause — Christopher Columbus being the most well-known example. I have not been able to determine if that was the case with Jemmy Jones, or if something else — head trauma, for example, or perhaps alcoholism — caused his demise.

But most people will agree that the world was a less colorful place after he left it.

Sources and Works Cited:
- *British Columbia Coast Names, a book by John T. Walbran, published in 1909 by Government Publishing of Ottawa;*
- *Lewis & Dryden's Marine History of the Pacific Northwest, a book by E.W. Wright, published in 1895 by Lewis & Dryden;*
- *Pacific Lumber Ships, a book by Gordon Newell, published in 1960 by Superior Publishing of Seattle;*
- *By Juan de Fuca's Strait, a book by James G. McCurdy, published in 1937 by Binford and Mort of Portland.*

WILLIAM JOHNSON:

PIONEER MOONSHINER.

Most people know Prohibition in the United States started in 1920 when the Volstead Act went into effect. But in Oregon, Prohibition started quite a bit earlier than that. Actually, it started before Oregon was even a state.

In 1844, the Oregon Territorial Government became the first in the United States to outlaw the use, manufacture or sale of "ardent spirits."

The full story of Oregon Territory's first experiment with Prohibition will probably never be known; not a lot of written history has come down to us from early 1840s Oregon, and what we have is often contradictory. But from a distance, it looks an awful lot like the whole thing was inspired, if that's the right word, by the commercial activities of one man — a fellow named William Johnson — and his product, a rough-and-ready distilled beverage marketed under a picturesque and, sources agree, accurate name: "Blue Ruin."

The introduction of Johnson's Blue Ruin to the Willamette Valley frontier community was followed almost immediately by America's first

FIRST HOUSE IN PORTLAND.—ERECTED IN 1844 AT FRONT AND WASHINGTON STS.

An engraving by Grafton T. Brown showing the first cabin in what would become the city of Portland — a cabin occupied by William Johnson, the Oregon Territory's original moonshiner and maker of the legendary "Blue Ruin." The location given in the picture is wrong, however; Johnson's cabin was actually in the area of Macadam Avenue and Curry Street. (Image: J. Gaston)

prohibition law — the preamble to which gives a few hints as to why lawmakers felt it was necessary:

"WHEREAS the people of Oregon now occupy one of the most beautiful and interesting portions of the globe," they wrote turgidly, "and are placed in the most critical and responsible position ever filled by men, having as they do important duties to themselves, to their century, to posterity and to mankind, as the founders of a new government and a young nation; and WHEREAS the introduction, distillation, or sale of ardent spirits, under the circumstances in which we are placed, would bring withering ruin upon the prosperity and prospects of this interesting and rising community, by involving us in idle and dissolute habits, inviting hither swarms of the dissipated inhabitants of other countries, cluttering emigration, destroying the industry of the country, bringing upon us the swarms of savages now in our midst, interrupting the orderly and peaceable administration of justice, and in a word producing and perpetrating increasing and untoward miseries that no mind can rightly estimate; THEREFORE be it enacted by the Legislative Committee of Oregon as follows...."

Fair enough. And yet the members of the Legislative Committee of Oregon were frontier men — they liked a little nip now and then. Why would they pass a law that most of them would subsequently be violating on a regular basis?

The answer lies coyly camouflaged among the references to "industry" and "prosperity." It's the part about "bringing upon us the swarms of savages now in our midst."

Which gets us right back to Mr. Johnson.

Mr. William Johnson, it seems, had settled in a little clearing by the river a dozen or so miles downstream from Willamette Falls in around 1842. Different sources give different accounts of Johnson: one says he was a deserter from a British man-of-war who'd settled there, hiding out from the Brits; others say he was a 50-year-old family man living in Champoeg in the late 1830s with a successful farm who, for some reason, abandoned his land claim and moved 50 miles down the river to stake out a new one. The explanation may be that there were two William Johnsons in the valley at the time — Farmer Johnson and Bootlegger Johnson. Or perhaps he did something to get tossed out of the Champoeg community; we just don't know.

In any case, Bootlegger Johnson very quickly figured out that an ambitious distiller could sell

The original text of America's first prohibition law. (Image: State of Oregon)

An 1800s painting showing Hudson's Bay Co. employees trading with Native Americans. (Image: Hudson's Bay Co./ Fulton Archive)

every drop of liquor he could squeeze out of whatever horrific precursor sugars could be had: table scraps, molasses, rotten tomatoes, floor sweepings from the nearest flour mill — whatever.

The bluish-clear substance that oozed out of his still was like a raw, searing mixture of unaged grappa, white whiskey and Everclear. It's also a good bet that, being keen to save resources, Johnson didn't bother to discard the "heads" (the first ounce or two that comes out of the still with each batch, which contains all the toxic hangover-inducing wood alcohols and other nasty chemicals).

But it was cheap, there was plenty of it, and it was good enough for Johnson's primary customers: The Native Americans.

Now, many of the leaders of Oregon's provisional government were former Hudson's Bay Company employees. They knew, from firsthand experience, that letting Native Americans buy as much whiskey as they wanted was a recipe for trouble. For whatever reason, be it cultural or genetic, the Pacific Northwest natives had virtually no ability to resist liquor, and would drink just as much of it as they could get, as fast as they could. It would transform them from peaceful, happy people into raging, brawling rioters. The best-case scenario was a sharp drop in their production of otter pelts; the worst-case scenario was bloodshed and property destruction.

So the old Hudson's Bay men were careful to prevent whiskey from falling into Native American hands. Yet those Native American hands were unusually eager to get the stuff. The laws of supply and demand being what they are, the arrival of Johnson — or someone like him — was inevitable.

Once Johnson's commercial enterprises came to the attention of U.S. Indian Agent Elijah White, the official journeyed to Johnson's place and destroyed his still. And it was around that same time that the provisional government convened and outlawed his trade.

Johnson's reaction to this seems to have been to find a better hiding place for his rebuilt still. He may also have raised his prices. He certainly didn't quit making deliveries.

Any questions about whether "Blue Ruin" was a genuine public menace are answered rather nicely in the memoirs of one of Johnson's erstwhile partners — a rough-and-ready French-Canadian gambler and all-around rascal named Edouard Chambreau (about whom, we'll have much more to say in the next chapter).

Here's how Chambreau remembers his first liquor run with Johnson:

"The next morning the skiff was made ready with a 20-gallon keg of Blue Ruin. This was hid under the things in the bottom of the boat. ... There were quite a number of Indians camped here, and they were anxious to 'swap for lumm' (the word for whiskey)....

"We made them sit down in rows with their different things they had to put their Lumm in, and whatever they had to pay for it. They were all on the beach about ten steps from the skiff.... We went to every one before we began to pour it out in their vessels, and agreed on what should be given for this and that measure full. Having done this, Johnson began to pour out and I carried the things to the boat. The principle things we got in exchange was Beaver and Otter skins, and Hudson's Bay blankets.

"An Indian, when he drinks whisky, he will drink as long as he can hold his breath. By the time [Johnson] was getting through with the last ones, the first ones were getting very funny. He shouted to me to run for the boat. I ran to the boat and shoved it until I was knee deep in the water. As he had the whisky, some of them followed him to the boat. He was retreating backwards with his keg under his arm and his long knife in the other (hand). In the meantime, I covered him with my rifle. Before it takes time to tell it, he threw the keg with what remained in it as far as he could toward the camp. This gave him a chance to get away from those who were immediately near him, and he got into the boat.

"We were almost in swimming water, with three Indians hanging yet to the boat. We knocked them over the head and shoved off just in the nick of time, because we had no more than had them loose from the boat than there was a gang of about 30 that came running and yelling with all their might. Then the fighting was among themselves.

"On this trip we made very near $500 apiece," Chambreau concludes.

"The reader can draw his own conclusions of what must have been the scene in that Indian camp with 20 gallons of that abominable stuff in them."

William Johnson died the following year. I haven't been able to find a source that will give a cause of death, but a couple of them hint that it happened during one of these deliveries … a fate that seems grimly appropriate, like poetic justice.

In any case, Oregon's prohibition law was repealed the year after Johnson died, and after that the booze flowed pretty freely, right up until the 1910s.

The still Johnson was running when Chambreau helped him make that 1847 delivery was tucked away in a gulley about four miles downstream from Oregon City, a setting much more in keeping with the spirit of an illicit moonshine still. But it's worth noting the location of the first one he set up — the one White destroyed when he learned the Native Americans were getting supplied by it. Most likely it was conveniently located by his cabin — in the area of what's now Macadam Avenue near the Ross Island Bridge, right in the middle of Portland. Johnson's was the first house in Portland … and, it seems, the first business.

Sources and Works Cited:
- Edward Chambreau: His Autobiography, *a Ph.D. dissertation by Timothy Wehrkamp, published in 1976 by University of Oregon;*
- Oregon: End of the Trail, *a book by the Federal Writers Project, published in 1940 by Metropolitan Press of Portland;*
- *Oregon provisional government charter, Oregon State Archives, arcweb.sos.state.or.us.*

EDOUARD CHAMBREAU:

GAMBLER AND SALOONKEEPER.

In its early years, Oregon was at the outer limits of the known world, and that remoteness attracted all sorts of interesting characters. There were Joe Meek types, driven by a spirit of adventure; there were guys like William Ladd, who came hoping to get in on the ground floor and become the next generation of business barons; and, of course, there were the Marcus Whitmans and Jason Lees, the state's spiritual forefathers, come into the wilderness to save souls.

But there was another kind of frontier Oregon character, too, to whom the remoteness of Oregon appealed: The criminal, looking to run away to a place where people's memories are short and hideouts are plentiful and laws are new and weak.

History has recorded plenty about the successful, hardworking folks who would, a few decades later, become Oregon's gentry. But history was mostly written by members of that gentry, people who wanted to cast Oregon in a positive, glorious light. The last thing they wanted to write about was what was going on in seedy saloons in places like Portland's North End

"Whitechapel" district, or the brothels and "cribs" of the Second Street "Court of Death."

Which is why the writings and recollections of Edouard Chambreau — pioneer bootlegger William Johnson's assistant, who wrote the account of the liquor delivery quoted from in the last chapter — are so valuable.

A portrait of Edouard Chambreau as a young man, based on a very early photograph that appears in Wehrkamp's dissertation. (Image: Leland John)

Chambreau, in middle age, wrote a long and heartfelt memoir as a sort of confessional — hoping by his example to turn future young men away from the path he had trodden for the previous 40 years. In his youth, he had been an itinerant swindler, gambler, gunfighter and, of course liquor peddler — one of the most scurrilous rascals in all the Oregon territory. Then, in his later years, he became one of its most earnest and effective reformers.

It was, one has to admit, an interesting story. And it sheds much light on the seedy underbelly of the frontier communities of the Oregon Country.

Chambreau was born in France in 1821, and moved with his family to Montreal in 1825. His parents had hoped he'd become a tailor, but he hated the work, and in 1838, at age 17, he ran away to join the circus.

He spent the following decade or so in circuses and blackface-minstrel troupes, and it was there that he learned the skills that he'd bring to bear so effectively on the Oregon frontier: fighting to win, cheating at cards and dice, and making money the old-fashioned way — by swindling people out of it.

He spent a little time in the Army of the West, fighting in the Mexican-American War, and it's that enterprise that brought him to Oregon for the first time, in 1847.

The Oregon Territory would never be the same.

Almost immediately upon arriving, Chambreau connected with William Johnson, the Oregon country's first bootlegger, whom we talked about in the last chapter.

As you can imagine, the British at Hudson's Bay Company soon identified this young French-Canadian barbarian as a threat, and a few months into 1848 they tracked him down and arrested him. So when the word of the discovery of gold in California reached the Oregon territory, Chambreau was in a Hudson's Bay Company prison in Fort Vancouver.

He immediately knew he had to go. So with the help of some friends, he broke out and fled southward to the gold fields.

But Chambreau had no intention of actually looking for gold — at least, not directly. Although he got in very nearly on the ground floor in the gold fields, it seems never to have occurred to him to try his luck as a miner. No, Chambreau's plan was to let the miners get the gold, and then swindle them out of it.

In San Francisco, Chambreau settled in with a pack of his friends from the old Army of the West — including James Lappeus, who would become the first Portland Chief of Police twenty years later (and whom we will talk a lot more about in the next chapter). The group of them formed themselves into a nativist gang that called itself "The San Francisco Society of Regulators," but quickly became known simply as "The Hounds."

The Hounds were at first kind of popular with the San Francisco community, much of which sympathized with their anti-Mexican racism; but their welcome wore out rather quickly. By early 1849 they were running an actual city-wide protection racket.

Then one night, Chambreau and fellow Hound Jim Beatty got into a shootout with a group of Mexican miners. When the smoke had cleared, Beatty was dead.

The Hounds decided some retribution was in order.

So a few nights later, their faces masked or blacked out with burned cork, the Hounds descended on the Mexican and Chilean mining camps for an out-and-out massacre. Miners were shot as they stumbled out of their tents, and then the tents were torn down and set afire. Chambreau does not say whether he participated in this atrocity, but he almost certainly did, since he was with Beatty when he was killed.

For a frontier town that had been suffering increasingly egregious acts of thuggishness from the Hounds for some time, this act of mass murder was too much.

The next day, "San Francisco had put on a different look," Chambreau wrote. "People could be seen in different places whispering together, and sizing up all those who were suspicioned of having taken part in the massacre."

And the day after that, with stunning speed, the group that would later become Sam Brannan's vigilance committee formed, about 400 strong and armed to the teeth, and fanned out over the city looking for Hounds. Their official goal was to arrest the Hounds, not to lynch them; but every Hound knew mob action was a real possibility.

Chambreau got out, but only just barely. He disguised himself as a hobo and stowed away on a schooner, whose first mate he bribed to help him get out.

The schooner took him to Stockton, where he again very nearly got lynched after being caught harboring a robbery suspect.

After that, he quickly headed into the gold fields, where law enforcement was sketchier and less organized and where gold by the ton was being hauled out of the ground by suckers, ripe for the plucking. Dressed like a miner to allay suspicion, the sharp-dealing gambler drifted from town to town, fleecing the real miners and then shooting, punching or knifing his way out of any trouble that resulted.

Around 1850 Chambreau dropped in to visit old friend Lappeus, who'd also made it out of San Francisco with his pelt unspoiled. Lappeus was running a saloon and general store called Ten Mile House, just north of Sacramento. Chambreau arrived just in time to help Lappeus deal with a large, angry cohort of drunken teamsters. He doesn't say, but the most likely explanation for this is that the teamsters had caught Lappeus cheating them; he and Chambreau were both masters of the art of swindling people at the card table or faro bank.

The two ex-Hounds drove the teamsters out of the building by throwing whiskey bottles at them.

"Some of them, after they got outside, they began to shoot," Chambreau writes. "In an instant we both had our six-shooters out, and you think it was not lively there for a little while? After we had driven them away from near the store, we retreated and barricaded ourselves inside and made ready for an attack, but they did not want any more of it. We were both hurt but nothing serious."

After this, Chambreau teamed up with another gambler and headed out to the mining towns again — "We had something new on the game of Monte, and before it would be exposed, we thought we would take a trip in the small mining towns," he wrote — and had a few more experiences of shooting and pistol-whipping his way out of the clutches of angry suckers before finally giving up and heading back toward Oregon.

By 1853, Chambreau was back in Portland, and was courting a local woman, a nice, respectable girl named Barbara Ann McBee, who was understandably terrified by his sinister reputation, but who also seemed to see something in him. She would be the cause of the big change in his life — but that change wouldn't happen for a full twenty years, and those would be eventful years indeed.

A cartoon by Thomas Nast from Harper's Weekly, published in March of 1874 at the height of the anti-saloon temperance movement. (Image: Library of Congress)

He did give a try at making some changes now, though. And when Chambreau popped the question, Barbara said yes — and so he soon had a young wife, and later a baby on the way. It was hard to imagine life as a hard-punching roving gambler, drifting from mining camp to mining camp with one hand on your poke and the other on your pistol, with a wife and baby in tow. It was time to settle down ... or at least, try to.

So Chambreau set up shop by the St. Charles Hotel on Front and Morrison, and hung out his shingle. He was now a saloonkeeper — not exactly the height of respectability, but a great improvement on his previous profession of itinerant gold-country scallywag.

Not that much was going to change as far as Chambreau's moneymaking

A cartoon drawn by John Chapin from Leslie's Illustrated Newspaper in February 1878, showing a group of temperance workers holding a prayer service outside a saloon, whose proprietor apparently had refused to let them in. (Image: John Chapin/Leslie's, Library of Congress)

techniques were concerned. "It (the saloon) was fitted up fine," Chambreau wrote, "having private gambling rooms attached to it."

But a few months later, Chambreau heard that a hotelier named Owen had made some very disparaging remarks about him to Barbara Ann, all but urging her to leave him. Furious, he waylaid the unfortunate fellow and proceeded to vigorously "cowhide" him, as he puts it — initiating a feud with Owen and his friends that more or less forced him to close down his saloon and leave town. He traveled to Vancouver, signed on with Ulysses S. Grant, and traveled up the Columbia River Gorge with the United States Army.

Chambreau's career in uniform was surprisingly successful, although it got off to rather a rocky start. A few months into it, he found out that the soldiers he was serving with wouldn't be paid for their service until they got back to Vancouver. That meant they were all flat-stony broke, and he wouldn't be able to swindle them out of any of their pay along the way — as he had anticipated being able to do. But he stuck it out, resisting the temptation to become a deserter, until his tour of duty was done.

Upon his return, Barbara Ann tried her best. She prevailed upon

Chambreau to become a farmer, but this lasted only a little while; he soon sold the farm and moved his family back to Vancouver. There, he served in the Army some more (where his command of Native dialects and his French heritage made him particularly useful) and eventually opened yet another saloon and gambling den. But Chambreau's time in Vancouver was wild and unruly, peppered with card games and the occasional gunfight.

"I had a good and loving wife, and she did what she could to keep me home, but it was of no use," he later wrote. "After I would be home a while, I would get a kind of a fever, and off I would go again."

It was like a pioneer version of an old Jerry Jeff Walker song — she was "losing him to that rodeo wind," as it were. And it happened again and again.

Eventually, again, the town just got too hot for him, and the Chambreau family — including, now, several children — moved to the Tygh Valley, near The Dalles, where Chambreau opened a trading post.

It was in the Tygh Valley that Chambreau's wild and rascally ways started to fade just a little, allowing glimpses of the kind of integrity for which he would be known later in his life. His business was an enormous success. His relations with the Native Americans — characterized by a then-rare degree of mutual respect — gave him a big advantage over any competitors as well. He quickly earned the respect and (mostly) admiration of the entire tiny Tygh Valley community, of both races.

Liquor was a part of his business in Tygh Valley, to Barbara's growing dismay — but only a part. Mostly, Chambreau was a storekeeper. A few years later, he was elected Justice of the Peace. Respectability loomed. It looked as though Barbara Ann's prayers were finally being answered.

Then came 1861, and some idiot struck gold at China Creek, and that rodeo wind started blowing again.

"My excuse was to go and make money, but really it was the excitement that I wanted," Chambreau wrote. "I have regretted this trip all my life."

He soon was once again running a gold-field gambling house amid a veritable swarm of frontier gold-field hooligans, all of them busy drinking and shooting and swindling each other as the real miners tried to hang onto their wallets and stay out of the way.

"It was almost the days of '49 all over again," Chambreau wrote.

For almost two full years Chambreau thrived in this petri dish of iniquity, giving as good as he got.

Then one day he had a terrible dream — a dream of his six-year-old daughter's death. It brought him back home to the Tygh Valley on the gallop, and upon his arrival, he found it to be true.

Moreover, while he'd been gone, the trading post had gone to ruin; the people hired to run it had stolen stock; the facilities had deteriorated.

Chambreau had taken a thousand-dollar bath in the "fire sale" of his saloon in the gold country, and couldn't afford to set it all straight. So he moved into The Dalles … and opened another saloon and gambling house.

He ran this for two more years, then moved to Portland.

In Portland, Chambreau, although almost flat broke, gathered together a small stake and went into the restaurant business. But if he was hoping that selling meals would be a quieter way to make a living than selling booze, he was disappointed.

"Here in this business I had as much trouble and as much fighting as I had in the saloon," he said. "Every old bum would come in, set down, eat all he could, and when he was through, he would say that he had no money to pay for it."

This cost Chambreau a lot of money — but not for the reason you might expect. It wasn't the cost of the food; it was the legal costs associated with thrashing the deadbeats, something it doesn't seem to have occurred to him to stop doing.

"I had already paid three fines for 'firing' men out because they would not pay for what they eat, until one day a tight one by the name of Buckskin Bill came in, called for a good meal, and when he got done eating, he said he would pay me another time," Chambreau wrote. "Well, I used this man up so bad he had to be taken off the sidewalk in a cart. The fine was $90."

Perhaps this was because the restaurant was in such a bad part of town. It was right next to a "free and easy dance house" and gambling hall in the North End — a joint he referred to as a "hell-hole."

Eventually, Chambreau gave up on the restaurant and went into partnership with the owners of the hell-hole.

Chambreau's autobiography is a little bit cagey and oblique in describing this gambling-dancing joint, which suggests it was probably more than just a gambling house.

"This was one of those places where 'everything went,'" he wrote. "This place was open for everything that talked, from the highest to the lowest of both sexes. Any one could be accommodated with fun, amusements and games of all kinds with cards or other devices."

It's hard to say for sure if Chambreau meant this to imply that his new saloon was also a bordello. Other than Chambreau's memoirs, documentation of this "hell-hole" is very scant. But the way he writes about it, and about his new partners — a man he identifies as "Sam R." and a woman whom he never names at all — suggests this might be the case.

In any case, Chambreau makes it quite clear that there were "girls" working there, and that their job was to fleece the suckers in some way — if not in bed, then certainly at the card tables or on the stage.

Chambreau wasn't long running this particular joint. Most likely, Barbara Ann put some pressure on him to get out of the "girls" business. He spent a little time as a freelance gambler, opened a sort of liquor-and-pawn shop, lost it in the great Portland fire of 1873, and then opened a new place, on Second Street near Pine, in the middle of the North End. Here, Barbara Ann didn't have to worry about him employing prostitutes — there would have been too much competition. "The saloons that were kept on each side of me were kept by 'bad women,'" he writes.

A flyer from the 1874 temperance crusade, meant to encourage temperance workers to persevere through the initial hostility of barkeeps like Edouard Chambreau. In his case, the prescription seems to have worked. (Image: Library of Congress)

Alas, Chambreau wouldn't get to keep this place too much longer. A few months later, it also burned. Chambreau, trying to hustle his valuables out of the upstairs, had a good view of about 50 loggers and sailors and unscrupulous neighbors who'd come running, eager to "rescue" some of the bottles and kegs in the bar.

A couple months later, despite his wife's tearful pleas, Chambreau was back in business at yet another saloon — this one a tonier place, on the corner of First and Washington, in the respectable end of town.

He was operating this establishment in March of 1874 when a group of ladies in their Sunday best stepped into his saloon.

This was unusual. In 1874, women might be seen in a saloon if they worked there, but ladies? Never.

But these ladies told him they were temperance crusaders, and they wanted to know if it would be OK for them to hold a prayer-and-hymn-singing service there, while he was serving his customers. (We'll have lots more to say about this particular group of ladies in the next two chapters, by the way.)

Chambreau said no. And the next time they came, he said no again. And again. And again.

But they kept coming. And finally, one day, he let them in.

The crusaders finished up their services, handed out fistfuls of temperance tracts and left. When the saloon closed that night, Chambreau was left with a pile of them, thinking about things.

The next night, Chambreau handed over the keys to his partner and quit the liquor-and-gambling business for good.

Sources and Works Cited:
- Edward Chambreau: His Autobiography, *a Ph.D. dissertation by Timothy Wehrkamp, published in 1976 by the University of Oregon;*
- Merchants, Money and Power, *a book by E. Kimbark MacColl, published in 1988 by Georgian Press of Portland.*

JAMES LAPPEUS:

GAMBLER, SALOONKEEPER, AND CHIEF OF POLICE.

"Any desperado who had the necessary abilities could always get himself elected city marshal," wrote Edouard Chambreau in his autobiography, sometime in the 1870s.

Chambreau would have known. At the very time he was committing the story of his life to writing, one of his old friends from the Gold Rush days was sitting at a desk downtown in the city offices — an old friend and onetime business partner named James Lappeus, Portland Chief of Police.

James Lappeus was, most sources agree, Portland's first police chief. And all sources I've found agree the position was — well, perhaps the most charitable way to put it is "ironic." For most of the time he was in office, Lappeus owned a combination saloon, variety theater and gambling house called the Oro Fino — this in an era when essentially all gambling houses were crooked, and a variety theater was often a front for prostitution. He was eventually canned over fairly credible allegations that he'd offered to let a convicted murderer escape from the city jail if his family could come up with a $1,000 bribe.

James Lappeus came to the West Coast in 1848 with a detachment of U.S. Army soldiers to fight in the Mexican-American War, and decided to stay. Luck had placed him at the epicenter of one of history's most fabulous wealth booms — the California Gold Rush.

Like Chambreau, had he staked a claim and started working the ground, there's a good chance he would have made good money. But, also like Chambreau, he went into a different business instead, joining the cadre of steely-eyed characters that preferred to let others mine the gold, and then take it from them afterward in rigged games of chance or celebratory drunken benders. Like Chambreau, he became, essentially, a crooked gold-field gambler — in the parlance of the day, a "blackleg."

Essentially, the term "gambler" was, in the Gold Rush days, synonymous with "crook." At that time, there was no regulation or governmental oversight, and honest men simply couldn't compete. In fact, the most popular frontier gambling game by far was Faro — a game that, today, is simply no longer played. That's because a gambler can't make money playing faro unless he cheats. The "house edge" is razor-thin, and the game depends so much on chance that skill, honestly applied, isn't very helpful.

Gamblers today solve these problems by not playing Faro. Gamblers back then couldn't do that, because it was what people wanted to play, so

The Oro Fino Saloon and Theater as they appeared in 1876. The Gem was also a saloon. These buildings were located on First Street between Oak and Stark. (Image: Oregon Historical Society)

they solved it by cheating. And if they didn't cheat, they quickly went broke.

By the turn of the century, cheating at Faro was so widespread that the Hoyle's rule book actually included the startling warning that *all* Faro games were crooked — period.

Well, all gambling establishments offered Faro games — at least, in 1850s Portland they did. So when, a year or two later, Lappeus came to Portland and built the Oro Fino Saloon and Hall, featuring specially built rooms for Faro banks to operate in, there couldn't have been too much doubt over which side of the law he belonged on.

A portrait of James Lappeus painted from a photograph made around the time he first became Portland's police chief. (Image: Leland John)

But then, in 1859, the old blackleg Hound started a law enforcement career. He was hired as city marshal.

Almost immediately, Lappeus got himself into trouble. When he got the job, there was a famous fugitive loose in the area: Danford Balch, a homesteader who had reacted to news of his stepdaughter's elopement by taking a shotgun and emptying both barrels into his new son-in-law. When Lappeus took the job, Balch had just escaped from the city jail, where he'd been held awaiting his murder trial.

Lappeus tracked Balch down and brought him back, and he was promptly tried, convicted and sentenced to hang. Then, after the trial, Lappeus apparently made the soon-to-be widow a proposition: "Cross my palm with $1,000 and I'll accidentally leave the jailhouse door unlocked one of these nights."

This offer can't be proven to have been made, but the widow's

HEROES and RASCALS of OLD OREGON.

A satirical cartoon that appeared in The West Shore magazine in the late 1800s. Moving clockwise from left to right around the "blind" policeman, we have gamblers playing Faro; a man being mugged while others look on insouciantly; an illegal Chinese gambling house; a speeding buggy driver running over a little girl; a drunk vomiting in the gutter; and a prostitute soliciting business at her "crib" window. (Image: UO Libraries)

subsequent fund-raising frenzy can, and a number of citizens swore out affadavits accusing Lappeus of making this offer. But ultimately, it fell short of its goal, and Balch was hanged in the first public execution in Portland history.

In spite of the rumors of this attempt, when the Oregon Legislature seized control of Portland police matters in 1870 to prevent a political rival from gaining control, it picked Lappeus as police chief. Most sources say he was the first chief; the police department's official history disagrees, saying the man who designed the department, Joseph Saunders, was chief for two weeks before the state seized power. This may be true, and it's easy to see why PPD wants to think so. Saunders was a good cop and had earned the right to be the city's first chief; Lappeus, on the other hand, was not, and certainly had not.

In power as chief, Lappeus was able to make some extra money by taking care of his friends. Chambreau wrote about how he'd work with Lappeus to make sure any suckers fleeced at his saloon didn't get anywhere when they complained to the cops. Lappeus also, on several occasions, arrested temperance workers for "disturbing the peace" by singing and praying on public sidewalks outside other saloonkeepers' establishments. It was a nice, cozy time for Portland gamblers and grog-shop operators.

Not that everything was always smooth. Lappeus was removed from office "for cause" in 1877, and replaced with a former City Councilor named Luzerne Besser (remember that name). But he was back in office again two years later, so the "cause" couldn't have been anything too egregious.

In 1883, though, Lappeus's law enforcement career ended for good — on a somewhat ironic note — after notorious Portland bordello madam Carrie Bradley testified that she'd paid him $500 in gold to look the other way after she and her employee, Dolly Adams, murdered a customer to keep him from testifying against them in a larceny trial.

You would think that would be enough of a reason to fire a police chief... but Carrie Bradley was very well connected in Portland, and Lappeus also had Carrie Bradley-related dirt on lots of local VIPs. Plenty of members of the city's elite were very interested in having these charges against Lappeus go away — and so they did. Instead, he was promptly cleared of all charges, and then, almost immediately, newly elected Mayor James Chapman suddenly and unexpectedly brought the Danford Balch case up again, and used it as a pretext to fire Lappeus.

In a final twist, Mayor Chapman put a cherry on top of this sundae of municipal corruption just a few weeks later, when he confessed that he'd actually fired Lappeus not because of the Balch bribe, or the Bradley bribe, or the alleged cover-up of a murder — no, none of these things were the real reason Lappeus lost his job. Lappeus had been fired because ex-Chief Luzerne Besser had slipped Chapman a fat bribe — $1,000 in gold — during his election campaign, in exchange for a promise to can Lappeus and appoint him (Besser) to the job.

Lappeus apparently took the hint, though, and disappeared from city politics for good after that.

Sources and Works Cited:
- Merchants, Money and Power, *a book by E. Kimbark MacColl, published in 1988 by Georgian Press of Portland;*
- Wicked Portland: The Wild and Lusty Underworld of a Frontier Seaport Town, *a book by Finn J.D. John, published in 2012 by The History Press;*
- Portland: People, Politics and Power, *a book by Jewel Lansing, published in 2003 by Oregon State University Press;*
- Edward Chambreau: His Autobiography, *a Ph.D. dissertation by Timothy Wehrkamp, published in 1976 by the University of Oregon.*

CAPT. WALTER MOFFETT:

Saloonkeeper.

The temperance movement, when it came to Portland in the early 1870s, really shouldn't have taken anybody by surprise. There had been plenty of warning signs plain to see for anyone paying attention.

What was surprising, though, was the form it took when it got there. Portland's temperance drama reached a climax in April 1874 with a genuine knock-down-drag-out riot on the streets of downtown Portland, as angry citizens exchanged punches and clobbered each other with chairs — while, the whole time, serene as if they were singing in a forest glade, a cluster of upper-class ladies in their Sunday best sang hymns and prayed for their souls.

And then, almost as soon as it appeared, the temperance movement was gone again from the public eye, apparently destroyed from within after some of the preachers who fancied themselves its leaders overplayed their hand.

Early in the spring of '74, word started reaching Portland of the great temperance movements in Ohio.

There were, of course, plenty of other temperance movements across the country, and there had been for some time. Mostly, they took relatively mild form, with women spending lots of time praying and singing in churches and exhorting their daughters to choose a "temperance man" for a husband. This last tactic, perhaps inspired by Aristophanes' play "The Trojan Women," might have worked a little better had there not been such a strong social stigma against unmarried women at the time; there were nowhere near enough "temperance men" for every girl to marry one. All in all, the movement was easily ignored.

Or rather, it had been easily ignored until now. With its new spirit of assertiveness and evangelism, the Ohio movement was different. Participants — most of them women, who were largely excluded from "saloon culture" but not from its effects on their husbands and sons — were no longer contenting themselves with praying in churches and "setting a good personal example in the home." They had started going out into the community to spread the word, and actually went to saloons to urge temperance upon their owners and customers. And they'd had some success at this — most notably in persuading saloonkeepers to leave the business.

In Portland, the mainstream newspapers — there were three of them at the time: the *Morning Oregonian*, the *Portland Bulletin* and the *Evening Telegram* — mentioned these events only briefly and occasionally. Likely they thought nothing of them; in 1874, three decades before Carrie Nation first picked up her hatchet, the concept of aggressive temperance workers was a new one on most folks.

But Abigail Scott Duniway, editor and publisher of *The New Northwest*, was paying close attention. Readers of her weekly paper, mostly women, were kept very much up to date on the temperance movement.

Duniway was a legend even in her own time, and her profile has grown since. The great passion of her life was a quest for legal equality of the sexes and voting rights for women. She saw temperance as an issue that would have been quickly resolved if 50 percent of the population were not forbidden to vote — in other words, as a symptom of the great social evil that she had devoted her life to overturning. She was the sister of legendary longtime *Morning Oregonian* editor Harvey Scott — who, due to some political machinations going on at that time involving railroad-and-stagecoach baron Ben Holladay, was then working as editor of the *Bulletin*.

(She would live to see her dream realized — but it took years, possibly even decades, longer than it probably would have if the "temperance wars" had played out differently in Portland.)

RASCALS.

This drawing, from Frank Leslie's publication, shows the Ohio ladies who were the Portland temperance workers' primary inspiration, singing and praying before a saloon in early 1874. This scene, sketched by S.B. Morton, is in Logan, Ohio. (Image: Library of Congress)

Plenty of Portland women read Duniway's newspaper. It was a lively read which prominently featured serial fiction stories (many of them written by Duniway herself), local news of interest to women, and tidbits such as recipes and funny anecdotes. Oh, and it had editorials. Duniway's editorials were every bit as assertive and hard-hitting as those of her male counterparts at the other Portland newspapers. Of course, they were viewed differently; a strong editorial written by a man was "powerful," whereas the same editorial under a woman's by-line was "waspish."

The New Northwest devoted considerable coverage to the temperance movement's successes back east. And that, ironically, is probably the primary reason the whole thing came to Portland in the first place. It's certainly why the fervor of the movement was so startling and unexpected to Portland men. They were nearly all caught off guard, because they were reading the wrong newspapers.

Nonetheless, those among them who happened to be preachers in temperance churches rose to the occasion with alacrity. Soon their churches were crammed to bursting with women yearning to do something about this terrible social evil.

Enacting outright prohibition was out of the question for the time being,

233

and the ladies knew it well. They had no voting rights with which to support it. A 40-year-old bum who had been neither sober nor fully employed since he was 13 was a voter; a 40-year-old published "authoress" teaching home economics at the state agricultural college was not. The drunks would vote to keep drinking. The ladies would have to take a different route.

They assembled in churches. Stirring sermons were preached. Invitations went out to men all over Portland to come and be inspired, and a pledge of abstinence from alcohol was circulated at each service. Hundreds of people signed.

Yet mere hundreds wouldn't change the course of history. Plus, those hundreds were most often already teetotalers. Then as now, the pub-crawling set wasn't seen much in church, or at least not in the kind of cold-water churches that would preach temperance and abstinence.

Inspired once again by *The New Northwest*'s dispatches of events in Ohio, the ladies of several Portland churches decided they needed to be more assertive. They and their pastors organized themselves into an interdenominational coalition — the Women's Temperance Prayer League — and made their headquarters at the Methodist Church on Taylor Street. There they decided, as the *Portland Bulletin*'s reporter put it, to "go forth and beard the lion in his den" — by going out two by two, as Jesus sent forth his disciples, to hold their temperance-church services in the saloons themselves.

A few of the more conservative ladies thought that was too much, and when the decision was made to do this, they dropped out. But there remained a total of 13 game sisters who were ready to go out there and change the world.

And so it was that on March 23, 1874, a team of fired-up ladies streamed out of the church and, in groups of two and three, fanned out across Portland.

The ladies' battle plan was simple. They would present themselves at each saloon and ask the proprietor if they might enter and lead a prayer service. Most of the time, the answer was yes — although that would change later. Then they'd pray, sing a hymn or two, circulate a pledge for the drunks to sign promising to abstain from alcohol, sing and pray some more, and leave.

For a Victorian-era lady, this was nowhere near as easy as it sounds to the modern ear. Laura Francis Kelly, one of the temperance crusaders, wrote a hand-written account of how it went:

"Can you imagine what it would be to go into a saloon to pray? Then you can imagine how we felt. I cannot tell you.

"The saloon keeper received us cordially, ushering us into the card-room.

As the song rose from trembling hearts: 'Holy Spirit, faithful guide, Ever near the Christian's side,' etc., the bar-room quickly filled with young men to whom the barkeeper freely dispensed his liquors. As we knelt in prayer, the clink of glasses well nigh drowned the petitions that rose from trembling lips. When the short service was over, the bar keeper invited us very pleasantly to 'come again.' Oh! how we hastened back to church and kindred spirits! But the pastor, George W. Izer, met us with, 'Back so soon? Did you visit only one saloon?' Then we saw what was before us."

At the end of the day, they were exhausted and demoralized.

This advertisement ran prominently in almost every issue of the Portland Bulletin, often right next to the newspaper's coverage of the temperance crusaders' efforts to deprive Mr. Fleckenstein of business. (Image: UO Libraries)

True, the ladies were treated courteously everywhere (with, the *Bulletin* sniffed, the notable exception of "the proprietress of a low doggery on Second Street" — and one other place, which we'll talk about shortly). But as crusader Kelly mentioned, saloons were noisy places. A pair of frightened ladies standing close together in a corner singing hymns was easily ignored. In the pubs where they were not ignored, they were treated as objects of curiosity, as if a circus act were visiting the saloon. Few if any of the men in the saloon even bothered to listen to their message, and more than one liquored-up wag made fun of them, pretending showily to be convinced and signing a fake name to the temperance pledge.

Back in the church, the ladies prayed for strength and then went home for the night.

This forbidding portrait of Abigail Scott Duniway was made later in her life, after she had won her forty-year battle to get women the right to vote. In 1874, she was still a young woman — but woe to the man who underestimated her.. (Image: J. Gaston)

The next day, things were a little different. That's because, after debriefing the previous day and discussing strategies, the ladies decided to change their tactics. Today, rather than fanning out across the city two by two, they would go in a group. All 13 of them would pay a call on a single saloon.

The ladies fortified themselves with a lengthy prayer service, then poured forth once again from the church into the mean streets of Stumptown's saloon district.

Today they descended upon the Mount Hood Saloon, owned by a chap named Thomas Shartle; he graciously let them in and gave them the run of the place. Shartle did not, however, turn off the taps, and was probably glad he did not. If two Victorian ladies in a saloon was a little like a circus act, thirteen of them was more like the whole circus. People poured into the Mount Hood.

On the surface, it looked like a repeat of the previous day's disaster, only on a bigger scale. Mr. Shartle did a brisk trade. The ladies got the same faux-hearty "best of luck to you, God bless you, here's to ya" response from the same saloon bums, and fielded the same fake signatures on the temperance pledge.

But this time, the "clink of glasses" was powerless to drown out their voices as they sang. There were, after all, a baker's dozen of them. They were too large a presence to ignore.

The ladies moved on, going downmarket a bit and visiting a rum house called the Evening Call. Again, they brought the proprietor plenty of business and left with very few legitimate pledges.

Back at the church, the ladies learned that word had gotten around the saloons that their presence represented a large business boom. One saloon owner actually sent them an invitation to come to his place, which — to his delight — they did the next day.

But the sense of demoralization was now utterly gone. The ladies knew they were onto something. If some people were laughing at them, at least they were now being heard; their seed might be falling on stony ground, but at least it was reaching the ground — rather than being drowned out by the clink of glassware the instant it was thrown.

They started going out every day, each day to a different saloon. And slowly, things started to change.

As March of 1874 drew to a close, the marauding squadron inspired a growing uneasiness among the businessmen of the liquor industry in Portland. The crusading ladies included the wives and daughters of some of their customers. And they were showing no signs of slowing down or calling it quits.

At first, the businessmen had been pleased; most of their customers had seemed to look on the prayer services as something akin to having live music in the pub. But within a week the money-making magic was fading fast. The crowd of idle, thirsty spectators that had once followed the ladies around from tavern to tavern dwindled away until it included only the idlest and thirstiest. After a week or so, the crusaders' arrival at a saloon stopped being an attractant. At the same time, the number of ladies participating in the "raids" swelled. Soon their arrival meant not a

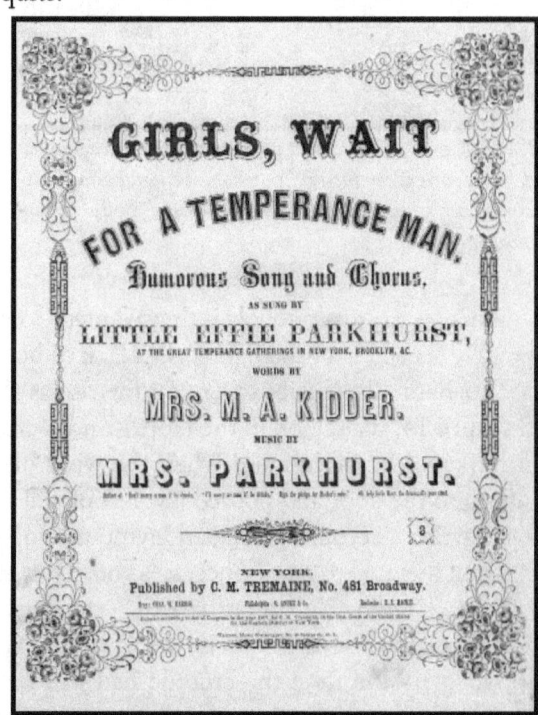

This piece of sheet music from the University of Oregon's collection is from 1867. Chances are good that the ladies participating in Portland's temperance crusade knew the tune. (Image: UO Libraries)

The Taylor Street Methodist Church, which served as a sort of headquarters for the multi-denominational effortof the temperance movement in Portland. (Image: www.cafeunknown.com)

lucrative afternoon of pouring drinks and collecting coin, but the effective shutting-down of the bar for as long as the ladies chose to stay.

More and more saloonkeepers began refusing to let the ladies come in. At first, when this happened, they'd move on, but soon — inspired by the actions of Walter Moffett (about whom more in a bit), they changed their tactics. When refused admission to a saloon, they'd stand in front of it on the sidewalk and hold a prayer-and-song service right there.

This was actually worse than letting them in, because it was like a picket line that customers would have to cross publicly if they wanted to enter the saloon. It also made a public spectacle of the barkeeper's lack of hospitality.

So, naturally, tensions were on the rise as the month of April wore on. On April 14, at a saloon in the North End, a proprietress slammed the door in the crusaders' faces, and when the wind blew it back open again, "she rushed to the door and poured a volley of abuse upon us," according to the hand-written account of one anonymous temperance worker.

But there were some successes too. That same hand-written account goes on: "Evening Call saloon closed — proprietor signed the Pledge." You'll remember the Evening Call as the rum shop visited on the first day of the crusade. (By the time the crusade had run its course, the ladies had also converted at least one other saloonkeeper — the notoriously rascally Edouard Chambreau, whom you will remember from a few chapters ago.)

By the middle of April, the warring parties had settled down into an uneasy sort of relationship in which the saloon keepers tried to keep as low a profile as possible — trying, if you'll pardon the anachronism of using a metaphor 100 years before its time, to stay off the ladies' radar.

Well, most of them did. There was ... one exception. And it's time to talk about him now.

Walter Moffett was one of Portland's most respected men, and by most accounts a decent guy. A Brit by birth, he went to sea as a young man and did well for himself; by the time he arrived in Portland, he was a ship captain. He settled down in Portland and married well — his wife was a daughter of the Terwilliger family. By the time he'd settled down with her, he was a man of property, owning several shipping interests as well as two saloons: the Tom Thumb and the Webfoot.

It was the Webfoot Saloon that was to be Ground Zero in Portland's temperance riots.

The Webfoot was located on the northwest corner of First and Morrison — just off the waterfront at its more "respectable" southern end.

How the hostilities between Moffett and the temperance crusaders got started is unclear; there are two very different accounts of the action — one from the *Portland Bulletin*, and one from author and journalist Frances Fuller Victor's little book, *Crusading in Portland*, published later that same year.

Both accounts agree that Moffett first met two of the temperance workers on that first day in mid-March when they were fanning out across the city two by two. But, that's all they agree on. The *Bulletin*'s story the next morning says Mr. Moffett greeted them courteously but declined to let them enter his bar. Fuller Victor, however, describes the interaction ... somewhat differently:

"The two ladies, trembling, but full of holy zeal, paused at the entrance on Morrison Street, and stepped into the saloon whose proprietor was as unknown to them as the proprietors of other saloons. As they entered, Mr. Moffett, on the alert, ... entered by the Front Street door, which brought him face to face with his visitors. Without giving them time to announce their errand, he seized each rudely by an arm, and thrust them out into the street, exclaiming, 'Get out of this! I keep a respectable house and don't want any damned whores here.'" *

She goes on to describe the ladies' shocked reaction to this reception, and the horror with which one of them recognizes him as a family friend:

"'Walter Moffett!' she exclaimed. 'Can this be Walter Moffett? Why,

---

* *In Fuller Victor's original text, the words "Damned" and "Whores" are written as "d——" and "w——." Ironically, the word "whorehouse" appears later in the same quotation, fully spelled out.*

Walter Moffett, I used to know you; and I prayed with your wife for your safety when you were at sea years ago!'

"'I don't want any of your damn prayers; I want you to get out of this and stay out; that's all I want of you. I don't keep a whorehouse!'"

Well then. These are words that even today would earn any man a lusty punch on the mazzard from pretty much anyone in a position to deliver one, male or female. The fact that Moffett didn't get one on the spot can probably be chalked up to the utter improbability of his behavior, which was so far out of line with Victorian-era norms of how respectable women were supposed to be treated that the ladies were too flabbergasted to do anything but make their way back to the Taylor Street church and tell their comrades-in-arms what had happened.

Their story galvanized the congregation there. Outraged and furious, they immediately moved his name to the top of their target list.

For the next week and a half they tried to wear down his defenses by putting in daily appearances at his saloon — requesting entry, being denied and moving on.

Finally, on the last day of March, they changed tactics. After being denied entry as usual, they lined up on the sidewalk and launched their prayer service right there, outside the door.

Moffett's response was almost as tone-deaf as his previous one had been: He emerged from his saloon wearing spectacles and holding himself with prim dignity, a copy of the Holy Bible in one hand. From this he proceeded to read a selection of passages which, taken out of context, sounded wildly offensive. (The only one of these specifically mentioned by the crusaders is Deuteronomy 23:1, which reads, "He that is wounded in the stones, or hath his privy member cut off, shall not enter into the congregation of the Lord.")

The ladies sang louder to drown him out. Moffett increased his own volume until he was actually shouting. This went on for some time, attracting — as you can imagine — a healthy crowd of spectators.

Finally, the ladies moved on. But before they left, one of them tearfully asked Moffett why he was behaving like this. His bellicose response was that he minded his own business and expected others to mind theirs, and he called the crusaders hypocrites.

That evening, the ladies discussed Moffett at great length. Was he simply incorrigible, a waste of their time? Should they simply leave him on his road to hell and focus their attention on more salvageable souls? Or — or was his bizarre, erratic and offensive behavior a subtle call for help?

Strange as it sounds, the "call for help" theory is the one that prevailed. Some of the ladies argued that his strange behavior must stem from an uneasy conscience, and that meant he was not beyond the reach of salvation. What Brother Moffett needed right now was not to be abandoned to his depravities and the blandishments of Satan, but rather to feel the tough, brave love of his true friends, who would be there to support his struggle for righteousness no matter how viciously he tried in his self-destructive madness to drive them away.

Looked at that way, leaving Walter Moffett alone would be a seriously sinful and selfish act, and one the ladies figured they'd be called to account for on Judgment Day. No, poor Brother Moffett would continue to receive his special treatment, along with earnest and loving prayers for his salvation, whether he wanted them or not.

In other words, Moffett's behavior had not only failed to persuade the ladies to leave him alone, it had put the full force of divine authority behind a mandate to continue pestering him. And the poor dolt clearly had no idea.

Moffett continued to show the world his stunning lack of good judgment by hiring some thugs and buying and stockpiling some firecrackers for the ladies' next visit, which came the very next day after the Bible-reading incident — April Fools' Day, 1874. When they arrived, Moffett's goon squad went into action, beating big Chinese gongs in their faces and tossing lighted strings of firecrackers under their feet.

It was another Rubicon crossed. Before this day, the only truly ungentlemanly behavior Moffett had engaged in had been a private conversation with two ladies whom he was ejecting from his bar, and some off-color Scripture readings a few days before. Now, in front of the whole city, he and his thugs were not only being very disrespectful, they were putting the ladies in danger of a broken ankle or even immolation — much of the clothing of the day was highly flammable. The crowd of onlookers was shocked. Then it started murmuring ominously and moving closer. The police, sensing that something ugly was about to happen, hurried in and persuaded the ladies to break off the engagement.

The tone-deaf Moffett seems to have taken precisely the wrong lesson away from this episode. Spared from the consequences his tactics were about to bring down on his head, he concluded that they were exactly the ticket to get the ladies to leave him alone.

In fairness, it probably seemed to be working, at least in the short term.

The ladies gave him a whole week — a longer break from their attention than he had yet enjoyed — before returning on April 7.

On that day, a force of 15 of them stationed themselves in front of the Webfoot and started singing and praying as usual.

Word spread like an electric current through Portland and in minutes the crowd of onlookers was blocking the streets and sidewalks, effectively shutting down the bar. Moffett, in a swift change of tactics — perhaps the gong-beaters and firecracker-throwers he'd hired had given up and gone home during the seven-day truce — got out his police whistle and started blasting upon it, summoning Portland Police Chief (and, as you'll remember, fellow saloon owner) James Lappeus to the scene.

Upon Lappeus's arrival, Moffett demanded that he disperse the praying women. They were, he asserted, disturbing the peace by attracting an unruly crowd of onlookers.

Oddly enough, it seems to have occurred to precisely no one to ask the crowd of onlookers to disperse. Instead, Chief Lappeus approached the ladies and asked them to leave. They declined. The chief told them that if they stuck around and a riot broke out, people could get hurt. They replied that that was up to God and to those people; they were just there to pray and sing.

So the chief arrested them.

Now remember, as the ladies themselves surely were well aware — Chief Lappeus was also Saloonkeeper Lappeus. In today's world, this kind of conflict of interest would be outrageous — one saloon owner helping out another saloon owner by arresting a dozen ladies who were clearly doing nothing illegal. In 1870s Portland, though, it was no big thing.

The ladies surely also knew Chief Lappeus's reputation. He was a little notorious, as you'll likely recall from the last chapter.

Even so, they were upright, law-abiding women. So off went the ladies in one of the most remarkable impromptu parades ever seen in a Portland street: the police chief at the front in the full dignity of office; fifteen fashionably corseted Victorian ladies in their finest attire gliding fabulously along behind; and a dangerously huge crowd of onlookers bringing up the rear. Moffett was left behind at his suddenly empty bar, perhaps wondering if he was experiencing the equivalent of the eye of a hurricane.

Almost magically, husbands and sons and fellow temperance workers materialized at the police station, all eager to bail the ladies out. The ladies, who had started singing hymns again, refused to take or give a nickel. They were accordingly loaded into the jail, where they spent another two or three

A lithograph of the scene on a bleary Saturday morning in the Portland city jail, published in The West Shore magazine in 1888. (Image: UO Libraries)

hours singing and praying. Meanwhile, court authorities, eager to get them out as fast as possible before the crowd got any uglier, frantically rounded up the requisite magistrate and officers of the court.

The ensuing hearing was very brief. Judge Denny dismissed the complaint almost immediately, ruling that standing on a public sidewalk singing hymns did not constitute "disturbing the peace."

The ladies visited the Webfoot saloon a week later, but stayed only for half an hour. Presumably, Moffett was not yet ready to join battle. But two days after that, on April 16, he was.

Moffett had tooled up for this showdown. In a rare display of wisdom, he'd gotten rid of the firecrackers, but he'd traded in his gongs for bigger and louder models and hired a couple of local urchins to beat on them. He'd also acquired a hand organ, the kind organ grinders used to crank away on while a trained monkey danced. And of course, there was his trusty police whistle.

When the temperance gang rolled up in front of the joint a little after 2 p.m., Moffett & Co. were ready for them ... and the fight was on. The boys whaled on the gongs. A local drunk hired for the event cranked furiously on the organ. Moffett's whistle shrilled away. Even before the ladies had started their devotionals, the streets of Portland were ringing with an unbelievable racket that brought spectators sprinting to the scene from blocks around.

"This hideous clamor continued for an hour, the Crusaders meanwhile calmly saying prayers and singing songs which not even those closest to them could hear," historian Malcolm H. Clark writes. "Fritz (the organist) grew arm-weary. The two boys, despite the encouraging shouts of their commander, were perceptibly weakening. Moffett's face had acquired a purplish cast."

(The "purplish cast" part almost certainly represents poetic license; I have been unable to find a primary source to discuss Moffett's complexion during this engagement. Clark tells a great story, and most of what he recounts is accurate, but one does have to watch out for embellishments like this.)

The bartender, J.F. Good, ducked out the door and found a street hydrant with a hose attached to it, used to fill the sprinkler wagons that kept the dust down on the dirt street during dry weather. Picking the hose up, he opened the hydrant and blasted water onto the front of the saloon; it ran down the front of the building and soaked the temperance workers with dirty water. Dripping wet in clothes that were probably ruined, they sang on.

By late afternoon the gong boys had given out completely, so Mr. Good grabbed one of the gongs and the erstwhile organist seized the other. According to the *Bulletin*, one of them soon thereafter lost his gong; beating it as hard as he could inches from the face of one of the ladies, a Mrs. Stitzel, he was surprised when she acknowledged his presence for the first and only time — by suddenly snatching the gong from him and "retain(ing) possession of it." The *Bulletin* doesn't mention what happened next, but according to Frances Fuller Victor, Moffett actually tried to recover the gong robber-style — he pulled out a pocket pistol, pointed it at her head, and demanded that she give it back. But Stitzel silently called his bluff. He wasn't going to murder her over a gong, and she knew it; so the gun went back in his pocket, and the gong stayed out of service.

The gongbeater involved in this little bit of pistol-waving drama was probably Mr. Good, because around 5 p.m. we know he was no longer operating a gong. We know this because that's the point at which he — after several trips into the saloon for yet another quick bracer, and now quite drunk — started swearing bitterly and profanely at the line of singing, praying ladies.

It was too much. You never know what's going to set a crowd off. In this instance, this display of drunken churlishness was enough for bystander

William Grooms — who, by the way, had been Portland's city marshal back in 1853.

Grooms now approached the sloppy, obscenity-sputtering Mr. Good, hauled off and flattened him with a powerful punch square in the middle of the face.

The crowd exploded. Fists and elbows flew. Uninvited guests surged into the Webfoot Saloon, and Moffett and his little band, finding themselves the targets of a vengeance-minded mob, backed away as best they could and sought refuge behind the bar. Glass broke and chairs flew. Moffett got his pistol back out of his pocket, and several others did likewise. How this whole affair managed to not end with anybody getting maimed or killed is a mystery, but the police must have been keeping a close eye on the situation, because they were on the scene within seconds. They didn't shut it down and they didn't ask the ladies to leave; they simply restored order and withdrew.

Moffett was down a gong and the crank organ had fallen victim to the mob as well. With a few tin cans and the one remaining gong, he and his crew carried on until 6 p.m., when the ladies quietly withdrew. On almost every possible level, they had won the day.

Pressing their advantage, the ladies were back the next day at 10 a.m., and word spread quickly; within minutes, the streets and sidewalks were jammed with spectators ready for the show. But inside the Webfoot Saloon, all was quiet. Instead of engaging the enemy, Moffett hustled down the road to the police station and swore out a complaint against the ladies for disorderly conduct, based on the riot that had broken out the previous day.

Chief Lappeus, never one to neglect to do a fellow saloonkeeper a solid, sallied forth once again to enforce it; and soon the procession of the previous week from the Webfoot to the courthouse was repeated.

At the courthouse, the ladies who had not been in the group the previous day were sent on their way. Remaining behind in Lappeus's custody were six women — once again under arrest for praying and singing on a public street.

This time the charges against them would actually stick; Moffett, Lappeus, and the other liquor men had had a week or two to get their legal theories in order and to lobby and schmooze (and, perhaps, bribe) the necessary public officials. But things wouldn't turn out quite the way they envisioned.

The legal concept of "disorderly conduct" was creaking under the strain of what the prosecutors were trying to get it to do. The idea was, although the ladies hadn't been personally disorderly, they had shown up and prayed on a sidewalk knowing full well that doing so would inspire others to disturb the peace by, for example, rioting and trashing the Webfoot Saloon. The fact that the rioters had actually been inspired more by the plaintiff's activities than the defendants' was conveniently overlooked.

It took a couple of days for the trial to finish up and for the jury to come to a decision. But one of the jury members was a saloon owner, and the other five were business owners of other types; their natural sympathy lay with the guy trying to sell beer, not the citizens outside interfering with commerce and trade by singing and praying in public. To no one's surprise, the verdict was "guilty."

The ladies were sentenced to spend a night in jail or pay $5. Offers to pay their fines poured in immediately, but like Socrates refusing to go into exile, they insisted on doing the time instead.

And so the six crusaders were carted off to the hoosegow, accompanied by a huge crowd of well-wishers.

All throughout that afternoon and into the evening, the Portland city joint was jumping. Hordes of visitors trooped in and out of the jail, to visit and to participate in impromptu prayer services; and the joint rang with the sound of six determined voices belting out hymn after hymn. Finally, visiting hours ended, and the ladies settled down for the night.

It couldn't have been more than half an hour later that Chief Lappeus stormed into the jail and ordered them all to get the hell out.

The ladies, assuming this was another attempt to cut them a break, hurried to reassure him that they were quite ready to stay the night like the judge had said. The chief didn't even let them finish.

"I'M THE BOSS HERE," he roared. "YOU LEAVE."

Some of the ladies had already dressed for bed. Lappeus roared at them until they scurried out of the courthouse, half put together and feeling scandalously immodest. For a Victorian-age man, it was a remarkably ungentlemanly thing to do; people in the 1870s were challenged to duels for lesser "offenses against Womanhood" than this.

"From first to last it was a farce, although a very serious one," wrote Fuller Victor. "The women had violated no laws or ordinances. They were arrested on a charge which only really applied to the man who had them arrested, and only to him.

"In this first trial, as in those that followed [against Moffett], the Crusaders, whether defenders or complainants, were treated as if they had been in every other sense what they are legally — infants or idiots. Their relations to society, as wives, mothers and daughters, were as completely ignored as their political rights."

After this episode, for a short period of time, the temperance ladies virtually owned Portland. Moffett was bedeviled on almost a daily basis, and his behavior continued to be odd and erratic. For the most part, knowing he was fighting a losing battle, he contented himself with "following his tormentors around, muttering imprecations and offering unsolicited advice," according to historian Clark.

However, on occasion he would do something actually aggressive. On May 1, he made history in what surely was the first use of tear gas in state history. On that day, he emerged from his saloon with a wet handkerchief around his nose and some sort of vile-smelling smoke pouring from the pockets of the old overcoat he was wearing. In them, he apparently had a mixture of tobacco and pepper, and the smell was almost suffocating; Moffett, free to move about, could leave the cloud of stinging smoke behind him, whereas the singing and praying ladies more or less had to stay in one spot and endure it as best they could. Moffett was hauled into court for this bit of chemical warfare, but on May 21 he was acquitted — "the jury were all liquor men," an anonymous crusader wrote.

On May 27, the same crusader reported, "Mr. Moffett of the 'Webb-Foot' still a tool for Satan, executing the designs of the devil with astonishing intrepidity." And as late as June, Moffett was still occasionally throwing firecrackers. But his tactics seemed to have shifted from pitched battle to isolated harassment.

Sadly, the chronicles are silent on the question of what impact his behavior had on his business. Did the drinkers of Portland rally around him, supporting him in his little war? Or did they start avoiding the Webfoot, uncomfortable with the ungentlemanly behavior for which it was fast becoming famous? We don't know.

As Election Day approached for Portland's City Council seats, a new newspaper, the *Temperance Star*, was launched — Abigail Scott Duniway's publication having been deemed not ideologically pure enough. This was absolutely true. Success had gone to the heads of the temperance-church preachers and other male leaders of the crusade, and they were starting to display a species of merciless, self-righteous swagger that Duniway immediately saw was public-relations poison. Forseeing the brutal comeuppance that was about to come their way, she was at some pains to distance herself and her favored cause — women's suffrage — from their movement. This did not go unnoticed.

Most of the Temperance advocates were practical enough to understand her position. They themselves were being forced to make similar compromises. They had drawn up a slate of Temperance candidates for the election;

but it was clear that in spite of the general support of the community for those brave crusading women who were battling for the soul of the Webfoot Saloon's customers and staff, there would not be enough votes to elect them. They would be going head-to-head with the Republican Party's slate of moderate, reform-minded candidates — who were generally friendly to the Temperance cause, but weren't part of the movement and probably woundn't rock the boat too much in pursuit of its goals; and a "People's Ticket," which was generally stocked with liquor-business-friendly candidates. (The Democratic Party did not put forth a slate of candidates in this election.)

The Temperance movement's leaders, in the end, decided to throw their support behind the Republicans rather than risking splitting the vote. None of them were happy with this decision, of course; they would much rather have had a slate of pure-hearted teetotalers to vote for. But they knew if they put one forward, the liquor ticket would ride to easy victory over a divided opposition.

But some of the more fanatical Temperance people were more than just unhappy with the move. One in particular seems to have been enraged by what he saw as the selling-out of the movement's purity.

That one was a man named Abraham Coryell Edmunds, and we will have lots more to say about him in one of the forthcoming volumes of the Offbeat Oregon History series. For now, suffice it to say that Edmunds was the kind of fanatic who is quite happy to make the perfect into the enemy of the good.

Shortly before the election, following this decision, Edmunds stepped forward with a small essay that he proposed to have printed and circulated on Election Day, which he assured his Temperance colleagues would tip the balance and assure them the win.

The circular was titled "The Voter's Book of Rememberance."

The Women's Temperance Prayer League met and considered, and Edmunds got the green light to have the circular printed.

The "Voters' Book of Remembrance" put the entire city into a cold fury. Its language doesn't sound too bad to the modern ear, but in 1874 it was outrageously unsubtle — and, what was worse, insulting.

"Voters of Portland, the Book of Remembrance is this day opened, and you are called upon to choose 'whom ye will serve,'" it starts out. "On one hand are found prostitutes, gamblers, rumsellers, whiskey topers, beer guzzlers, wine bibbers, rum suckers, hoodlums, loafers and ungodly men. On the other hand are found Christian wives, mothers, sisters and daughters of the good people of Portland. You cannot serve two masters. You must be numbered with one or the other. Whom will ye choose?"

The circular went on to accuse Portland's police of being "devoted to the protection of prostitution, drunkenness and debauchery, and the persecution and punishment of virtue" and claiming that "whiskey advocates employ prostitutes to insult Christian women while praying and reading the Holy Bible."

After a few more similar paragraphs of high dudgeon, the little circular added, "Remember that persons are known by the company they keep. Birds of a feather flock together."

In other words, as historian Clark puts it, "any citizen low enough to vote against the Temperance candidates was a supporter of Sin, an un-American scoundrel, and an arch-foe of Home and Mother."

Remember, this was a pre-Suffrage election, so it was to be decided by men. Most men, in 1874, had at one time or another participated in saloon culture — some of them on a daily basis, others very occasionally. And although it was a particularly hard-drinking age, not every Portland man was a souse. Responsible drinkers have always been with us, and in 1874, as in most times, they represented a great majority of the male population. Now here came these Temperance scolds to tell Joe Sixpack-A-Week that he must either dry out completely or "be numbered with" hookers, swindlers, loafers, thugs, day-drinkers, and "ungodly men."

No sale, Reverend.

The Temperance-backed Republican candidates, who 24 hours before the election had looked like shoo-ins, were trounced. The Women's Temperance Prayer League vanished, its constituents slinking away from the public-relations fiasco that someone had signed their name to. It was replaced by the Women's Christian Temperance Union, which lasted for years but never had the same kind of influence.

Edmunds left town immediately after this fiasco; his flyer was widely blamed for the disaster, and some fairly credible rumors started to circulate that he had done it deliberately to punish his allies for having been willing to work with the ideologically impure Republican reformers.

Ironically, probably the biggest loser in the whole thing was the woman whose newspaper had catalyzed the whole movement. Abigail Scott Duniway now got to watch her worst fears become real: The women's suffrage movement became irrevocably tied to the temperance movement in most Portlanders' minds, and the temperance movement was now painted in the popular imagination as preachy, self-righteous, meddlesome and generally insufferable. It would take decades for this association to dissipate.

Speaking of dissipation, let's turn back to Walter Moffett for a moment. He started wasting away just a few months after the election. Then he sold his saloons and sailed off to the South Seas — a relatively unremarkable thing to do today, but a fairly odd action for a middle-aged married man of property to take in 1875; in that era of small, vulnerable sailing ships, sketchy navigation and nonexistent weather forecasting, people didn't go to sea unless they had to.

In any case, Moffett died en route. His cause of death was officially something else, but it's at least possible that he was suffering through the final stages of syphilis, which in that era caused many a middle-aged man to become mentally unhinged and then die early. Certainly that would explain why a man who had clearly once had enough good judgment to build several successful businesses suddenly thought it would be OK to throw firecrackers at praying ladies on the street and call them "damned whores."

But, of course, we can't ever really know.

Sources and Works Cited:
- *The Women's War with Whisky; or, Crusading in Portland,* a book by Frances Fuller Victor, published in 1874 by Himes the Printer of Portland;
- "The War on the Webfoot Saloon," an article by Malcolm Clark Jr. published in the March 1957 issue of Oregon Historical Quarterly;
- "He Was a Starter but Got No Further: Careers of A.C. Edmunds," an article published in the June 1983 issue of Oregon Historical Quarterly;
- Edward Chambreau: His Autobiography, *a Ph.D. dissertation by Timothy Wehrkamp, published in 1976 by the University of Oregon.*
- *OHS Archive document folders MSS 1535 and 550;*
- *Archives of* The New Northwest *and* Portland Daily Bulletin, *March—July 1874.*

HANK VAUGHAN:

GUNFIGHTER AND LIVESTOCK RUSTLER.

Crime, they say, does not pay.
    Yet it's pretty easy to look back through history and find examples of a certain kind of criminal for whom it did, handsomely, and for decades. With charisma, moxie and a seemingly endless supply of good luck, these characters sometimes even manage to cheat karma and die a natural death. And somehow, after these criminals are gone, people remember them with a kind of fascinated fondness, and say things like, "well, we'll never see another like that again."

The second half of the nineteenth century saw such a man in a larger-than-life Wild West character named Hank Vaughan.

Hank Vaughan is remembered by folks who met him sober as a slender, wiry fellow with a sober look, a full set of whiskers and a Prince Albert-style coat, very affable and charming, but with gray-blue eyes that seemed to hold you. Most people liked him, even if they were a little afraid of him.

Others didn't like him much at all — especially the owners of the horses and cattle that would reliably vanish when he came around their herds. Hank

Hank Vaughan in his Sunday best, posing for a portrait photo when he was roughly 30 years of age. Vaughan favored the Prince Albert- style coat because it hung down far enough to conceal his pistols.

was, for most of his life, a horse thief and a rustler — possibly the most successful rustler in the history of the Old West.

And then there were the folks who met Hank when he was drunk. Some of these didn't survive the experience. Hank Vaughan was in at least a dozen gunfights in his life. There are old saloon buildings in The Dalles, Pendleton and Athena that still have .45-caliber slugs embedded in their woodwork from his Colts, and gouges on their floors from his horse's hooves.

Writing in the late 1800s, historian Noah Brown, a former employee at The Umpqua House saloon in The Dalles, describes a typical scene from Vaughan's heyday — as quoted in Jon and Donna Skovlin's excellent biography of this "hell-raising horse trader":

"On (Vaughan) entering the saloon drinks were ordered for the house," he writes. "Needless to say a crowd ambled up to the mahogany and foot rail in the sampling of Old Crow until the room was full to overflowing. It was not a great while until nearly every individual was in the same fix ... A shot fired from a six-shooter in a frolicksome way pierced a hole through a back-bar mirror. Tabs were kept on all drinks, damage to furniture, incidental expenses added and by the next evening those typical early-day Western trailblazers and pioneer characters ... paid ... the full lucre for their gentle-manly tete-a-tete of their own liking in the year of 1881."

In riotous barroom scenes like this, Vaughan was first among equals. He was a fun if dangerous friend, happy-go-lucky and fearless in any kind of fight. His skills as a horseman were legendary, and he could drive nails with a pistol from 20 yards away. But if you were a horse rancher or a cattle drover, he was the last guy you wanted to see.

Hank Vaughan was born in 1849 near Brownsville, in the Willamette Valley. He was one of the very first babies born in the old Oregon territory — although some historians would later try to claim he was really from Missouri, motivated apparently by a desire to keep the Beaver State's reputation free of the stigma of having produced such a rascally native son.

Hank's family moved to Canyon City when he was about 12 or 13. By age 15 he was an active horse trader with a chip on his shoulder and a pistol on his hip — with which, that very year, he made his first attempt to kill somebody. A customer named William Headspot, to whom Hank had been foolish enough to sell a horse on credit, tried to buffalo the boy by jeering at him and claiming the horse he'd bought from him was stolen. (It probably wasn't, but it might have been.) Hank, incensed by the insult, pulled his Colt and used it to carve a bullet-shaped furrow across Headspot's scalp; half an inch lower, and Hank would have been facing a murder rap.

He was arrested and charged, but he didn't really face much risk of being convicted because of Headspot's behavior. However, a few months later, free on bond, Hank saw the man who'd signed the arrest complaint walking into a saloon in which he was drinking. Out came the six-shooter again ....

The wound Hank inflicted on his antagonist with his pistol doesn't seem to have been very serious, but now Hank's situation was. It was one thing to reply to an insult with gunfire; the Canyon City miners and cowboys didn't approve of that, but they understood, and most of them figured Headspot had had it coming. But to retaliate in semi-cold blood against a man for doing his duty as a citizen was entirely different. Had Hank's aim been better, or his victim's reflexes slower, he almost certainly would have been lynched that day.

As it was, he spent four months in jail, at the end of which he copped a plea: A one-dollar fine and an agreement to join the First Oregon Volunteer Infantry.

That lasted just a few months. Six weeks after Hank mustered in, the Army spat him out. He left with a dishonorable discharge, but it saved him from the state pen and left him free to get back to the business that was already clearly his life's sacred calling:

Horse theft.

It was just three months after Hank left the Army that he and a friend, Dick Bunton, traveled to the foothills of the Blue Mountains, stole a few good horses from a ranch there, and headed for Idaho Territory with them.

But Umatilla County Sheriff Frank Maddock and Deputy Jackson Hart were hot on their trail. The two lawmen got the drop on them one night while they were camping by Swayze Creek near the Burnt River, close by the Idaho border. And when the two lawmen slipped up to the sleeping boys and yelled for them to throw up their hands, they both woke up shooting.

The ensuing gunfight was short, but very eventful. Deputy Hart was killed on the spot. So was Hank's companion, Dick Bunton. Sheriff Maddock was wounded badly, a bullet actually passing through his skull and breaking his jaw and wrecking his inner ear, and was knocked unconscious. And Hank was hit in the thigh and scalp.

Bunton was dead. Hart was dead. Maddock was still alive, but sure looked dead. Hank, thinking he was the only survivor, fled the scene.

But it's hard to stay on the lam with a bullet in your leg, so Hank was soon captured. Dragged back to the notoriously rope-happy town of Auburn to stand trial, Hank was nearly lynched by an angry crowd, and had it not been for the intervention of future U.S. Rep. John Hailey — who stood between the crowd and the jail with a cocked Colt in each fist until they gave up and dispersed — that would have been the end for Hank.

The trial was fast and the outcome not much in doubt. The Dalles Weekly Mountaineer reported its outcome on June 16, 1865:

"Henry Vaughan, the boy thief and murderer, arrived at The Dalles yesterday in custody of an officer on his way to the penitentiary, where he is to pass the remainder of his life. This fellow is a youth … yet he is steeped in crime, and regarded as one of the worst villains that ever cursed the country. It is to be hoped that he is not permitted to escape, as in the event of his return to this county he is sure to be hung" — and by "hung," of course, the reporter means "lynched."

And so to prison Hank went. He was under a life sentence, but he would only serve five years. Some accounts have claimed that prison turned him from a wild but good-hearted boy into a hard-eyed monster, which is a fairly common pattern in such cases; however, the Hank Vaughan that emerged from prison seems to have been *less* dangerous rather than *more*. He definitely was more successful in his rustling endeavors after he got out.

Prison seems to have given Hank the discipline and social skills he'd need to survive and thrive in the 1870s and 1880s on the Oregon frontier. The Hank Vaughn who, at the age of 21, walked out of the Oregon State Penitentiary a free man (his mother having successfully lobbied the governor

Canyon City as it appeared from a nearby bluff in 1885. This was the town in which, 20 years earlier, Hank Vaughan got in his first serious trouble with the law after he shot two people — one for calling him a thief, and the other for signing an arrest warrant. (Image: Baker County Library)

for a pardon) was very different from the punk who'd swaggered in five years before. He was more sober, more mature, far more competent — and quite a bit more dangerous. Prison had taught him the skills he'd need to survive another 25 years in the Oregon country. And although he'd get in plenty of trouble over that time, he'd never face a lynch mob again.

Hank was, first and foremost, a horseman — quite possibly the most gifted horseman in the history of the state. ("One-Eyed Charley" Parkhurst doesn't count, for reasons you will know if you've read Chapter 3.) So he naturally went straight back into the business of horse trading — and, of course, horse theft.

Shortly after his release from prison, Hank developed what would become his regular hustle: Using money made either by running stolen stock or leaning on family and friends, he'd set up a prosperous and ostensibly legitimate horse ranching business as a front. He'd run that business with diligence and competence, and it would thrive. But by night, in the backcountry, Hank would be prowling the land, looking for stock to rustle and quietly adding it to his herd — after keeping it secreted away in a hidden valley for a year or so to allow the animals' brands to heal over.

This was in the heyday of the open range, all over the West. That meant there were vast expanses of unfenced land that cattle and horses would just wander across, and occasionally ranchers would take their animals on long drives to markets or to better food supplies. When they did this, a few of the animals would always stray off from the herd, melting into the woods one or two at a time. Cowboys would ride through a day or two later collecting the strays, but they often wouldn't find them all. The way this was supposed to work was, when they were found, the animals would be recognized by their brands and returned to the rancher who'd lost them.

But it didn't always work out that way. Especially when the person who found the animals was Hank Vaughan — who was known to actually follow cattle drives closely so that he could gather up the strays before the cowboys could round them up. Hank also was known to cut a few animals out of herds when he found them unsupervised.

Operating on the border of the Umatilla Indian Reservation, Hank would then lead the stolen animals into the reservation and mingle them with the Indians' herds. It was a beautiful swindle, and worked nicely for a long time.

Of course, this wasn't the sort of thing that a fellow could do forever without someone getting wise.

On the day someone did, Hank was gambling and drinking in a saloon in the Central Oregon town of Pilot Rock when a group of stockmen walked in, fresh from having tracked a group of their strays straight to Hank's corral, and confronted him with the evidence.

Jon and Donna Skovlin, in their book, describe the scene that followed: Hank very coolly told them he didn't know what they were talking about; then he leisurely picked up his poker chips and strolled toward the bar to cash them in, riffling them as he walked.

Halfway there he abruptly released his grip on the poker chips, whirled round to face the stockmen, and froze. They realized his gun was out, cocked and pointed straight at them. There was a split-second of silence, followed by the cacophonous clatter of the poker chips hitting the floor. Hank had turned, drawn and was ready to shoot, all in less than the time it took a handful of poker chips to fall three feet.

The shocked stockmen backed away, hands in the air. Hank backed away too, toward the door, and then ducked through it and ran for his horse.

Hank's horse was always the best in town. Through his own operations and through his thefts, he was able to basically take his pick, and he always picked the best. Today that attention was going to be crucial, because as soon as his pistol was no longer covering them, the stockmen were running for their own horses and shouting for a posse to gather together and go catch him.

A sheepherder drives a flock down the old stock road near Pilot Rock. The bluffs in the background of this photo are the ones Hank Vaughan rode his horse off of to escape an angry posse in the late 1870s. (Image: Gifford Collection/OSU Libraries)

Out of town Hank galloped with the posse just a few hundred yards behind. He was making for a big bluff that overlooked the town — not a cliff per se, but it might as well have been; the ground sloped away at a good 75 to 80 degrees.

When they saw where he was headed, the posse slowed a bit and fanned out, seeking to cut off Hank's avenues of escape. Their plan was to pin him against the edge of that bluff, from which he'd have no alternative but to surrender or be shot.

What they didn't know was that Hank had planned for this moment. He'd scouted a line down the bluff and practiced it with his horse until the animal was perfectly comfortable taking it.

And so, as the posse closed in, they saw Hank's horse leap over the edge of the bluff like Pegasus taking off.

Rushing to the rim, they looked down through the dust, expecting to see horse and rider in a broken pile of flesh and bone at the bottom, and instead saw Hank's horse galloping away at its foot. There was nothing for it but to go back to town and recover as much of their property as Hank had left behind.

It was the events of that day — played for high drama in an almost Vaudevillean way — that cemented Hank Vaughan's reputation as a masterful horseman and terrifyingly swift gunfighter. Hank's flair for the dramatic served him well; many a future opponent, having had such a clear demonstration of his skills, opted not to risk challenging him because of it.

Not that all of them would. Hank was involved in at least a half dozen more gunfights over the following years, including two that left him fearfully wounded and one that resulted in some premature obituary notices in local newspapers.

Hank spent those years drifting around the dry country of the Pacific Northwest, buying and stealing and selling horses and cattle. He had a hideout deep in the Wallowa Mountains to which he'd drive stolen stock, there to wait for their skin to heal over the old, legitimate brands before rebranding them and driving them out and selling them in Boise. Today, that hideout is known as Vaughan Basin.

But by 1883, Hank could see the writing on the wall. The open range was closing up. The future would belong not to the cowboy and his riata, but to the farmer and his plow. So following a marriage to a Umatilla Indian woman named Martha Robie, Hank prepared to lead the country into this transition to a more settled life on a 640-acre wheat farm near Pendleton.

It wouldn't be all that settled, though. Not with Hank Vaughan involved.

Hank's new bride, Martha, was a widow, and had inherited a comfortable sum from her late husband, along with the wheat farm.

So Hank, as Martha's husband, now turned his considerable managerial talents away from livestock rustling and toward wheat-farm management. The results were surprisingly gratifying.

The farm was in the Pendleton-Athena area, which meant both those towns were going to be seeing a lot of Hank Vaughan over the following dozen-odd years. Hank quickly developed a reputation as a real local character. He also became known as somebody to never lend money to. For the most part, once Hank had borrowed money, the only way he'd pay it back was through legal proceedings. But Jon and Donna Skovlin tell of one constable in Pendleton, Billy Mays, who figured out how to collect: He'd simply ask Hank for a loan in the same amount as what was owed. Hank would never refuse, nor would he ever remember to ask for it to be paid back, so it was all good.

Hank became most famous for his Saturday-afternoon excursions to Athena, then called Centerville. According to former resident Lute Lane as quoted in *The Dalles Chronicle* in 1926, he'd "patronize the various bars until he attained his Western frame of mind, and then he would ride up and down the streets shooting out the few lights or go in stores, two guns on his hips, and take without pay whatever he wanted. The merchants never worried over this, for Monday morning Hank was sure to come to town with a repentant headache, and ask the various storekeepers what he had "charged" Saturday. He would then pay what they asked and go out without a word."

When in Pendleton, Hank would request service at the Bureau Saloon, his favorite watering hole, by putting a bullet through the transom window over the door, showering the floor of the bar with broken glass. This was the bartender's signal to drop everything and hustle out onto the front stoop with a shot of Old Crow for Hank; if he moved too slow, Hank might ride his horse into the bar and start shooting glasses and bottles off the back wall. He'd pay for everything, of course, but the hassle and drama was best avoided, and so Hank always got the promptest possible service.

Hank's pranks weren't always drunken revelry, though, and they weren't always really pranks. On one occasion, when he learned a judge was holding court (without his permission) in a building he owned, he charged into his building and evicted everyone inside — during the trial of a man accused of a stabbing. The prisoner slipped away in the confusion, and there's some reason to suspect that may have been the real purpose of the whole affair — that the defendant was a friend of Hank's, and the timely eviction was intended to rescue him from prosecution.

Something else happened about that time, too, that no one could have predicted. The livestock business had started consolidating into the hands of a small cadre of cattle barons — men like Peter French and Henry Miller. They displaced and undercut local cattle producers and feuded with settlers over property boundaries, and they considered themselves to owe nothing to the local communities near which they operated other than the stingy wages they paid to the local cowboys who worked for them. Resentment started to grow among the small farmers and homesteaders, and Hank found it convenient to harness that resentment to get in one last great glorious round of industrial-scale stock theft at the expense of the big out-of-town operators.

By late 1885, though, the local support for this sort of thing had subsided into a fresh outbreak of vigilantism, inspiring Hank to actually leave town for a few weeks on a "camping trip," as he said (in December, no less) to give the vigilantes time to cool down. After that, although he certainly didn't stop rustling, he became much more discreet about it.

In 1886, Hank tried one of his favorite pranks — the old "dance, varmint" routine familiar to us from so many old Western movies and Yosemite Sam cartoons, in which he'd inspire his victim to step lively by shooting at his feet — on a newcomer to town, one Bill Falwell. Falwell turned out to be a former member of the Younger Brothers gang, a hot-blooded Southern outlaw who would not let such a humiliation go unanswered. Hustling out of the bar, he spotted a man packing a massive .50-caliber cap-and-ball revolver and traded his saddle horse for it. Then he hustled back into the saloon and without further ado opened fire on Hank.

Hank soaked up one of the balls using his right arm — his shooting arm — which was shattered. In spite of this, he surged out from behind the bar when the shooting stopped, collared his assailant and was busy pummeling him when the sheriff arrived. Falwell got four years in the state pen for this assault, and Hank had to spend about that much time learning to shoot with his left hand.

The "dance, varmint" routine backfired on Hank another time, too, with less damaging (but more humiliating) consequences. Hank picked a big burly railroad bridge builder as his dancer, and after his bullets ran out and the dancing subsided, this fellow stepped up to Hank, grabbed his gun with one hand, and flattened him with a powerful roundhouse punch with the other. Then he handed the gun to one of the bystanders and walked unhurriedly away.

Hank earned a lifetime free pass on the railroad after foiling a robbery attempt one day. He was napping on the train when a trio of robbers appeared and started robbing the passengers in the car. Martha, who was traveling with him, reached up under his Prince Albert coat and unbuckled his gun belt, and as the pistols fell to the floor he caught the butts and flipped the muzzles up. A split second later, two of the three robbers suddenly decided to call the robbery off and legged it, bullets whizzing past their ears as they ran. They left the third robber behind, dead on the floor.

Another story about Hank is a trick he played to get clear title to the 640-acre farm. The land was reservation land, and the authorities — tribal or federal — had decided to auction it off rather than continuing to let tribe members use it as Martha and her husband had been doing. Accordingly, an auction was scheduled.

Hank hired a lawyer to represent him in the auction. He had, he said, some other urgent business to attend to.

Then, by some odd coincidence, the exact moment when Hank's wife's ranch was on the block and the bids were starting to be called, a gunshot rang out behind the building — and another. The sound of men shouting cut through the air. Forgetting all about the auction, the crowd hurried around to see what was going on, and found that it was Hank and another fellow. They were running, ducking for cover, and shooting at each other. It sure looked like a gunfight. But, nobody was getting hit.

Finally, the two of them ran out of bullets and the situation settled down. The bidders returned — and found the Robie land had sold. And the price had been extraordinarily cheap, because the only person bidding on it had been Hank's lawyer ... everyone else had been watching the gunfight-show, which Hank had been staging with one of his friends to distract them.

Eventually, the wild chances Hank took every day caught up with him. While galloping wildly through downtown Pendleton, his horse slipped — there are all kinds of explanations for what it might have slipped on, ranging from a muddy street to a railroad track to "Pendleton's first concrete sidewalk," so apparently nobody knows for sure. In any case, slip the horse did, and fell heavily to the ground, landing on top of Hank. His head whiplashed into the rocky ground, hitting it hard enough to fracture his skull and force his right eyeball partway out of its socket.

A week or so later, on June 15, 1893, at the age of 44, Henry Clay Vaughan slipped away from the land of the living and took his place in the pantheon of Western legendry.

> *Sources and Works Cited:*
> - Hank Vaughan: Hell-Raising Horse Trader of the Bunchgrass Territory, *a book by Jon and Donna Skovlin, published in 1996 by Reflections Press of Cove, Ore.;*
> - Outlaws of the Pacific Northwest, *a book by Bill Gulick, published in 2000 by Caxton Publishers of Caldwell, Idaho.*

CHARLES "BLACK BART" BOLTON:

STAGECOACH ROBBER.

Charles Bolton was a man with many friends, a charming, gentlemanly member of society in the brand-new frontier town of San Francisco.

If you asked him, he'd tell you he was the owner and manager of some mining concerns in the Sierra Nevadas, up near the Oregon border. If you pressed for more details, he'd talk vaguely and change the subject, like a successful fisherman trying not to divulge the location of his favorite fishing hole. That was nothing unusual; plenty of successful mine operators were similarly cagey.

It also didn't raise any eyebrows when Bolton left San Francisco for extended trips into the mountains, ranging in time from a few days to several weeks. Other mine owners did the same thing, going off to inspect their mining operations, making sure they weren't being stolen from and maybe doing a little strategic prospecting too, or inspecting other mines for possible purchase.

But with Bolton, it was different. When he went off into the mountains, he didn't bring a pick and gold pan. He brought a heavy ax — and a shotgun.

Once safely out of sight from the city, Bolton would take off his gentlemanly attire and put on crude, homespun clothes and a stained-up linen duster. Like Lamont Cranston stepping out as "The Shadow," the suave, gentlemanly Charles Bolton would transform into "Black Bart," outlaw terror of the Oregon-California Wells Fargo stagecoach line.

Charles Bolton may not have had much luck as a miner, but Black Bart was quite possibly the most successful stagecoach robber in history. His string of robberies lasted for more than eight years: from July 1875 to November 1883.

Black Bart — he took the name from a character in a popular dime novel — would promptly head for a rugged, wild place like the Siskiyou Mountains on the border between Oregon and California, moving quickly and quietly through the wilderness on foot. This was a major reason for his success: he was a master woodsman. Also, he knew that if he took a stagecoach, people would see him and possibly remember him afterward; if he rode a horse, someone would absolutely remember the horse. So he did neither. Black Bart moved across the landscape like a fox, on foot, avoiding people and often traveling by moonlight.

The goal was to get to a spot where the stagecoach was most vulnerable — a steep, rocky incline overlooked by close trees and underbrush. The

A scale model of a Wells Fargo Concord stagecoach on display at the Wells Fargo History Museum in Sacramento. The model was created by Jim Means. (Image: Jack Snell)

reason Black Bart liked the Siskiyous so much was, that kind of terrain was common along the stage routes there.

After carefully scouting the stage road, Black Bart would carefully arrange some sticks to look like rifle barrels aimed at the road, then pull a flour sack over his head with eyeholes cut in it so he could see, and hide behind a bush with his shotgun and wait for the stage to come. When it did, he'd step out into the road and, with exquisite courtesy, ask if the driver would be so kind as to throw down the Wells Fargo strongbox and the mail sacks.

Over the years, that courtesy became a Black Bart hallmark. He always said "please" and "thank you," and he made a point of never bothering passengers. Several times, when frightened passengers tried to surrender their booty to him, he handed it back to them with urbane smoothness.

"It is Wells Fargo that I am robbing, not the passengers of this stage," he told one woman as he handed her purse back to her.

Black Bart also became known as a poet, although not a very good one. At two of his robberies, he left notes including bits of doggerel. But, of course, the average armed robber didn't go much in for fine literature, so Black Bart's slim, uneven output really made him stand out in the ranks of desperado-poets.

The express box was where the action was — that, and the mail sacks. Most stagecoach robbers robbed the passengers as well, but a key part of Black Bart's success was that he never did that; passengers, after all, were usually armed, and the last thing Bart wanted was a gun fight; plus, if he could keep them from turning against him, he would never be outnumbered.

Once the box and the mail sacks were on the ground by the stage, Black Bart would motion the driver to move on, and then he'd get his ax out and break open the express box, take whatever was inside and be on his way — moving, usually, at top speed on foot through the densest possible brush for 12 to 24 hours, and leaving any trackers far behind, scratching their heads and wondering how he did it.

Oregon was farther away from Black Bart's home base, but he made some of his most lucrative hauls from stages robbed on the Beaver State side of the pass. That's because they were heading south — toward the gold fields instead of away from them — and therefore most stagecoach robbers figured they wouldn't have any gold aboard. They were so seldom robbed that it didn't make sense to guard them heavily.

But one key part of Black Bart's success was that he specifically targeted stagecoaches that would be carrying money rather than gold. As an old

Charles Bolton, a.k.a. Black Bart, as he appeared in the early 1880s. (Image: Calaveras County Historical Museum)

miner himself, Black Bart knew raw gold was dangerous. A good assayer could look at it and know what part of gold country it came from, and a stranger bringing in a big haul of gold from different regions would raise suspicions. Plus, it was always well-guarded by men who expected robbery attempts, meaning it was a lot more likely that Bart would have to kill somebody — which he took considerable pains, on more than one occasion, to not do.

He also depended on stage drivers to cooperate with him, knowing his reputation as an easy robber. With Bart, you threw down the strongbox and you were on your way. Everybody knew this, and few drivers were willing to risk the wrath of his shotgun knowing that was all he wanted.

As time went by, Wells Fargo started chaining or bolting the express box to the coaches. This resulted in Black Bart having to climb up onto the stagecoach with shotgun and ax and batter his way into it, an activity that surely gave more than one driver a chance to get the drop on him; but that didn't happen until that November day in 1883, when an armed rider came upon the stagecoach as Bart was trying to get into the box. The driver hastily borrowed the rider's pistol and sent a bullet singing past Bart, who leaped from the stage and disappeared into the underbrush. Unfortunately for Black Bart, he left behind a bloody handkerchief — he'd cut his hand on the ax while attacking the express box with it — and some personal effects. The handkerchief had a laundry mark and the Wells Fargo detectives lost little time in making the rounds of every laundry in San Francisco, asking whose it might be.

Eventually, the trail led the detectives to Charles Bolton. Asked if he was the notorious Black Bart, Bolton tried to bluff his way out with a haughty "Sir, I am a gentleman." Alas, once detectives started looking closely at his financials, and checking into the timing of his trips into the field to "inspect mining operations," it was all over for Bolton.

Bolton's real name, as it turned out, was Charles Boles. He'd been a moderately successful prospector and miner in the California gold rush, and later in the Eastern Oregon rush of the early 1860s, leaving behind a wife and four children to pursue his golden dreams like so many others; but at some point in the early 1870s, he had a negative experience with Wells Fargo, and, swearing to get even with them, he vanished from his family's sight, leaving them to conclude that he'd died — and remade himself as Charles Bolton, Mining Engineer.

Boles drew an eight-year sentence for his crime, but was released early for good behavior. His health had deteriorated in prison; he'd visibly aged, gone deaf in one ear, and was having trouble with his eyesight — possibly the victim of a stroke. He

A poster advertising a 1948 "B Movie" titled "Black Bart." Although the movie's title character shares Black Bart's real name (Charles Boles), the movie's plot bears no resemblance to the real Black Bart story.

BLACK BART'S POETRY:

LEFT AT SCENE OF A ROBBERY, AUG. 3, 1877:
I've labored long and hard for bread,
For honor and for riches;
But on my corns too long you've tred,
You fine-haired sons of bitches.

LEFT AT SCENE OF A ROBBERY, JULY 25, 1878:
Here I lay me down to sleep
To wait the coming morrow,
Perhaps success, perhaps defeat,
And everlasting sorrow.
Let come what will, I'll try it on,
My condition can't be worse;
And if there's money in that box
'Tis munny in my purse.

was released in January 1888, but complained that Wells Fargo agents wouldn't leave him alone. They apparently weren't convinced that he was done robbing stages.

The following month he checked into a hotel in Visalia, Calif., then disappeared into the wilderness — this time for good. But no body was ever found, and of course rumors flew thick and fast: was he faking his medical condition? Had he started a new life for a third time? Was he perhaps even now robbing stagecoaches under another fake identity?

Theories abound: Black Bart moved to New York and settled down; Black Bart moved to Montana and resumed robbing stagecoaches; Black Bart shipped out and lived the rest of his life in Japan ... but as with the final disposition of legendary skyjacker D.B. Cooper, no one really knows, and no one is ever likely to find out.

Sources and Works Cited:
- Outlaw Tales of Oregon, *a book by Jim Yuskavitch, published in 2007 by Twodot Press;*
- Black Bart: Boulevardier Bandit, *a book by George Hoeper, published in 1995 by Quill Driver Press of Fresno, Calif.*

DONALD MCKAY & AL.:

PATENT-MEDICINE SHOWMEN.

The two decades following the Civil War were something like a golden age of charlatanry in the West, and Oregon was no exception. From swindling tourists at a gambling parlor, to fleecing miners in a tent-city saloon, to peddling stock in nonexistent gold mines, the opportunities for a morally-flexible fellow to make a stack of ill-gotten greenbacks were probably never higher in the Beaver State than they were back then.

One of the most popular ways for a con man to steal a buck or two was with a medical-miracle scam. An enterprising con would mix up a concoction containing a few substances with dramatic effects — red pepper, raw alcohol and opium were popular ingredients — and mix in a few different flavoring agents to give it the proper medicinal taste: eucalyptus oil, for example. Then, into a bottle it would go, and the con, calling himself by a credential-heavy alias like "Dr. Scruggs" or "Professor Smith," would roll from town to town selling it as a secret-recipe folk remedy for whatever seemed most likely to coax the most gold out of the pockets of the local suckers.

This basic scheme was demonstrated in one of the more famous episodes of *The Lone Ranger* radio show, from 1938 — in which "Doc Stubbs" rolls into town selling a product called "Snake Oil Tonic," which does nothing but put the residents to sleep so that his accomplice can pick their pockets while they're out cold.

Unfortunately, there aren't many stories of specific medico-cons in the historical record. Touring the country under false names and often a skip or two ahead of the law, these swindlers did their best to stay out of the history books as long as possible.

But the legitimate physicians in the towns they visited have left us some pretty colorful accounts of their general business methods.

"Do you see that open barouche coming down the street with a torch on either side ... and two California sharpers sitting just back of the driver?" wrote Dr. William L. Adams, an eclectic physician working in Portland in the 1870s. "They wear stovepipe hats and are neatly dressed in broadcloth with high standing collars, and wear massive watch chains washed with oroids and glistening in the light of their torches.... They stop on the corner of First and Alder streets. By this time, attracted by the torches and the music of a fiddle, there has gathered around them a crowd. The orator stands up in the barouche. He takes in the character of the crowd and begins his oration: He has a medicine for sale that will cure catarrh, asthma, epizootic, and all other diseases.

"He is a ventriloquist. Here he lifts up his 'Punch and Judy' and makes her sing a song about Henry Ward Beecher, which amuses the crowd. He then makes her say something about the value of his medicine in curing all diseases....

"He makes an eloquent speech with loud intonations and violent gestures. 'This medicine is a sure cure for asthma, consumption, catarrh, or anything else you happen to have. Anyone who buys it and is not satisfied will have his money refunded. We sold 5,000 packages here in Portland last year at a dollar a package and if there is a man here who was not satisfied, let him walk up and return it and we will refund the money.'

"Of course nobody does. This satisfies the crowd that the medicine is a good thing, and one poor laboring man walks up and hands over a dollar and receives an ounce bottle of magnesia, table salt and red pepper, nicely mixed. 'Now take a pinch of that,' shouts the doctor, 'and see if it doesn't clean out your nose.' The victim obeys and sniffs, sneezes, snorts until the tears run down his cheeks and then laughs. He proudly shoves the package

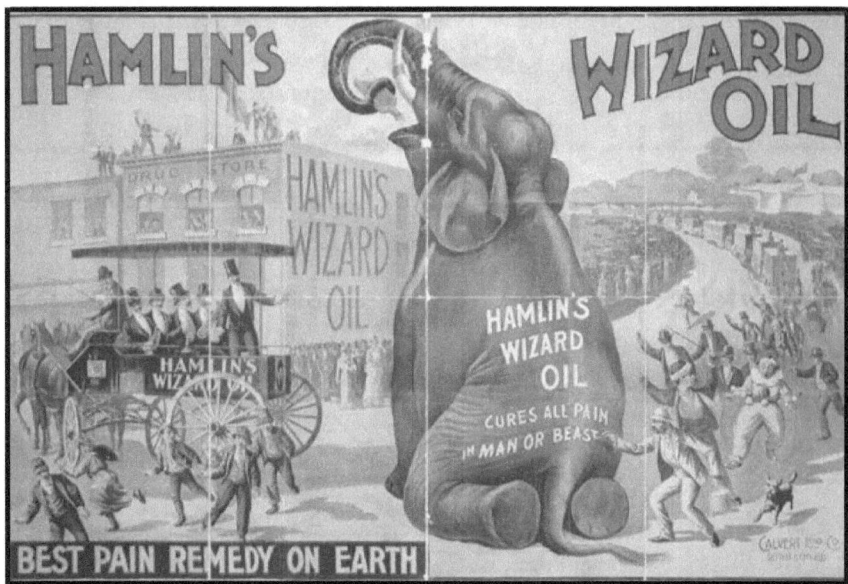

Hamlin's Wizard Oil was one of the earliest of the patent-medicine-show products; it was first produced in 1861. The stuff was 65 percent alcohol, with oils of cloves, sassafras, camphor, and turpentine added for medicinal flavoring.

into his breeches pocket, with an expression on his face that shines out through dirt and tobacco juice, which the crowd reads as saying, 'By golly, I think that medicine ain't no humbug.'

"Now the sharper shouts out: "Gentlemen, if you are skeptical of this medicine, I don't blame you. You have been humbugged and robbed by your doctors until you have no faith in medicines.'

"Here he snatches up a package of his stuff and, extending it to the crowd, proceeds: 'Gentlemen, we humbug nobody. We believe in dealing on the square. Please, walk up and try some for yourself. This may be your last chance to get a medicine for a dollar that will do you more good than a thousand dollars spent on a doctor. You may not be diseased now, but you may be within a week after we have gone back to California, and when we come back next year you may be down in your graves, or on your beds past cure. You know that millions of souls have been eternally lost because they failed to get religion when the preacher invited them. Don't make the same fearful mistake. Get medicine when you have a chance. Don't wait until it is too late.'

"At this point, the rattle of dollars dropping into the collection box sounds like a gambler's table. It is now 10:00 and the intelligent fellow-citizens are tired. The doctors bid them an affectionate good-night, promising to be back tomorrow night, and in the meantime they can be found at their room at the hotel where they will be pleased to relieve as many sufferers as choose to call.

"On reaching their rooms, their piety evaporates. They don't even say their prayers and go to bed, but proceed to open their bag and count out 57 webfoot dollars, as the result of their night's work. At four other doctors' stands the receipts range from $20 to $80. The doctors crawl into their beds happy, and ... the ventriloquist says, 'Jim, they told us the truth in California, didn't they?'

"'How's that?'

"'That there are more doggone fools in Portland than anywhere else.'

"Jim replies, 'You bet! It's a good place to gather goose feathers up here in Webfoot.'"

Dr. Adams was describing a scene from the early- to mid-1870s. By the 1880s, scenes like the one he described were getting rare. That wasn't because the public was getting wise — it was because the operators who remained in the game were starting to realize that the best way to keep the public from getting wise was to develop more finished and professional presentations and products, and more believable back-stories.

So the shows started to get really elaborate. And the patent medicines they were peddling started to get more elaborate as well: distinctively blown glass bottles and elaborately printed labels served as a testimony to buyers that, whether the medicine worked or not, it wasn't a DIY mixup of "magnesia, table salt and red pepper, nicely mixed" — it was a real factory product, usually with a fancy guarantee printed right on the label.

One of the most popular of these fancy remedies was a product painstakingly brewed by members of the Warm Springs Indian tribe of Central Oregon, using natural ingredients harvested from the beautiful virgin forests and fruitful plains of their home hunting grounds ... or so the manufacturers of "KA-TON-KA, The Great Indian Medicine" would have their customers believe.

"The ingredients of Ka-Ton-Ka are all gathered by the Warm Springs Indians in Oregon and Washington Territory," exults Page 5 of "The Warm Springs Indians and their Medicine," a 36-page booklet published by the company in the late 1880s. "They prepare them in their own peculiar manner; and no druggist can duplicate that simple Indian preparation."

No specifics are offered about those ingredients, of course; but each bottle of Ka-Ton-Ka gives full details about what kind of benefits one can expect from regularly taking it: "A cure for all blood diseases, stomach and

A bottle of Ka-Ton-Ka, with the box that it came in (in a protective plastic sleeve). The mountain man in fringed buckskins is Donald McKay. (Image: Smithsonian)

liver difficulties!" it shouts. "Such as — Dyspepsia; Biliousness; Syphilis; Scrofula; Salt Rheum; Erysipelas; Catarrh; Liver Complaint; Rheumatism; Enlargement of the Liver; and Diseases of the Kidneys!"

And, at the bottom, in bold type: "OREGON INDIAN MEDICINE CO." — followed, in the smallest letters on the entire label, by the line, "Corry, Pa." — the actual city where the stuff was actually made, by the ton, in a factory.

Ka-Ton-Ka Tonic was, of course, a simple patent medicine, barely different from the thousands of other alcohol-based medicated tipples with which the country was awash by this time. Unlike

Col. T. A. EDWARDS,
MANAGER WARM SPRING INDIAN MEDICINE CO.

"Colonel" T.A. Edwards, the "Buffalo Bill Cody" of the Oregon Indian Medicine Company, as shown in a portrait printed in an advertising pamphlet. (Image: Archive.org)

some others, Ka-Ton-Ka was at least fairly harmless; it was made with sugar, aloes, and baking soda, dissolved in water and alcohol (20 percent). And by the late 1880s it was one of the most popular patent remedies, sold by traveling troupes of Native American entertainers at elaborate wild-west shows staged at small-town community halls and parks all over the rural parts of the country.

The product, and the company, was the fruit of a partnership between a colorful New York native named "Colonel" T.A. Edwards, and a native Oregonian — a half-Cayuse mountain man named Donald McKay.

Donald McKay was the son of Hudson's Bay Co. trapper Thomas McKay and She-Who-Rides-Like-The-Wind Umatilla, a member of the Cayuse tribe. The young McKay worked early in life as a trapper and trader, then as an Indian interpreter for the U.S. Government.

Then in 1872, McKay was put in charge of the Warm Springs Indian Scouts (a detachment of the U.S. Army) and sent to do battle with Kintpuash, better known as "Captain Jack," the leader of the Modocs — who were then in the process of humiliating the regular Army by hiding out in the lava beds of Southern Oregon and defeating every force sent against them.

In 1873, the Modocs were defeated with the help of McKay and his Scouts — and news of the action, spun as heroic Wild-West action stories, made McKay nationally famous.

It was about that time that he met Edwards, who was working for the

U.S. Secret Service and had been sent out to Oregon to help with the Modoc situation.

Edwards was one of those larger-than-life promoter types with which the Wild West seemed to abound. Portraits of him from the time show keen eyes, long hair combed back, a walrus mustache and an "Imperial" goatee — very much like "Buffalo Bill" Cody. And, in every way that counts, he was in the same business as Buffalo Bill.

Capitalizing on his half-Native scout friend's momentary fame, Edwards squired McKay around the U.S. and Europe on an exhibition tour as the "Hero of the Lava Beds." This was at about the same time Buffalo Bill was doing the same thing on a grander scale; Wild West shows of the type that would soon make Buffalo Bill famous were just getting started.

But rather than taking his Western Hero and going into direct competition with Buffalo Bill, Edwards chose another path. In the mid-1870s he organized the Oregon Indian Medicine Company, with Donald McKay as a sort of hero-mascot; and got to work peddling Indian folk remedies, the formulas for which McKay supposedly learned at his grandmother's knee.

Ka-Ton-Ka was the first one, of course, and it was soon joined by a whole fleet of spurious Warm Springs medical breakthroughs: Nez Perce Catarrh Snuff, Indian Cough Syrup, Modoc Oil, War Paint Ointment, Warm Springs Consumption Cure,

The cover of a pamphlet produced by the Oregon Indian Medicine Company, prominently showcasing Donald McKay and filled with pictures and feature stories about Warm Springs Indians, their customs, and their medicines; most of the stories, of course, were made-up. (Image: Archive.org)

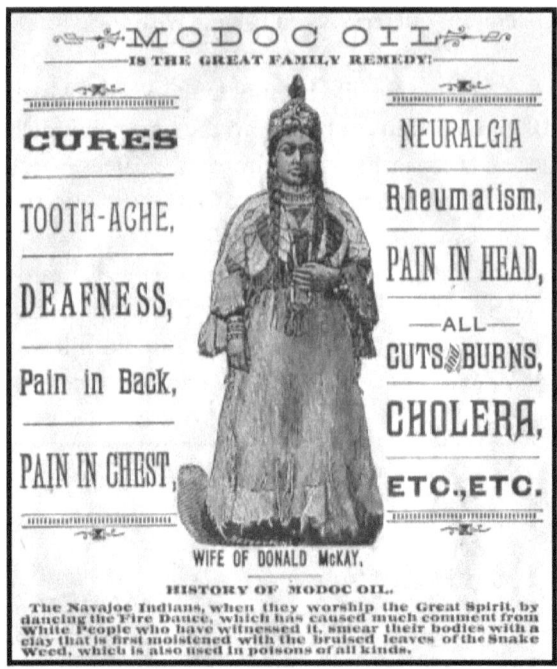

An advertisement for "Modoc Oil," one of the Oregon Indian Medicine Company products. (Image: Archive.org)

Wasco Cough Drops, Quillaia Soap, something called Mox-Ci-Tong, and Donald McKay's Indian Worm Eradicator.

This last, by the way, consisted of large pills made of rolled-up waterproof paper. In the stomach, the candy coating would dissolve and the paper would unravel, so that at the sufferer's next "call of nature," there would be visible "evidence" of tapeworm eradication in the toilet bowl. One imagines Donald McKay not being too happy about that particular medicine being the one chosen to bear his own name.

But none of these nostrums had any real medical value beyond their alcohol content, except as antacids. And perhaps McKay's ego was soothed a bit by the extraordinarily flattering full-color portrait of himself in buckskins printed on the side of each box of Ka-Ton-Ka, with the words "DONALD McKAY, Greatest of Living Scouts" at the top.

To sell all this pseudo-Indian hokum, Edwards and McKay started out by hiring troupes to go forth and stage Wild West Indian Medicine shows around the country — so basically, taking the basic setup of the "California Sharpers" described by Dr. Adams, but making it bigger and more professional and Indian-themed.

At first, the story of the Indians brewing medicine in the primeval forest proved a powerful one. But Edwards and McKay's centrally controlled sales model didn't scale up quickly enough to slake all the market demand that it stimulated in time to establish market dominance. So their main competitor in the Indian medicine racket, the Kickapoo Indian Medicine Co., promptly borrowed the concept and refined it into traveling Indian encampments complete with dozens of painted tipis, a fast-talking bottle-waving "Indian Agent" to do the selling, and a bubbling cauldron supposedly full of "medicine" that people could actually watch the "Indian medicine men" brewing. They literally hired more than 500 players — real Indians from any and every tribe, and Native-looking white people — to pretend to be Kickapoo Indians for these shows. They were peddling something called "Kickapoo Indian Sagwa," a tonic almost identical to Ka-Ton-Ka.

And with that, the Indian Medicine Craze of the 1880s was off and running.

(By the way, the Kickapoo Indian Medicine Co. never produced a product called "Kickapoo Joy Juice" — that was a fictional beverage invented by Al Capp, the cartoonist who drew "Li'l Abner" from 1934 to 1977. It was probably a winking reference to the many drinkers who used patent

Warm Springs Indian Scouts in the field at the scene of the Modoc War, in 1873, pose for a photograph. Their leader, Capt. Donald McKay, is the man standing in the front. (Image: U.S. War Dep't)

medicines like Sagwa, Ka-Ton-Ka and Jamaica Ginger to get drunk during the years of Prohibition.)

Edwards decided that instead of continuing to face the Kickapoo challenge head-on — a strategy that would almost guarantee Ka-Ton-Ka would play second fiddle, at best — his company would instead corner the market on supplying independent medicine-peddler troupes with product to sell, along with copious amounts of promotional posters and fliers, and let them do the legwork. He'd get a smaller slice, but there would be no central-office bottleneck to slow Oregon Indian Medicine's growth.

Soon all over the rural parts of the country, from tent-revival-like Indian circus shows and on the stages at community opera houses, in a thousand different ways, traveling medicine shows hawked Oregon Indian Medicine.

The idea of these shows was, basically, the same one that was used in the old single-sponsor early radio and TV shows like "Oxydol's Own Ma Perkins" or "DeSoto/Plymoth's You Bet Your Life with Groucho Marx." There would be copious entertainment — musical performances, sketch comedy, maybe a ventriloquist — followed by a pitch man urging everyone to get their wallets out.

This, of course, was before radio or television, and many little towns that were visited by these traveling shows were so grateful for the entertainment that they would buy whether they felt they needed it or not. And it certainly didn't hurt that Ka-Ton-Ka worked just as well as Tums to settle an acid stomach. It wasn't truly useless — although it certainly wasn't going to help syphilis sufferers, as the label promised, it was fine for "dyspepsia."

But it's worth remembering also that in the late 1800s, traveling troupes of Vaudeville players had a terrible reputation, especially in rural communities. So many of them were fronts for gangs of card sharpers and prostitutes that the very name "Theatre" became poisonous; if you've ever wondered why the old turn-of-the-century community theater building in towns like Elgin and Salem is called an "Opera House" despite likely never having hosted an opera in its entire existence, that's why. Rural America is peppered with other "opera houses" for the same reason.

But if a traveling Vaudeville company wasn't welcome for moral reasons, a traveling troupe of healers selling medicine was fine. For one thing, one knew exactly what they wanted — to sell bottles — and didn't have to worry about immoral hidden agendas; for another thing, if a troupe turned out to be a front for depravity, the company could be appealed to.

So these elaborate sales pitches were giving rural Oregon, and rural America, something they didn't trust anyone else to give them. Ironic as it sounds, the patent medicine swindlers were the only entertainers the public felt they could trust, because they had made peace with their particular swindle. No one was going to go to Hell for having bought a bottle of useless medicine, but plenty of rural Americans would consider themselves or their loved ones in grave danger of damnation if they succumbed to the charms of a Vaudeville tart after a variety-theatre show.

But over the first couple decades of the twentieth century, that changed. First, stock theatre troupes like Baker's Players in Portland started reclaiming the respectability of the stage; and then came motion pictures. By the outbreak of the First World War, not even the most straight-laced community had to resort to getting its entertainment from sales pitches.

By then, the Indian medicine shows were already showing their age. McKay died in 1894, although his portrait stayed on the boxes till the end. Colonel Edwards died 10 years later. The company soldiered on, dwindling in size and changing hands several times, until it sort of faded away just before the First World War.

Sources and Works Cited:

- Step Right Up, *a book by Brooks McNamara published in 1975 by Doubleday;*
- *"William McKay's Journal: 1866-67: Indian Scouts, Part I," an article by Keith Clark and Donna Clark published in the June 1978 issue of* Oregon Historical Quarterly
- The Doctor in Oregon, *a book by O. Larsell, published in 1947 by Binford and Mort of Portland;*
- *"Frontier Humor: Plain and Fancy," an article by Erik Bromberg published in the September 1960 issue of* .

JEFFERSON "SOAPY" SMITH:

SWINDLER AND RACKETEER.

August 1, 1882. On a sunny streetcorner in the middle of the rough-hewn, stump-strewn frontier town of Portland, a fresh-faced, wholesome-looking 22-year-old fellow named Jefferson Smith, nattily attired, sets up a big valise atop a portable tripod.

He opens it up. It's full of little packages, wrapped with paper. He pulls out his billfold and extracts several banknotes: some ones and fives, a ten, a twenty.

Then he looks around at the gathering crowd of curious onlookers, and starts his spiel. He has the most wonderful soap, he exults; it's lightly scented and possessed of wonderful cleansing properties. Moreover, this soap, he assures the bystanders, can make them a tidy sum of money — if they watch him carefully.

He picks up the $10 bill and a cake of soap, wraps the bill around the cake, deftly re-wraps the whole thing in paper and drops it into the valise.

"Watch me closely, gentlemen," he prattles — or words to that effect — as he scoops up another cake. This one he wraps with a $5 bill, and drops it back in the valise.

Jefferson "Soapy" Smith as he appeared in around 1890, around 30 years of age.

Finally, out comes a $20 bill — worth $440 in today's dollars — and into the bin it goes, wrapped around a cake of soap.

Dozens of eyes watch the $20 cake as the young man gives the contents of the valise a desultory stir with his left hand, while gesturing emphatically with his right as he extolls the wonders of his product.

Then he begins his closing pitch. His wonderful soap costs just 50 cents per package, or three for $1. (One dollar in 1882 was worth about $22 today.)

And in the crowd, watching with interest, is a reporter for the *Portland Daily Standard*.

The presence of that reporter is how we know about this street scene today. In his news story, the reporter didn't actually quote Smith's sales patter; he simply referred to him as "a 'fakir' whose tongue appears to be hung in the middle and run at both ends."

"During about 10 minutes in which (the reporter) was watching him, he took in about $20," the article noted. "The whole business is one of the most transparent frauds imaginable and should be stopped."

Apparently this advice was taken to heart by someone in Portland, because less than 10 days later, Smith had moved on up the river to Albany.

This article is the first documentation of the streetcorner swindle that would make Jefferson Smith rich and famous — and would give him a nickname: "Soapy" Smith, the late, lamented, too-soon-martyred patron saint of Old West con artistry, the most famous "bunco man" of his time. From the prize-package soap racket he would move on to ever more audacious criminal enterprises, eventually making his name as a political fixer and an organized-crime boss with multiple businesses specializing in fleecing "greenhorns" — and anyone else he could get away with fleecing.

All that was in the future, though, on this day in Portland. Young Soapy was still a bit of a greenhorn himself, relatively inexperienced, traveling from town to town as an itinerant swindler of a fairly common type. His skills were still rough, too, by his later standards. Toward the end of his Oregon run — late October — he got in a fistfight with some disappointed soap buyers in Eugene. An older, smoother Soapy would never have let that happen.

Soapy's Oregon run is hard to reconstruct in detail. It was early in his career, and as an itinerant swindler, he didn't keep very good records; nor did the newspapers of the day take much notice of streetcorner hawkers. But the kind of operation he was running at that time was a turf-burner, meaning that he couldn't stay too long in one spot; eventually the marks would get wise, and the city cops would start dreaming up charges on which he could be jailed. For a successful con artist, half the game was knowing when it was time to disappear in the middle of the night. Guess wrong, stay just one day too long, and you could end up with a brand-new coat of tar and feathers ... or worse.

Despite these challenges, Jeff Smith, Soapy's biographer and great-grandson, was able to place him in Astoria in early July; Portland in late July

Soapy Smith at the bar in his saloon, "Jeff. Smith's Parlor," in Skagway in February 1898. Note the light bulbs proudly displayed; electric light was a rare luxury in the 1890s, especially in Alaska.

to early August; Albany in mid-August; Salem in mid-September; and Eugene in mid-October. And by Feburary of 1883, he was in Utah, having apparently left the Beaver State for good.

But the Beaver State wasn't done with Soapy yet. Oregon still had one more role to play in Soapy's story — and it was a role that would not have pleased him much, had he known.

In later years, Soapy would develop the prize-package soap swindle to a science. Working with a team of "cappers," or secret confederates, he would set up his valise — a specially built case with a secret compartment inside, which would enable him to sort the soaps on the fly — and start his routine, wrapping a dozen or so cakes of soap with bills ranging from $1 to $100. The $1 cakes would occasionally go to a mark; the larger denominations, though, would be pulled out of the valise only when one of the cappers made a purchase. The capper would joyfully "discover" a $10 bill in his soap and go frolicking off with it. Soapy would glibly point out that the $20 and $100 packages were still in play, and resume his sales.

As the number of bars in the valise dwindled, Soapy would switch to an auction format, and people would bid up the price of the remaining soaps. From there, it was simple enough. Near the end of the soap supply, Soapy would simply sell the $100 package to a capper, and the crowd, disappointed, would melt away.

It was a few years after leaving Oregon that Soapy Smith settled down in Denver to build the first of his three major organized-crime empires. He seems to have realized that rather than living on the lam, one step ahead of the law or the vigilance committee, he could establish himself in a morally flexible town which a lot of greenhorns pass through. He could then fleece those out-of-town suckers to his heart's content, while leaving the locals strictly alone and building their trust and goodwill with copious local philanthropy.

Soapy built elaborate criminal empires first in Denver, then in Creede, Colorado, and finally, after the Klondike Gold Rush broke out, in Skagway, Alaska. At their peak, these operations ran multiple crooked saloons and gambling dens, lottery shops, auctions for imitation jewelry and watches, and even fake stock exchanges.

But as he got older, Soapy's bad habits started to catch up with him. Throughout his mid-30s, his drinking problem worsened, and when drunk his temper was terrible. The morale and discipline of his confederates — the "Soap Gang," the cappers and assistants whose loyalty was always Soapy's

The town of Skagway as it appeared in the 1910s. The Juneau Wharf, where the shootout between Soapy Smith and Oregonian Frank Reid took place, is the one at center-left. (Image: Postcard)

number-one asset — started to go to seed.

It all came to a head on July 8, 1898, on the Juneau Wharf in Skagway. Three members of the Soap Gang had swindled a miner out of $87 in a game of three-card monte. Wanting more money to play, he offered some gold dust from his bag, which contained $2,700 worth; one of the swindlers snatched the bag and and ran.

A vigilante group demanded that Soapy return the money; Soapy refused, loyally standing behind his men's claim that the miner had lost it all fair and square playing three-card monte. The vigilantes were meeting on the pier to decide what to do about it when Soapy loaded his Winchester rifle and went down to the meeting in an apparent attempt at intimidation.

When he got there, he found the vigilantes had posted four guards to bar any Soap Gang members from the meeting. One of them, the only one of the four who was armed, was an Oregonian: Frank Reid, a teacher from Linn County who had joined the gold rush a year or two before. (It's tempting to wonder if Reid might have bought some soap from Soapy when he was working the marks in Albany 15 years earlier; he was, at the time, 48 years old, so he would have been in his early 30s.)

The three unarmed guards stepped aside for Soapy, who was almost certainly liquored up and in a bad humor. The fourth, Reid, did not. Soapy went for Reid with the rifle, either to clobber him with it or shoot him; Reid pulled his revolver; and a second or two later, Reid was mortally wounded and Soapy was stone dead. Soapy's last words were, "My God, don't shoot!" — but, unfortunately for him, he was addressing them to a man who likely knew he was about to die of wounds that had just been inflicted on him by Soapy.

Soapy Smith was just 38 years old when he died. His passing was largely unlamented at the time, but in subsequent years his career would be refurbished in nostalgic memory in the typical manner of American bad guys from Jesse James to D.B. Cooper. Today, remembering the copious philanthropy that was always necessary to ensure the support of the local population, he is sometimes depicted as a sort of fast-talking Robin Hood, stealing from the rich and giving to the poor. And the true story of Soapy Smith can sometimes be hard to pick out from among all the legends that have developed.

The world was probably a better place after Soapy Smith was removed from it. But it was, without question, a less interesting and colorful one.

Sources and Works Cited:
- Alias Soapy Smith: The Life and Death of a Scoundrel, *a book by Jeff Smith, published in 2009 by Klondike Research of Juneau;*
- The Reign of Soapy Smith, *a book by William Ross & al., published in 1935 by Doubleday.*

MAUD MYRTLE JOHNSON:

ACTRESS AND INSURANCE SCAMMER

When D.C. Davis first met Hazel Petterson, she was lying, frail and sickly, in a hotel bed in Yacolt, Washington. She'd been taken there following a horrifying mishap on the Northern Pacific Railroad on April 9, 1909.

It seemed someone had left a suitcase in the aisle, and the train's crew hadn't noticed. As the train had pulled into Yacolt, there had been a sudden lurch, and poor Mrs. Petterson, her baby in her arms, had been thrown forward and tripped over the suitcase. Crashing to the floor with a horrible scream as she held her baby safely away from harm, she'd writhed there in agony, spitting teeth and blood and clutching her side.

Hastily removed to the hotel bed in which she now rested, they had learned the extent of her injuries — and they were astonishing. Her ankle appeared to be broken, with a bone out of place, although it had not yet started swelling. She appeared to have at least one broken rib. One of her pupils was dilated while the other was normal — a known sign of either eye injury or brain trauma. And she'd spat two teeth out upon the floor of the

Maud Myrtle (Wagnon) Johnson, "Queen of Fakers," as she appeared in court during her 1909 trial for swindling $1,250 out of the Northern Pacific Railroad by pretending to be injured. (Image: UO Libraries)

train amid a welter of blood, the apparent result of a lung hemorrhage, possibly punctured by the broken rib.

This was bad. And it kept getting worse. Davis had learned that Mrs. Petterson was a wealthy widow from Calgary, the sort of person who could be expected to take legal action against the railroad if she felt unfairly treated. Davis's job was to make sure she didn't.

Davis spent nearly a week attending to poor Mrs. Petterson. A local doctor examined her, confirmed her injuries and set her ankle in a plaster cast.

As the railroad's claims agent, Davis's first priority was to forestall any litigation and attendant bad publicity. So as soon as he could, before any additional symptoms could manifest themselves, he hurriedly started negotiating a settlement with the injured woman. She finally accepted a payment of $1,250, and he wrote a bank draft out on the spot.

Then he set about getting her ready to go home to Calgary. She was loaded in a stretcher on a baggage car and sent to Vancouver (Washington); then she was placed in an automobile and gingerly driven down into Portland, in the care of two nurses hired by the railroad. They first took her to the railroad's banking house, where Davis vouched for her identity and she cashed the draft — taking most of it in gold.

This was probably the moment when the first hints of doubt started to cross Davis's mind. Why would a wealthy widow faced with nothing more than a week-long train trip home want the trouble of lugging five pounds of gold along with her?

Mrs. Petterson checked into a hotel. Davis went out, at her request, to find an attorney for her, make an appointment with an eye specialist, and arrange accommodations on a train back to Calgary.

Then Mrs. Petterson asked her nurse to go and make travel arrangements. She'd be OK for an hour or two until the nurse could return, she said.

Immediately after the nurse departed, Mrs. Petterson hopped out of bed and made a phone call. Within minutes she'd left the hotel — and disappeared into the night.

When Davis returned, she was gone.

Following a quick series of inquiries to Calgary by telegraph, the dismayed Mr. Davis learned that there was no recently widowed Mrs. Petterson. He also learned that a very odd thing had been found in Mrs. Petterson's hotel room in Yacolt: A small packet of red powder, which had been recognized as fake blood.

There could now be no doubt: D.C. Davis had been taken for a ride. And, worse yet, he knew exactly who had conned him. All the railroad claims agents, all over the West, had been talking about her. She could be none other than the "Queen of Fakers," Maud Myrtle Johnson — a smooth and talented actress who over the previous few years had bilked railroads and streetcar companies all over the western United States out of at least $200,000.

And, in what must have been a particularly bitter revelation to poor Mr. Davis, it turned out that the train she'd been riding on had been carrying Maud Johnson away from the courthouse in Seattle, where she'd just been acquitted on charges of soaking the Seattle streetcar company for $600 in precisely the same way.

Maud Johnson was born Maud Myrtle Wagnon, on a farm near Albany. After her mother died, her father left her in a convent in Salem and moved to Portland, where, in an ironic twist, he became a police officer.

Maud undoubtedly had some abandonment issues related to this. As a teenager, she seems to have been something of a hellion. When she was 14, she sued a man for seduction under promise of marriage, and at 16 ran away from the convent into whose care she had been committed with another man.

She soon drifted into a life of crime and Vaudeville — a combination that would turn out to be rather lucrative for her over the subsequent years. And at the same time she was becoming well known to the police departments of Salem, Portland, and Pendleton, she was also acquiring a very unusual set of skills.

By 1906, Maud could dislocate an ankle, a knee, and a rib at will. Endowed with a slightly misshapen chest, she learned to pose it to maximize an illusion of brokenness. One of her eyes was noticeably different in appearance than the other, and she could exacerbate that by dilating its pupil at will. And she developed a macabre ability to bite on her gums in a way that produced blood on demand.

As a side note, it really is very hard to ignore the possibility that Maud's peculiar bodily idiosyncrasies were the lingering legacy of a history of horrific physical abuse. The most likely way to end up with asymmetrical pupils is brain damage from head trauma; the most common way to end up with an asymmetrical rib cage is broken ribs left unset. The most likely explanation for the ability to produce a mouthful of blood on demand is jagged fragments of teeth broken off below the gumline. An ankle and a knee that can be dislocated at will, these are not things that just grow that way — there has to have been a first time when someone dislocated them. It's possible that she developed this set of skills and abilities in a more innocuous way ... but it's far more likely that someone *broke* Maud Myrtle Wagnon, not once but many times and over a period of several years when she was young and flexible enough to survive it all.

Regardless of how she came by her abilities, once she figured out how to put them to work, Maud took her show on the road. Adopting a foundling baby from an orphanage to use as a prop — she knew a settlement would be far more likely if a baby were involved — she set out with a small group of accomplices, bilking railroad and streetcar companies all over the country and living high on the hog from the proceeds. Sometimes, after a particularly horrific-looking pratfall, she would even call for a lawyer and minister and "make out a will" on the spot. (This was great for convincing railroad agents that she was rich, and therefore dangerous.)

She was good enough that she might have gotten away with this for many years if she'd been just able to dope out a way to keep the marks from getting wise. She knew to stick around after being paid was courting trouble; for instance, can you imagine if she'd stayed an extra day in D.C. Davis's care, after they found that fake blood she'd left in her room in Yacolt?

And yet, every time the delivery of a stack of cash transformed her from a catatonic cripple into a hale and hearty specimen leaping aboard an outbound train, the party she'd swindled couldn't help but get wise to her game, and set about collecting clues to try to catch her or prevent her from doing it again.

Her performances were so lucrative, and her abrupt departures so obvious and galling to the freshly fleeced, that the railroad agents actually formed the Pacific Claim Agents Association specifically to try to spread the word of her antics and share information that might lead to her capture.

And that's exactly how she was caught. Something she did or said in

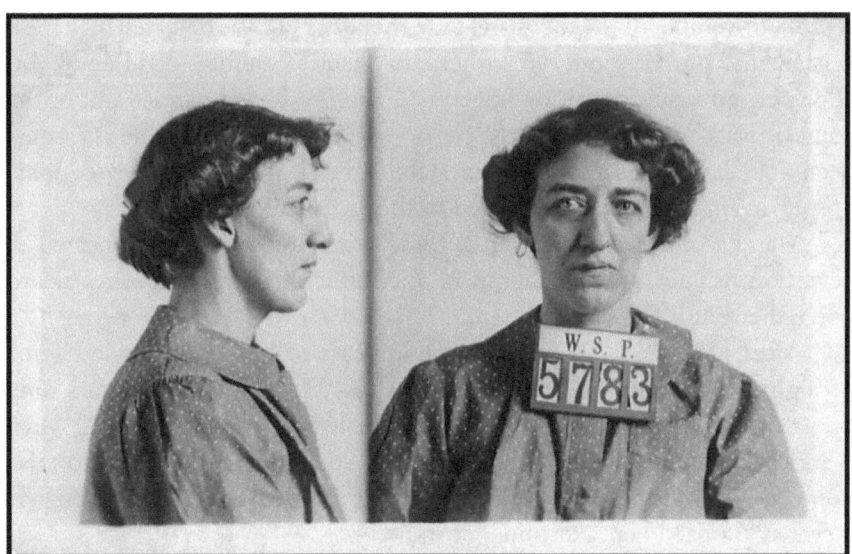

Maud Myrtle Wagnon Johnson's prison mugshot from her time in Walla Walla State Prison. Notice her slightly protruding right eye. (Image: Washington State Archives)

Yacolt gave her away, and authorities caught up with and arrested her in San Francisco.

Her subsequent trial in Vancouver turned into a big event. It was a bit like a reunion tour for all the claims agents she'd defrauded in her long and distinguished career. The prosecutor paraded them before the jury, one after the other, describing her performances — the horrible falls, the "blood" gushing from her mouth and nose, the sickening misalignments of knees and ribs, and always the poor wailing baby who was frightened but uninjured in the crash.

The outcome was never in doubt. Off to the penitentiary at Walla Walla went Maud Johnson to serve a five-year sentence, leaving the baby she'd adopted with her family.

But even in prison, Maude never stopped working the angles. She "platformed" a deadly illness with a letter to the warden inquiring if she would be allowed to bring her medicine into the joint ("as I am in ill health, having a fibroid tumor.")

She then used this documentation of an imaginary ailment to rally a group of outside supporters, who lobbied for her early release. Team Maud scored a stunning triumph the following year, in May 1911, when they actually got Gov. Oswald West of the state of Oregon to write to Washington Gov. Marion Hay to endorse her early release. Gov. Hay, who was by now wise to the game, replied with a short, courteous note declining to intervene.

In November of the following year, though, Hay was defeated by Ernest Lister, who proved more sympathetic to Maud's carefully-peddled plight. The new governor promptly intervened and got Maud paroled out of the joint (it wasn't technically parole per se — this was before parole as a penal technique had been adopted by the state — but it was a post-release monitoring arrangement that amounted to the same thing).

Maud promptly ditched her P.O. and skipped town and disappeared. A few months later, she was caught in Snohomish County, and sent back to serve the rest of her sentence.

After her release, Maud Johnson appears to have more or less gone straight, immersing herself fully into show business. She appears only sporadically in the newspapers after that, including one time in 1922 when a minstrel's troupe she'd joined disbanded suddenly and she had to raise some cash by kiting bad checks. But as far as I've been able to learn, she never again tried her fake-injury swindle.

Or ... maybe she did, having learned from previous mistakes. If so, we'll likely never know.

Sources and Works Cited:
- *"How This Early Northwest Con Woman Became 'Queen Of Fakers,'" a radio newsfeature by Allie Ferguson produced on KNKX Radio on April 22, 2017;*
- *"Maud Johnson: Queen of Fakers," an article by Logan Camporeale published on thelocalhistory.com on Nov. 13, 2016;*
- *"Smooth Woman Swindler on Coast," an un-by-lined article published in the July 31, 1909, issue of* Electric Traction Weekly;
- *"Fakir Queen Makes Living Falling from Trains," an un-by-lined article published in the May 27, 1914, issue of* The Day Book;
- Portland Morning Oregonian, Pendleton East Oregonian *and* Albany State Rights Democrat *archives, 1896-1922.*

EDWARD F. LEE:

PATENT MEDICINE SWINDLER.

PLEASE NOTE: This story is the only one in this collection that contains strong profanity — an "F-bomb" in the context of an extremely coarse anatomical reference. In the original newspaper article on which this story was based, this had to be danced around, of course, but the conventions of books are different.

Not much is known about Edward F. Lee, the Albany-based swindler sent up the river for mail fraud in 1919. In fact, Edward F. Lee may not even have been his real name; he may have assumed it as an alias to encourage people to confuse him with a highly respected and trusted Seattle-area businessman and shipbuilder of the same name.

Lee's career as a huckster started out relatively mildly. In the early 1910s, his small classified ads frequently appeared in the Portland *Morning Oregonian*'s business section, and their content was only slightly scammy. "$8 EVERY DAY selling ORANGEADE POWDER, the new drink," reads one from May 1915. "It's the craze; everybody buys; sample package 10 cents; makes a gallon; send today: EDWARD F. LEE, Kennewick, Wash."

Of course, 10 cents was a lot of money to pay in 1915 for a packet of Kool-Aid powder, but it's not against the law to charge high prices.

That can't have been all he was doing, though, because in 1916 Spokane County authorities arrested him for committing fraud through the mails. His advertisements in the Oregonian stopped for a time, and the next time they appeared in the Oregonian, they were slightly different:

> VALUABLE FORMULAS and trade secrets. List free. EDWARD F. LEE, Albany, Oregon.

These formulas, such as they were, included recipes for home production of liquor, which had been outlawed in Oregon several years previously. But that wasn't what got Lee in trouble with the law — that would come from the other ads he was running at the same time, in publications far distant from Lee's new home city of Albany. Ads like this one, quoted without attribution in the *Journal of the American Medical Association's* report on his case:

> MEN OF ALL AGES—STOP GROWING OLD. You can recover and retain your youthful vigor and vitality without dangerous drugs and appliances. OUR NEW METHOD tells how. Send for free letter. The P. Presto Company, Albany, Oregon.

This ad was, as you have likely guessed, a carefully coded appeal to men suffering from erectile dysfunction. At the time, ministering to this cohort of men was an extremely profitable and popular line for scammers of all types. For many men of that era, impotence was almost a fate worse than death; it was a severe blow to their masculine pride. They were desperate enough to try nearly anything in quest for a cure. And, even better, erectile dysfunction was a disease that most commonly struck affluent men in their 50s and 60s — meaning they'd have plenty of money to throw around to find that cure.

The hucksters rose to the occasion, peddling everything from fake folk remedies to the "electric belts" that were supposed to jolt men's reproductive apparatus back to life. There was even a quack surgeon in Little Rock, Arkansas, who offered to surgically implant a piece of a goat's testicle in patients.

Potential patients who had ingested dangerous drugs or blasted their most sensitive parts with electrical currents without noticeable effect read Lee's advertisement with considerable interest. And best of all, the price was right; so many of them took the time to write a letter to Lee requesting more information.

In response, he would send them a form letter. In this letter, Lee described the benefits of his remedy in much blunter language:

Safe and sane and scientific, it is what every young, middle-aged or old man should know, as our system will enlarge, lengthen and strengthen the organs, making the weak strong and the strong stronger, and bring back the firmness of youth unlike any other method.

The letter then announced that the price of the treatment was $2, but the patient need only send half the money up front. Upon receipt of the first dollar, Lee would mail the "copyrighted new method" to the patient with a bill for the remaining dollar, to be paid only if the patient was 100 percent satisfied.

In point of fact, Lee never expected to see that second dollar from his patients. When they took his bait, here's what they received in the mail from him:

To build up, to strengthen and increase the blood and nerve supply to the testicles, they should be stretched by placing one hand on each side of the scrotum above the testicles, and stretch them (the testicles) away from the body, moving the hands from side to side in a swaying motion while pulling. The above treatment frees the circulation in the many feet of arteries, veins, etc., and causes a strong flow of blood and nerve force to the parts. Stretch the penis the same way. Also stretch the skin of the scrotum strongly with the tips of the fingers. Above treatment should also be used for variocos le (a common cause of male infertility), but should be given quite gently at first.

It gets worse:

Should the impotency have been caused by prostate gland enlargement," Lee's letter continues, "anoint the first (index) finger in Vaseline or mild oil and, inserting the finger in the rectum, manipulate well the prostate gland, which lies right in front of the rectum and behind the lower portion of the bladder.

And, of course, the second page contained a bill for $1.

In other words — and it's very hard to imagine that Lee didn't think of it in exactly this way — once he got a sucker's dollar, he responded to it by sending step-by-step instructions on how the mark might "go fuck himself" — along with a bill.

Lee knew he could get away with this sort of stunningly gratuitous disrespect because of the shame his victims felt about their conditions. No man who sent away for a patent cure for impotence would ever dare to say a word about it.

But Lee's downfall seems to have come from a different product: a compound he called "Vivian," which he was selling as a birth-control product. Birth control of any kind was, in 1919, against the law; but it was widely practiced, and there wasn't nearly as much social stigma associated with it as there was with impotence. Women who were swindled with a sugar-pill birth control formula could not be depended upon to keep their mouths shut about it, as he apparently assumed they would.

And so it was that Edward F. Lee found himself, on August 4, 1919, facing a federal judge after having been found guilty of misuse of the mails.

Lee's attorney, of course, tried his best to get his client a decent deal — but the prosecution had an ace up its sleeve: The prosecutor had found out about Lee's conviction for mail fraud up in Spokane County.

Now knowing he was dealing with a repeat offender, Judge Wolverton threw the book at him, sending Lee to serve an 18-month sentence in federal prison.

What became of him after his release I have been unable to learn.

Sources and Works Cited:
- Nostrums and Quackery, *a book by Arthur J. Cramp, published in 1921 by Press of American Medical Association of Chicago;*
- Portland Morning Oregonian *archives, 1915, 1917, and 1919.*

JONATHAN BOURNE JR.

POLITICAL BOSS.

T he 1896 election had been good to Portland businessman and politician Jonathan Bourne Jr. He had gotten himself elected to a seat in the Oregon House, with a good chance to become speaker.

Of course, there had been some — ahem — irregularities. But then, of course there had. This was Oregon, after all.

Bourne was in his early 30s, outgoing and well liked, with cocky eyes and a moustache that had to be seen to be believed. His father owned Bourne Mills, a clothing manufacturer in New Bedford, Mass., and also a small fleet of whaling ships. Young Jonathan had dropped out of Harvard — or possibly he had been been kicked out; a fairly believable rumor had it that he had hired a burglar to break into the administration building and steal his grades, and was caught in the act.

In any case, after leaving Harvard, he had gone to sea on one of his father's ships, and ended up shipwrecked off China. It was on his way home from Hong Kong, in 1885, that he discovered Portland.

Something about the town's wide-open character appealed to young

Jonathan. According to a letter from fellow legislator Abraham Lafferty, upon arriving he arranged to tour the town by hiring a cab and driving around town "accompanied by the leading lady of a traveling show, and with an ice bucket filled with champagne bottles sitting in front of them in the cab."

As you can imagine, Bourne soon had a motley collection of good friends and kindred spirits along the town's shady waterfront — especially its notorious "North End" north of Stark Street, where by popular consensus all the hard-core vice operators were supposed to stay, tucked out of the sight of more respectable Portlanders. Sailors' boardinghouse operator and shanghai artist Larry Sullivan was probably the best known of the bunch; the owners of numerous seedy waterfront saloons and whorehouses and opium dens made up the others. Together, these shady entrepreneurs and entrepreneuses catered to the lowest caste of people in Portland — sailors and hobos, along with itinerant loggers and lumbermen.

Clever lad that he was, Bourne had quickly figured out that those desperate wastrels, scorned by many as the dregs of society, were the source of tremendous political power. Starting in 1884 or so, he set about tapping that power to advance his political career.

By the the election of '96, Bourne was as close to a political-machine boss as Portland would ever get. And in that election, he tapped that power to the fullest.

Following a now-familiar playbook, hundreds and hundreds of sailors, just-passing-through loggers, hookers and saloon bums turned out, eager earn the price of a drink or six by casting ballot after ballot for Bourne and his friends — a plan that now propelled Bourne to power in the House of Representatives accompanied by enough friendly faces to make it pretty likely he'd be named speaker.

Ensuring the re-election of his pick for U.S. Senate, John Mitchell, was quite a bit more expensive, but just as easy; in those days, the state legislature picked the state's senators, so all he had to do was secure written pledges of support for Mitchell from a majority of legislators and pay for those pledges with fat campaign contributions underwritten (to the tune of $225,000) by the Southern Pacific Railroad. Easily done, and quickly too.

By the day after Election Day, Bourne could look back on the whole operation as a big success. But a few days later, Bourne learned that something was about to happen that would utterly ruin it for him.

That's when he started hearing rumors that U.S. Senator John Mitchell planned to abandon his support for the silver standard for U.S. currency, and switch his allegiance to gold.

Why, you may ask, would Bourne care about something like that?

RASCALS.

Jonathan Bourne Jr. as he appeared a few years after arriving in Portland in 1885. (Image: Oregon Historical Society)

Well, Bourne was the owner of several silver mines in Eastern Oregon and Idaho. He was passionately committed to the silver standard because, well, it was great for the silver business. Hearing that Senator Mitchell was about to switch allegiance and throw his lot in with the "gold crowd" was a shocker. The next time Bourne saw Mitchell, he asked him straight out, and Mitchell reluctantly admitted it.

It was a serious double-cross, and both men knew it. But elder-statesman

Mitchell must have been a bit taken aback by the youthful Bourne's reaction:

"I looked him straight in the face and I said, 'You are not going to be elected by this legislative body that meets next January,'" Bourne recalled, according to former governor Walter Pierce's account.

"The Senator replied, 'Jonathan, you can't [stop me],'" Bourne recalled. "'You took the pledges from the men who were candidates when you gave them the money for their expenses for the campaign, and you took those pledges to the Southern Pacific Railroad which put up the $225,000 that you distributed among candidates for the legislature. Those pledges have been signed. They are locked up in the Southern Pacific Railroad safe.... You can't help it. I will be elected.'"

Bourne knew Mitchell was right about one thing: There was nothing he would be able to do to change the way the vote would go when the subject of Mitchell's re-election came up. Odd though it sounds to the modern ear, the politicians who signed those pledges in return for Bourne's bribes considered them to constitute their word of honor as gentlemen, even though in signing them they had been violating several federal laws and essentially swindling their constituents. Regardless of Mitchell's changed plans, they would vote for him.

However, if the Legislature failed to elect *anyone* in time for inauguration day, the law stipulated that the governor would appoint someone to the vacant post. And the governor at that time — Republican William P. Lord — was a friend and ally of Bourne's. All Bourne had to do was figure out how to prevent the Legislature from voting until inauguration day.

How might he do that?

He did it with classic Bourne flair. First, he collected together about $80,000 — including $10,000 skimmed from the operations of his North End friends' waterfront gambling joints, opium dens, brothels and shanghai boardinghouses — and used it to throw a massive, six-week-long drunken party for his fellow legislators in the state House of Representatives.

The party would rage for forty days and forty nights, in an unholy if unconscious parody of the Biblical account of Jesus' time of temptation in the wilderness.

"I ... hired the best chef in the state of Oregon; sent him to Salem to fix up apartments in the Eldridge Block; things to eat and drink and entertainment," Bourne later recalled. "I said to the chef, 'I pay all expenses. I want to take care of all my friends in the lower House who signed pledges with me, the friends of silver.'"

The chef probably didn't come from the North End, but some of the "entertainment" clearly did. The Eldridge Block quickly developed some colorful new nicknames: "Bourne's Harem" was one; "the Den of Prostitution and Evil" was another. State Senator George C. Brownell of Oregon City wrote disapprovingly that legislators at Bourne's party "were kept drunk and intoxicated for days."

Of course, how much of this was an accurate assessment of the event, and how much was the disgruntlement of those left off the guest list for the hottest party in town, cannot really be known. The party was, of course, restricted to House members who were "friends of silver."

This was the 40-day debauch that went down in song and legend as "the hold-up session."

By Inauguration Day, nothing had come out of the state House at all — on Mitchell's re-election or any other topic. So, as Bourne had planned, Governor Lord announced the appointment of one of Bourne's closest political allies, Henry Corbett, to Mitchell's Senate seat.

Corbett was delighted, of course. He had been a Senator, years before, and had long cherished hopes of being elected to the Senate again. Alas, when he arrived in Washington he met a chilly reception. Stories of the hold-up session had preceded him and Capitol Hill was a-twitter with them. The U.S. Senate refused to seat him.

A crestfallen Corbett had to return to Portland, and Oregon's second Senate seat remained vacant for two full years. Finally, in late 1898, a special session of the Legislature elected Joseph Simon — another close associate of Bourne's — to Mitchell's seat.

Mitchell was done for, at least for the time being. (He would come roaring back a few years later, and we will have quite a bit more to say about him in the next chapter.)

Jonathan Bourne had won — and had earned for Oregon a reputation for political corruption that wouldn't fade for decades.

Sources and Works Cited:
- Merchants, Money and Power: The Portland Establishment, 1843-1913, *a book by E. Kimbark MacColl, published in 1988 by Georgian Press of Portland;*
- Memoirs of Walter M. Pierce, *a book by Walter M. Pierce, published in 1981 by Oregon State University Press.*

JOHN M. HIPPLE, A.K.A. JOHN H. MITCHELL:

EMBEZZLER, BIGAMIST, AND U.S. SENATOR.

When you're watching a melodrama, you know right away who the villain is. That's him over there, twirling a sinister handlebar moustache beneath a sleek silk stovepipe hat and telling the pretty widow and her nine orphan children to kiss their beloved homestead goodbye.

But that's melodrama, right? And the next scene is always one in which the hero arrives just in time to squelch the villain's evil plan. "Zounds! Curses! Foiled again!"

Ah, but this scene wasn't melodrama. It was real life.

The poor widow was Mary Jane Balch, widowed wife of the late Danford Balch, the first man legally executed in the history of the state of Oregon (and, you may remember, the fellow Portland City Marshal James Lappeus reportedly offered to spring from jail for a $1,000 bribe).

The old family homestead she was being turned out of included much of what's now Portland's Northwest Heights neighborhood and a goodly swatch of Forest Park — some of the most valuable real estate in the state.

The classic Snidely Whiplash-style melodrama character.. John H. Mitchell was probably as close as Oregon has come to a real historical figure who fits this stereotype. (Image: Leland John)

And the crafty, mustache-twirling villain was an attorney Mrs. Balch had hired to help her sell the property, who had craftily arranged the paperwork so he could gobble up nearly all the proceeds — and he was none other than Oregon's very own Snidely Whiplash: Future U.S. Senator John H. Mitchell.

As a member of the U.S. Senate, Mitchell enjoyed the official title of "The Honorable John H. Mitchell," but, well, that title really didn't quite suit him. For one thing, "John Mitchell" wasn't his real name — it was an alias that he adopted as a fugitive from justice. For another, relative to the "honorable" part ... well, perhaps I should just tell his story.

John H. Mitchell's real name was John M. Hipple — "Mitchell" was his middle name — and he was born in 1835 in Pennsylvania. After graduating from college, he embarked on a career as a schoolteacher there.

Then, in the mid-1850s he got one of his students, 15-year-old Sadie Hoon, into some family-style trouble, a situation he resolved in the usual way — by marrying her.

A few years later, the Hipples had two additional children. John proved hardworking and ambitious, although he wasn't the sort of fellow who lets a little old thing like a wedding ring slow down his social life; within a few years of his marriage, if that, he was discreetly (or, if you believe Sadie's account, not so discreetly) keeping a mistress on the side.

By 1857, John M. Hipple was a practicing attorney, well on his way to making a nice life for himself and his little family.

And then ... he vanished. He took his youngest daughter and his mistress, "borrowed" $4,000 belonging to the law firm he was working for (which he did pay back, much later), and set out across the continent to start a new life in California, leaving his wife and other children behind and penniless.

Then in 1860 he did it again, abandoning the mistress in San Francisco and moving to Oregon with his daughter. Perhaps he was tired of the mistress; but the timing of this move suggests a more likely reason: In 1859 the first telegraph line was installed connecting San Francisco to the East Coast, which meant it was now much harder to hide out from the Pinkerton detectives and other law-enforcement types after having embezzled that $4,000 (which was worth more than $100,000 in modern currency). And yes, there were private detectives actively looking for him. Now that San Francisco had a telegraph wire, they could very easily check to see if he was living there, and, after learning that he was, show up on his doorstep unexpectedly at any time.

So unless he was ready to cough up the cash, answer some very tough questions and possibly serve some hard time, John M. Hipple needed to make himself a whole lot harder to find, right quick.

Portland in 1860 was about as far away from anywhere as you could get without living in a log cabin and having to kill stuff for your dinner. As other men had before him and others would again after, he found refuge from a checkered past in this frontier city, a place to start a new life. And with a new life came a new name: John Mitchell Hipple was now calling himself John

Sen. John Mitchell as he looked when, as a young railroad attorney, he was first elected to the U.S. Senate, in the 1870s. (Image: Joseph Gaston)

John H. Mitchell as he appeared in the 1870s, when he was in his 30s. (Image: J. Gaston)

H. Mitchell, Attorney at Law.

It was shortly after arriving that Mitchell fleeced the widow and orphans Balch. At around the same time, the still-married Lothario started romancing the daughter of a blacksmith in Oregon City; he subsequently married her without having bothered to first divorce Sadie, an oversight that would come back to haunt him later.

Now, to be fair about this, John H. Mitchell was playing a very high-stakes game, and he knew it. He'd probably skipped San Francisco just a week or two ahead of the law. It was a matter of time, and not much of it, before they tumbled to Portland as a possible next place to look for him; and once they did, the new name wouldn't fool them for long. He had an unknown amount of time — it could be years, it could be months, or it could be a matter of days — before he would be called to account for the $4,000 he'd stolen. And the only way to win the game he was playing was to get so big, so fast, that he could pay the money back with interest and make it worth his benefactors' while to decline to prosecute him for the theft.

The race was on, and Mitchell had bet his life on the outcome — figuratively as well as literally, given the conditions in the Oregon State Penitentiary at the time. Mitchell could not afford scruples if they delayed his reaching that critical mass of wealth and power that would keep him out of prison. And over the next few years he would stop at nothing, or nearly nothing, to make it big enough.

RASCALS.

Mitchell was, by all accounts, as charismatic as he was rascally. He soon made the acquaintance of another newcomer to Oregon: the controversial and flashy Ben Holladay, the Gilded Age stagecoach-and-railroad magnate who rocked the Portland establishment with his energetic, take-no-prisoners approach to business, especially his Oregon & California Railroad. Mitchell became Holladay's personal attorney, which was most certainly a lucrative job, and soon he was Portland's leading railroad-and-timber lawyer.

But where Mitchell made his big money, early on — and the job that probably saved him from the consequences of the $4,000 theft — was in a deft swindle pulled in 1868, which left him and few of his friends with clear title to half of downtown Portland.

Before Portland was more than a clearing on the river, a woman named Elizabeth Caruthers and her son, Finice, had taken out a 640-acre homestead claim just south of the "town." The property, clearly in the path of progress, was already skyrocketing in value. Elizabeth Caruthers considered herself a widow — her husband had disappeared and was presumed dead — so the land claim was in her own name.

Both Carutherses subsequently died, with no known heirs and no will. Mitchell and some promoter friends saw their chance.

They went on a hunt for a man who answered to the name of Joe Thomas — the name of Elizabeth Caruthers's vanished husband — who would be willing, for a fee, to swear to be *the* Joe Thomas, the missing husband himself.

They found such a man in St. Louis. Although his real name turned out to be John C. Nixon, he was willing to lie about that, which was good enough to get the job done.

Nixon was brought to Portland, where he was sworn in and faithfully did his bit of perjury. Then, after receiving an

John H. Mitchell in 1898, two years after Bourne's machinations had successfully ousted him from his seat in the U.S. Senate. (Image: Oregon Historical Society)

$8,000 payoff for his services (and remember, that's about 200 grand in modern currency), he deeded the land over to Mitchell's group.

Easy money.

By the 1870s, Mitchell knew well how profitable it could be to mix business and politics. He'd gotten himself elected to the state senate in 1862, almost immediately upon arriving in the state.

Ten years later, he was able to clinch the prize he was really after: A seat in the U.S. Senate. He set his sights on Henry Corbett's Senate seat. But, that's the moment at which he was nearly undone by a blast of karma. It had come to the attention of his political enemies that he'd abandoned most of his first family in Pennsylvania, was living under an alias, and was a bigamist.

It's certain that by the time these revelations developed, Mitchell had already made amends for the $4,000. In fact, he likely took care of that the minute he could financially swing it. Particularly after he started working with Ben Holladay, any injured party contemplating prosecuting him after he'd paid back the money and a generous "interest payment" would have to think long and hard about whether he could afford to make such a powerful enemy.

In any case, by the time Mitchell's troubles were being unpacked in the Portland *Morning Oregonian* (which was, at the time, owned by Mitchell's Senate-race opponent, Henry Corbett himself) the folks Mitchell had stolen the $4,000 from were calling it a loan and making it very clear that they considered everything to have been 100 percent aboveboard.

So that meant all that was left to worry about was the bigamy charge, and the abandonment of his family. This, though, posed a pretty serious issue. Sadie had been forced to go to work as a domestic housecleaner, and had spent the previous 15 years on her hands and knees scrubbing. Her health had broken down, she was wracked with arthritis, and she was most happy to discuss her feelings about the whole matter to the reporter her estranged husband's newspaper-owning political enemy sent out to visit her.

Mitchell had gotten wind of the affair, and had dispatched an envoy to somewhat high-handedly offer her $500 to keep her mouth shut and give him a divorce. It was the first time she'd heard from him since he'd walked out on her. This, too, she divulged to the Oregonian's reporter. It was a royal mess, from a public-relations standpoint.

Luckily for Mitchell if not for his adopted state, the Senate decided these things weren't deal-killers, and seated him.

Once ensconced there in Washington, Mitchell turned on the legendary charm, and a few months later when the U.S. Attorney in Portland started investigating allegations that Ben Holladay had bribed the state house and senate to get him elected (this was back when U.S. senators weren't elected directly; they were appointed by state legislatures) he already had accumulated enough influence to get the investigation quashed.

(Actually, Holladay had intended the Senate seat for himself. Mitchell had double-crossed him in the preparations for it, and Holladay had been forced to play along, or see Henry Corbett re-elected. It was, truth be told, extraordinarily well played.)

John H. Mitchell would spend the next 30 years of his life in and out of the U.S. Senate — feuding with Corbett and charming his way out from under the wages of his many sins. In 1878 he lost his bid for re-election, but won his seat back six years later; shortly after that, the Oregonian got hold of, and published, several love letters that he'd written to his wife's sister. This was embarrassing, but it didn't prevent him from serving two consecutive terms in the Senate.

During that time, he did accomplish some notable good things for the state. His efforts got the Cascade Locks funded, as well as a number of Oregon's complement of life-saving lighthouses.

However, Mitchell worked tirelessly to promote the interests of his clients in Washington, including Ben Holladay and, later, the Southern Pacific Railroad. He also never seemed to weary of trying to get the federal government to renege on treaties made with South Coast Native American tribes, whose heavily timbered lands development companies coveted.

In 1896, Mitchell lost his Senate seat through the machinations of his former ally, Jonathan Bourne Jr. (see the last chapter for the details of how this was done). But he staged a dramatic comeback in 1900.

It was during that 1900-1906 Senate term, though, that Mitchell found his Waterloo. This occurred as a result of his involvement in one of the biggest land swindles of American history — and his role in that swindle would finally bring him down.

In the early years of the 1900s, federal public lands in Oregon were available to individual homesteaders in 160-acre chunks for a tiny fraction of their true market value — $2.50 an acre. Large timber companies like Booth-Kelley and Weyerhaeuser wanted to buy vast swaths of it, and felt they should be free to do so — but they weren't.

So they simply made arrangements with "front men," often hobos, who would file a claim on 160 acres, pay the $400 for it with company money, and sign it over to the big outfits.

In the process of making these arrangements, the companies got some help from Mitchell — for which they paid him bribes. And when a federal investigation by Theodore Roosevelt appointee Francis Heney started looking into the matter, it was all over for the white-bearded Grand Old Man of Oregon politics. He had done something unthinkably stupid: He'd accepted and cashed a check for payment of one of those bribes.

In previous years, this would have been no big deal. Doubtless Mitchell had done this many times before. But there was a new sheriff in town now: Theodore Roosevelt was President, and abuse of public lands was no longer being winked at.

Mitchell was convicted and sentenced to serve six months in prison and pay a $1,000 fine — which sounds beefy in 1903 dollars, although the bribe he was being convicted of taking was twice that.

In any case, he died from a dental abscess while the case was on appeal, so he never actually served any prison time. To this day, he's one of less than half a dozen Senate members in U.S. history who have been convicted of a crime while in office. And as far as I know, he is the only U.S. Senator who has ever served in the Senate under an AKA.

Sources and Works Cited:
- Merchants, Money and Power, *a book by E. Kimbark MacColl, published in 1988 by Georgian Press of Portland;*
- *"How they Stole the Oregon Land," an article by William Boly published in the July 1976 issue of* Oregon Times;
- The Saga of Ben Holladay, Giant of the Old West, *a book by Ellis Lucia, published in 1959 by Hastings House.*

SYLVESTER PENNOYER:

GOVERNOR OF OREGON.

If there were a category in the Guinness Book of World Records for the state with the crankiest former governor, Oregon would surely hold the title.

The state would have earned the record in 1886, when it elected Sylvester Pennoyer. And Pennoyer would have clinched it seven years later with a telegram he shot off to the President of the United States of America telling him, in essence, to mind his own damn business.

His precise words:

> WASHINGTON: *I will attend to my business. Let the president attend to his.*
> — Sylvester Pennoyer, Governor of Oregon.

The telegram was in response to a note from the president, Grover Cleveland, urging western governors to take steps to make sure no Chinese people got hurt in riots or demonstrations following the renewal of the Chinese Exclusion Act. The president had sent the same telegram to the governors of Idaho and California and gotten very different replies. (Washington wasn't a state yet.)

But then, Pennoyer was no friend of the Chinese. Or any other ethnic minority either, for that matter. In fact, he owed his governorship to an incident in 1886 in which he and a mob of workers crashed an outdoor meeting being held by the mayor of Portland and turned it into a loud, rowdy anti-Chinese rally. He was also — 25 years after the Civil War — an advocate of slavery.

He was also an advocate for workers' rights, which might have seemed odd; he was a lumber baron who regularly wore very formal suits with swallowtail coats and carried himself stiffly, like an aristocrat. But shortly after he took office, Oregon became the first state in the union to declare Labor Day a holiday. He also refused to call out the state militia after railroad workers in Albany formed an angry mob in response to their employers' refusal to pay them. If they got their paychecks and rioted anyway, he told the railroad managers, he'd call out the militia — but otherwise, he'd let nature take its course.

What he was most famous for, though, was snubbing presidents. There was, of course, the telegram incident, but his petulance didn't end there. A year or two before that, he'd refused to leave Salem to welcome the president of the United States (Cleveland's predecessor, Benjamin Harrison) when the nation's leader arrived in Oregon on a railroad tour in 1891. "I have no business to go to pay homage to him," Pennoyer told a newspaper reporter at the time. "On the contrary, when he visits Oregon, he should rather pay his respects to me." Pennoyer subsequently relented and agreed to leave the capitol building to meet Harrison at the Salem train depot, where he kept the commander-in-chief and a large crowd of onlookers waiting in the rain and arrived 10 minutes late.

But Pennoyer had a special animosity for Grover Cleveland. Cleveland was the leader of the libertarian, pro-business Bourbon Democrats, and the Bourbon Democrats were dead set against the free silver movement, which was possibly Pennoyer's number-one policy goal (more on that in a bit).

When Cleveland was nominated, Pennoyer was so upset that he bolted the Democratic Party and joined the Populist Party, becoming the second Populist Party governor in history (and the only Populist Oregon governor). And when Cleveland won the election, Pennoyer refused to let the Oregon Democratic Party use the official state cannon to fire a salute in celebration.

"No permission will be given to use state cannon for firing a salute over the inauguration of a Wall Street plutocrat as president of the United States," he said, and locked the thing up under armed guard.

The Democrats won this standoff by their wits: They forged a court order commanding the sheriff to confiscate the cannon as collateral for the payment of an imaginary unpaid bill for blacksmith work — then got it from him and fired the salute. One imagines they likely took special care to fire it within earshot of the governor's office — but on that point, the record is silent.

A few months later came the Thanksgiving debacle, in which Pennoyer essentially arranged for Oregon to have two Thanksgivings. Here's how that went down:

A woodcut portrait of Sylvester Pennoyer as he appeared in the late 1880s. (Image: Univ. of South Florida)

In late October of 1893, Pennoyer was getting ready to deliver his annual Thanksgiving Proclamation speech. He'd scheduled it for Nov. 1, in what seemed an obvious attempt to get ahead of President Cleveland's national Thanksgiving proclamation.

As mentioned, Pennoyer's number-one priority as a politician was the Free Silver movement, which sought to add a silver standard to the existing gold standard of U.S. currency. The gold standard was causing all sorts of trouble in the early 1890s, because the economy was growing faster than the money supply, causing deflation. Deflation was a serious problem for borrowers, who had to pay back their mortgages and notes with dollars that were worth more than the ones they'd borrowed; people were losing their homes and farms because of it.

Pennoyer's preferred solution, and that of other Agrarian Democrats and Populists, was to use silver as well as gold to peg the dollar. The wealthy elites — who controlled most newspapers, including the Portland *Morning Oregonian* — saw this idea as a dilution of their financial power, and opposed it bitterly.

The problem was being exacerbated by a compromise bill called the Sherman Silver Purchase Act of 1890, which required the government to buy a certain amount of silver each year at a certain price. The problem was, that price was higher than the market price for silver; so clever traders were making a killing buying silver off the open market and selling it to the government for dollars. Because the gold standard meant that every dollar represented a specific amount of gold in Fort Knox, this was depleting the government's gold reserves with alarming speed.

Cleveland, seeing this, pushed for and got the Sherman Act repealed. This was the right thing to do — but the optics were terrible; at the same time the nation was entering a deflationary spiral, he was actually tightening the money supply. Pennoyer, enraged, called for Cleveland's immediate impeachment — something that's become pretty common for a U.S. politician in the years since President Clinton's second term, but a real eyebrow-raiser in the more decorous 1890s.

Repealing the Act might have stopped one source of bleeding, but it made another one worse, and after that, the country slid with sickening speed into the worst depression in its history. The depression of 1893 — mostly known today by the anodyne term "panic of 1893"— has been mostly forgotten by modern Americans, but it was, in human terms, as bad as or maybe even worse than the one that hit in 1929, because there was no "safety net." The 1893 depression was the last time significant numbers of American women were forced to choose between prostitution and starvation.

Pennoyer believed (correctly, according to modern economic theory) that the depression was precipitated largely by fidelity to the gold standard. In addition to its toxic effects on family farmers and small businessmen, it made American dollars attractive as an investment, and after a revolution in Argentina unsettled the European investing community, foreign investors started buying large quantities of dollars; the system, already straining, couldn't absorb this extra layer of abuse, and the result was a vicious spiral of plunging prices that made hoarding dollars a better financial strategy than investing them.

So it was against this backdrop that Pennoyer stepped up to the rostrum to deliver his Thanksgiving Proclamation of 1893.

"I do hereby appoint the fourth Thursday of the present month as a day of thanksgiving to Almighty God for the blessings he has bestowed upon this commonwealth during the present year," he droned. "God has indeed been most beneficent to our state and nation, and yet unjust and ill-advised congressional legislation, having made gold alone full legal tender money, has so dwarfed and paralyzed business that the bounties of Providence are now being denied to hundreds of thousands of people within the national domain who are not only without employment, but are also without the means of procuring food, rainment or shelter."

"While, therefore, the people of Oregon return thanks to God for His goodness," he continued, "I do most earnestly recommend that they should devoutly implore Him to dispose the President and the Congress of the United States to secure the restoration of silver as full legal tender money."

Now, granted, it was a bit odd to actually ask God to intercede with national monetary policy. But the man had a point. Ordinary people were suffering because of that policy, and the plutocrats who owned newspapers were not at all pleased at being chided for it. But fortunately for them, Pennoyer had also said something else ... a minor thing ... insignificant really. He'd proclaimed the wrong date for Thanksgiving. The holiday was traditionally held on the *last* Thursday of November; Pennoyer had said the *fourth* Thursday of November. Most years, it came to the same thing; this particular year, it did not.

Pennoyer, in other words, had proclaimed Thanksgiving a week early.

The newspapers pounced.

"Not satisfied with telling the President of these United States to mind his own business, Oregon's estimable governor has, figuratively speaking, given Grover Cleveland another slap in the face," intoned the Oregonian with high-minded sarcasm.

Nationwide, the tone was considerably harsher.

"Everything that this gubernatorial freak has done hitherto has been characterized by execrable taste and bad manners, but this, we believe, is the first time that he has been publicly and flagrantly sacrilegious," huffed the *Chicago Journal* — sounding, somewhat hilariously, as if it were implying that God Himself had ordained the gold standard and that publicly praying for its repeal was like praying for the salvation of Satan.

Amid such a response, any attempt by Pennoyer to correct his error in fixing the date of Thanksgiving would be unthinkable (to him, at least). So he did what politicians of his style usually do — he doubled down: The rest of the country could do as it pleased, he announced. Oregon would celebrate Thanksgiving on his day.

So, how did that go? It's hard to know. The newspapers of the day claimed that "Pennoyer's Thanksgiving" was mostly ignored except for a few state agencies, and that the following Thursday, Oregon families sat down with the rest of America to the traditional feast. But then again, those newspapers weren't exactly impartial observers in the fight.

In any case, just to prove he'd meant what he said, the governor did the same thing again in 1894, proclaiming Oregon's Thanksgiving a week early.

The following year, there were once again only four Thursdays in November, and Pennoyer's calendar once again called for Thanksgiving on the same date as the rest of the nation. By the time another five-Thursday month of November came around, Pennoyer was safely out of office, and nothing further was heard about Oregon's second Thanksgiving.

But had Pennoyer still been around in 1941, he probably would have smiled when President Franklin D. Roosevelt officially changed the date of Thanksgiving from the last Thursday of the month, to the fourth Thursday. (It would give people more time to shop for Christmas, he said.) The change was controversial, but it stuck. Pennoyer's Thanksgiving was now the nation's standard — as it remains to this day.

By that time, the gold standard was also history — Roosevelt dropped it in 1933 in response to the next massive depression, a move that would definitely also have made Pennoyer smile.

Nonetheless, the idea of having two Thanksgivings has a certain appeal. We could do worse than to resurrect this maverick Oregon tradition, celebrating Pennoyer's Thanksgiving a week before the real thing as a sort of rehearsal.

During his time in office, Pennoyer's cantankerousness earned him the nickname "Sylpester Annoyer" from pioneer judge Matthew Deady, and the Portland Oregonian took to referring to him in editorials as "His Eccentricity." For a time there was talk about running him on a presidential ticket, but such talk died instantly, of course, after he bolted the Democratic Party.

Among voters, though, Pennoyer was still hugely popular. After his two terms as governor, he went on to become mayor of Portland. There, in an ironic twist, he presided over the dedication of the city's new water system sourced from the Bull Run River — which has, ever since, enjoyed a nationwide reputation for purity.

As governor, Pennoyer had vetoed the legislation that gave the city of Portland authority to sell bonds to raise the money for Bull Run. Portlanders were furious; before Bull Run, the city's water came from the Willamette River, which, by the time it arrived in Portland, carried with it the toilet-flushings of Salem and Eugene as well as several dozen other upstream towns. It was making people sick; and here was the governor — who, being as he lived in Salem, was one of those upstream flushers — trying to block them from doing something about it. It would, he claimed, "cause goiter in the fair sex of Portland" because it originated in glacier water.

Luckily, the city had other financial resources, and it called upon them and got the project built ... just in time for its greatest opponent to preside over the dedication as Mayor of Portland.

At the ceremony, Pennoyer was given the first cup of water from the new system so that he might take the first sip from it. This he did, and then, putting the cup down, he declaimed, "No flavor. No body. Give me the old Willamette."

Pennoyer set the tone — in ways both good and bad — for politics in Oregon for decades. In the early 1900s, Oregon would become known as a land of people like Pennoyer — crotchety mavericks, proudly libertarian and frankly populist, friendly to workers so long as they were of northern-European descent, with a sometimes slippery interpretation of the rule of law. You'll still hear echoes of that spirit in Salem to this day.

Sources and Works Cited:
- Oregon: Her History, Her Great Men, Her Literature, *a book by John B. Horner, published in 1919 by the Corvallis Gazette-Times;*
- *"His Eccentricity,"* an article by Dick Pintarich published in Great Moments in Oregon History, *a book edited by Dick Pintarich, published in 1987 by New Oregon Publishers of Portland;*
- New York Times *archives, May 1891;*
- Portland Morning Oregonian *archives, 1893-1895.*

JOSEPH "BUNCO" KELLEY:

SHANGHAIER AND UNDERWORLD ENTREPRENEUR.

In the shadowy world of late-1800s Portland waterfront folklore, there's nobody who quite cuts the figure of a man named Joseph Kelley — better known by the nickname he carefully cultivated: Bunco Kelley.

Kelley was best known as a crimp — that is, one of those tough waterfront characters involved in the trade of furnishing sailors, willing or not, to ship captains in need of a crew. But really, Bunco Kelley was into any business that promised easy money — from smuggling opium up to and including shanghaiing.

He was also an easy liar with a real flair for a dramatic story — which means it's often difficult to tell his fact from fiction. And any discussion of Bunco Kelley has to deal with both the historical facts of his life and deeds of, if you will, derring-don't; and the almost-as-historical tall tales that sprang up around him, with considerable assistance from the man himself.

So let's take those two topics one after the other, starting with the biographical facts of Bunco Kelley's life as best we are able to know them:

THE FACTS.

Joseph Kelley came to Portland on a sailing ship, from somewhere back east — either Liverpool or Dublin or somewhere in Connecticut, depending on whom you asked — with his brother, William. Almost immediately upon his arrival, he went into the sailors' boardinghouse business — probably starting as a "runner" for one of the existing boardinghouses.

Sailors' boardinghouses were dingy, unsanitary hovels kept close to the waterfront, ostensibly as a place for sailors to live while their ships were in port; technically the sailors could stay on board, in the cramped and smelly forecastle cabin where they lived while at sea, but very few of them ever wanted to do that.

Each boardinghouse would employ one or more "runners," who functioned as basically an outside-sales force. When a new ship came into port, the runners would run out to meet it and, using cigars and bottles and personal charm, try to convince the sailors that their boardinghouse was the best and most pleasant housing option on the West Coast. They were paid, of course, on commission.

Part of the boardinghouse pitch was that it was free to stay there — sort of. Room and board charges were "on credit," and this was a key part of the business model. Typically, a man would run up a bill for room and board that he couldn't pay off, and he'd be more or less forced to discharge the debt by signing onto a sailing ship, whose captain would pay his lodging bill as an advance against his meager future earnings.

So this was the industry into which Joseph Kelley applied himself.

Now, a successful career in the boardinghouse business required a few key elements, chief among which was a pair of hard fists; there was a reason all boardinghouse owners were prizefighters or legendary brawlers. Rarely did a sailor go back to sea voluntarily.

A sailors' boardinghouse operator (known to his friends as a "boarding master" and to his enemies as a "crimp") also needed to have a very high degree of what you might call moral flexibility. After all, the business was basically a human trafficking operation based on swindling people into indentured servitude — a whisper away from outright slave trading.

That Kelley met both these requirements isn't in any doubt at all, as a number of his appearances in the cops-and-courts listings of the *Morning Oregonian* during that time readily show.

Kelley kept a boardinghouse for a while, but seemed to prefer the life of a freelance underworld entrepreneur, chasing after anything that smelled like easy money.

Notorious shanghai artist Joseph "Bunco" Kelly, as drawn by the Portland Evening Telegram's staff artist during his trial for murder in 1894. (Image: UO Libraries)

Through the late 1880s and early 1890s, he developed a reputation as a boarding master of last resort. When the usual boardinghouses were empty, you came in desperation to Kelley, who would go out and find somebody to fill out your crew — often by finding, befriending and shanghaiing some luckless hobo. (History-storyteller Stewart Holbrook claims he had a special knockout-drop formula that he called "Kelley's Comforters" that he used to do this. But there's at least an 85 percent chance that Holbrook simply made that detail up.)

This hobo-shanghaiing activity appears to be how Kelley came by his name; in 1887, the skipper of the British barque *Jupiter* wrote a letter to the Oregonian complaining that the seaman he hired through Kelley's good offices (probably delivered to him unconscious and wrapped in a tarp, although he does not specify) was "a perfect cripple by rheumatism," and referring to Kelley as "Bunco Kelley." The name stuck — with, it seems, considerable encouragement from Kelley himself.

As the late 1880s ripened into the early 1890s, the Portland crimping scene came increasingly under the control of a remarkably well-connected, socially polished prizefighter named Larry Sullivan. Sullivan and Kelley worked together for years, with Kelley representing Sullivan's boardinghouse as a runner, going out to ships and talking the incoming sailors into staying at Larry's place rather than someone else's.

But at some point in the early 1890s, Sullivan discovered that he could make serious money by selling the services of every sailor in port at election time as a "repeater," or serial voter. (This discovery likely came to him through one of his political patrons, Jonathan Bourne Jr., whom you'll remember from several chapters ago.) Keeping that illegal money train chugging along meant keeping Portland's ruling Republican elite, including Bourne, happy with his services, something it was getting hard to do with the flashy, notorious, proudly Democratic Kelley on his payroll.

And Kelley really became a liability in 1893, when the doors were blown off the Blum-Dunbar opium smuggling gang, an industrial-scale operation that for a time supplied most of the opium to the West Coast with the help of Portland chief customs official James Lotan — who happened also to be the head of the Oregon Republican Party at the time.

Lotan's little side hustle was exposed by the incompetence of his partners (Nat Blum and William Dunbar), and in a trial that held Portland spellbound throughout December of 1893, Lotan found himself facing serious federal corruption charges — and the whistleblower accusing him, Nat Blum, was one of Kelley's cronies. To make matters worse, Kelley was called to the stand as a witness for the prosecution — testifying against the head of the Oregon Republican party — and testified that he was "in partnership" with Sullivan.

Lotan's party friends saved him from prosecution. But Kelley's involvement had probably cost Sullivan a great deal of money, and the two of them were bitter enemies after that.

The end of Kelley's career as a Portland underworld figure came in 1894, when Kelley was accused of having murdered an old man named George Sayres — a generally well-liked former saloon-keeper. Significantly, his co-defendant was Bob Garthorn, who had been one of the other key lieutenants in the Blum-Dunbar opium gang. The prosecution alleged that the two of them had been involved with Sayres in a scheme to swindle some Chinese people by selling them a large shipment of fake opium. Things had gone sideways, and Kelley had tried to solve the problem by shanghaiing Sayres; the attempt was bungled, and Sayres ended up dead — that was the prosecution's story.

Kelley maintained to the last that it was a frame-up engineered by Sullivan, and that he had nothing to do with the killing — and there are compelling reasons to believe him. Sayres' body, when fished from the river, was still carrying his gold watch and some jewelry; neither Kelley nor Garthorn was the type to let that sort of loot get just thrown into the river. Also, the suggestion that an experienced shanghaier like Kelley would be unable to handle kidnapping a 73-year-old man is highly dubious. And it also seems unlikely that a pair of longtime opium pushers like Kelley and

Merchant barques of the grain fleet lined up at the wharves in Portland in 1904. Ships like these were the primary customers for shanghaiers in the 1890s. (Image: Robert Reid Pub.)

Garthorn would burn their bridges in Chinatown by selling fake dope, even if they'd had the skills and resources to make the little cans that opium came packaged in and to label them with the proper Chinese characters.

But, innocent or no, the verdict was guilty, and after that Kelley was shipped off to the state penitentiary in Salem.

This moment was the apex of Kelley's notoriety. Crowds thronged at railroad stations, hoping for a glimpse of Portland's most notorious bad guy.

Kelley spent 13 miserable years in the joint before being pardoned by the governor in response to a petition signed by some of the same people who'd sought to put him away years before.

He promptly set out to capitalize on his reputation with a book tour. Unfortunately, in the intervening 13 years, so much water had rolled under the bridge that few people remembered him, and he soon found himself crawling back into the underworld — this time in San Francisco. Historian Barney Blalock found a reference to him in coverage of a 1908 trial of a San Francisco gangster for whom he was apparently working. What became of him after that, I have not been able to learn.

And that, in broad strokes, is the life of Joseph "Bunco" Kelley, the most notorious shanghai artist of 1890s Portland. You will immediately notice that there's not much to this biographical sketch that would justify such notoriety, other than his wonderful nickname. That justification would come from less historically rigorous sources — from the tall tales, myths and stories of the old Portland waterfront, cleaned up and augmented and carefully spun by one of the most skilled storytellers who ever hung his black deerskin gloves and snappy Fedora in the Beaver State: Stewart Holbrook.

THE LEGENDS.

Most of the myths and legends of Bunco Kelley come down to us through a series of conversations held in a local watering hole in the early 1930s between Holbrook and an aging waterfront thug named Edward "Spider" Johnson.

Johnson had, in his youth, also been a "runner" for sailors' boardinghouses. So he clearly knew what he was talking about. The question is, did he tell it straight, or exaggerate a few things to make a better story, to keep Holbrook interested and thereby keep the drinks coming? And did Holbrook write his stories as he told them, or did he exaggerate a few things himself? Remember, this was at the height of the Great Depression, and Holbrook was paying the bills with his pen. How well he would eat the next month depended on how compelling his copy was.

(As a side note, it's illuminating to compare Holbrook's accounts of Bunco Kelley's adventures as written for a nationwide audience in *The American Mercury* in the late 1940s with the original articles from the Portland *Morning Oregonian* fifteen years earlier. Thrilling details are added, conversations are re-created, and key facts are changed.)

In any case, most of the stories that came out of the Holbrook-Johnson drinking dates have proven to be highly suspicious. And nowhere is this more clear than in the legends of Bunco Kelley.

According to Johnson, Kelley actually earned his name — "Bunco" — by one evening snaffling the big wooden Indian at a local cigar store and, after wrapping it in a tarp, selling its services to a particularly thick ship captain as an "A.B.," or Able-Bodied Mariner.

Writing in *The American Mercury*, Holbrook says Bunco did this by slipping aboard ship with the big wooden thing (which, by the way, stood a foot and a half taller than Bunco, who was five-three) and hauling it directly to the forecastle, where the sailors slept. He stuck it in a bunk, covered it up with blankets, and only then did he seek out the captain to collect his $50 fee.

So, did it happen? Well ... maybe.

Johnson recalled that Bunco established a boardinghouse deep in the North End shortly after arriving in Portland in the 1880s, but quickly learned that he could make more money in other ways. A naturally charming man, he soon made fast friends with the proprietresses of the North End's finer bordellos. Such entrepreneuses as Nancy Boggs, "Liverpool Liz" Smith, and Mary Cook would often receive customers who had no local connections and wouldn't much be missed if they vanished over the bar aboard a China-bound barque. So, Johnson tells us, when a skipper placed an order for manpower with Bunco Kelley, Bunco would immediately go forth to visit his ladyfriends and see if any anonymous loggers, itinerant hobos or gawky farmboys were being entertained in one of their girls' cribs. If there were, they stood a pretty good chance of waking up aboard ship, well out at sea.

In broad strokes if not in fine details, this claim is probably true. That's not the case, though, for this next one:

It's the most notorious Bunco Kelley story, and it involves dead guys. Lots of dead guys — either 24 or 39 (depending on whether Holbrook is writing in 1933 or 1948); but either way, that's a lot of dead guys.

It seems while on the prowl for a big order of A.B.s for a ship called the *Flying Prince* in late 1893, Bunco was having a run of tough luck. He visited the bordellos, as usual, but the ladies were having a slow night. He visited his saloonkeeper friends, hoping to find a stranger or two to chat up and "drink with," but — no luck. He was just on the point of giving up when he smelled something funny while leaving the Snug Harbor Saloon on Morrison street.

Investigating, he found the smell was coming from the basement of the Johnson & Sons Undertaking Parlor. It seemed two or three dozen men had broken into the basement, thinking they were in the saloon next door, and had gotten started drinking from the barrels of alcoholic-smelling liquid which they found there — which, as it turned out, were full of formaldehyde.

By the time Bunco found them, half of them were dead and the other half were dying.

"By God!" Bunco gasped, according to Holbrook. "Them stiffs has been drinkin' undertaker's dope!"

Bunco's shock didn't last long, though, as his crafty mind turned, as was its wont, to thoughts of commerce. Hastily closing the door so that his new friends would not be discovered and rescued by some night-stalking do-gooder, he quickly got to work. First he rounded up a posse of friends and associates to help him with the task of muscling dozens of dead guys around. Then he hired a fleet of hacks to haul his catch to the waterfront; and finally, he and his friends stowed the corpses securely in the bunks in the forecastle of the "Flying Prince."

Then, having collected $30 apiece for them, Bunco went on his way.

"Long before noon (the next day) the first mate made the hideous discovery in the forecastle," Holbrook writes. "The ship put in at Astoria, where the corpses were removed. Astoria newspapermen soon had the story on the wires. The sensation following the discovery of the dead men made a great rumpus in Portland."

So Holbrook writes. There are, of course, a few reasons not to take him at his word. For one thing, there's no sign of any of the businesses he named in any historical record I've been able to find: No Snug Harbor Saloon, no Johnson & Sons Undertaking Parlor. There's no record of any British ship called Flying Prince. I personally spent three and a half hours going through The Daily Astorian archives on microfilm, for calendar year 1893, and found no reference to the "great rumpus" at all. And during the extensive newspaper coverage of Bunco Kelley's murder trial the following year, there was not even a passing mention of it.

So, what really happened? Anything? Nothing? Your guess is as good as mine. My guess, if you're curious, is that the story grew out of an accident, in which Bunco accidentally overdosed a group of shanghaiing victims — not 39, surely, but maybe four or six — and came up with the "undertaker's dope" story to avoid being charged with murder, and the rumors just snowballed from there. But really, who knows?

Who knows, indeed? Apparently not even Spider Johnson. After recounting this tale in the 1933 article, he added, "No, I don't know positive that that story is true, but it's one you'll hear from any of the old-timers."

Still, even though they can't tell us what really happened, we could do a lot worse than to study the stories of those old-timers — not as historical accounts, but just as stories, as a part of a colorful and long-gone waterfront culture — like Paul Bunyan stories of the sea. And as a wonderful possibly-partly-true-but-probably-not piece of historical Portland folklore, the adventures of Bunco Kelley have no equal.

Sources and Works Cited:
- *Portland's Lost Waterfront, a book by Barney Blalock, published in 2012 by The History Press;*
- *"Shanghai Days in the City of Roses," an article by Stewart Holbrook published in the Oct. 1 and 8 issues of the* Portland Sunday Oregonian;
- *"Bunco Kelley: King of the Crimps," an article by Stewart Holbrook published in the October 1948 issue of* The American Mercury;
- Portland Morning Oregonian *archives, October 1894—January 1895;*
- Portland Evening Telegram *archives, December 1893;*
- Daily Astorian *archives, calendar year 1893.*

F. WALLACE WHITE:

MINING-STOCK SWINDLER.

When it comes to attracting swindlers and charlatans, there's nothing quite as effective as gold.
And nowhere in Oregon was that fact more clear than in the bustling boomtown of Bourne — what today is a tiny ghost town, seven miles out of Sumpter along the banks of Cracker Creek.

Bourne was named after one of Oregon's most notorious rascals, Jonathan Bourne, Jr., who was invested heavily in silver mines nearby. Bourne himself had nothing to do with the municipal swindle that would make his namesake town famous — he was far too subtle a rogue for that sort of thing — but it wasn't entirely out of sync with his style.

The mines, as mines do, started out very productive and over the years became less and less so. But Bourne wasn't going to let that stop progress. In 1900, Bourne was the home of several hundred people, along with a large collection of promising-looking but relatively unproductive mines, and a printing press that, in historian Miles F. Potter's words, "hardly had an opportunity to cool off for six years." Its glory days ran from 1900 to 1906,

HEROES and RASCALS of OLD OREGON.

The town of Bourne as it appeared in 1921, looking out from the front porch of the White mansion. (Photo: Baker County Library, Baker City)

when the mastermind of its multi-million-dollar municipal swindle skipped town just hours ahead of the law.

Here's the story:

In the late 1800s, miners started discovering massive veins of gold in the rugged, remote regions of Oregon's Blue Mountains.

In short order, towns like Granite and Sumpter sprang up from the rocks, mining companies started setting up shop, and representatives of a species of rugged, hard-drinking, hard-punching men drifted into the region to work the mines.

By this time, technological breakthroughs had made it possible to get a lot more gold out of a promising vein than the hopeful prospectors of 1849 had been able to, but it cost a lot of money to do it. That meant mines were more valuable to big industrial mining concerns than to individual prospectors. And with the fortunes that were being cracked out of the earth at the time, big industrial mining concerns were springing up on stock exchanges all over the world. Financiers in London were buying, sight unseen, mines in places like Cornucopia and Sumpter. And they were doing really well.

It was probably inevitable that someone in the mining district would figure out, sooner or later, how to work this system to mine a different resource: not gold from the ground, but "investments" from suckers. It was simple supply and demand: There was a market for mining-opportunity fantasies. And into that market stepped F. Wallace White.

White worked the system like the pro he was. First, he hauled that printing press up Cracker Creek to Bourne, which by that time was a fading sister city to nearby Granite and Sumpter. A few hundred miners lived there and worked nearby mines, but those mines were playing out and the freelance miners weren't having as much luck as their colleagues in the other towns.

For White, it was the perfect opportunity. After all, he wasn't in the market for mines that actually produced; why pay extra for something you don't need?

Soon his printing press was in motion. Its main purpose was to crank out two newspapers. One, for local consumption, served as a typical small-town weekly paper and was more or less truthful.

The other, distributed nationally wherever suckers might congregate, contained almost nothing but lies — a gold-mining fantasy that would have been worthy of Walt Disney himself — had Walt been a swindler. It was designed to look exactly like a real, honest small-town weekly newspaper, kind of like Main Street U.S.A. at Disneyland was designed to look like a real, honest small-Missouri-town main street.

This publication spun fantastic but convincing tales of mammoth gold strikes, of huge capital construction projects, of rich shipments of bullion. And, of course, it offered readers opportunities to buy into this fairyland investment opportunity.

With a $7.5 million stock offering, White launched The Sampson Company Limited, with offices in London, New York City and Bourne.

A photo of downtown Bourne, Oregon, during the boom years of hard-rock gold mining and swindling the suckers back east, circa 1905. (Photo: Baker County Library, Baker City)

He bought up the playing-out mines in the Cracker Creek area. When investors came to visit, he put on a dazzling show for them at his rustic-but-lovely terraced mansion with its formal dining room and ballroom; at the mouths of promising-looking mines guarded by burly men with steel in their eyes and shotguns in their hands; and on tours of mines carefully salted with rich ore.

And the money poured in.

Meanwhile, other shysters were working the suckers too, and the marks were starting to get a little smarter — or perhaps it was just that so many people had been ripped off that they couldn't fool themselves any more.

Local resident Lee Robertson at upper level entrance to the North Pole Mine, located less than a mile north of Bourne, probably sometime in the 1920s. (Photo: Baker County Library, Baker City)

In fact, the legitimate mine financing industry was having trouble raising capital too, because so many investors simply thought any gold mine was crooked. The governor of Pennsylvania actually threatened to outlaw the sale of any Oregon mining stock in his state.

In response, the scammers spent ever more money. Full-page newspaper ads started appearing: "You can enter the temple of fortune by purchasing HIAWATHA MINING STOCK," screamed one. (There is no record of the Hiawatha having ever produced anything.) "Buy CONSOLIDATED STANDARD ... Dividends are sure to follow as day succeeds night. $500,000 worth of rich ore waiting to be processed," promised another. (Consolidated Standard produced only a tiny trickle of gold.)

But as for White, by 1906 he was starting to get nervous. What he was

RASCALS.

The ruins of F. Wallace White's house in Bourne as they looked in 1928. This photo was taken 22 years after White, having swindled millions of dollars from investors in phony gold mines, skipped town in the middle of the night just a few steps ahead of federal investigators. (Photo: Baker County Library, Baker City)

doing with his printing press constituted mail fraud, and in his six rich and productive years of mining far-distant suckers he'd made himself a small army of enemies, many of whom had friends in important places.

So one night, White simply disappeared from Bourne. He left everything behind but the money. Authorities did finally catch up with him, many years later, still diligently operating mail-fraud swindles and no doubt muttering to himself that after this next big score, he was going to quit for real this time.

As for Bourne, the town melted away. There wasn't enough gold to keep the place busy. Most of the miners went downstream to Sumpter or across the ridge to Granite, or out of the hills to Baker City. A few families remained. Today, though, it's empty, and it's not coming back — it's part of a national forest.

Sources and Works Cited:
- *Oregon's Golden Years: Bonanza of the West, a book by Miles F. Potter, published in 1982 by Caxton Publishing of Caldwell, Idaho;*
- *The Far Corner, a book by Stewart Holbrook, published in 1976 by Comstock Press of Sausalito, Calif.*

ELLIS HUGHES:

METEORITE PIRATE.

The old playground doctrine of "finders keepers" does not apply to meteorites. At least, that's what the Oregon Supreme Court said in 1905, when deciding who got to keep the Willamette Meteorite — the largest meteorite ever found in the United States, before or since.

Here's the story:

Ellis Hughes, a settler in the West Linn area, near the Tualatin River, was out prospecting for minerals with a friend in 1902 when he spotted a projecting rock in the forest that looked promising. Hughes tried to chip off a piece with his rock hammer — it bounced off with a metallic "ting." The thing was solid iron!

Well, the two of them were really excited at first. They figured this was a "reef" sticking out of the top of a massive vein of iron that could make them both very wealthy. But they soon made two sobering discoveries: First, it was an isolated piece, just sitting on the soft ground, obviously from somewhere else. Its shape was definitely suggestive of it being a meteorite.

HEROES *and* RASCALS *of* OLD OREGON.

Two small boys clown around in the holes of the 16-ton Willamette Meteorite, where it sits on display in the Americvan Museum of Natural History in New York in 1911. (Image: Library of Congress)

And second, it wasn't on Hughes' property. They'd strayed over onto the neighboring plot, owned by — ironically, given what it was obviously made of — the Oregon Iron and Steel Company.

Hughes kept mum and tried to buy the land. Nothing doing. So he, his wife and his 15-year-old stepson toiled for a solid three months at dragging the 32,000-pound mass across three-quarters of a mile of forest floor and onto Hughes' property. This done, he announced his find, built a shed over it and started charging admission to see it.

I haven't been able to learn how the Oregon Iron and Steel Company found out the meteorite had been moved. Probably Hughes' attempts to buy the land aroused some suspicion and prompted company officials to investigate. In any case, figure it out they did, and filed a lawsuit demanding that Hughes give it back.

Which he eventually did — but not without a fight. Hughes appealed the case all the way up to the Oregon Supreme Court, which decided in late 1905 that he would indeed have to give it back.

Oregon Iron and Steel took possession of the meteorite just in time to haul it up to Portland for the 1905 Lewis and Clark Exposition, at which it was displayed proudly and drew much notice. Afterward, it was purchased by Sarah Dodge and donated to the American Museum of Natural History in New York City — where it remains to this day.

So, how did it get there, in the woods by West Linn? The meteorite apparently fell on a glacier during the last ice age. During the Missoula Floods, the ice in which it was embedded formed an iceberg and roared down the Columbia River Gorge, eddying back up into the Willamette Valley and finally ending up in West Linn when the ice melted away, depositing it gently onto the forest floor there.

In Oregon, there are two replicas of the meteorite on display: one at the United Methodist Church in West Linn, near where it was found; the other outside the University of Oregon's Museum of Natural and Cultural History in Eugene. The original is composed of 91.65 percent iron, 7.88 percent nickel, 0.21 percent cobalt and 0.09 percent phosphorous.

The local Native American tribes had treasured the meteorite, calling it "tomonowos" — "visitor from the moon." In 1990, they sued for its return. But they came to an agreement with the museum in 2000 that let them come visit the meteorite in New York and hold private ceremonies around it; the deal also says if the museum ever takes it off permanent display, the tribes will get it back.

The Willamette Meteorite on display at Ellis Hughes' homestead, where he was charging admission to view it. Shortly after this postcard image was made, Hughes was forced to give it back to the Oregon Iron and Steel Company, off of whose property he had laboriously and surreptitiously dragged it. (Image: Brück & Sohn Postcard)

A member of the state House of Representatives weighed in seven years later by introducing a bill that would have demanded its return to the state of Oregon. The tribes said no one had talked to them about it, but they were happy with the arrangement they'd made and did not support the new bill. So, as Willamette Week put it in an editorial that year, "neither the bill nor the 16-ton meteorite went anywhere."

Sources and Works Cited:
- Images of America: West Linn, *a book by Cordelia Becker Seigneur, published in 2009 by Arcadia Publishing;*
- *Volume 6 (the 1906 issue) of* American Museum Journal*;*
- *Oregon House Joint Resolution 30 (2007).*

FRANK "THREE MINUTE" WAGNER & AL.

PRISON ESCAPEES.

Escapes from Oregon's state prisons are very rare events today, and have been for years. But there was a time, not that long ago, when an average of one prisoner every month made a break for freedom, and one or two of them actually succeeded in staying gone for a good long time.

The criminal population in Oregon's prisons has also changed a lot. One of the most noticeable ways is the type of criminal housed there. In 1912, there were a lot more of a particular sort of criminal professional who specialized in breaking into vaults — safecrackers, or, in the slang of the time, "yeggs."

Possibly because they made a living solving puzzles of this sort, yeggs seemed to make up a disproportionately high percentage of escapees.

One such professional was Charles Drocker, who was sent up the river in May 1915 to serve a 10-year term for burglary. After he'd served a year of this sentence, Drocker vanished one morning. He was there at breakfast, but at the noon count, he was gone.

A postcard image showing the front gate of the prison in 1913. Quite why travelers wanted an image of the state prison on the backs of the postcards they were sending home is unclear, but clearly they didn't mind.

Prison officials searched for him for two days, and found not a sign. Meanwhile, among the inmates the rumor grew that Drocker had crawled under a truck and pulled himself up into its chassis someplace, riding out through the front gates of the prison under the very noses of a half-dozen armed guards before dropping to the ground and slipping away.

And perhaps that's what he did — but to this day, nobody knows for sure.

Nothing was heard until the following year, when word came back to the Beaver State that the intrepid Mr. Drocker was now a war hero. He had snuck out of the country and joined the military in France — perhaps the French Foreign Legion — in the middle of the First World War.

One assumes that a grateful French nation made him a citizen, and all that unpleasantness in Oregon was put behind him. On the other hand, it's also possible if not likely that "Charley" went back to his old profession in his new country, or that — patched up and sent back to the front lines — he fell before a German Mauser like so many of his compatriots. In any case, as far as I've been able to learn, nothing more was heard from him.

Another yegg who proved hard to hang onto was Frank Wagner, whose first of two escapes offers a surprising echo of the Stephen King novella (and, later, movie) "The Shawshank Redemption."

Wagner was a member of the safecracking elite, possibly the most skilled yegg on the West Coast. His nickname was "Three Minute Wagner," and the moniker referred to his ability to get into any vault in under 180 seconds.

Getting out of the "big vault" took a little longer than that. But Wagner figured out how to get the job done.

In the summer of 1914, he and his cell mate, a fellow German named Carl Weinegal, discovered that the thick brick walls of which their cell block was built were not as impenetrable as they seemed. The mortar was soft and crumbly.

So the two of them got to work on it. They bored a man-sized tunnel into the wall and down through the floor. This was the wall between their cell and the prison hallway, so it had to be a rather tight fit; when they were done with it, there was only one row of bricks between their hole and the hall. But it was big enough for them to slip through.

During the months of work on this project, the two crooks disposed of the extra bricks and mortar by hiding them in their pockets and in their "cell bucket," or chamber pot; in 1914, the cells did not have toilets in them. Inmates were responsible for emptying their own buckets, so they didn't have to worry about the maids tattling on them for sneaking out building materials.

They hid their work in progress by setting their cell up with dozens of pennants and fancy doilies and other wall decorations, and keeping it neat as a pin. During cell inspection, nobody thought to check behind that one big girly doily that hung on the wall near the cell door. If the guards had, they would have discovered that, like Andy DuFresne's poster of Rita Hayworth in "Shawshank," it was hiding a very interesting secret.

On their big night, Wagner and Weinegal pushed through the last layer of bricks and burst through into the prison basement. Unfortunately, they were not able to do this under controlled conditions. The first of them fell through space and lit on the concrete basement floor, hitting his head hard enough to be knocked unconscious for some time. The other managed to land on his feet, but twisted one leg badly enough that walking was extremely painful.

But there was no turning back now; the hole in the ceiling they'd come out of was accessible only to birds and bats. Onward and outward the two cons hobbled, hoping for the best.

The two of them got most of the way off the prison grounds before a dog started barking, attracting the attention of one of the guards, who opened fire on them from a great distance. This had the chief effect of inspiring the two of them to hobble away at superhuman speed. They remained at large for two days before being recaptured.

Wagner served the rest of his sentence without incident, but as soon as he was released he got right back to work, and six months later was back in prison. This time, he simply slipped away from a guard while working in the brick yard. He was found three months later at a cabin in Clatsop County — ratted out, apparently, by the woman he was living with there. When the posse tried to retrieve him, a firefight broke out, and Wagner was killed.

Sources and Works Cited:
Sensational Prison Escapes from the Oreogn State Penitentiary, *a book by "Prisoner No. 6435," published in 1922 in a book with no publisher listed.*

HARRY VIRTUE:

SWINDLER AND QUACK DOCTOR.

It was sometime in the late summer of 1912 that Dr. Jean Barber first heard the rumors: Her husband, whom she had not seen since 1904, had reappeared in England, and was apparently in some trouble there.

And this has to have been a surprise to Dr. Barber, because when she'd last seen her husband, eight years earlier, he had been dead.

Dr. Richard Barber, back in in 1904, had been the male half of a husband-wife team of physicians operating the local hospital and clinic in the Winchester Bay area at the mouth of the Umpqua River.

The two of them were originally from England; in 1890, when both were in their mid-20s, they emigrated to the rough-cut new city of Portland with their young son, Eric. Richard was a recent med-school graduate and was on the English medical register as a licensed physician. Jean had attended medical school too, but had not yet been admitted to practice; so they were, when they first arrived, a "Dr. and Mrs." couple.

This Jean soon set about rectifying, and in 1894 she was able to take her place as Dr. Jean Barber, Richard's colleague as well as his wife.

Meanwhile their practice was thriving in their new home town. But then came the Spanish-American War, and the newly naturalized Dr. Richard left his practice to take a commission as a lieutenant in the Oregon Volunteers, and was deployed to Manila.

When Dr. Richard returned, "his health was shattered," as Oregonian reporter Addison Bennett put it. This likely meant he'd contracted malaria, which made Portland — with its marshy riverside wetlands and nasty Gilded-Age-city smogs and miasmas — a bad place for him to live. So the couple moved south in the valley, to the clean, fresh-aired timber town of Sheridan; and then, a few years later, to Yoncalla, in northern Douglas County; and finally to the coastal town of Gardiner, near the mouth of the Umpqua, to establish the hospital and clinic there.

They were big fish in a small pond, and they seem to have been happy there. But Dr. Richard didn't have much time in which to enjoy his new life and his returning health. Less than a year later, on the night of Dec. 2, 1904, a messenger arrived from Florence, 28 miles up the beach. A young man had been operating a jackscrew when it had cut loose, dealing him a terrific blow on the head. He needed a surgeon, stat. Dr. Richard was his man.

Dr. Richard saddled up and rode off into the night.

What happened next is mostly educated guesswork. When Dr. Richard arrived at the mouth of the Siuslaw River, he apparently thought it was the flood-swollen waters of the Siltcoos (a.k.a. Tenmile Creek) — which his horse had crossed without his noticing — and instead of turning along the bank to catch the ferry at Glenada, he urged the beast into the water to swim the river. In the darkness, he didn't realize that it was a good half a mile to the other side.

By the time they reached the other side of the river, Dr. Richard was suffering from full-blown hypothermia. He staggered ashore on the jetty; found a shack; tried and failed to force open the door; somehow managed to retrieve a flask of liquor from his saddlebag; tried and failed to get the cap off; and, finally, fell through a gap in the jetty landing, 10 or 15 feet down onto the rocks and shallow water below.

The fall probably killed him, but if it didn't, the cold did. They found his body there the next day.

The heroic nature of Dr. Richard Barber's death, and his immense popularity in every community in which he had practiced, guaranteed widespread publicity. A glowing editorial praising him, and country doctors in general, graced the *Morning Oregonian*'s opinion page a few days later. And poor Dr. Jean, his widowed partner and wife, had to carry on with their work at the hospital alone.

She was, of course, a very busy woman; and it didn't occur to her that she might need to write to the medical authorities in England to let them know of Dr. Richard's death.

Which is why, a year and a half later, no eyebrows were raised when "Dr. Richard Barber" notified the authorities that he had returned from abroad and re-established himself in Dear Old England — in Liverpool.

Harry Virtue, impersonator of Dr. Richard Barber, in 1917 after he had been caught practicing medicine without a license and embezzling funds, as seen in a picture from the Liverpool Echo. (Image: thequackdoctor.com)

The fake Dr. Barber was an English mountebank named Harry Virtue — or if that was not his real name, it works as well as any of the many others he adopted during his colorful career. He was the same age as Dr. Jean — born in Manchester in 1865 — and, like the Barbers, emigrated to the U.S., where he practiced (without a license) as a veterinary surgeon in various places. He moved around a lot; his success was hampered by his lack of actual medical training, and by his sticky fingers — once he even stole a horse and buggy from an employer.

One of the places Virtue briefly worked was Oregon, and while there, he met Richard. And when word of Richard's death reached him — doubtless he read one of the glowing accounts of the country doctor's heroic end — he saw his opportunity. Booking passage back to England, he sent that letter off to the medical authorities, dusted off his shingle, and went into practice as "Dr. Richard Barber."

The problem was, the personality traits that had gotten him into trouble as an unlicensed veterinarian had not disappeared. And now he was in a civilized country rather than a rough-sawn frontier community. When he burned a bridge as "Dr. Richard Barber," he couldn't just cross a state line and get a fresh start under a new name somewhere else, like he'd been able to do in the Oregon country.

He got by at first by taking positions as an assistant to actual competent, trained physicians, and not staying with any one doctor for long enough for suspicions to form. But eventually, he got cocky, and set up his own practice in Treeton in South Yorkshire, hiring an MD assistant of his own: Dr. Henry Bond.

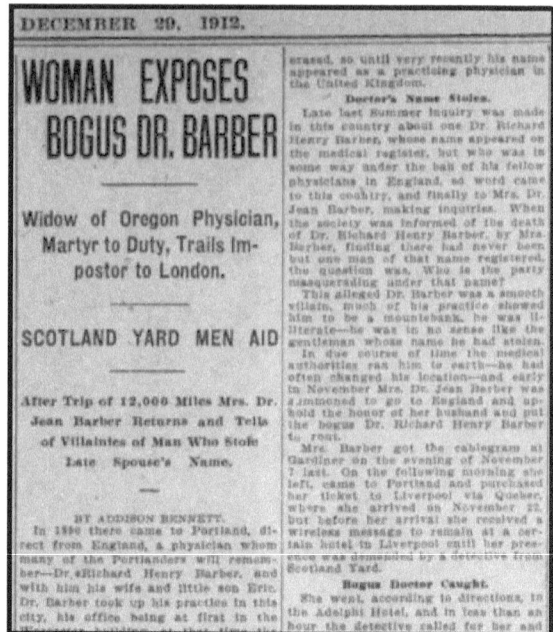

An article that appeared in the Portland Morning Oregonian after Harry Virtue was arrested for impersonating the late Dr. Richard Barber in England. (Image: UO Libraries)

After a time, Dr. Bond realized that his boss was avoiding medical topics in conversations with him, and was relying on him, Dr. Bond, for all the complicated surgeries that came their way. He started wondering if "Dr. Barber" was actually competent. And he reported his suspicions to the medical authorities — who responded with a letter to "Dr. Barber" asking for some information about his Oregon practice.

And so it was that, on one late summer day, "Dr. Barber" opened this letter and knew the jig was up. He slipped away that very night; Dr. Bond never saw him again.

But he couldn't just change his name and open a new practice somewhere else. This wasn't Oregon, and he wasn't a vet any more. This was England, and the only name that he'd be allowed to practice under was Richard Barber's. So he had another crack at it, hanging out his shingle in Liverpool — but the cops were ready for him, and he soon found himself in their custody.

And that's when they telegraphed for Dr. Jean Barber to come and "identify" him.

Harry Virtue didn't go down easy. He made a last-minute attempt to sign onto a freighter bound for Brazil as "Dr. Charles Thompson," apparently hoping to continue his itinerant quack-doctor lifestyle in another far-flung frontier community; but the police were just a little too quick for him, and he was once again nicked. He made an almost-successful attempt to leap from the train and escape, but with the help of some bloodhounds and local residents who couldn't help but notice the handcuff locked around his wrist, he was recaptured, tried, and sentenced to nine months in prison.

After the First World War broke out, Virtue took advantage of the tumult to hop back into the fake-doctoring racket, renaming himself Dr. Harry Siddons, forging a captain's commission, and wangling his way onto the Birkenhead Military Medical Board, where he got busy taking bribes in exchange for military medical deferments and other favors until 1917, when he was once again caught with his hand in the till. And on the eve of his trial for these new charges, Virtue committed suicide by cutting his own throat with a doctor's scalpel — dying, one might say, as he had lived.

As for Dr. Jean Barber, she returned home to Gardiner and resumed her life of healing the sick and saving the lives of the injured. She died in 1927.

Sources and Works Cited:
- Portland Morning Oregonian, *6-12 Dec 1904, 29 Dec 1912;*
- Roseburg Evening News, *26 Nov and 30 Dec 1912;*
- *"The Alleged Dr. Barber: A Case of Identity Theft in 1912,"* an article by *"Quackwriter" (pseudonym) published on thequackdoctor.com, 10 Oct 2018.*

GEORGE L. BAKER:

VAUDEVILLE IMPRESARIO, MAYOR OF PORTLAND.

George L. Baker, the big, bluff, hail-fellow-well-met owner of Portland's Baker Theater, was flabbergasted. As he and his fellow Portland Rosarians were getting ready to march in the 1917 Rose Festival parade, a courier had run up to him with a cryptic message:

"The grand marshal's car awaits," the messenger puffed. "Hurry and get in and don't delay the parade."

"Why, I'm not grand marshal," Baker replied, puzzled.

Just then his friend Gus Moser, who was in charge of the parade that year, hustled over. "George, hurry up," he said. "Get in the grand marshal's car. You're the grand marshal."

"Since when?" Baker replied.

"Oh, all the time," said Moser breezily. "We just made you grand marshal. But we couldn't get you on the phone and we forgot to tell you after the meeting. You've been grand marshal all along."

And Moser showed Baker a copy of the parade program. Sure enough, he was listed as grand marshal.

As Moser had clearly planned, the surprise honor had lowered Baker's shields a bit, and he allowed himself to be bundled into a massive, flag-draped, chauffeur-driven car. Promptly the door was shut and the car moved out with the parade column, headed for the streets of town with him stuck inside, all by himself.

"But some of you fellows ride with me!" Baker wailed, no doubt suddenly realizing he'd been pranked.

But nobody did, and Baker had to endure the entire Rose Parade all by himself — and the jibes of the other Rosarians afterward.

"You fellows always want a fellow to be a good dog in a pinch, but this time it wasn't so funny," he grumbled afterward.

But this wasn't just any local businessman the Rosarians were pranking. Baker was within a week of being sworn in as mayor of Portland. And the fact that the Rosarians felt comfortable enough to pull a stunt like this at his expense is a good illustration of what was different about Mayor George Luis Baker.

By the time he'd finished his run as mayor of Portland, George L. Baker was probably the most famous mayor of an American city in the world. But most modern Oregonians interested in Portland history don't quite know what to make of him.

Baker served longer in the office of Mayor of Portland than anyone ever has, before or since. He was hugely popular among most Portlanders for most of that time, becoming known for a kind of adorably bluff teddy-bear boisterousness.

But he also resorted to fascist tactics in opposing labor unions and other "subversives"; he was famously friendly

Mayor George Baker around 1930, on the front steps of City Hall. (Image: Oregon Historical Society)

with the Ku Klux Klan; and during Prohibition, his police department ran an outright protection racket among illegal speakeasies and kept City Hall generously furnished with seized liquor.

He was a big, boisterous man, a classic early-1920s show-biz man of the cigar-chomping, back-slapping type. During his candidacy, the *Oregon Voter* magazine had proclaimed him "the World Champion Loud Noise of the Northwest." He had big black expressive eyebrows which he probably darkened with charcoal, as old Vaudevilleans used to do, and his face seemed always set in a happy smile.

Mayor George Baker of Portland as he looked shortly after his swearing-in in 1917. (Image: Oregon Historical Society)

Baker's life story was like something out of a Horatio Alger novel. Born to a poor family in The Dalles, he dropped out of school when he was 9 to shine shoes and deliver papers in San Francisco, to help support the family after they'd moved there. He soon found a steadier job in a Vaudeville theater, and with that, he'd found his life's calling. A gifted impresario, he quickly worked his way up through the ranks, and when he moved with his family to Portland, he soon was working at Cordray's Theater at Third and Yamhill streets — tending the animals there.

It was a low-ranking position, but it was a foot in the door. One thing led to another, and by the late 1890s George was managing theaters and running for Portland City Council — first winning election in 1898.

In 1901 young George struck out on his own as the proud owner of his own theater — Baker Theater — and set about building a Vaudeville stock troupe with a nationwide reputation. Within a matter of months the Baker Theatre was Portland's premier theatrical venue.

But hardly anyone today understands how important that was. And the fact is, one can't understand Mayor George Baker without knowing what his theater meant to the Portland of the 1910s.

Stock theatre is something most Americans today know little about. It still exists; but it's a faded and impoverished ghost of what it was at the turn of the twentieth century. Usually it's seen in the form of local repertory theatres like the Oregon Shakespeare Festival in Ashland.

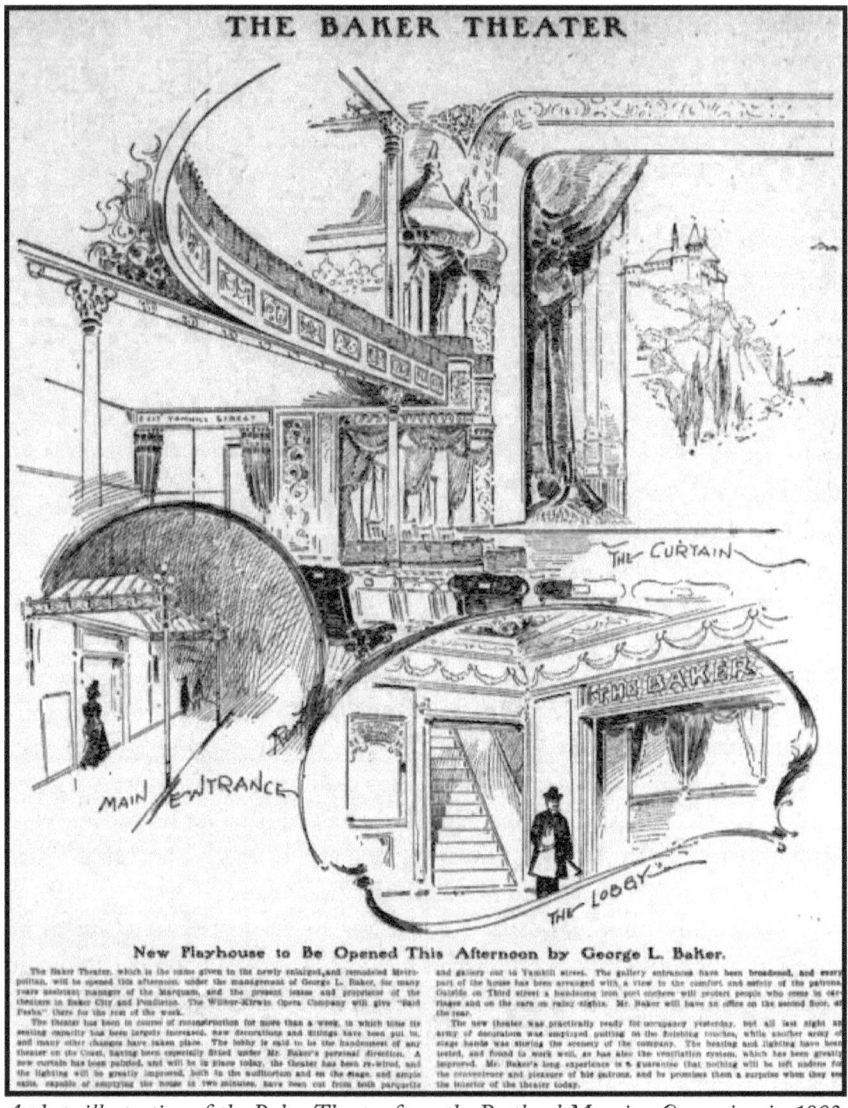

A photo illustration of the Baker Theatre from the Portland Morning Oregonian in 1902. (Image: UO Libraries)

It's something of a niche art form, patronized by a small but enthusiastic cohort that tends to pride itself (not without reason) on its cultural refinement.

But in 1901, when George first hung out the shingle over his very own stock-theatre playhouse, that wasn't the case at all. Stock theatre was a mass-media enterprise, and it was huge — likely one of the five or ten most important industries in the city.

A drawing of the Baker Theatre when it first opened, from the Portland Morning Oregonian in 1902. (Image: UO Libraries)

It was, however, an industry with a bit of a lingering reputation problem, dating from the years just after the Civil War.

Vaudeville had always had a bit of a disreputable edge, and never more so than in the 1870s in the American West. Companies toured around the country like circuses or carnivals. The shows they performed were often poorly written and crudely ribald, the theatres they played in sometimes doubled as bordellos. The players were widely considered fast and disreputable, and although they usually weren't, it only took a few examples to reinforce those stereotypes.

But local resident players, back in the early days, were often worse. Vaudevilleans usually weren't prostitutes and card-game swindlers. In the frontier town of Portland just after the Civil War, local players often were. Venues like the Oro Fino — owned and operated, of course, by our old friend James Lappeus, Portland's first chief of police — actually had little rooms upstairs for "private theatrical performances," and trained mountebanks staffing the gambling tables downstairs to fleece the suckers and tenderfoots and keep the regulars winning just enough to keep them coming back. Particularly in saloon settings like the Oro Fino, the women on stage sometimes would come out and vamp audience members between sets, cajoling them into buying them drinks which they would dump discreetly into spittoons. (Getting drunk would, of course, be a bad idea for a con artiste working on a mark.)

As the town got bigger and more respectable, though, so did the theaters. And by the time George Baker was entering the field, circa 1888, there were basically two kinds: Vaudeville houses, offering cheap shows by the traveling troupes; and big upmarket mainstream houses, less cheap but by no means expensive, which hired their own professional staff or "stock" of players.

In this era, live theater was the preeminent visual storytelling medium. When the movies came to prominence after the First World War, it was live theater that they essentially replaced. Live theater supplied the stories and narratives that Portlanders used to define themselves and their world, and it was the most accessible source of the East Coast culture that middle-class Portlanders felt the lack of rather keenly in their rough-hewn frontier city.

For all of the first decade of the century and most of the second, the Baker Stock Theatre was the center of Portland's mainstream social and cultural life. Baker positioned it as a great unifying force: it was not too high-brow for the average longshoreman to appreciate, but not too frivolous for an erudite lawyer to enjoy. It brought the upper and lower classes together, gave young people a place to meet and get to know one another, and performed a community-building function of which Baker was obviously very proud.

It was strictly G-rated: Mindful of the sketchy reputation of his industry, Baker took pains to make his theaters as clean and wholesome as possible, and his players — who were part of the community, of course — shared that vision. Entire families made it part of their weekly routine, and on Wednesday matinees, babies and children under 5 were allowed.

Baker's players, especially the leading ladies and men, quickly became celebrities. Some went on to actually be national celebrities; Izetta Jewel, the Baker Stock Company's leading lady until 1909, was, in later years, President Woodrow Wilson's favorite actress, and (so far as is known) the first woman to address a national political convention, the Democratic Party's convention, in 1921.

Others contented themselves with being locally famous.

"We belonged to them," said Fay Bainter, the leading lady after Jewel left, in an interview many years later. "We were a part of their lives. Our position was enviable. Why, I never had to use a streetcar or taxi. Someone would always stop and take you where you wanted to go."

"Don't you remember the way it was?" former leading man Howard

Russel asked an Oregonian reporter years later. "Why, if the right people did not occupy the seats we were accustomed to seeing them in, we would ask (from on stage), "Where is so-and-so tonight? I don't see them in their regular seats!' It was like a family party."

It's this picture of Portland — an overgrown small town, rough-hewn but with high cultural aspirations, a town in which workers and business executives moved in the same circles and knew one another's families and laughed at the same jokes and enjoyed the same diversions — that has to be kept in mind when considering the things Baker became most notorious for after he was elected mayor of Portland in 1917. Because within just a few years of his election, that "belle epoque" Portland was lost and gone. And Baker very much missed it.

A s mayor, Baker was a wonder. He could be wildly inappropriate in the most adorable way, as in the time he almost caused an international incident by taking advantage of the reverent silence at France's Tomb of the Unknown Soldier to launch into a political stump speech, or when he welcomed international opera star Mary Garden with a big, publicly-bestowed kiss. (Historian Karl Klooster once quipped that part of his political legacy was "public bussing.") He personally saw Oregon soldiers off at the railroad station with tears in his eyes, bellowing, "God bless you, boys!" as they pulled out. He was a tireless and persistent booster of his city. The vast majority of Portland residents loved him.

Yet there was a dark side to Mayor Baker too. Every time trouble started brewing between workers and their employers, he would be found reliably on the bosses' side, and he'd bring every resource at his disposal — including, as he did during the 1922 dock strike, swarms of "Mayor's secret police" and "Portland Vigilance Police" officers to break up strikers. Claiming a violent revolution was imminent, he more or less suspended the U.S. Constitution for a mass arrest of all known union activists, trying (successfully, as it turned out) to break the power of the radical International Workers of the World (I.W.W., the "Wobblies") in Portland.

His patriotic enthusiasm, forged in the First World War and tempered like lethal steel in the Red Scare era afterward, made him almost a poster boy for the "100 Percent Americanism" movement that brought the Ku Klux Klan to Oregon. In fact, there's some reason to suspect he may have been a member of the Klan; he was an inveterate joiner of fraternal organizations and societies, from the Shriners to the Elks, and the Klan was not regarded as much different from those clubs in the early 1920s — at least until it was revealed as a nest of hypocrisy and corruption in the "bridge scandal" of 1924. Certainly he accepted and encouraged the Klan's support — Baker is the mayor who appears in a famous photograph, published in the Portland Evening Telegram in 1923, of city officials posing with two robed-and-hooded Ku Klux Klan officials.

Then, too, there were the constant rumors (and, later, more than rumors) of corruption in City Hall — the liquor tippling and trading, the payoffs by vice operators, the bribes and kickbacks. It wasn't entirely clear that the corruption went all the way to the top, but at the very least, some of Baker's lieutenants showed great moral flexibility.

After about 1924, Baker started losing popularity as the corruption of his administration started rubbing off on him. It didn't help that, after hearing rumors that he didn't plan to run for re-election for financial reasons, the president of the electricity-and-streetcar monopoly passed a kitty to raise a slush fund for him, which the donors used to pay off his mortgage.

In 1932, a recall petition was on the ballot. It accused Baker of "failure to enforce the laws against various social evils" and thereby giving "aid and comfort to the denizens of the underworld and to official graft and corruption connected therewith."

Baker survived the recall attempt, but 47 percent of Portland voters were now on record as wanting him out. A few months later, perhaps taking the hint, he announced he wouldn't run for re-election.

By the end of his time in office, in 1933, Baker was basically a spent force. Perhaps that's because his theater company, which he hadn't really been able to run personally while serving as mayor, went out of business in 1922. The golden age of stock theater was over; its primary functions had been taken over by the new Hollywood feature-length movies. And by 1933 there was a whole generation of Portlanders who had never been to Baker's theater, never met him working the crowd on opening night, and knew him only as a back-slapping character about whom rumors of disreputability occasionally swirled, presiding over one of the more corrupt City Halls on the West Coast.

The old Baker magic just didn't work any more. To borrow an analogy from a far later time, video had killed the radio star.

George Luis Baker died in 1941 at his home in The Tides, a resort that he owned in Seaside. He's still remembered today, with a little help from the golden light of nostalgia, as one of Portland's most beloved and colorful mayors ever.

But with an eye on the corruption, crypto-authoritarianism and xenophobia that marred his time in office, he's also frequently cited as one of the worst mayors in the city's history.

George knew, and had presided over, the golden past that the cultural

RASCALS.

King Kleagle Luther Powell, center, and Exalted Cyclops Fred Gifford pose for a picture in the Portland Evening Telegram with (left to right) H.P. Coffin of the National Safety Council; Senior Police Capt. John T. Moore; Police Chief L.V. Jenkins; District Attorney Walter H. Evans; United States Attorney Lester W. Humphries; Multnomah County Sheriff T.M. Hurlburt; U.S. Department of Justice Special Agent Russell Bryon; **Portland Mayor George L. Baker;** *and Scottish Rite Masonic Lodge Sovereign Grand Inspector General P.S. Malcolm. (Image: UO Libraries)*

reactionaries yearned for as the "Red Scare" dawned in 1919. He looked at union representatives fighting to get their members treated fairly, and saw out-of-town troublemakers trying to turn brother against brother for their own personal gain; so he hired a secret crew of thugs to fight them. He saw ethnic minorities and newly emancipated women influencing and changing the culture he'd helped create in ways he didn't like, so he threw his support behind the "100 percent Americanism" of the Ku Klux Klan. This is, of course, no excuse for his quasi-fascist behavior throughout the 1920s; but it's important to know these things in evaluating this fascinating and controversial ex-mayor.

Sources and Works Cited:
- Round the Roses, *a book by Karl Klooster, published in 1987 by Klooster Enterprises of McMinnville;*
- The Growth of a City, *a book by E. Kimbark MacColl, published in 1979 by Georgian Press of Portland;*
- Portland: People, Politics and Power, *a book by Jewel Lansing, published in*

2003 by Oregon State University Press;
- *"The Baker Stock Company and the Community,"* an article by Kenneth W. Waters *published in the September 1981 issue of* Oregon Historical Quarterly.
- Portland Morning Oregonian *archives, June 1917 and May 1941.*

PAUL REMALEY & AL.:

BOOTLEGGERS AND JAILBREAKERS.

In the pitchy darkness after midnight on a blustery February morning just off the Oregon Coast, the 36-foot powerboat *Sea Island* was in big trouble.

The *Sea Island* was a Canadian rumrunner out of Vancouver, B.C. It was February 8, 1932; Prohibition, as everyone by then knew, was an utter failure, but it still had another year to go before it would be officially repealed. Until it was, there was still big money to be made running boats and ships like the *Sea Island* down from Vancouver to meet up with waiting trucks at remote locations on the West Coast of the U.S., smuggling in tons and tons of bonded Canadian liquor.

One such remote location was Whale Cove, a mile or so south of Depoe Bay — which is where the crew of the *Sea Island* now found themselves. And they were in some trouble. After they'd safely delivered their delicious cargo on the beach at the back of the bay, they had gotten most of the way out of the harbor entrance when the engine had started missing badly — just at the moment it was most needed. It was now firing on only one cylinder, and barely making any power, as the crew struggled to guide their boat out

An aerial shot of Whale Cove on a sunny day, showing clearly the location of Bootlegger Rock and the beach on which the booze was buried. (Image: Bryce Buchanan/ODOT)

of the mouth of the cove and into the open sea — through actual breakers.

Now, Whale Cove was almost everything a crew of smugglers might want in a rendezvous spot — remote, with no houses or settlements nearby, partly protected from the open sea. The only problem was, it was so dangerous as to be almost unnavigable. In particular, there was a big rocky reef jutting out of the middle of the entrance to the little bay, and that reef took some very fancy navigating to stay clear of.

Bringing the *Sea Island* in and out of Whale Cove in broad daylight with full power would be a real test of a skipper's skills; doing it in the middle of a moonless night with an almost-dead engine was a virtual impossibility.

The Canadians did their best, but it wasn't enough, and a big breaker soon picked the *Sea Island* up and dashed it against the rock. Then another one repeated the performance.

Now here's where the story gets muddled — or, rather, one of the places. The *Sea Island*'s crew later testified that, working from the theory that maybe the engine was out of fuel, one of them grabbed a gasoline can and started pouring fuel into the boat's main tank ... forgetting all about the cigarette dangling from his lips. The fumes ignited, the gasoline can dropped and spilled, and suddenly the *Sea Island* was also on fire.

Well, maybe. It seems likely, though, that they were lying about that, trying to explain how their boat ended up half burned up on the beach. For one thing, it's hard to imagine an accident like the one they described not ending in serious injury for the man holding the gas can. It seems more likely that the fire wasn't set until after they'd beached the boat — but I'm getting ahead of myself.

At that point, fire or no fire, the crew — William Kerr, Charles Ryall and Arthur Babcock — gave up on the situation as hopeless, and with water pouring into the hold, drove for the beach as fast as their failing power plant would push them.

By the way, it's entirely possible that this accident happened on the way into the bay rather than on the way out — which would explain why they didn't just let the boat sink in the middle of the bay rather than trying so hard to reach the beach. Letting the boat quietly sink and swimming to shore would have very effectively and discreetly hidden the wreck, and they probably would have made it back to Canada unnoticed if this had been done. But, of course, if the whole cargo — 400 cases of liquor and 900 gallons of straight tanker-truck ethanol (190 proof, in 15-gallon cans) was still in the hold when the wreck happened, that would have been unthinkable. The men themselves were not much help on this issue; their claim was that their engine failed and the tide miraculously washed them into the cove.

Nor is it entirely clear whether their cargo of booze was already buried

The beach at the back of Whale Cove as seen from some of the rocky outcroppings beside it. This beach is where the liquor was buried. (Image: Bryce Buchanan/ODOT)

in the sand, or whether they now had to bury it by the light of their burning boat. It seems most likely that burying the booze was their regular M.O. — Whale Cove is right between Depoe Bay and Newport, and although there wasn't much action there in 1932, there was enough traffic that a fleet of heavy trucks hanging around the area might be noticed. Most likely the system was, they'd bury it on the beach, and their local associates would dig it up during "picnic lunches on the beach" and bring it out in the trunks of their sedans.

If so, the booze would already have been buried, and the only thing on their minds would have been to put as much asphalt between themselves and the scene of their shipwreck as humanly possible before the cops got wise.

They attempted to light the boat back on fire again, hoping it would burn the rest of the way. In this, they were only partly successful. After all, it was early February on the Oregon Coast; getting anything to burn was a tall order. But they didn't stick around to make sure it worked. Two members of their local loading crew were there with a sedan, and the five of them now piled into this and made themselves scarce. Their chances of making it back to Canada, already slim, were getting slimmer by the minute. There was a good 400 miles of twisting two-lane roads between them and the border.

Roughly 365 of those miles were still untraveled when disaster struck again. The driver of the car got a little too eager, or perhaps he'd tipped a glass or two of the *Sea Island*'s cargo before they left the scene of the wreck; in any case, near Hebo he ran off the road and wrecked the car — actually overturned it.

Luckily, nobody was hurt. The five of them made their way to town, where the two locals managed to disappear; the three Canadians, though, were still on the lam and hoping to get home, so they bought tickets on a morning bus bound for Portland.

But by the time they'd gotten there, the wreckage of the *Sea Island* had been found. The Depoe Bay locals, who found it first, knew exactly what had happened the minute they saw the half-burned hulk on the beach. Nor did it take a whole lot of imagination to figure out what had happened to the *Sea Island*'s cargo. Local Depoe Bay-area residents flocked to Whale Cove, shovels in hand.

(Knowing how rumors are, it's at least possible that the rumrunners' operations in Whale Cove were already suspected. An operation like theirs would be hard to keep truly secret for long, so close to a small town.)

Meanwhile, Trooper Johnson of the Oregon State Police, responding to investigate the car wreck in Hebo, discovered that the abandoned car's

The Portland Morning Oregonian ran these mugshots of William Kerr, Charles Ryall and Arthur Babcock, the three-man crew of the rumrunner Sea Island, after their capture. (Image: Oregonian)

license plates had been switched — and the game was up. The three Canadians had been seen in Hebo as they boarded the bus; a description was promptly wired to Portland, and when the bus arrived at the station there, a delegation of bluecoats was ready and waiting to welcome them.

Depoe Bay's "Whiskey Galore" moment was all too brief. The Lincoln County Sheriff's men were soon on the scene, and the party was mostly over from there. Federal and state Prohibition agents arrived with shovels and spent the better part of a week uncovering the cache — they were delayed by a nasty storm that arrived just after they did. Of course, locals tried to slip onto the scene at night, and despite the feds' best efforts, some of them succeeded.

Either that storm was a real humdinger and moved a bunch of sand and bottles around, or this wasn't the first time the rumrunners had buried booze on this beach — because after the feds left with all the booze they could find, there remained several dozen cases of very good liquor buried hither and yon up and down the little strand, and for the next several months the beach at Whale Cove was a very popular recreation spot; visitors wandered around probing the sand with metal rods. They promptly named the rocky reef that had precipitated their good fortune upon them "Rumrunner Rock."

The three Canadian rumrunners were taken to the county jail in Toledo and locked up to await their trial. But anyone who thought the story was over was in for a surprise. A little over a month after the *Sea Island* wreck, the boat's crew members escaped from the county joint in one of the most spectacularly audacious jailbreaks in all of Oregon history.

THE JAILBREAK.

Act II of Oregon's adaptation of "Whisky Galore" started at around 10 p.m. on the night of Saturday, March 19, 1932 — just a few months before Prohibition was ended — when four vehicles rolled furtively into the little Coast Range town of Toledo, which was then the seat of Lincoln County.

A big, important-looking sedan led the caravan, followed by two large trucks and finally a sleek Buick coupe. In the coupe, two men sat cradling machine guns.

The nine men in those vehicles weren't tourists. They'd come to Toledo to get three of their business associates and bring them back home to Canada — with their luggage.

It wouldn't be an easy rescue, though. Their friends weren't staying in a Holiday Inn. They were locked away in cells at the Lincoln County Jail. And their "luggage" was more than a couple of beige Samsonite bags, as by now you are well aware — all of it locked securely away in the jailhouse evidence room.

The three men in the jail that night were, of course, the crew of the *Sea Island*. And now their friends were there to bust them out of the joint in proper gangster style.

The party was delayed a bit when a Lincoln County Sheriff car rolled into town, passed them, and pulled into the county garage. But, a few minutes later, the deputy pulled out again and was gone. Around 11 p.m., the coast was clear, and it was showtime.

The smaller of the two trucks pulled up near the jailhouse, and Portland resident S.U. Carrick lugged an oxyacetylene cutting torch into the building. In about 15 minutes he had the locks cut off of all the intervening doors, and the three prisoners were once again at liberty.

The entrance to Whale Cove, as seen from the headland at its southern end. This image was made at high tide, so the rocky reef — Bootlegger Rock — is mostly covered, but can be seen to the right just past the rocky sides of the cove; the beach behind is probably where the whiskey was hidden. (Image: Offbeat Oregon)

There followed a lively debate, according to the testimony of the other prisoners. The three Canadian mariners felt that breaking out of jail was a bit much; they thought it would be better to stay and face the music. But the leader of the rescue party, international motorcycle racer and Portland resident Paul Remaley, assured them that they couldn't be extradited for a mere jailbreak. Once they got home to Canada, he assured them, they'd be home free — so long as they didn't try to re-enter the U.S. again.

The jailbirds weren't too hard to convince. They didn't really want to stick around.

Meanwhile, Carrick had already gotten busy cutting his way into the evidence locker, and once this was done the other nine men hastily started lugging boxes of booze out to the waiting trucks. All the while, the men in the Buick peered over the front sights of their machine guns into the darkness, watching and listening for any signs of trouble.

Luck was with them (more luck than they could probably imagine, actually), and a few minutes later the Canadians, reunited at last, were piling into their vehicles. The gunmen in the Buick, their job done, disappeared into the night; and the others got their rigs started and pointed them north, toward home.

Meanwhile, unbeknownst to all, they had been ratted out. A vague, anonymous phone call had come in to Portland authorities warning that something was going to happen in Toledo that night. The warning had been passed on to the state police, and a couple of squad cars had been dispatched to check things out.

The state cops were about 20 minutes from Toledo when they passed the caravan rolling northward: one sedan and two large trucks. It wasn't unheard of for legitimate trucking companies to be hauling stuff around at night, but it was unusual enough to be noticed as the cops — who still didn't know anything had happened in Toledo — approached the town.

But when they got there, and learned what had happened, they figured it out right quick. They jumped back into their cars and raced out of town in pursuit.

The trucks had a long head start on them. But they had one huge advantage: The vehicles had passed each other in the dark of night, and the drivers of the caravan hadn't been able to see any of the details of the two cars that had passed them as they drove out of Toledo. They had no idea that the heat was on. So they continued driving northward at normal speeds. Then they stopped the two trucks. The smaller truck, with the welding kit in it, needed gasoline; and the cans of gas for the trip were in the larger truck. So the bootleggers got busy refueling.

They were still refueling when two carloads of Oregon State Police troopers rolled up on them, guns drawn.

The cops quickly learned that the sedan had gone on ahead. They were pretty sure that if they pulled up behind it in their cop cars, the driver would hit the gas hard and might actually get away; or a rolling gunfight might break out, and someone could get hurt or killed. So instead of risking that, several of the troopers who were in civilian dress hopped into the trucks and drove on into the night. They figured by the time the people in the sedan figured out that they weren't who they thought they were, they'd be covering them with their service revolvers and the jig would be up.

The ruse worked. They soon caught up with the sedan, which had pulled over to wait for them, and by the time the people in the car realized what was going on, they were already looking into the barrels of .38s.

The Lincoln County jail facilities no longer being in suitable condition to receive guests, the bootleggers were brought to the Benton County jail in Corvallis instead.

In court, the Canadian gangsters and their local associates were affable and colorful. They promptly posted bond — ringleader Remaley used his one phone call to tell someone named Frank to grab $13,500 in cash and come to Corvallis to bail him out. Carrick, the one who had cut the locks off the jailhouse doors, cheerfully offered to fix the jail for them, free of charge; since he wasn't going anywhere for a while anyway, he might as well make himself useful, and he held a boilermaker's-union card. He could, he added, make the Lincoln County Jail break-proof if they wished.

He went on to compliment Lincoln and Benton counties on their accommodations. "If you want a real jail experience, go down to Louisiana, where they feed you molasses and cornmeal and sowbelly," he said. "I know; I've been there."

The men were all convicted, of course, on various liquor and prison-break charges, both federal and state offenses. But by the time they'd served their relatively short state sentences, Prohibition had been repealed, and the federal charges were dropped.

Several sources add a few final details to this story. According to these, the jailbreakers had in fact started a fire that damaged the Toledo jail heavily, and in lieu of prison some of the Canadians were sent back to Toledo to help repair it. When Prohibition was repealed in April of 1933, they were set free, and they headed back to Canada with many handshakes and expressions of friendship. It's a fun little detail, but I haven't been able to confirm it in any of the newspaper accounts, so I'm not sure it's true.

Even without that detail, though, it's a remarkable tale — one of the most audacious jailbreaks in history, perpetrated by one of the most colorful gangs of rogues ever. And they probably would have gotten away with it if they'd done a better job keeping their mouths shut while preparing for it — or if they'd contented themselves with just breaking their friends out of jail and left the booze alone.

But it's worth mentioning that the whole caper could easily have gone bad — very bad. If the state cops had arrived in Toledo just 20 minutes earlier, there's a real possibility that a gangland-style firefight would have broken out with the two gunmen in the Buick coupe. If that had happened, people would have been killed — probably some or all of the cops, possibly several of the jailbreakers.

It's interesting to contemplate how history might have changed if those cops had left Portland just a few minutes earlier.

On the other hand — it's at least a possibility that the Buick coupe never actually existed. This sinister, powerful car with its two machine-gun-toting Al Dillinger types is exactly the sort of detail that sometimes gets added to stories like this for propagandistic purposes — to reinforce to members of the public that these bootleggers are bad guys and they are not to be rooted for. It fits all the patterns of a detail made up by a public official hoping to spin some moral clarity into a narrative: two bad, dangerous gangsters, heavily armed with "Chicago typewriters" and driving a distinctive-looking car, vanish into the night and are never seen again; nor is there any noticeable interest by law enforcement in finding them. Of all the vehicles present that night, theirs is the only one identified by make — as though, when making up the story, the storyteller felt a need to add a realistic detail to make it more believable.

Really, it's far more likely that this was just a case of seven affable, audacious Canadians trying to bust their pals out of the klink. And for us, looking back on this story from a safe future distance, that arguably makes it all the better.

Sources and Works Cited:
- Top Deck Twenty! Best West Coast Sea Stories!, *a book by Stan Allyn, published in 1989 by Binford & Mort;*
- Portland Morning Oregonian *archives, March—July 1932.*

ROBERT G. "OREGON WILDCAT" DUNCAN:

RADIO TALK-SHOW HOST.

The first radio broadcaster ever to be sent to prison for cursing on the air was a hard-charging early shock jock known as "The Oregon Wildcat," who kept the city of Portland and surrounding regions glued to their radio sets every evening for most of the first half of 1930.

Robert Gordon Duncan was the Wildcat's name, and he'd broadcast his scandalous but highly entertaining tirades every single day over Radio KVEP (K-Voice of East Portland), 1500 AM.

The radio station was originally started in 1927 by William Schaeffer, who ran it in the customary way for several years and achieved a modest popularity with listeners. It shared time on the 1500-kilohertz frequency with several other stations, so it had designated hours during which it was supposed to be off the air so others could broadcast.

Then came 1929, and the onset of the Great Depression, and suddenly KVEP was losing money for Schaeffer. In desperation, he struck a deal to transfer control of the station (and later ownership, although the federal

369

This political cartoon ran on the front page of the Portland Morning Oregonian on May 30, 1930, with a story about KVEP's license revocation. The snake on top of the cabinet is supposed to resemble an old-fashioned loudspeaker, which in 1920s radios looked like a curved trumpet mouth sticking up out of the top. (Image: UO Libraries)

government intervened before those plans could be implemented) to The Oregon Wildcat: Robert Gordon Duncan.

Duncan was a populist firebrand with what passed, in the late 1920s, for a very dirty mouth. His primary focus was on "chain stores" — outfits like Woolworths and Piggly Wiggly that would open a store in a local community and, with the advantages of bulk-buying power and economics of scale, run the local "mom-and-pop" operations out of business. Duncan was running for the Republican nomination for Congress, and he had a little money at his disposal; Schaeffer was nearly out of money, but he had a platform that lots of voters listened to. It seemed like a match made in heaven.

It wasn't.

Schaeffer soon wished he'd never met Duncan. Once the contract was inked, Duncan pretty much took over, and rebuffed any attempt by Schaeffer to rein him in. And as 1929 blossomed into 1930, the Voice of East Portland started drawing community attention like a train wreck in progress.

There were several factors that kept 'em tuning in:

First off, The Cat's vision of how an advocate should behave frequently crossed the line into outright protection-racketeering. On the air, the Wildcat demanded contributions from local merchants to help him fight the chain stores, and if the checks they sent in were too skimpy, he'd sometimes accuse them — over the air — of peddling bad merchandise or cheating their customers.

Secondly, after Duncan lost the Republican primary to incumbent Franklin Korell, his attacks on the Congressman became even more vitriolic, and he could be counted on to light into the lawmaker in distinctly ungentlemanly terms at least once a day.

Korell, trying to gear up for what looked to be a hard general-election fight with his Democratic opponent — future governor, retired U.S. Army major general, and certifiable Horrible Person Charles

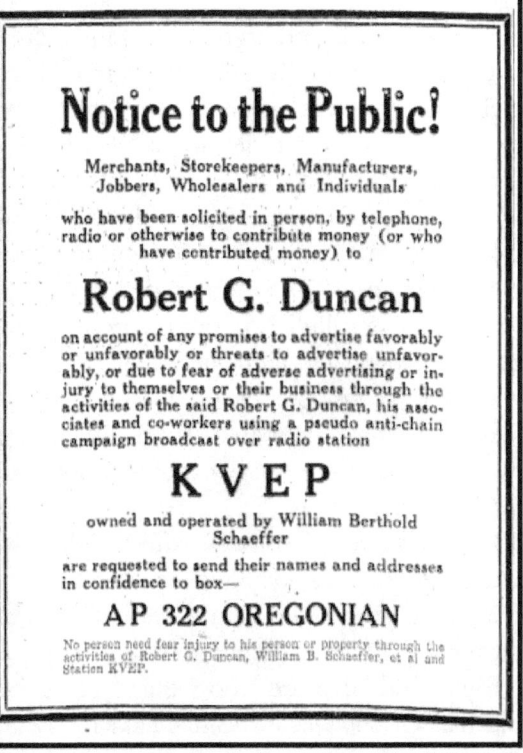

This newspaper ad ran in the Oregonian on April 15, 1930, in an attempt to put together a group of merchants to legally oppose the fund-raising tactics of "Oregon Wildcat" Robert Duncan. (Image: UO Libraries)

H. Martin, who would in fact win the seat — was baffled by this continued attention. "Who is paying Duncan to continue these attacks on me now that the primary campaign is over?" he wondered, during one of the many judicial hearings that followed.

Nobody, apparently. It seemed The Wildcat was just on a tear, and one of his favorite topics was a rather frank speculation about Korell's sexual orientation.

"Korell is a bachelor, and when he was asked why he doesn't marry he says, 'I don't care for women,'" The Cat once thundered, according to the testimony of witnesses who heard the broadcast (tragically, there are no recordings; tape technology wasn't available in 1930). "What do you know about that? Isn't that a strange statement for a natural man to make? ... It must be explained thoroughly, and in ways that I can understand, to free the man who says it from the charges of practicing the vices that caused the destruction of Sodom and Gomorrah."

Then, perhaps thinking that was putting it too subtly, he went on to claim Korell had been "the roommate and bed-fellow" of a man named Clarence Brazell, and urged all "natural men" to honor the women in their lives by voting for Korell's Democratic opponent (Charles Martin — a plainly heterosexual he-man who, by the way, will be discussed in some detail in Volume 3 of this series, titled "Bad Ideas and Horrible People of Old Oregon") in the fall.

A third attractant to the Wildcat's broadcast was the entertainment value of good, imaginative swearing. By modern standards this was fairly tame ("He's a son of a mother who scratched her ear with her hind foot!" "You undiapered kid!" "He's a convention grifter and a rum-soaked scamp!"), but it was peppered with "hells" and "damns" and occasionally lapsed into what many considered actual blasphemy: "I can make a six-shooter sing 'Come to Jesus,'" he roared into the mic one night just before the election he was about to lose, "and I'm going to shoot the next crook that comes into my office to bully me."

But although Duncan's daily broadcast was attracting eager listeners like a bare-knuckle boxing match, it was also making some big waves in the Portland business community. The chain stores, of course, loathed him with great cordiality, and the mom-and-pop operators understandably felt that a friend and advocate who regularly practiced extortion on them wasn't much of a friend and advocate. That left, essentially, nobody in the Wildcat's corner.

And KVEP was also making waves in the broadcasting community, because the Wildcat had quit respecting the time division agreements with other stations and was now just broadcasting his rants for as long as he pleased; Radio KUJ Longview could just wait until he was done, thank you very much.

Letters and telegrams from all these aggrieved groups, plus some V.I.P.s whom the Wildcat had slandered on the air, started pouring into the Federal Radio Commission, which — clearly shocked by the volume and fervor of the correspondence — took the matter in hand immediately.

At the resulting hearing, Portland judge J.C. Kendall was serving as counsel for a remarkably vast and diverse array of civic organizations and prominent individuals, including the American Legion, the Chamber of Commerce and a big bevy of church groups, all petitioning the FRC to shut KVEP down.

"There is a mad dog loose in the City of Portland," Kendall fulminated. "For two hours every night we have had a persistent series of talks so utterly indecent that they offend every human sensibility."

He then went on to demand Schaeffer be sanctioned as well, because "for the past three months he has had his hand on the faucet of this filth without attempting to turn it off."

The F.R.C. members were shocked by what they heard, and moved to slam the door on KVEP in jig time. Then they initiated prosecution against Duncan himself, taking him into federal custody.

While Duncan was under arrest in the federal building, one young man, the son of deceased Oregonian editor Edgar Piper, tracked him down, burst in on him and socked the 60-year-old Wildcat in the teeth. It seemed Duncan had said some rather uncharitable things about the elder Piper on the air shortly after his death, when the newspaperman's corpse had barely cooled; and the deceased's son had been listening at the time. A U.S. marshal tried to intervene, Piper punched *him*, and a general melee broke out, which ended with the 1930s equivalent of a blackstick beatdown for Mr. Piper — who was, of course, thereupon arrested.

A sympathetic court subsequently fined the young lad the modest sum of $50 for this crime, to which he freely admitted; he had been, he said, overcome with fury at the criticism of his freshly dead father, and determined to have his punch, come what might.

"This young man would rather be a toad, and feed upon the vapors of the dungeon, than allow such procedure to go unpunished," his attorney explained to the apparent approval and sympathy of the entire court. "It is fortunate that he was unarmed, or were it not so this polecat would be lying today under six feet of earth."

Duncan himself got no such sympathy on his day in court, and a short time later The Oregon Wildcat found himself convicted of indecent broadcasting and sentenced to a six-month term in the county jail.

After his release, Duncan tried to launch a magazine to continue his anti-chain-store crusade, but it went nowhere. Eventually he gave up on public life, and in the early 1940s, historian Malcolm Clark found him running a nine-hole golf course near Troutdale — "an inoffensive, frail, rather courtly gentleman who was old before his time," Clark recalls.

Duncan died at the age of 73, in 1944. He had, as it were, clawed his way into the history-of-broadcasting textbooks with cutlass in one hand and pistol in the other, a 60-year-old political pirate from the crazy maverick state of Oregon. And whatever you might think of his anti-gay prejudice and his sketchy practices as a broadcaster, you just have to respect that kind of chutzpah.

Sources and Works Cited:
- Radio Cultures, *a book by Michael C. Keith, published in 2008 by Lang of New York;*
- Dirty Discourse, *a book by Robert L. Hillard, published in 2009 by Wiley of New York;*
- "Self-Appointed Anti-Chain Lobbyist," *an article by Malcolm Clark Jr. published in the Dec. 20, 1982, issue of the* Portland Oregonian.
- Portland Morning Oregonian *archives, May–June 1930.*

"BIG JIM" ELKINS & AL:

RACKETEERS.

I f you were a fan of the classic ABC television sitcom "Happy Days," you know Arthur "The Fonz" Fonzarelli had a special relationship with two particular machines: His trusty '49 Triumph motorcycle, and the pinball machine in Al's diner.

But it may surprise you to know that when Fonzie was playing that pinball machine, in 1950s Milwaukee, Wisconsin, he was breaking the law — and so was Al, by having the machine in his restaurant.

It's a bit hard for younger Oregonians to believe, but just a few dozen years ago pinball was illegal in most large American cities — including Portland. But, of course, pinball machines were everywhere ... furnished and controlled by organized crime.

W hen coin-op pinball was first developed, it was mostly a game of chance, not skill. Early machines didn't even have flippers, so there was no way for the player to affect the game's outcome.

But even after controls were added in the late 1940s, authorities still looked at a pinball machine as a straight-up low-stakes slot machine with some extra gewgaws attached to it to fool players into thinking it was a game of skill.

And they may have been right about that — at least, in some cases, and in a small way. There were taverns and bars in which extra games won playing pinball could be cashed in at the bar for small amounts of money. That, of course, doesn't seem like the kind of high-stakes, high-profit game that would attract much law-enforcement attention, and for the most part it didn't.

But after 1949, the illegal status of pinball was going to have some profound effects on Oregon's underworld, especially in and around Portland. It would set the stage for a semi-comical battle between two of the Beaver State's scuzziest — and most rascally — racketeers.

Games like pinball had been around since at least the 1700s, but the coin-operated variant that we know as pinball was developed in the early 1930s. By the end of the Great Depression they were a familiar sight in bars and malt shops pretty much everywhere.

But slot machines of the "one-armed bandit" type were getting to be a familiar sight in bars and malt shops, too. And as city authorities started cracking down on these in the 1940s, they also took a look at the pinball games.

To be fair, in the early years it wasn't unfair to lump pinball machines in with slots; as mentioned, pinball gameplay was mostly luck-based at first. That made it great for gambling operators, since it provided protection against some wizardly player coming to the table and using his or her mad skills to break the bank. So a number of bars had started letting patrons place bets, and cash in extra games that they might win.

They'd mostly quit doing that by the late 1940s, though, as improvements to the games had dramatically increased the amount of skill that was involved in the game and decreased the role of luck. But by then it was too late. The public-relations war had already been lost.

So in '49, when the city of Portland outlawed the silver balls, pinball's reputation was dark and sordid — and alluring. Authorities considered them "gateway machines" used by wicked, scheming men to lure innocent youths into the underworld of one-armed bandits, covert blackjack tables, friendly-but-expensive trollops, and other darkly gleaming tidbits of underworld wickedness. Rebellious youths, attracted by the forbidden-fruit effect, considered them great fun and a great way to freak out the parents.

All of which meant that by the mid-1950s — the beginning of pinball's glory days — pinball in the Portland area was strictly an outlaw enterprise. Games were supplied by criminal syndicates, sometimes in collaboration with corrupt local officials. And when those syndicates started fighting for market share, things could get pretty exciting.

The pinball wars in the north Willamette Valley mostly centered around two racketeers, who supplied the machines that restaurants and bars used. There was Stan Terry, an old bootlegger whose pinball-and-slots syndicate covered mostly establishments south of Portland, in the Milwaukie area; and "Big Jim" Elkins, the self-styled vice boss of Portland itself.

The two of them, in a nutshell, coveted one another's rackets. And they were both the kind of guys who go after what they want.

They started out in the early 1950s with surprise raids. Elkins, with five or six heavily armed goons, would barge into a bar with Terry's machines in it, take all the money and as many of the machines as they could haul, and disappear into the night. Then Terry would respond in kind. Apparently nobody got hurt in any of these tit-for-tat raids, but then again, they weren't getting anywhere either.

So around 1955, Elkins escalated the battle by traveling to Seattle and asking the Teamsters Union for help. The Teamsters Union at that time was essentially an organized-crime syndicate, and was already running some machines in Portland under the direction of a short, stocky crook named Tom "Blubber" Maloney.

Elkins couldn't get an appointment with the head of the Teamsters in Seattle, so he reached out to Maloney instead. Holed up in the Roosevelt Hotel on Park Street, the two of them hatched a scheme: They'd set up a Teamsters-affiliated pinball operators union, lock Terry out of it, and shut him down by denying him access to union trucking services and by throwing picket lines around his customers' joints.

This was soon done, and a few weeks later, the Coin Machine Men of Oregon was formed. Almost immediately, it moved on the enemy: It summoned a picket line of Teamsters around the Mount Hood Café, a place with a bunch of Stan Terry's machines in it.

It was looking like the end for Stan Terry. Once the Teamsters started shutting down his customers, his remaining clients would leave in a hurry.

In desperation, he went and talked to an old underworld buddy who'd worked for legendary former head Portland racketeer Al Winter before that well-connected gentleman had left to open the Sahara Casino in Las Vegas.

He was in luck. Terry's friend had another friend who knew Hy Goldbaum, the pit boss at the Flamingo Casino — the mobbed-up joint in Vegas that had been started by the late Bugsy Siegel. Goldbaum personally escorted Terry to Seattle and introduced him to the head of the Teamsters — that's right, he introduced him to the guy Elkins hadn't been able to get an appointment with.

Some cash changed hands, and then a telephone rang in the Portland Teamsters' office — and the pickets were pulled from around the Mount Hood. Just like that, Elkins had lost, and now the Coin Machine Men of Oregon was the group on the outside, facing the prospect of pickets and "hot cargo" restrictions on its slots and pinball machines.

At that point, it was checkmate: Elkins had no choice but to sell his machines and routes to Terry for whatever he could get. Terry, with the Teamsters, had run him out of the business.

But Elkins wasn't done yet. He had another scheme up his sleeve to get the business back. All the business — whether the Teamsters liked it or not. And it was very simple.

Elkins had made the acquaintance of a square-jawed goon named Herman "Bugsy" Burns. Now, he called up Bugsy and told him he had a job for him: He and some associates would pose as pinball-machine repairmen and start making the rounds to every joint with one or more of Stan Terry's machines in it. Elkins already had the trucks and fake IDs that they'd need, and had lined up a big warehouse in North Portland where the machines could be hidden afterward. Everything was ready to go.

When the crew got to each joint, they'd tell the owner pretty much what The Grinch told Cindy Lou Who in Dr. Seuss's classic *How The Grinch Stole Christmas*: The machines were being updated, so they were collecting the old ones, and another truck would be along in an hour or so with the new replacements.

Elkins figured if they were efficient, they could collect every single Stan Terry pinball machine before anybody figured out the scam, and then Terry would be out of business.

And it probably would have worked, too. But they'd never find out. Because Bugsy and his friends got bored while waiting for the signal to start the collection run, and decided to pass the time by jacking up a nearby Safeway. Of course, they got caught and arrested.

Stan Terry kept his machines, and kept paying the Teamsters for the privilege. Big Jim Elkins was stuck on the outside looking in, perhaps thinking — as historian Phil Stanford wryly comments in his book, *Portland Confidential* — that "as ever, good help is so hard to find."

Sources and Works Cited:
- Portland Confidential, *a book by Phil Stanford, published in 2004 by ptown books of Portland;*
- Dark Rose: Organized Crime and Corruption in Portland, *a book by Robert C. Donnelly, published in 2011 by University of Washington Press.*

ALLEN MIDGETTE:

ANDY WARHOL IMPERSONATOR.

On the evening of Oct. 5, 1967, students were pouring into the doors of one of the biggest rooms in the University of Oregon's Erb Memorial Union.

It was a big day. The one and only Andy Warhol was scheduled to appear, for something he called an "illustrated lecture." For the students, it was a once-in-a-lifetime chance to see and talk to one of the most influential characters in the art world.

At last the man of the hour stepped out on the stage with already-legendary film director Paul Morrissey. With his crazy-cut white hair, his ever-present Ray-Ban Wayfarers and his stylish cigarette, the speaker was instantly recognizable.

But almost immediately, the lecture got off to a rocky start. The two men on the stage started an "art film" showing a young fellow running through crowds in New York City yelling, "I love you! I love you!" to everyone whose eye he could catch. The film, of course, had no narrative arc or plot — the absence of any such bourgeois conventions was *de rigeur* in the avant-garde art of the day — so basically it was just several dozen minutes of meaningless action, until the film ran out of the spool. Then the lights came up, and Morrissey asked if anyone had any questions.

The questioners started out curious, but soon they were sounding baffled and by the end of the evening some of them were actually angry.

"I don't know how to say what my meaning is," the white-haired artist told one student. "I guess it means to me that I film it, mostly."

"That is one of the big questions," he told another, after being asked why he made films. "Let's just say we do it to keep us off the streets."

As the questions got tougher and more specific, Morrissey started breaking in and fielding them, to the annoyance of students who had wanted a response from Warhol.

By the end of the event, the students from the University of Oregon School of Journalism and Communication were starting to make their presence known, firing zingers at the white-wigged swinger on the stage. "Sir, do you give a damn?" one of them demanded. (Former students and colleagues of the U of O's late, legendary journalism professor Bill Winter will instantly recognize the pedigree of that question.) The by-now-beleaguered speaker replied, hesitantly and vaguely, "Sure ... (about) all kinds of things. It changes all the time."

The Oregon students didn't know it, but they were looking at one of their own up there on the stage: A University of Oregon-trained actor named Allen Midgette who was now one of Warhol's cronies in the Factory art loft in New York City. Midgette had been dressed to look like Warhol and sent out west to do a series of four college lectures for him. Warhol himself had never left New York.

The U of O appearance was the last stop on the tour, and it represented a distinct turn for the worse. At the University of Utah, where it had started out, the reception had been warmer; but almost as soon as he'd left, faculty members were wondering if it was really Andy Warhol. The student newspaper there stepped up and started pulling together evidence, including a candid shot that one of their photographers had snuck of him during the visit — "Warhol" had been very insistent that no pictures be taken, but one of the student journalists there had used a twin-lens Rolleiflex camera (one of the type one looks down into and shoots from waist level) to surreptitiously snap one anyway, likely intending it only as a personal souvenir. Close examination had left faculty members convinced that unless Warhol had had a nose job while nobody had been looking, the speaker had been someone else.

And so it was that a few days after "Warhol" spoke, Chris Hougham — then the editor of the University of Oregon's student newspaper, the *Oregon Daily Emerald* — got a phone call from an editor at the University of Utah's student newspaper, the *Daily Utah Chronicle*, asking if there had been any suspicion of Warhol's identity. Hougham assured her that it had been Warhol who appeared at the U of O; but after the phone call, *Emerald* staffers started connecting the dots as well.

By this time, of course, "Warhol" was well away from the Scene of the Crime, and back in New York.

Allen "Andy Warhol" Midgette's whirlwind tour through Oregon had started the day before the U of O appearance, when two students from Linfield College in McMinnville picked him and Morrissey up from the Portland airport. Initially they'd anticipated an afternoon round-table discussion; but "Warhol" wanted to spend the afternoon checking out Portland thrift stores.

"Let's save all that for the evening," he said, and so, accompanied by the two baffled college boys, the Peter Pan of Pop Art hunted through the used clothing and knickknacks at the Salvation Army on Northeast Martin Luther King Jr. Boulevard (then called Union Avenue); then they made their way out Burnside in quest of another store.

Finally, the four of them made their way back to McMinnville and set up for the show.

In contrast to what was coming the following day in Eugene, the reception at Linfield was not particularly hostile, according to the recollections of Mt. Angel College art professor Leland John, who traveled to McMinnville to attend. John recalled that "Warhol" responded to many of the questions by simply issuing an ironic laugh or giggle. When he did reply, it was with a degree of glib wittiness that tended to distract the questioner's attention from the fact that his/her question was not being answered (remember, Midgette is a theatre guy; improv is his thing.)

"Some people say your films are crude or promiscuous," one questioner began.

"Yes, I think they are, a lot of them," the faux Warhol replied smoothly. "But most of those haven't been shown."

"Some people say your film 'Harlot' is a joke on the straight world," another said; "what do you say?"

"It isn't," Midgette shot back. "It's just a joke. Period."

"Would you explain why you're dressed and groomed the way you are?" asked another.

"Mainly because I like the way I'm dressed and groomed," Midgette

Andy Warhol in Moderna Museet, Stockholm, before the opening of his retrospective exhibition there. This photograph was taken right around the time the truth about his lecture was coming out. (Image: Lasse Olsson/ Pressens bild)

said. "I won't model for you, but I like it. You explain why you dress the way you do."

The performance went over reasonably well with the crowd, all things considered. There were a few actual artists in the crowd, and some of them were a little dissatisfied with having come for an art talk and been served an arch, cryptic bull session lightly spiced with junior-grade media theory; but for the most part, the audience members figured it was just yet another piece of avant-garde Andy Warhol art that they couldn't fathom, and out of fear of being identified as a stupid Phillistine, they nodded and smiled and golf-clapped when it was finished.

Perhaps it was just as well that Midgette saved the University of Oregon for last, because that one didn't go nearly so well.

But soon Midgette and Morrissey were on their way back to the Eternal City with their thrift-shop treasures, no doubt yukking it up about the gullibility of the Western rubes.

Meanwhile, Chris Hougham at the Oregon Daily Emerald had been in contact with Register-Guard reporter Don Bishoff, and Bishoff just happened to know somebody who could help him get to the bottom of it.

"We had an aging hippie working on our copy desk, named Bill Thomas," Bishoff recalled later. "Somehow he had the number for the pay phone on the wall at The Factory. So I called the number — and Paul Morrissey answered it."

Morrissey had made a variety of arrangements in case the "rubes" got suspicious, but apparently it had never occurred to him that any of the hinterland yokels would be hip enough to actually know the phone number of the Factory's ironic pay phone. Caught by surprise, Morrissey stammered a bit, then put Warhol on the line. And, after some head-scratching over how Bishoff could know it was the real Warhol this time, the artist confessed the whole thing.

"He was better than I am," Warhol told Bishoff. "He was what the people expected. They liked him better than they would have liked me."

"His explanation of how he sent the guy didn't make sense," Bishoff recalled. "I still think to this day he was pulling another Andy Warhol spoof, and proving a point that people wouldn't know the difference."

The student journalists in Utah, whose skepticism led to the full unmasking, were distinctly unimpressed. In a telephone interview, Morrissey told Chronicle Assistant Editor Kay Israel that impersonating each other was just regular hijinks for the art world's self-styled avant-garde golden boys.

"We do it a lot in New York," he explained breezily.

"Well, being from the West, I don't think we're quite used to it," she shot back.

Paul Cracroft, the director of lectures and concerts at the University of Utah, was even more acerbic about the whole thing. Cracroft, who had learned of the scam early enough to withhold payment for it, said he'd be open to having other pop artists come and talk at the U of Utah — "if they're wonderful and can assure us somehow that they're coming themselves." Asked how that might be accomplished, he quipped, "Blood tests and fingerprints."

Sources and Works Cited:
- *"The Fake Warhol Lectures," an article by Greg Allen published April 6, 2007, on his blog at greg.org;*
- *Portland Oregonian, Eugene Register-Guard and Oregon Daily Emerald archives for October and November 1967;*
- *Personal recollections of Don Bishoff and Leland John, January 2009.*

www.ingramcontent.com/pod-product-compliance
Lightning Source LLC
Chambersburg PA
CBHW020937180426
43194CB00038B/212